Horace

OKLAHOMA SERIES IN CLASSICAL CULTURE

Oklahoma Series in Classical Culture

SERIES EDITOR
Ellen Greene, *University of Oklahoma*

ADVISORY BOARD
Ronnie Ancona, *Hunter College and CUNY Graduate Center*
Carolyn J. Dewald, *Bard College*
Nancy Felson, *University of Georgia*
Helene P. Foley, *Barnard College*
Thomas R. Martin, *College of the Holy Cross*
John F. Miller, *University of Virginia*
Richard F. Thomas, *Harvard University*

Horace

Epodes, Odes, and *Carmen Saeculare*

Translated and Edited by Stephanie McCarter

UNIVERSITY OF OKLAHOMA PRESS : NORMAN

Publication of this book is made possible through the generosity of the University of the South's Department of Classics.

Latin text is from C. Edward and H. W. Garrod, *Q. Horati Flacci Opera* (Oxford: Clarendon Press, 1901).

Library of Congress Cataloging-in-Publication Data

Names: Horace, author. | McCarter, Stephanie, editor, translator.
Title: Horace : Epodes, Odes, and Carmen saeculare / translated and edited by
  Stephanie McCarter.
Other titles: Oklahoma series in classical culture ; v. 60.
Description: Norman : University of Oklahoma Press, 2020. | Series: Oklahoma series in
  classical culture; volume 60 | Includes bibliographical references. | Summary: "A verse
  translation of Horace's Epodes, Odes, and Carmen Saeculare that preserves Horace's
  stanzaic structures and line numbers while marrying them to English iambic meter.
  Latin text faces English translation with explanatory footnotes at the end of each page,
  along with a detailed introduction, maps, and glossary of rhetorical terms"—
  Provided by publisher.
Identifiers: LCCN 2019042783 | ISBN 978-0-8061-6487-8 (paperback)
Classification: LCC PA6394 .M35 2020 | DDC 874/.01—dc23
LC record available at https://lccn.loc.gov/2019042783

Horace: Epodes, Odes, *and* Carmen Saeculare is Volume 60 in the Oklahoma Series
in Classical Culture.

For Sandra and Carl McCarter

CONTENTS

A NOTE ON THE TEXT

The Latin texts are from the edition of Wickham and Garrod (1901), except as follows:

Epodes 7.12	*numquam* for *umquam*
Epodes 9.17	*at huc frementis* for *ad hunc frementes*
Epodes 13.13	*pravi* for *parvi*
Epodes 17.22	*relinquor* for *reliquit*
Epodes 17.42	*vicem* for *vice*
Odes 1.6.19	*cantamus, vacui sive* for *cantamus vacui, sive*
Odes 1.7.27	*auspice Teucro* for *auspice: Teucri*
Odes 1.8.2	*te deos oro* for *hoc deos vere*
Odes 1.9.4	*acuto?* for *acuto.*
Odes 1.16.6	*Pythiis* for *Pythius*
Odes 1.25.20	*Euro* for *Hebro*
Odes 1.28.21	*rabidus* for *rapidus*
Odes 1.35.17	*saeva* for *serva*
Odes 2.2.14	*pellas* for *pellit*
Odes 2.4.18	*dilectam* for *delectam*
Odes 2.9.1	*Histricos* for *hispidos*
Odes 2.13.28	*belli.* for *belli!*

Odes 3.4.14	*Aceruntiae* for *Acherontiae*
Odes 3.4.46	*umbras* for *urbes*
Odes 3.4.69	*Gyges* for *Gyas*
Odes 3.5.15	*trahenti* for *trahentis*
Odes 3.14.11	*non* for *iam*
Odes 3.27.18	*Orion?* for *Orion*
CS 29	*Tellus* for *tellus*
Odes 4.2.49	*tuque* for *terque*
Odes 4.4.17	*Raetis* for *Raeti*
Odes 4.7.15	*pius* for *pater*
Odes 4.9.31	*silebo* for *sileri*
Odes 4.10.5	*Ligurine* for *Ligurinum*

ACKNOWLEDGMENTS

This project began when two colleagues and I decided to include Horace's Cleopatra Ode (*Odes* 1.37) in a team-taught humanities course at the University of the South in Sewanee, Tennessee. Finding no translation that accomplished everything I wanted, I decided simply to translate it myself. That first prose translation eventually grew into this book. I am indebted to numerous friends and colleagues for offering me various kinds of feedback, wisdom, and encouragement, including Paul Holloway, Eric Thurman, Shelley MacLaren, Matthew Irvin, and Stephanie Batkie. Jim O'Hara offered invaluable "kibbitzing" that greatly improved the final product (and saved me a few embarrassments). I owe a particular depth of gratitude to Christopher McDonough, who is simply an extraordinary colleague and frequent coteacher. He has offered me support throughout this and so many projects. Thank you to Adam Ross and the team at the *Sewanee Review* for giving me the opportunity in their pages to explore some of my thinking about translation. Adam Hawkins keeps my work life running smoothly, and I appreciate all he does.

I had the opportunity to test these translations with a group of talented and thoughtful Latin students in an advanced Horace seminar in the fall of 2018. They were keen critics who helped me identify many ways to improve the poems, and they deserve to be thanked individually: Bramwell Atkins,

Julia Harrison, Kathryn Hicks, Emma Jacobs, Ford Peay, Celeste Shibata, Jackson Smith, Hpone Myint Tu, Jackson Yates, and Zachary Zimmerman. Talking through the knots of translation with these wonderful students was an utter delight.

I am grateful to everyone involved with this project at the University of Oklahoma Press, especially Alessandra Jacobi Tamulevich and Stephanie Evans, who expertly guided the book through its various stages, and Brian Bowles, whose sharp editorial eye helped bring the manuscript *ad umbilicum*. The anonymous readers for the press were tremendously generous in their criticism, helping me iron out inelegance and making sure I knew all the pertinent scholarship. I am enormously appreciative of the evident time they took to review the proposal and manuscript. All remaining infelicities and errors are, of course, entirely my own.

To all of those who have taught me about Horace, I will remain in your debt always: Sara Myers, Edward Courtney, John Miller, Tony Woodman, Jenny Strauss Clay, Elizabeth Sutherland, and David Rohrbacher.

This translation would not have been possible were it not for the immense support my family gives to me. Daniel Holmes, my husband and fellow classicist, has patiently read these poems and listened to me read them over and over again. He has been a tremendously caring and encouraging partner, as well as a wonderful coparent to our beloved young children, Rory and Edie, every step of the way. This book is dedicated to my parents, Sandra and Carl McCarter, who have driven more miles than I can count between Sewanee and Knoxville the past few years to help in so many ways. I have no words to thank them adequately for their unwavering love, so I will steal and slightly adapt some of Horace's: *quod spiro et placeo, si placeo, vestrum est.*

INTRODUCTION

This book contains Latin texts and English translations of the lyric poetry of Horace, one of the most admired writers of Roman antiquity. His mark on the literary tradition is indelible, both for his transformation of Greek poetic forms into Latin verse and for his influence on later poets and writers. Even those who do not know his name repeat his words in their exhortations to "seize the day" or observe the "golden mean." His lyric poetry engages us with political, ethical, poetic, and aesthetic ideas and invites us to see these spheres as complexly intertwined. This introduction places Horace's lyric poetry in its cultural and literary contexts and provides a foundation for those approaching the poems for the first time.

LIFE AND WORKS OF HORACE

Our knowledge of Horace's life is stitched together chiefly from information he himself provides in his poetry, although how much of this is simply poetic fiction is unclear.[1] A short biography of the poet by Suetonius, who lived in the principate of Hadrian (117–38 C.E.), supplements the poems, but its reliability is likewise dubious, and at any rate it seems to be based

---

1. On Horace's biography, see esp. Armstrong (1989) and (2010), Nisbet (2007), and Günther (2013a).

largely on the poems themselves. Familiarly known in English simply as Horace, his full Latin name was Quintus Horatius Flaccus. He was born on December 8, 65 B.C.E. and spent his early childhood in Venusia, a town in the Southern Italian region of Apulia, to a father he describes in both the *Satires* and *Epistles* as a freedman and to a mother whom he never mentions.[2] Horace's father worked as a *coactor,* a figure that handled the financial transactions between buyers and sellers at auctions, from which profession he earned enough money to give his son a prestigious education in Rome alongside the sons of the senatorial and equestrian elite.[3] Horace thereupon went to Athens, where he studied philosophy at the Academy before joining the losing side of Brutus and Cassius in the civil war against Antony and Octavian (later Augustus) at Philippi in 42 B.C.E.[4] While in the army he attained the rank of *tribunus militum* (military tribune), a position that brought with it equestrian standing.[5]

Following the general amnesty issued after Philippi, Horace returned to Rome but seems to have suffered diminution of his estate in the ensuing property confiscations, for which reason he turned to writing poetry.[6] He nevertheless possessed enough wealth to purchase a prominent post as *scriba quaestorius,* clerk of the public treasury, an expensive acquisition that belies his poetic claims to poverty at this time.[7] Horace came into real prominence through his position as friend and client of Maecenas, Augustus's advisor and "right-hand-man," to whom he was introduced by the famous poets Varius and Vergil.[8] His friendship with Maecenas is a topic

---

2. Horace's precise birthdate is given in Suetonius's *Life of Horace*, and the poems verify both the month (*Epistles* 1.20.27) and the year (*Epodes* 13.6, *Odes* 3.21.1). On Horace's birthplace see *Satires* 1.5.77 and 2.1.34 as well as *Odes* 3.4.9–16, 3.30.10, and 4.9.2. He mentions his father's freed status throughout *Satires* 1.6 and at *Epistles* 1.20.20.

3. For Horace's early education and his father's role therein, see *Satires* 1.6.71–88.

4. *Epistles* 2.2.41–48.

5. *Satires* 1.6.48.

6. *Epistles* 2.2.49–52.

7. On his position as scribe, see *Satires* 2.6.36 and Suetonius's *Life of Horace.* On Horace's equestrian rank and position as scribe, see esp. Armstrong (1986).

8. Horace recounts his first meeting with Maecenas and the subsequent invitation to join the great man's circle of friends at *Satires* 1.6.54–62. Maecenas's precise position and role in Rome is hard to pinpoint. To quote DuQuesnay (1984), "he was at this time the second most powerful man in Rome; yet he remained an elusive and

he revisits frequently throughout his poems, and it is to this patron that he dedicates the *Epodes, Satires* 1, *Odes* 1–3, and *Epistles* 1. Their friendship was further cemented when Maecenas, as seems likely, bestowed Horace with the gift of the Sabine farm in the countryside to the northeast of Rome or else with the means to acquire it.[9] This farm provided Horace with the leisure necessary for directing his thoughts to poetic composition, and he speaks of it gratefully as giving him the means of living a sound, ethical life free from both ambition and want. As Horace's poetic success grew, he found himself increasingly attracting the notice of Augustus, by whom, according to the Suetonian biography, he was asked to compose the *Carmen Saeculare* for the Secular Games of 17 B.C.E. In the final period of his life—especially after Vergil's death in 19 B.C.E.—Horace was the most prominent poet in Rome, a position he would enjoy until his own death on November 27, 8 B.C.E.[10]

Although the general sweep of this biography probably reflects real events of his life, many of the autobiographical details Horace provides are no doubt poetic fabrications.[11] Horace's celebrated poverty, for instance, probably owes more to poetic fiction than to fact, since poverty is a style of life professed by more than one lyric poet in the Greco-Roman tradition, including, for example, Archilochus, Theognis, Hipponax, and Catullus. For these poets poverty is a means of expressing the lyric persona's self-effacement and of contrasting the small scope of their poetry with the grander claims and sweeping scale of epic verse. Horace employs poverty, moreover, as an important ethical marker; it symbolizes the simplicity, satisfaction, and moderation that form the moral heart of his lyric poems,

---

enigmatic figure, a *privatus* and an *eques* whose power resided in his *amicitia* with Octavian" (26).

9. Horace never explicitly credits the benefaction of the farm to Maecenas, though many scholars see this implied at *Epodes* 1.31–32. For Horace's gratitude, see the opening of *Satires* 2.6, where Horace attributes the farm to *Maia nate* ("Maia's son," that is, Mercury), which, as Bowditch (2001, 153) points out, strongly recalls in sound the ablative of Maecenas, *Maecenate*. For the opposing view that Horace purchased the farm independently, see Bradshaw (1989).

10. Suetonius's biography provides us with his death date.

11. For an introduction to Horace's poetic self-representation, see Harrison (2007b). For studies that consider the poetic construction of Horace's lyric persona, see Davis (1991), Lowrie (1997), and Oliensis (1998).

but this does not necessarily reflect Horace's lived experience. Much of his autobiographical information, moreover, seems heavily crafted to suit the genre in which it is presented. In *Odes* 2.7, for example, Horace offers the enticing detail that he lost his shield during the Battle of Philippi. The veracity of this is called into doubt when we remember that Archilochus and Anacreon each claim to have lost their shields in battle, and a similar story is recounted about Alcaeus.[12] The loss of his shield says less about Horace as a historical person than it does about him as a lyric construct.

Horace's self-presentation in the *Epodes* and *Odes,* furthermore, draws from the complex lyric tradition on which he models himself. He is variously a misogynist like Semonides of Amorgos, a lover like Mimnermus, or a politically engaged citizen like Alcaeus. He can adopt different or even contradictory modes of life in different poems, at times retired from political life and at others addressing the citizenry, at times too old for love and at others attempting to seduce. Horace creates and recreates himself from poem to poem as the literary occasion demands, and the "I" whose beliefs and thoughts these poems purport to voice is best thought of as a meticulously crafted literary persona.

It is not only with his own life that Horace takes such poetic license. The famous portrait of his freedman father, for instance, is heavily indebted to the poetic and thematic concerns of his hexameter poetry. In this view, his father is carefully crafted as a protosatirist who provided his son with the moral authority needed to write satire, yet as a freedman he also fuels the poet's status anxiety that is a major theme of both the *Satires* and *Epistles.*[13] This beloved father, moreover, is nowhere to be found in the lyric poems. Many other figures that inhabit Horatian poetry should similarly be read more as literary characters than accurate reflections of historical figures— especially Maecenas. Although Maecenas was undoubtedly a real person, the poems do not give us incontrovertible or uncontroversial evidence for the historical relationship between the poet and patron or the actual events of

---

12. Archilochus fr. 5 and Anacreon fr. 51. For Alcaeus, see Herodotus 5.95.
13. On Horace's father, see esp. Schlegel (2000). For status anxiety, especially in the *Epistles*, see McCarter (2015).

their lives. *Epodes* 1, for example, offers enticing evidence for some scholars that Maecenas and Horace were present for Octavian's victory at Actium in 31 B.C.E., but this evidence contradicts what is found in other authors, such as the historians Appian, Cassius Dio, and Valleius Peterculus, nor does Horace explicitly mention Actium in the poem.[14] Scholars have consequently tied themselves into knots trying to reconcile conflicting accounts. It is likely more productive to focus on the ways in which the opening epode introduces the poetic themes of war and male friendship that run through the *Epodes* rather than search for historical veracity.

Horace's poetic output can be divided broadly into two metrical categories: lyric and dactylic hexameter works. The former, written in a variety of lyric meters that date back to archaic Greece, consist of the *Epodes, Odes,* and *Carmen Saeculare,* all of which are contained in this volume. The latter, comprising short poems written in dactylic hexameter, include the two books of *Satires,* the two books of *Epistles,* and the *Ars Poetica.* Horace moved back and forth between lyric and hexameter throughout his poetic career. The earliest works we have from his pen are the first book of *Satires,* published in 35 B.C.E. Often referred to as the "smiling" satirist, Horace pokes fun at the moral foibles of those around him, opines on literary and poetic matters, reveals his own faults and eccentricities, and fashions those around Maecenas as an idealized circle of friends who enjoy frank philosophical conversation. A second book of *Satires* followed in around 30 B.C.E., and in it Horace frequently hands over the role of satirist to others, including the inept Stoic Damasippus (2.3) and his outspoken slave Davus (2.7). Perhaps the best-known satire of this book is 2.6, a celebration of the Sabine farm and a recounting of the fable of the country and city mouse.

Concurrent with *Satires* 2 is the book of *Epodes,* published also in 30 B.C.E. These are short lyric poems written in the tradition of Greek *iambus,* a form of poetry known chiefly in antiquity for abusive invective. Horace's magnum opus, the first three books of *Odes,* was published as a unit in 23 B.C.E. In these

---

14. Appian (*Bella civilia* 4.50), Cassius Dio (49.16.2 and 51.3.5), and Valleius Paterculus (2.88.2) all suggest that Maecenas stayed behind to manage Octavian's affairs in Rome.

poems Horace models himself on the great lyric poets of ancient Greece and crafts a powerful vision of post–civil war Augustan Rome. Horace follows this lyric achievement by returning to hexameters, publishing in 19 B.C.E. the first book of *Epistles,* a collection of twenty verse letters addressed to a variety of real and fictitious people. Horace adopts a more mature voice in these poems and takes up a heightened ethical and philosophical focus. He resumes lyric with a choral ode, the *Carmen Saeculare,* for performance at Augustus's Secular Games in 17 B.C.E. and with a fourth book of *Odes* in around 13 B.C.E. At this point Maecenas begins to retreat to the background of the poems and Augustus and his family to emerge to the forefront as a sharper imperial emphasis unfolds.[15] Horace addresses the *princeps* himself in the so-called *Epistle to Augustus* (*Epistles* 2.1), in which he takes up literary matters, including the role of the poet in the state. This literary focus is retained in *Epistles* 2.1 (addressed to a young poet named Florus) and the *Ars Poetica,* a highly influential verse letter on the craft of writing poetry. These later epistles are generally dated to the final years of his life, from 13 to 8 B.C.E.

AUGUSTUS AND THE EARLY PRINCIPATE

Although Horace's poems should not be read primarily as conclusive historical evidence, they nevertheless were not written in a historical or cultural vacuum. It is in fact impossible to imagine any of these works being written in a different time or place than the Rome that witnessed the rise of Augustus, the first emperor. From the expressions of anxiety about civil war in the *Epodes* to the cautious optimism about peace and moral renewal of the *Odes,* these poems reflect and reflect on the momentous changes in Rome as it transitioned from republic to empire. It is therefore worthwhile to offer a sketch of the historical context to better grasp how Horace's poetry mirrors as well as participates in the formulation of the ideals of Augustan Rome.[16]

---

15. Some have tried to use Maecenas's eclipse from the works as evidence that he fell from Augustus's favor, but no consensus on this question has been reached. See, for example, Williams (1990) and White (1991).
16. The bibliography on the late republic and early empire is immense and can be daunting. For those interested in going beyond this cursory summary, good starting points would be von Ungern-Sternberg (2014) on the late republic, Eder (2005) on the rise of Augustus, and Gruen (2005) on the early Augustan principate.

Horace came of age in a Rome and Italy divided by factional strife. By the time he was born, violence had been an instrument of political action for decades, beginning with the deaths of the tribunes Tiberius Gracchus in 133 B.C.E. and his brother Gaius Gracchus in 121 B.C.E., both of whom died at the instigation of an angry senate. All-out civil war erupted throughout the Italian peninsula with the Social War of 91–88 B.C.E. as the Italian allies of Rome successfully fought the capital city for full Roman citizenship. It was in this war that Horace's father may have experienced a period of enslavement.[17] During this time a series of strongmen arose, each competing to become the foremost man in Rome and each employing violence and military might to this end. Marius (157–86 B.C.E.), Sulla (138–78 B.C.E.), and Cinna (died 84 B.C.E.) inaugurated the use of private armies, proscription lists, and land confiscations as tools of civil war; their use would be resumed more than once during Horace's life.[18]

Two final bursts of civil bloodshed, each occurring in Horace's youthful years, would bring an end to the republic and usher in the principate. In the 50s B.C.E. three men were jockeying to be the foremost man in the state: Crassus, the wealthiest man in Rome; Pompey, the most brilliant and successful general; and Julius Caesar, a popular general and orator who ultimately sought to surpass both. These three agreed to combine their collective influence and in 60 B.C.E. formed the First Triumvirate, a private alliance designed to overcome any possible opposition to their political and military agendas. Caesar was elected consul in 59 B.C.E. and received an extraordinary five-year command (renewed in 55) as the proconsul in Gaul, where with his private army he proceeded to amass enormous amounts of wealth and prestige and thereby cemented the loyalty of his soldiers. After the military defeat and death of Crassus in Parthia in 53 B.C.E., the alliance between Caesar and Pompey became increasingly insecure, and civil war grew inevitable.

In 50 B.C.E. an alarmed senate called on both Caesar and Pompey to disband their armies, an act that Caesar refused, choosing instead in January of

---

17. For this theory see esp. Williams (1995).
18. In proscriptions, a list of individuals was drawn up, and anyone who killed or aided the killing of these individuals received a share of their property as a reward, with the rest going to the state.

49 to march his men across the Rubicon into Italy in a virtual declaration of civil war. The decisive battle of this war would be held at Pharsalus in Greece in 48 B.C.E., where Caesar's army defeated the much larger force of Pompey. Following the defeat, Pompey fled to Egypt, where he was killed as his boat came to shore at the initiative of the young ruler of Egypt, Ptolemy XIII, the brother of the famous Cleopatra VII, with whom Ptolemy was himself involved in a civil war for the throne. This murder so angered Caesar, who prided himself on his clemency, that he thereupon allied himself with Cleopatra against her brother, eventually fathering a son, Caesarion, with her. In 44 B.C.E. Caesar declared himself *dictator perpetuus,* commonly translated as "dictator for life." Although the dictatorship was a traditional office intended for times of crisis, it had a term limit of six months, and Caesar's open-ended possession of this position caused considerable alarm, especially in the senate. Fearful that he aimed at becoming a king, a group of about sixty senators led by Brutus and Cassius assassinated Caesar on the Ides (15th) of March, 44 B.C.E., championing themselves protectors of Roman liberty.

Caesar's will revealed that he had adopted his eighteen-year-old great-nephew Octavian, who immediately set out to claim his inheritance. The young Octavian's attempts to accede to Caesar's position quickly brought him into conflict with Mark Antony, who was Caesar's coconsul and staunchest ally. The senatorial opponents of Mark Antony, especially Cicero—who considered Antony a potential tyrant and published a series of speeches, entitled the *Philippics,* harshly denouncing him—hoped that Octavian would be a malleable tool against Antony's rise, and indeed the young Octavian initially lent his aid to this senatorial opposition, helping to defeat Antony at Mutina in April of 43 B.C.E. Cicero and the senate did not, however, take Octavian seriously enough. Cicero was rumored to have called him a *laudandum adulescentem, ornandum, tollendum* (a youth to be praised, honored, and gotten rid of), a remark that made its way back to Octavian and roused his displeasure.[19] Octavian in fact quickly proved

---

19. *Tollendum* here is ambiguous, since it can mean "gotten rid of" or "exalted." The context of the letter (*Ad Familiares* 11.20.1), however, makes it clear that Octavian read it as a dismissive insult.

himself a force to be reckoned with when in August of 43 B.C.E. he marched on Rome with eight legions and was accordingly elected consul at a record nineteen years of age.

In November of 43 B.C.E. Octavian formed an alliance known as the Second Triumvirate with Antony and Lepidus, another powerful ally of Caesar. Unlike the First Triumvirate, this was a legal arrangement whose chief goal was to defeat the assassins of Julius Caesar. Antony and Octavian together controlled an enormous number of soldiers—twenty legions each, with four thousand to five thousand men per legion—and now sought ways of paying so huge an army. A new set of proscriptions took place, and at Antony's behest Cicero's name was placed on the list of the proscribed. The orator was killed in December of 43 B.C.E. and his severed head placed on the speaker's platform in Rome. The triumvirs defeated the army of Brutus and Cassius at the Battle of Philippi in 42 B.C.E., whereupon both of the assassins committed suicide. Present at the battle and fighting on behalf of Brutus and Cassius against Octavian and Antony was Horace.

After the victory at Philippi, Octavian returned to Italy to take up the tasks of settling veterans via land confiscations and defeating the prorepublican fleet of Sextus Pompey, son of Pompey the Great. Antony meanwhile remained in the east, where he famously undertook a political alliance and sexual affair with Cleopatra. This affair would ultimately result in the birth of three children, a set of twins named Alexander and Cleopatra and a son named Ptolemy Philadelphus. We have inherited from the Romans a portrait of Cleopatra as a beautiful, dangerous femme fatale, a characterization that we would do well to regard with suspicion. The enormous amount of Roman propaganda against her has permanently and indelibly distorted the image of this formidable monarch and has reduced her to a stereotypically power-hungry female whose potent sexuality emasculates the men around her, including Antony. Horace draws extensively on such propaganda in his famous poem about the defeat of Cleopatra, *Odes* 1.37.[20]

Despite Antony's affair with Cleopatra and the building tension between him and Octavian, the triumvirate was reinforced in 40 B.C.E.,

---

20. On Augustan propaganda and image-making, see especially Zanker (1988).

when Antony married Octavian's sister, Octavia, and in 37 B.C.E., when the alliance was renewed for another five-year period. After Lepidus fell from favor in 36 B.C.E, Rome stood divided between Antony in the east and Octavian in the west, and a hostile propaganda campaign between the two ensued, with Octavian depicting himself as an upholder of traditional Roman values against an easternized and decadent Antony. Civil war became inevitable, and in 31 B.C.E. Octavian declared war not on Antony, but on Cleopatra. In September of that year, Octavian defeated Antony and Cleopatra in a sea battle at Actium on the western coast of Greece. Antony and Cleopatra fled to Alexandria, which fell to Octavian the following year with little resistance. Antony committed suicide by falling on his sword, and Cleopatra took her own life nine days later, a (now romanticized) act that Horace in *Odes* 1.37 suggests she undertook in order to avoid being marched as a captive in a Roman triumph. Octavian annexed Egypt as his own personal province, declaring himself pharaoh, in order to prohibit any further potential rival from gaining control of this wealthy and fertile region. He returned to Rome in 29 B.C.E., whereupon he celebrated a famed triple triumph for his victories in the east.

After his victory at Actium, Octavian emerged as the sole ruler in the Roman world, a position he would retain for over four decades until his death in 14 C.E. In 27 B.C.E. the senate bestowed on him the honorary title Augustus, under which name he has come to be known to us. Yet he would shirk any title aligning him with monarchy or one-man-rule, preferring the term *princeps* (first citizen, whence comes the term "principate") and arguing that his power derived more from *auctoritas* (influence) than any changes to the traditional republican constitution. He thus framed his victory not as the end of the republic but as its restoration. He operated within the existing republican framework, albeit in unprecedented ways, occupying, for example, the consulship continually from 31 to 23 B.C.E. A new arrangement was formed in 23 B.C.E. (the same year *Odes* 1–3 was published), traditionally called the "Second Settlement," whereby he permanently relinquished the consulship and all other magistracies, thus allowing competitive and ambitious Romans to compete for these positions. Instead, he retained up to his death the power of a tribune (*tribunicia potestas*), which gave him authority to veto acts of the senate, sacrosanctity, and popular appeal. In 12 B.C.E. he was given the lifelong position of *pontifex maximus,* chief priest, a position that invested him with significant moral authority, and in 2 B.C.E. he was honored with the title *Pater Patriae* (father of the fatherland).

Romans had a strong tendency to explain civil and political crises as stemming from the moral failures of the populace and its leaders, and consequently Augustus undertook a program of religious and moral renewal.[21] These reforms were aimed at restoring old-fashioned ancestral customs, the *mos maiorum,* which moralizing Romans felt had been compromised as expansion brought in wealth, luxury, and foreign customs. Augustus built or restored over eighty temples, including a new temple to Apollo on the Palatine Hill in thanksgiving for his victory at Actium. One of the keywords of this period of renewal was *pietas,* translated variously as "duty" or "piety," which was properly directed toward parents, fatherland, and gods. Vergil's *Aeneid,* published upon the author's death in 19 B.C.E., puts forth Aeneas as a hero exemplifying such *pietas,* who exercises this virtue by placing the demands of the state and the divine above his own private desires. Such *pietas* is designed in many ways as an antidote to the grand, personal ambitions of individuals that had so imperiled the state during the civil wars.

Augustus brought about his moral agenda through legislation as well, creating a series of new laws aimed at regulating sexual morality, especially among the elite.[22] The *lex Iulia de maritandis ordinibus* of 18 B.C.E. restricted marriage between certain social groups (such as between senators and freedwomen) and placed steep financial penalties on those who would not marry or remarry. The *lex Iulia de adulteriis* of the same year harshly criminalized adultery by mandating divorce from adulterous wives, the prohibition of adulterous women from reentering into legitimate marriage, steep financial penalties against both woman and adulterer, and the exile

---

21. The connection between personal *mores* and the Roman state features prominently in the Roman historians Sallust, Livy, and Tacitus.
22. On Augustus's legislation promoting marriage and childbirth, see especially Dixon (1988, 71–103). For his legislation on adultery, see especially Edwards (1993, 34–62).

of both to separate islands. The *lex Papia Poppaea* of 9 B.C.E. offered political and financial incentives for men and women who bore three or more children. These moral reforms were motivated also by the practical goal of restoring the population of Rome, which had been depleted by war, especially among the equestrian and senatorial ranks. Augustus's moral legislation was targeted especially at women, since unrestrained female sexuality was considered especially dangerous to the well-being of the state. He put forth the female members of his own household, including his wife Livia and sister Octavia, as exemplars of ideal, chaste Roman womanhood. He furthermore invoked these laws even against the women of his own family when he exiled first his daughter and then his granddaughter, both named Julia, for adultery. It is this moral climate that we see reflected repeatedly in the *Odes,* especially the six so-called Roman Odes that open book 3.

Augustus characterized his restoration of peace as a second founding of Rome and indeed as a renewal of the mythological Golden Age. In 17 B.C.E. he revived the *Ludi Saeculares* (Secular Games), meant to inaugurate a new Roman *saeculum* (age), an event thought to recur every 100 to 110 years. This three-day event was, to quote John Miller, "one of the most spectacular religious celebrations that Rome had ever seen."[23] It involved prayers, processions, sacrifices, feasting, and hymns. As a centerpiece of the event, a chorus of boys and girls performed Horace's *Carmen Saeculare* (Secular Hymn), written specifically for this occasion.

Despite his involvement with bloodshed, civil war, and the politics of personal ambition, Augustus's restoration of peace put a badly needed end to a century of upheaval and violence. Not everyone, however, would unambiguously welcome the new political reality. The senatorial male elite in particular would lament the reduction of personal and political *libertas* (freedom) that accompanied the advent of Augustus, especially in the sphere of free speech. The Roman historian Tacitus, writing at the start of the second century C.E., characterized the elite as eager slaves to the new regime: *at Romae ruere in servitium consules, patres, eques* (At Rome there rushed into slavery the consuls, the senators, the equestrians)

---

23. John Miller (2009, 253).

(1.7).[24] The republic, especially its idealized early period before the civil wars, would remain an object of Roman nostalgia throughout the imperial period, including already in Horace's own works.

Horace takes up the political events of his lifetime both directly and indirectly in his poetry, and these events form a major backdrop against which both the *Epodes* and *Odes* must be considered. Readers should, however, be cautioned against scrutinizing these poems for Horace's unambiguous personal views toward the new regime, whether positive or negative. In addressing the *princeps* or articulating the nature of his rule, the Horatian persona takes up a number of different roles; he is by turns a critic, an advisor, a champion, a stern moralist, a hedonist, a coward, a staunch nationalist, and a disengaged nonparticipant. He models in these poems the many different and even contradictory reactions one could have to the political upheavals of this period and seeks out a variety of explanations and solutions for them. It is therefore best to consider how Horace fashions a complex and nuanced dialogue between his poems and the principate rather than to attempt to uncover the unambiguous mind of the man writing the poems.[25]

THE *EPODES*

The seventeen poems of the *Epodes,* along with the second book of *Satires,* were published in 30 B.C.E. in the immediate wake of Octavian's victory at Actium.[26] By this time, Horace's friendship with Maecenas, to whom he dedicates the first poem and thus the collection, is firm, and through this friendship Horace is connected to Octavian's inner circle. In these poems Actium and the civil war form a major backdrop, especially in poems 1, 7, 9,

---

24. For an illuminating study of how the language of freedom and slavery was used to characterize the relationship between *princeps* and his subjects, see Roller (2001, 213–87).
25. For an overview of Horace and Augustus, see Lowrie (2007). On the problems and limitations of pro- and anti-Augustus interpretations, see Kennedy (1992).
26. Useful introductions to the *Epodes* are Watson (2007), Mankin (2010), and Günther (2013b), as well as the introductions to the commentaries of Mankin (1995) and Watson (2003). Recent book-length studies include Johnson (2012) and the volume of papers edited by Bather and Stocks (2016).

and 16.[27] The poems, moreover, present us with a series of themes implicitly embroiled with the larger societal upheaval, from the narrator's own loss of masculine virility to the dangerous sexual voracity of hags and witches and the upstart ambitions of social climbers. Yet Horace does not allow such social chaos, enmity, and antagonism to run entirely unchecked through the poems, opposing these divisive forces with evocations of friendship (especially that between Horace and Maecenas) and by softening and mitigating the harsh invective potential of his verse. The result is a collection of poems whose tone is ambiguous and subject to vacillation as at different moments they mimic the larger turmoil within Rome, point to a variety of solutions, and question the efficacy and desirability of the very solutions they propose.

In order to understand this complex tone, it is helpful to consider how Horace transformed the ancient genre to which the *Epodes* belongs, *iambus*. Its chief practitioner in the Greek tradition was Archilochus, who lived in the seventh century B.C.E. In all of his poetic endeavors, Horace prided himself on his originality, a term that for the Romans had less to do with inventing something anew than with taking up a long-standing Greek literary form and handling it in a new way. In *Epistles* 1.19, published about ten years after the publication of the *Epodes,* Horace describes how he had transformed his iambic model thus:

> Parios ego primus iambos
> ostendi Latio, numeros animosque secutus
> Archilochi, non res et agentia uerba Lycamben.

> I first showed Parian iambs
> to Latium, following the meter and spirit of Archilochus,
> not his subject matter and the words that harassed Lycambes.

Horace alludes here to the popular legend that Archilochus attacked Lycambes, who had promised his daughter Neobule to him in marriage and then reneged on that agreement, so viciously in his poetry that both father and daughter committed suicide. It is impossible to verify this story from

---

27. On the references to the civil war in the *Epodes*, see especially Nisbet (1984).

the fragmentary remains of Archilochus's poetry, but such invective, that is, harsh verbal aggression, is very much on display in these fragments. Attack was in fact the chief characteristic associated with invective poetry in antiquity, and Horace's choice of this genre, together with the mitigation of its abusive speech and personal rancor, must be read within the larger context of the civil war.[28] As Watson remarks, "*iambos* typically arises in times of social change or political stasis: the iambic poet hence feels empowered to preach to the populace at large appropriate behavior at crucial junctures in their history."[29] The restrained invective of the *Epodes,* while partaking of the aggressive ethos of civil war, also enacts a curbing of it as a necessary antidote to violence. Furthermore, the breakdown of societal systems resulting from civil turmoil is met in these poems with a desperate, though not always effective, attempt to reinforce social hierarchies, both of male over female, as in 8 and 12, and within the highly stratified system of Roman *amicitia* (friendship), with its delicate but inescapable negotiations of power and authority.[30] The first epode, for example, places Octavian, Maecenas, and Horace in a clearly hierarchical relationship and assigns suitable social roles to each according to rank.[31]

Yet the curbing of invective attack is itself problematic for Horace's iambic persona. *Iambus,* with its potent verbal hostility, is marked as especially masculine, whereas the Horace we encounter in these poems seems to experience a crisis of virility, as if the loss of invective force is a result not of

28. Horace's characterization in *Epistles* 1.19 of Archilochean *iambus* is, however, overly simplistic. The iambic tradition from which Horace draws is much broader than just the invective mode, and Archilochus, like Horace, uses his iambic as a vehicle for themes of friendship and ethics. In toning down iambic aggression, Horace follows an iambic mode already taken up by the Alexandrian poet Callimachus in his *iambi.* See most recently Morrison (2016). On Horace and the iambic genre, see also Barchiesi (2001), Harrison (2001), Hutchinson (2007), and the commentaries of Mankin (1995, 6–9) and Watson (2003, 4–19).
29. Watson (2007, 96).
30. In his definition of Roman *amicitia*, Saller (1982, 1) emphasizes the asymmetrical nature of the relationship, since it almost always involves two parties of unequal status, that is, the patron and client. Romans, however, avoided openly acknowledging this hierarchy, designating both parties with the term *amicus* (friend).
31. On the hierarchical configuration of Octavian, Maecenas, and Horace in *Epodes* 1, see Oliensis (1991, 127–28).

commendable restraint but of enervation and powerlessness. In this view, his words lack the power to drive Lycambes to suicide not because he has purposefully toned them down but because in his hands *iambus* has lost its potency. The persona's chief characteristic is in fact impotence, both sexual and verbal, especially in the face of female opposition, such as that of the "old hags" of *Epodes* 8 and 12 or of the witch Canidia in *Epodes* 5 and 17. In the face of such powerlessness the persona's only recourse is to the utterance of curses, which are a traditional element of iambic poetry but which also suggest the ineffectiveness of masculine action.

Horace's crisis of masculinity can be understood in a number of ways. On the one hand, it is a reflection of the general social crisis, at the center of which stood, according to Augustan propaganda, an enervated Antony and sexually potent Cleopatra. On the other hand, the curbing of Horace's aggressive free speech—which is one connotation of the Latin word *libertas* (freedom)—also suggests anxiety about the emergence of Octavian in post-Actium Rome. In a society wherein the right to speak was synonymous with masculine power, speech is necessarily one sphere that becomes diluted and diminished in the face of one-man-rule, and the poems cast doubt on the efficacy of unrestrained, free speech as a tool of masculine action suitable for the new political reality beginning to take shape. Horatian impotence in the *Epodes* thus has complex literary and political nuances, and it is therefore not easily reduced to a single, coherent meaning.[32]

Whereas Horace toned down Archilochus's invective hostility, his claim to have followed Archilochus's *numeri* (meter), indicates his conformity to the technical and metrical requirements of the genre. Although the origins of *iambus* are murky, it can be understood as one subcategory of the broad poetic form commonly designated as "lyric," an umbrella term often used to describe nonepic and nondramatic forms of ancient poetry.[33] *Iambus*

---

32. On Horatian impotence in the *Epodes,* see especially Fitzgerald (1988), Oliensis (1991), and Watson (1995). On the issues of gender and power in the poems, see also Gowers (2016).
33. Some scholars prefer to use a narrow definition of the term "lyric" as referring only to the "melic" poetry accompanied by stringed instruments such as the lyre. On this type of lyric, see below under the *Odes.* Elegy is the third type of poetry

was written in a variety of meters, but Horace's *Epodes* takes its name from its epodic meter. This arrangement, attributed to Archilochus, consists of "epodic couplets," that is, two lines of different metrical length and sometimes different metrical structures. The first ten poems of the collection form a metrical block, with couplets consisting of a line of iambic trimeter followed by a line of iambic dimeter. In Latin, meter is quantative, based on long and short syllables, so the metrical scheme for these poems would be as follows:

$$\times - \breve{} - \times \| - \breve{} - \times - \breve{} \times$$
$$\times - \breve{} - \times - \breve{} \times$$

Just when readers have grown accustomed to this metrical regularity, however, the final seven epodes offer a burst of metrical variety as Horace demonstrates his virtuosic skill at adapting native Greek rhythms to the Latin language and stretches the metrical limits of *iambus* by incorporating elegiac and dactylic elements into his verses.[34] The final epode disrupts our metrical expectations entirely as Horace abandons the couplet form and closes the collection with repeating lines of iambic trimeter. Although working in a definite tradition of Archilochean epodic meter, it is clear that Horace exploits this inheritance with a great deal of originality and variation. Indeed, Horace's claim to be the first to attempt such a metrical enterprise in Latin is entirely true.[35]

The *Epodes* have long lived in the shadow of Horace's other works, especially the *Odes*.[36] It may be that the aggressively virulent yet often ineffectual narrator seems too unlike his (usually) restrained counterpart in the

---

commonly categorized under the broad definition of lyric, but there is no indication that Horace practiced this form.

34. Elegiac poetry employed a metrical unit known as a *hemiepes* ($- \breve{} \breve{} - \breve{} \breve{} \times$), a unit Horace incorporates into *Epodes* 11 and 13. Dactyic hexameter, consisting of six dactyls ($- \breve{} \breve{}$) or spondees ($- -$) makes up one line of the epodic couplet in *Epodes* 12, 13, 14, 15, and 16.

35. On Horace's handling of Archilochean meter in the *Epodes*, see especially the introductions of Mankin (1995) and Watson (2003) as well as Bather and Stocks (2016, 8–14).

36. On the "afterlife" of Horace's *Epodes*, see especially Oliensis (2016).

Odes, who emphasizes decorum and moderation. The violent misogyny and obscenity of poems 8 and 12 have particularly disquieted many readers for a variety of reasons. Some of the poems have been much more widely read and translated than others, especially the perennial favorite *Epodes* 2, whose celebrated praise of the countryside it is tempting to want to see as Horace's own despite its being put into the mouth of a hypocritical urban moneylender, a fact not revealed until the closing epilogue.[37] Horace himself suggests in a later epistle that at least *some* people prefer his *Epodes* to his *Odes: non omnes eadem mirantur amantque; / carmine tu gaudes, hic delectatur iambis* (not all like and admire the same things; you enjoy odes, but this person takes delight in my iambs) (*Epistles* 2.2.58–59). It is precisely because the Horace we meet in the *Epodes* makes readers a bit uncomfortable or is a bit too unfamiliar that these poems should be taken into greater account. These are complex poems written for a complicated time, and we ignore them to the detriment of our understanding of the full arc of Horace's poetic career as it developed alongside momentous political and social upheaval.

THE *ODES*

The *Odes,* including the first three books published in 23 B.C.E. and a fourth that followed a decade later, are products of a more established stage of Augustus's consolidation of power and of Horace's poetic career. Just as Augustus's power in the Second Settlement of 23 B.C.E. rested more and more on his unquestionable *auctoritas,* so too in the *Odes* do we perceive Horace adopting a more authoritative voice, going so far as to predict his own poetic immortality already in the opening poem, albeit somewhat teasingly. His is often (though not unfailingly) the voice of experience as he takes up the role of wise advisor in matters of love, art, and politics. The *Odes,* like the *Epodes,* mirrors the larger political period in a number of important ways, emphasizing, for example, morality, moderation and

---

37. Not all imitations contain the same hypocrisy as the epode. For example, John Dryden's imitation of the epode, "To My Honor'd Kinsman, John Driden," omits the epilogue revealing Alfius's identity entirely.

decorum, the ties of friendship, and Roman supremacy, all of which favor stability over rancor.

Here again we find Horace breathing new life into an ancient poetic form and creating something original and relevant out of very old ideas. The *Odes* represents a different category of ancient lyric poetry than do the iambic *Epodes.* The *Odes* are "melic," a term derived from the Greek word *melos,* simply meaning "song"—whence comes the English word "melody." Melic poetry in the archaic Greek period was sung to the accompaniment of stringed instruments such as the lyre, barbiton, or cithara, and "lyric" as a narrow term is often used to designate only this type of poetry. Although we should think of the *Odes* more as published (and thus read) than performed (and thus sung or recited) poetry, Horace nods to their traditional musical setting by referring to them as *carmina* (songs), and by repeatedly mentioning accompanying musical instruments, such as the *Lesboum barbiton* (Lesbian barbiton) of *Odes* 1.1.34. Moreover, melic poetry was performed at a variety of public and private events, from grand, statewide religious festivals to semiprivate events such as weddings and funerals to the private, male-oriented symposium that formed the hub of aristocratic life and provided a venue for erotic, philosophical, and political activity.[38] The Horatian ode similarly spans a wide range of public and private situations as we see the narrator advising men about their personal erotic and ethical lives as well as the city at large about matters of political import.

The foremost practitioners of melic poetry in the Greek archaic period were Sappho and Alcaeus, both of whom lived on the island Lesbos, whose chief city was Mytilene, during the seventh century B.C.E. The surviving fragments of Alcaeus show him steeped in the male, aristocratic life of the city. Politics are at the heart of his poems, even those meant for performance at the private symposium or "drinking party," as this was a venue central to the life of the *hetaireia* (political club), an important elite social unit. His poetry is furthermore suffused with the erotic and philosophical

---

38. The women who attended symposia were *hetaerae* (prostitutes—often enslaved) used for sex by the male participants. The symposium was also a venue for homoerotic, pederastic sexuality between older and younger men.

subject matter we would expect to encounter at the symposium. Sappho differs from Alcaeus most obviously in being a woman, one of the very few female poets whose works survive (albeit in a fragmentary state) from Greco-Roman antiquity. Her poetry takes up politics and, more famously, private eroticism but is less tied to the symposium by virtue of her exclusion from that male institution. Although Sappho and especially Alcaeus are Horace's chief lyric models in the *Odes,* these poems are indebted to the whole canon of Greek lyric poets, both melic and nonmelic. Pindar's encomiastic praise poetry holds a special place in book 4, in which Horace's poetry takes a marked turn toward celebration of Augustus and other members of the imperial family, including the future emperor Tiberius and his brother Drusus. Elsewhere, Horace takes his cues, for example, from Mimnermus when comparing human life to the cycle of seasons, from Tyrtaeus in encouraging martial bravery and patriotism, and from Archilochus in articulating the proper response to the ups and downs of human life.[39] Readers engaged by Horace's *Odes* are urged to consult the Greek lyric poets directly in order to appreciate the full extent of his debt to his predecessors.[40]

Just as in the *Epodes,* one of Horace's greatest debts to the Greek lyric tradition in the *Odes* is metrical. The complex lyric meters that he employs all go back to his Greek antecedents and are therefore not native to the Latin language, a fact that makes his achievement all the more impressive. Whereas the *Epodes* ends with a burst of metrical variety, the *Odes* opens with one, with the first nine poems all written in a different meter. This metrical group, often referred to as the "Parade Odes," shows off Horace's metrical brilliance and gives us a glimpse of the variety of verse forms we can expect in the poems to come. Another metrical group, this time based

---

39. Mimnermus fr. 2 contrasts seasons with human life, as in, for example, *Odes* 1.4 and 4.7. Horace's famous claim at *Odes* 3.2.13 that dying for the fatherland is *dulce et decorum* (sweet and seemly) draws on ideas in Tyrtaeus fr. 10. Archilochus fr. 128 urges us to respond to the "rhythm" of human life by avoiding extremes, as in *Odes* 2.10.

40. An accessible annotated anthology of Greek lyric in English translation with a good selection of poems is Andrew Miller (1996). On Horace's debt to Greek lyric in the *Odes,* see the volume of papers edited by Paschalis (2002) as well as Hutchinson (2007), Clay (2010), Davis (2010), and Race (2010).

not on variation but on correspondence, is the "Roman Odes" that open the third book (3.1–6), all of which are in Alcaic strophe. Other metrical arrangements include the alternating Alcaic and Sapphic strophes of 2.1–11 and the ring produced by the shared meter (first Asclepiadean) of 1.1 and 3.30, which open and close the published unit of *Odes* 1–3. Although I do not attempt to replicate Horace's meter, it is worthwhile at least to look at scanned examples of two of Horace's favorite lyric meters, the Alcaic and Sapphic strophe, alongside examples of English poems in the same meter so that readers can at least get some idea of these ancient lyric rhythms. Bear in mind, however, that Latin poetic meter is quantitative, based on long and short vowel quantities rather than on stressed and unstressed syllables, as in the qualitative meter of English poetry. Remember too that, in Latin, every vowel (or diphthong) is pronounced, so *favete,* for example, consists of three distinct syllables:

Alcaic strophe:

Ōdī prŏfānŭm vŭlgŭs ĕt arcĕo.

Făvĕtē līnguīs: carmĭnă nōn prĭŭs

    audītă Mūsārūm săcerdōs

      vīrgĭnĭbūs pŭĕrīsquĕ

        cantō. (3.1.1–4)

"Milton, Alcaics," Alfred Lord Tennyson:

O mighty-mouth'd inventŏr ŏf harmónies,

O skill'd tŏ sing of Time ŏr Éternĭty,

    God-gifted órgan-voice ŏf Éngland,

      Miltŏn, ă name tŏ resoúnd fŏr

        ages. (1–4)

Sapphic strophe:

Aurĕām quīsquīs mĕdĭŏcrĭtātĕm

dīlĭgīt, tūtŭs cărĕt obsŏlētī

sordĭbūs tēctī, cărĕt invĭdēndā

    sōbrĭŭs aūlā. (2.10.5–8)

"Writing in the Manner of Sappho," John Tranter:

Writĭng Sápphĭcs wéll ĭs ă trickў busĭnĕss.

Lines bĕgín ănd énd wĭth ă pair ŏf trochĕes;

in bĕtween thĕm dozĕs ă dactyl, rhythm

    rĭsĭng ănd fallĭng. (1–4)

As Tranter's poem attests, it is extremely difficult in English, as in Latin, to produce these rhythms that were native to ancient Greek, a difficulty confirmed by the rarity of these verse forms in English and by the fact that no Latin poet before Horace had attempted a collection of melic lyric on this same scale.[41]

The four books of *Odes* contain, at 103 poems, considerably more material than the *Epodes,* and the range of themes these poems explore is likewise broader and more complex. It therefore may be helpful to lay out some of the most significant and most interconnected thematic concerns in the *Odes.* The following themes are by no means an exhaustive list, and readers will no doubt make their own thematic observations as they move through the poems.

The Ethical Life

How, given our brief span of mortal life, can we live as well as possible? To answer these questions, Horace draws widely from disparate philosophical systems, especially Epicureanism, with its emphasis on hedonistic withdrawal and freedom from ambition, and Stoicism, with its championing of virtue and the engaged life of action.[42] His ethical source material is poetic and traditional as well, deriving from the Greek lyric poets as well as popular wisdom. The result is a uniquely Horatian brew that contains four chief emphases:

- **Carpe diem**: Horace coins this famous tag, commonly translated as "seize the day," in *Odes* 1.11. *Carpe,* however, means to "pluck" or "harvest" the day as though it were ripe fruit. Although modern interpretations too frequently make of this an endorsement of hedonistic and sexual excess, Horace's message is much more restrained and concerned with the simple enjoyment of the pleasures at hand. Each moment,

---

41. Catullus employs Sapphic strophe in poems 11 and 51, but this is not a strong enough precedent to prohibit Horace from declaring himself the premier Roman lyricist at *Epistles* 1.19.32–33.
42. A good introduction to Horace's use of philosophical material is Moles (2007).

whatever the circumstance, offers enjoyment. Rather than focus on what one does not have, accept life as it is and relish the good in it.

- **The golden mean:** Horace champions this virtue in *Odes* 2.10 and develops it in two ways. On the one hand, it is the avoidance of equally bad extremes (such as destitution and excess wealth), but it also entails the ability to withstand sudden changes in circumstances that make extremes temporarily unavoidable. Moderation can be temporarily suspended, however, in the face of extraordinary circumstances, such as the defeat of Cleopatra in 1.37 (a call to get drunk) or the return of Pompeius in 2.7 (where his friend's homecoming calls for an unrestrained celebration).

- **Decorum:** Variously translated as "honor," "beauty," "suitability," or "seemliness," *decorum* forms the key to appropriately gauging one's action in accordance with one's circumstances, such as age or rank, the season, or the political situation. In *Odes* 1.4, for instance, the return of spring calls for decorous behavior (dancing and sacrifice) that befits the changed circumstance. In *Odes* 3.2 the youthful virility of a Roman soldier makes military courage and virile action commendable, with Horace famously stating that for him it is *dulce et decorum* (sweet and seemly) (13) to die for his country. *Decorum* is furthermore closely tied to aesthetic principles. In *Odes* 1.38, for example, Horace calls for a simple, unadorned myrtle garland that befits both the small-scale, sparse poetry he writes as well as the contented moderation with which he lives his life.

- **The contented life:** Closely aligned with all of the foregoing principles is the moral superiority of the simple life of satisfied contentment. Horace often uses keywords such as *satis* (enough), *tenuis* (slender), *modicus* (modest), and *pauper* (poor) to evoke this concept. The contented life readily facilitates moderation, enjoyment of the moment, and *decorum,* and it significantly acts as an antidote to the personal ambitions that had so ensnared the state in civil war. Horace's small-scale ambition furthermore corresponds to the small-scale compass of the lyric poem.

Morality and Religion

The ethical life is not necessarily equivalent to the moral one, since in Roman thought morals were closely bound less to modes of personal conduct than to conformity to social norms and customs, especially the old-fashioned *mos maiorum* (custom of the ancestors) through which the well-being of the state was thought to be ensured. Religion and the *mos maiorum* are, for example, at the heart of the so-called Roman Odes (*Odes* 3.1–6), in which Horace takes up the role of advisor or even a priestly figure (*vates*) correcting the moral failings that led to civil war, and the moral project of these odes is closely aligned with Augustus's larger religious and moral revival.[43] Female morality is a special concern, especially in 3.6, which mirrors Augustus's larger concerns with marriage and the family. The Cleopatra Ode (1.37) is a powerful demonstration of how greatly unleashed female license can imperil the state.

Friendship and Patronage

From the opening lines of the very first ode, where Horace calls Maecenas his *praesidium et dulce decus* (protection and sweet adornment), friendship (*amicitia*) is front and center. *Amicitia,* however, is hard to define and here encompasses both the idea of affectionate companionship, as we tend to think of it today, and the highly stratified world of patronage that wove together Roman public life. As his social superior and patron, Maecenas offers Horace security and distinction (*praesidium . . . decus*), whereas as his friend he provides Horace with the sweetness and pleasure (*dulce*) that make enjoyment of life possible. Maecenas is not the only friend to whom Horace addresses his odes, for the poems are almost all addressed to people who can be described as his "friends," and these people are sometimes historical people known to us and sometimes names he has no doubt simply fabricated for poetic purposes. The hierarchical configurations shift from poem to poem, as Horace addresses at times his social superiors and at times those who, such as women, sit well below him on the social spectrum. Each poem, however, contains important social dynamics that need to be taken into account.

---

43. On the Roman Odes, see Syndikus (2010); and on gods and religion, see Griffin (2007).

Wine and the Symposium

Horace's lyric odes, like the Greek poetry on which they are modeled, refer often to the symposium.[44] Wine and the symposium function frequently at the symbolic level in these poems, as drinking in the company of friends becomes synonymous with the good life. To *carpe diem,* for example, is to "strain wine" in 1.11, whereas in 1.20 the ethical value of moderation is denoted through "cheap wine" in "modest cups." Wine indeed can symbolize poetry itself, as again in *Odes* 1.20, where the cheap Sabine wine offered to Maecenas is stored in a Greek jar. This humble wine suggests the narrow scope (at only twelve lines) of the poem itself, which comes encased in a Greek metrical form, that is, the wine jar.[45]

Erotics and Gender

Although Horatian lyric is not love poetry per se, it has a significant erotic dimension.[46] Horace often presents himself as just past the suitable age for erotic activity, and he can therefore take up the role of advisor to younger men for whom sex and sexuality are appropriate. For example, in the Pyrrha Ode (1.5), Horace can counsel an inexperienced youth on the erotic heartache awaiting him because he himself has just retired from the life of love. At other times, however, Horace finds himself drawn back against his will into erotic pursuits, as in *Odes* 4.1, or he exposes the mendacity behind his pose as a detached observer of amorous foibles. In *Odes* 1.13, for instance, he gives banal advice about avoiding acrimony in love affairs while himself suffering from fiercely physical erotic desire. Horace uses erotics and gender especially to explore the idea of *decorum,* as sexual affairs are suitable only to one's youth. It is particularly unbecoming for women—or at least for the prostitutes and nonaristocratic women for whom sexual affairs were permissible and who inhabit Horace's lyric world—to extend their sexual availability beyond this period, as in *Odes* 3.15, or to postpone it unduly, as in 1.23.

---

44. On wine and the symposium in the *Odes,* see Commager (1957) and Murray (1993).
45. For this interpretation of *Odes* 1.20, see especially Putnam (1969) and Race (1978).
46. On erotics and gender in the *Odes,* see especially Ancona (1994) and Oliensis (2007).

Female sexuality, especially among elite women, comes across as dangerous not only to the state, as in *Odes* 1.37, but also to the individual men within it. In *Odes* 1.8, for example, Lydia's sexuality threatens to destroy the young Sybaris entirely as it distracts him from his proper masculine pursuits. Elite and "respectable" Roman women were expected to keep their sexuality firmly in check, focusing it instead on producing virile sons for the state. In *Odes* 3.6.39–40, for example, it is the *severa mater* (stern mother), not the sexually voracious woman playing the prostitute to her husband's pimp, who produced the sort of hardy Romans that once defeated Hannibal and other foreign foes.

It is often hard to identify the social standing of Horace's female characters, most of whom we can assume were poetic fabrications. Many of these women appear to be prostitutes, given their frequent presence at the male symposium and their involvement in erotic entanglements. How much sexual and legal autonomy such women would have had is not always clear, and certainly prostitutes were very often slaves and freedwomen who occupied a low rung on the social ladder. On the one hand, the Lydia of 1.25 seems empowered to choose her own lovers, yet, on the other hand, these women are frequently vulnerable to physical and emotional abuse; in 1.17, for example, Horace promises he will not be like Tyndaris's would-be lover Cyrus, who jealously assaults her and rips away her clothing. Horace (or his persona) sometimes romanticizes, furthermore, what we would regard as rape. In 2.4, for example, a young man named Xanthias is in love with his own slave, Phyllis, who would of course possesses no power to turn him away.

Death and the Passage of Time

Horace repeatedly exploits the parallels and contrasts between human life and the seasonal cycle of nature.[47] The moral urgency of these poems, moreover, derives from the fact that the cycle of human life, unlike that of nature, can never be repeated and death awaits us all. For this reason everyone, both rich and poor, must enjoy each season of his or her life to the fullest, but the types of enjoyment that befit each season are different.

---

47. On seasonal imagery in the *Odes*, see Ancona (1994).

In *Odes* 1.4 springtime offers the occasion for the youthful pastimes of dancing and lovemaking but also brings work, whereas winter offers the plowman and flock a chance to relax by the fire. Horace's constant evocation of the movement of time in human life reminds his reader that every springtime leads ineluctably to old age and death, so one must not wait to enjoy the present moment. In *Odes* 4.7, for example spring's arrival leads the speaker's mind almost immediately to the inevitability of death and prompts the warning that we remember our own mortality.

Rural versus Urban Life

Horace has a complex relationship with the city and the country in all of his poetry. In the *Odes,* the country, especially his Sabine farm, forms an idealized locale for ethical contemplation and poetic composition.[48] This modest retreat testifies to his lack of ambition and advertises his practice of the ethical principles he espouses. It furthermore connects him to the old-fashioned agrarian values on which rested the *mos maiorum.* Yet it also necessarily removes him from the sphere of friendship found in the city. In poems 1.20 and 3.29 Horace invites Maecenas to abandon his urban anxieties and join him in rustic simplicity, but there is no poem describing such a visit. Despite his professed love of the countryside, Horace maintains strong ties to the city and the men within it, and his poems repeatedly place us in its midst, from the Tiber's flood in 1.2 to the Capitoline in 3.30 and the temple of Janus in 4.15. Neither city nor country offers undiluted enjoyment of life, and the best approach is to seek pleasures from each as the circumstance and decorum dictate.

Romans and "Barbarians"

At the heart of the *Odes* sits the question of what constitutes Roman identity, *Romanitas.* Like many Romans before him (and many after him), Horace's response to this question involves establishing, often imaginatively, a series of outsiders and "others," particularly foreign others, against whom Rome could be defined. The term the Romans most frequently applied to these

---

48. On the city/country antithesis in Horace's poetry, see Harrison (2007c).

non-Romans was "barbarians," a word originally coined by the Greeks to describe those peoples who did not speak their language. This term of course has played a long and ugly role in the subsequent history of Western imperialism and colonialism, and we already see it being used in this prejudiced and hostile manner in Horace's poems. Horace employs the word not just to designate foreign peoples but also as a derogatory synonym for "wild" or "uncivilized," that is, those who warranted Roman imperial control.

Horace displays particular anxiety about Romans acting like barbarians or being ruled by barbarians, that is, of losing their essential Romanness. For example, in the Regulus Ode (3.5) Horace imagines and laments that Crassus's defeated, captured Romans have adopted Parthian families and customs. He celebrates and repeatedly emphasizes, moreover, the subjection of "barbarians" to Roman authority. This is especially prominent in book 4, where the victories of Tiberius and Drusus in the Alpine regions (4.4. and 4.14) sit alongside and further enhance those of Augustus on the other edges of the empire (e.g., 4.5). This focus on "the other" must also be read in light of Roman civil war, through which hostilities had long been directed internally. Horace now seeks to redirect Roman aggression outward, and his repeated and insistent focusing of his reader's gaze onto the margins of the empire suggests that his anxieties about civil war linger still.

Poetry and Aesthetics

Horace's preference for the small-scale poem and its refined aesthetics finds repeated expression across the *Odes*. One refrain we find again and again, for example in 1.6 and 4.15, is Horace's inability to take up grand epic or panegyric poetry, an inability he blames on his own lack of poetic prowess—a claim we can hardly take seriously since Horace's lyric mastery belies it. Such a repudiation of higher genres of verse is nowadays called a *recusatio* (refusal) and has a long literary history going back to the Alexandrian Greek poet Callimachus, who lived in the third century B.C.E. In Callimachus's *Hymn to Apollo,* the long poem is like a rushing river that carries with it much refuse, whereas the small-scale poem is likened to the purest trickle of water. This combination of "cleanness" and poetic refinement is nicely expressed by the Latin word *munditia,* which suggests both freedom from filth as well as the avoidance of excess in general. Horace, for example, uses this word in *Odes* 1.5.5 to describe Pyrrha, who with her sleek hairstyle is *simplex munditiis* (simply elegant). Like Horace's poetry, her hair eschews unnecessary refinement and is pared back to a polished minimalism. Horace uses this word again in *Odes* 3.29.14 to describe the modest dinner that Maecenas can expect to enjoy on the Sabine farm, but here it is tied to the ethical ideal of the simple life of contentment. We therefore see strong links between Horace's ethical and aesthetic principles, which we find expressed again in *Odes* 2.16.14, where Horace celebrates his *mensa tenuis* (slender table), which at once describes the humbleness of his life and the slim scope of his lyric poetry.[49]

The impact the *Odes* made from the moment of their publication cannot be overstated.[50] These poems, like Vergil's *Aeneid,* became an instant classic and have remained a core part of the literary canon throughout many areas of the world ever since. Horace's survival has been ensured by his central place in the schoolroom, which was true already in the ancient Roman period and remains so today. He has been a persistent object of scholarly inquiry, with commentaries being produced on his poems as early as the third century C.E.[51] He has, perhaps most significantly, been a perennial inspiration to later poets, from antiquity to the present day. Already in the first century C.E., the Latin poet Statius wrote two Horatian lyrics, one in Alcaics (*Silvae* 4.5) and one in Sapphics (*Silvae* 4.7). In the Victorian period, to name just one much later example, Tennyson became especially adept at creating Alcaics in the manner of Horatian odes, as in "Milton," the first four lines of which are quoted above.[52] Some English imitations of Horace's poems have become as famous as the originals, such as Dryden's version

---

49. For the *recusatio* and the links between Horatian aesthetics and ethics, see Mette (2009).
50. Horatian reception is a vast scholarly topic. Those interested should start by consulting the edited volumes of Martindale and Hopkins (1993) and Houghton and Wyke (2009). Introductions to Horatian reception can also be found in the companion edited by Harrison (2007a). For an introduction on the *Odes* in particular, see Edmunds (2010).
51. The chief ancient commentators on Horace were Acro and Porphyrio, and remnants of their work survive in later medieval collections of scholia that were attributed to them.
52. On Tennyson's Alcaics, see Talbot (2004).

of *Odes* 3.29 or Milton's rendering of the Pyrrha Ode (1.5). It is difficult to imagine English poetry without the "carpe diem" theme as Horace articulated it. Andrew Marvell's "To His Coy Mistress" and Robert Herrick's "To the Virgins, to Make Much of Time," to name just two famous examples, are the undeniable literary heirs of Horace's *Odes* 1.23 or 1.25. Even more recently, Seamus Heaney in his poem "Anything Can Happen" looked to Horace's *Odes* 1.34 to inspire his rumination on the world-changing events of September 11, 2001. The extent of Horatian influence on later literature is much too enormous a topic to try to cover here, but it would not be an overstatement to say that without Horace the subsequent history of poetry would look very different indeed.

THE CURRENT TRANSLATION

The current translation has its genesis entirely in the classroom, and with it I have tried to assemble a volume that I myself would find desirable for my students to use. Although I envision its primary audience as students reading these poems in translation for literature classes, it is designed to be highly accessible to general audiences as well. Its primary goal is to present readers with a literal but also poetic and metrical translation of Horace's Latin and to provide them with the tools necessary to dive into a deeper analysis of the poetry if so desired. It is not meant to be read in place of the Latin original but alongside it, and I therefore provide a facing Latin text. I attempt to communicate not just the language and thought of Horace's poems but also to illustrate some of their rhetorical effects and to provide interpretive notes to guide readers through these often challenging works.

Friedrich Nietzsche, in "What I Owe to the Ancients," brilliantly describes Horace's lyric poetry as a "mosaic of words," suggesting that each word is meticulously placed by Horace for a specific aesthetic and rhetorical purpose. Although no English version can hope to recreate this mosaic, this translation's driving force is to respect Horace's original architecture as much as English felicity will allow. I do not change the stanzaic structures of the poems, and I keep Horace's rhetorical effects, such as enjambment, anaphora, and repetition, intact wherever feasible. I make stylistic observations on Horace's Latin with some frequency in the notes and provide a glossary of rhetorical terms, where the bolded terms in the notes can be found. I moreover try to make sure that each word is translated, since each is meaningful, and have attempted to add nothing extraneous to the text, not wanting to detract from the stylistic economy at the heart of these poems. Readers are at times urged in the notes to take account of the Latin on the left side of the page in the belief that even those with little to no Latin can appreciate the aesthetic beauty of a Horatian ode or epode. Navigating the triad of Latin, English, and explanatory notes may slow readers down as they move through the poems, but this is an advantage. Horatian lyric demands a slow reading.

Every translator must make difficult choices, and this is especially true for anyone attempting Horace's lyric poems. One hard decision that confronts a translator of Horace is how to contend with the question of meter, and three options present themselves: (a) to try to recreate Horace's difficult lyric meters in English; (b) to ignore meter altogether and write in free verse or stacked prose; or (c) to adopt a meter that is more at home in the English language. I have opted for the last of these choices, keeping iambic rhythms throughout the translation. The basic unit is the pentameter, but this is lengthened and shortened to reflect the length of Horatian lines. In Sapphic strophe, I have kept the closing adonic rhythm (– ˘˘ – ×, *dum diddy dum dum*), as this is a distinctive and pleasing feature of those stanzas. I chose this route because I wanted the poems to sound *like poetry* to an English speaker, and iambic rhythms are very much at home in English verse. A re-creation of Horace's lyric meters, on the other hand, would be much less easily perceptible to the ear of an English-speaker and would unduly limit the translator's verbal flexibility. I admit, however, that the use of iambs perhaps gives a false impression of metrical regularity, so I have provided in the notes to each poem the name of the meter in which Horace writes. I am of course not alone in having made the decision to render Horace in iambs, and I offer as precedent for this such celebrated poets as Ben Johnson, Alexander Pope, William Cowper, John Dryden, and Lady Mary Wortley Montagu, among many others.

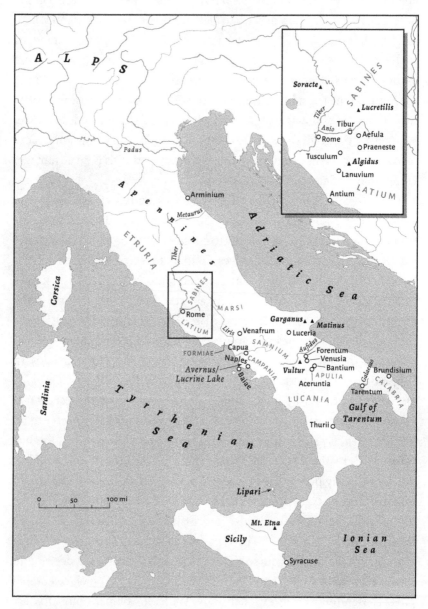

MAP 1. Horace's Italy. Map by Erin Greb Cartography.

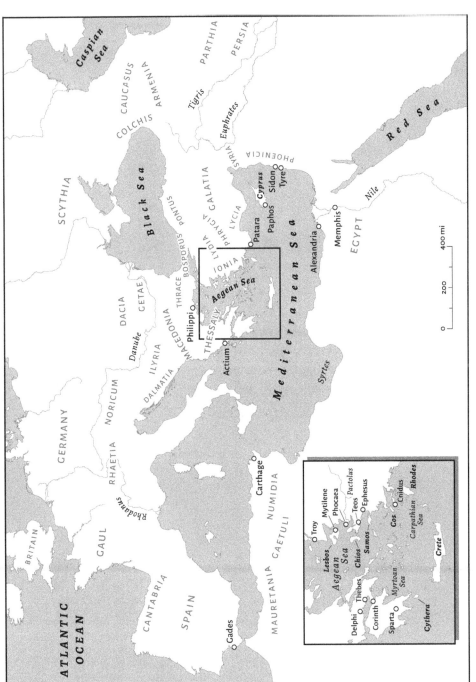

MAP 2. The Roman Empire in the Age of Augustus. Map by Erin Greb Cartography.

EPODES

EPODES 1

Ibis Liburnis inter alta navium,
    amice, propugnacula,
paratus omne Caesaris periculum
    subire, Maecenas, tuo.

EPODES 1[1]

You'll go[2] upon Liburnians,[3] my friend,
    amid the ships' high-rising bulwarks,[4]
prepared to undertake all Caesar's[5] danger,
    Maecenas, even with your own.

[handwritten marginal note: Maceras / ii goy / to war]

---

1. *Epodes* 1 (*Iambic Strophe*): This poem is simultaneously a dedication and send-off (*propempticon*) to Maecenas as he goes on campaign, most likely to Actium (although Horace does not here mention Actium and scholars remain divided as to whether Maecenas was present at the battle). The poem thus has the dramatic date of early 31 B.C.E., though it was no doubt written after Augustus's victory. Horace seems to suggest that he himself will accompany Maecenas to war, though there is no additional evidence for Horace's presence at Actium. He certainly took part in other campaigns, particularly Philippi in 42 B.C.E. Throughout the *Epodes* my notes are indebted to the commentaries by Mankin (1995) and Watson (2003).
2. **You'll go**: The word *ibis* ("you will go" or "embark") forms a nice contrasting ring with the final word of the *Epodes, exitus,* which can mean "ending" or "outcome."
3. **Liburnians**: The small but fast warships used by Octavian (the future emperor Augustus) at Actium (for which see *Odes* 1.37.30).
4. **ships' high-rising bulwarks**: It is not clear if these ships refer to those of Antony (i.e., Maecenas will sail on Octavian's Liburnians into the midst of Antony's ships) or those of Octavian (i.e., he will be on one Liburnian in the midst of many more).
5. **Caesar**: This refers to Octavian, the future Augustus, who was the great-nephew and adopted son of Julius Caesar. "Caesar" would later become a title for the emperors of Rome.

35

quid nos, quibus te vita si superstite   5
    iucunda, si contra, gravis?
utrumne iussi persequemur otium,
    non dulce, ni tecum simul,
an hunc laborem, mente laturi decet
    qua ferre non mollis viros?   10
feremus et te vel per Alpium iuga
    inhospitalem et Caucasum
vel Occidentis usque ad ultimum sinum
    forti sequemur pectore.
roges, tuum labore quid iuvem meo,   15
    imbellis ac firmus parum?
comes minore sum futurus in metu,
    qui maior absentis habet;
ut adsidens implumibus pullis avis
    serpentium allapsus timet   20
magis relictis, non, ut adsit, auxili
    latura plus praesentibus.
libenter hoc et omne militabitur
    bellum in tuae spem gratiae,
non ut iuvencis illigata pluribus   25
    aratra nitantur mea,

But what of me?[6] My life, if you are safe,
    is pleasant, but if not, a burden.
Should I, as ordered, keep pursuing leisure
    (not sweet unless it's spent with you),
or bear[7] this labor with a mind that suits
    how men who are not soft would bear it?
Bear it I will, and through the Alpine heights
    or Caucasus unkind to guests
or even to the West's remotest bay
    I'll follow you with steadfast heart.
You ask how with my labor I, not warlike
    or very strong,[8] can profit yours?
As your companion I'll be less afraid
    since fear is greater for the absent,
just like a bird that guards unfeathered young—
    she dreads the slithering of snakes
more when they're left alone, not that she could
    bear them more help if they were close.
Gladly will this and every war be fought
    in hopes of winning your goodwill,
but not so that, attached to extra bullocks,
    my plows might carry out their work,

5

10

15

20

25

---

6. **what of me**: Although I have translated with "me" and "I," Horace in lines 5–14 actually uses the word *nos* (we). Roman writers employed the "royal we" with much greater frequency than modern English speakers, and it can often be translated as an equivalent to "I." Others suggest, however, that Horace's use of the plural here indicates his more official, public role as a member of Maecenas's retinue rather than his capacity as a private friend or that he is speaking on behalf of Maecenas's whole circle rather than himself as an individual. By line 15, however, Horace drops the plural and speaks of himself in the singular simply as "I."

7. **Bear**: The repetition of "bear" in lines 9–11 and 22 translates the Latin words *laturi, ferre, feremus,* and *latura,* all from the same root word. Such repetition of the same root in different inflections is called **polyptoton**.

8. **not warlike or very strong**: It is common for poets, especially those writing in the lighter genres such as lyric or elegy, to describe themselves as physically weak and thus not suited to war or to epic poetry about war.

pecusve Calabris ante sidus fervidum
    Lucana mutet pascuis,
neque ut superni villa candens Tusculi
    Circaea tangat moenia.   30
satis superque me benignitas tua
    ditavit: haud paravero,
quod aut avarus ut Chremes terra premam,
    discinctus aut perdam nepos.

nor so, before Dog Days,[9] my flock might change *Farming*
    Lucanian pastures for Calabrian,[10]
nor so a gleaming villa might adjoin
    high Tusculum's Circean walls.[11]   30
Enough and more has your munificence
    enriched me.[12] I will not acquire
something to hide in earth, like greedy Cremes,[13]
    or else to waste, a lavish spendthrift.

---

9. **Dog Days:** The Latin here says *sidus fervidum* (seething star), with reference to Sirius, the Dog Star, whose appearance above the eastern horizon just before sunrise in July signaled the now proverbial "Dog Days" of summer.

10. **Calabrian . . . Lucanian:** Two districts of Italy. It would indicate great wealth if one had sufficient land to provide different summer and winter pastures for sheep.

11. **Tusculum's Circean walls:** Tusculum was a popular spot in the Alban hills for the villas of the wealthy. Its legendary founder was Telegonus, son of Odysseus and Circe.

12. **enriched me:** Most likely a reference to the Sabine farm that Maecenas is widely regarded as having given to Horace not long before the publication of the *Epodes*.

13. **Chremes:** a miser; he was comedic **stock figure**, as is the spendthrift of the following line.

EPODES 2

"Beatus ille, qui procul negotiis,
     ut prisca gens mortalium,
paterna rura bubus exercet suis,
     solutus omni faenore,
neque excitatur classico miles truci,   5
     neque horret iratum mare,
forumque vitat et superba civium
     potentiorum limina.
ergo aut adulta vitium propagine
     altas maritat populos,   10
aut in reducta valle mugientium
     prospectat errantis greges,

EPODES 2[1]

"Happy[2] is he who, far away from duties,

      just like the ancient race of mortals,[3]

works at his father's farm with his own oxen,

      freed from all interest he owes.[4]

No soldier whom the savage trumpet wakes,   5

      nor bristling at the angry sea,

he shuns the forum and the pompous thresholds

      of citizens more powerful.[5]

And when the layerings of vines mature

      he weds them to the lofty poplars,[6]   10

or in a distant valley he surveys

      the herds of mooers as they wander,

---

1. ***Epodes* 2** (*Iambic Strophe*): This is perhaps the best known and most anthologized of the *Epodes* poems. It is a long **encomium** of the rustic life of a farmer, but we do not know until the poem's epilogue that it is delivered by a money-lender named Alfius, who has no real intention of ever taking up residence in the country. This new information compels us to reassess the seemingly sincere praise we have just read and to search out clues for Alfius's hypocrisy or ignorance. Alfius's major fault is *mempsimoiria*, discontent with his own lot and envy of another's, a major obstacle to equanimity that Horace takes up again and again in his poetry. The question of the poem's tone remains disputed.
2. **Happy**: This is a word with two meanings: on the one hand, it suggests "happy" in an ethical sense; on the other hand, it means "wealthy." Alfius pays lip service to the former while in reality pursuing the latter.
3. **ancient race of mortals**: The speaker evokes the Golden Age. In earlier Greek writers, such as Hesiod, this was a period of spontaneous production prior to the advent of farming (cf. *Epodes* 16), but other versions of the myth locate an agricultural Golden Age in pristine Italy where farmers enjoyed the earth's easy bounty. Such an idea shows up, for example, in Vergil's *Georgics* 2.458–540, a text contemporaneous with Horace's *Epodes*.
4. **interest he owes**: An early hint of Alfius's hypocrisy; as we learn later, he is in fact the one who lends money on interest.
5. **pompous . . . powerful**: Alfius invokes the world of Roman patronage, wherein clients were expected to attend the morning "salutation" that took place in front of the patron's door. The adjective "pompous" is a **transferred epithet**.
6. **layerings . . . poplars**: Vines were supported by trees and were often referred to as being "married" to the tree. The "layerings" of the vine refer to a technique for propagating a new vine from its parent vine.

inutilisque falce ramos amputans
    feliciores inserit,
aut pressa puris mella condit amphoris,   15
    aut tondet infirmas ovis;
vel cum decorum mitibus pomis caput
    Autumnus agris extulit,
ut gaudet insitiva decerpens pira
    certantem et uvam purpurae,   20
qua muneretur te, Priape, et te, pater
    Silvane, tutor finium!
libet iacere modo sub antiqua ilice,
    modo in tenaci gramine:
labuntur altis interim rivis aquae,   25
    queruntur in silvis aves,
fontesque lymphis obstrepunt manantibus,
    somnos quod invitet levis.
at cum tonantis annus hibernus Iovis
    imbris nivesque comparat,   30
aut trudit acris hinc et hinc multa cane
    apros in obstantis plagas,
aut amite levi rara tendit retia,
    turdis edacibus dolos,
pavidumque leporem et advenam laqueo gruem   35
    iucunda captat praemia.

and, pruning sterile boughs off with a sickle,
      he grafts on ones producing fruit,
or in clean jars he stores away pressed honey,   15
      or else he shears the feeble sheep.
Or when Autumnus in the fields lifts up
      his head bedecked with ripened fruit,
how he exults in picking grafted pears
      and grapes whose crimson vies with dye—   20
presents for you, Priapus, and for you,
      father Silvanus,[7] boundary-guard!
It's pleasant[8] to lie down beneath an ancient
      oak tree or on the matted grass,
while meanwhile in deep brooks the currents gush   25
      and birds sing dirges in the woods
and flowing water clamors in the fountains.
      All this entices gentle slumber.
But when the wintertime of thundering Jove
      delivers storms of rain and snow,   30
with many dogs on every side he drives
      fierce boars into obstructing snares[9]
or stretches loose-knit nets upon smooth poles
      as ruses for voracious thrushes[10]
and nabs a frightened hare and migrant crane[11]   35
      using a trap—delightful spoils.

---

7. **Priapus . . . Silvanus**: Alfius evokes the famed piety of the smallholding farmer,
who dedicates his first fruits to the gods of the country. Priapus, whose chief
characteristic was his oversized, erect phallus, was associated with gardens, whereas
Silvanus was a tutelary deity of flocks and herds.

8. **It's pleasant**: Alfius presents in the following lines a standard portrait of a *locus amoenus*.

9. **obstructing snares**: Roman boar-hunting consisted of driving boars into
pre-positioned nets.

10. **voracious thrushes**: The thrushes are gluttonous because they enter the nets
to reach bait placed inside.

11. **migrant crane**: As commentators point out, cranes inhabited Italy in the summer,
not winter, so Alfius reveals here his ignorance of country life.

quis non malarum, quas amor curas habet,
    haec inter obliviscitur?
quodsi pudica mulier in partem iuvet
    domum atque dulcis liberos,   40
Sabina qualis aut perusta solibus
    pernicis uxor Apuli,
sacrum *vetustis* <u>exstruat</u> *lignis* **focum**
    lassi sub adventum viri,
claudensque textis cratibus laetum pecus   45
    distenta siccet ubera,
et horna dulci vina promens dolio
    dapes inemptas apparet;
non me Lucrina iuverint conchylia
    magisve rhombus aut scari,   50
si quos Eois intonata fluctibus
    hiems ad hoc vertat mare,
non Afra avis descendat in ventrem meum,
    non attagen Ionicus
iucundior, quam lecta de pinguissimis   55
    oliva ramis arborum

Among such things as these who'd not forget
　　　　the dreadful cares that love creates?
But if a modest wife should do her share,
　　　　tending the home and pleasant children—　　40
such as a Sabine woman or the sunburnt
　　　　wife of a lithe Apulian[12]—
and <u>heap</u> the **sacred hearth** with *ancient wood*[13]
　　　　before her weary husband comes,
and pen the fertile herd in woven fences,　　45
　　　　then drain their swollen udders dry
and, drawing this year's wine from its sweet jug,
　　　　prepare them feasts not bought with cash—
I would not be more thrilled with Lucrine oysters[14]
　　　　nor with a turbot or a wrasse,　　50
if winter, raging on the eastern waves,
　　　　should detour any toward this sea.
I'd gobble down no bird of Africa
　　　　or partridge from Ionia
with greater pleasure than the olives plucked　　55
　　　　off of their trees' most laden boughs

---

12. **Sabine ... Apulian**: Alfius cites two rural areas that were especially dear to Horace, the Sabine territory where he had his farm and Apulia, his birthplace. Sabine women were famous from the myth recounting their rape in the early mythological history of Rome; they became paragons of female virtue in settling the competing claims of their husbands and fathers. The Apulian woman's sunburnt skin suggests not only her work outdoors but also a disregard for her appearance that underscores her modesty and chastity.
13. **sacred hearth ... ancient wood**: A **chiastic** arrangement similar to the **golden line** (ABVBA) normally found in epic hexameters. The hearth was the religious center of the home where the household gods were kept.
14. **Lucrine oysters**: Alfius here enumerates two gastronomic lists, one of culinary delicacies (such as these oysters from the Lucrine Lake on the Bay of Naples) found in the city and one of the simple foods afforded by the country. Food had a wide range of moral associations, and through this celebration of a country diet Alfius suggests that he adheres to old-fashioned ethical standards. As Mankin (1995) suggests, however, his potentially gluttonous preoccupation with food throughout the poem casts doubt on this.

aut herba lapathi prata amantis et gravi
  malvae salubres corpori,
vel agna festis caesa Terminalibus
  vel haedus ereptus lupo.   60
has inter epulas ut iuvat pastas ovis
  videre properantis domum,
videre fessos vomerem inversum boves
  collo trahentis languido,
positosque vernas, ditis examen domus,   65
  circum renidentis Lares!"
haec ubi locutus faenerator Alfius,
  iam iam futurus rusticus,
omnem redegit idibus pecuniam,
  quaerit Kalendis ponere.   70

or meadow-loving sorrel greens and mallow,
    which can restore a clogged-up body,[15]
or lamb slain for the Terminalia[16]
    or kid retaken from a wolf.   60
How pleasing it would be amid such feasts
    to see the pastured sheep rush home,
to see the worn-out oxen drag along
    the upturned plough on drooping necks,
and homebred slaves, a wealthy house's swarm,[17]   65
    seated around the shining Lares!"[18]
After this speech the lender[19] Alfius,
    ever about to be a farmer,
collected all his money on the Ides—
    but on the Kalends seeks to lend it.[20]   70

---

15. **a clogged-up body:** Sorrel and mallow were used as laxatives.
16. **Terminalia:** The Terminalia was a festival held in February for the rustic god Terminus, an Italian god of boundaries.
17. **homebred slaves . . . swarm:** A *verna* was a slave born from a female slave. Authors tend to idealize them as prized and well treated, though of course in actual practice they would have been vulnerable to physical and sexual abuse.
18. **Lares:** Household gods.
19. **lender:** The word *faenerator* (lender) connects us back to *faenore* (interest) in line 4. As Watson (2003) notes, "to be a *faenerator* . . . was to practice a despised profession." Mercenary activity was generally looked down on by respectable Roman gentlemen.
20. **collected all his money . . . to lend it:** Most scholars interpret this to mean that he collects all the principal on the money he has lent out in order to purchase a small farm, but within about a fortnight he has changed his mind and reverts to lending. The Ides fell on either the thirteenth or fifteenth of the month, and the Kalends on the first.

EPODES 3

Parentis olim si quis impia manu
      senile guttur fregerit,
edit cicutis alium nocentius.
      o dura messorum ilia!
quid hoc veneni saevit in praecordiis?   5
      num viperinus his cruor
incoctus herbis me fefellit, an malas
      Canidia tractavit dapes?
ut Argonautas praeter omnis candidum
      Medea mirata est ducem,   10
ignota tauris illigaturum iuga
      perunxit hoc Iasonem;
hoc delibutis ulta donis paelicem
      serpente fugit alite.

EPODES 3[1]

If henceforth anyone with impious hand
    should break his parent's aged neck,
let him eat garlic, deadlier than hemlock.[2]
    What hardy bowels must reapers[3] have!
What is this poison raging in my gut?   5
    Did I not note the viper blood
cooked in these greens? Or was Canidia[4]
    the one who made these evil feasts?
Medea,[5] since she marveled at the leader
    gorgeous beyond all Argonauts,[6]   10
before he hitched the strange yokes to the bulls,
    anointed Jason with this stuff.
With presents soaked in this she avenged her rival
    and fled upon a flying serpent.

---

1. **Epodes** 3 (*Iambic Strophe*): A poem humorously bewailing the intestinal discomfort caused by eating an excessively garlicky dish. It shows Horace and Maecenas in the context of one of the venues most associated with Roman patronage, the dinner party. It has been taken as evidence for the close friendship between the two men, with each ready to laugh playfully at the other's expense. Maecenas, most scholars suggest, intentionally served the dish as a kind of practical joke, and the poem is Horace's reprisal.

2. **hemlock:** The deadly poison from the hemlock plant was administered in cases of capital punishment (most famously that of the philosopher Socrates) in ancient Athens.

3. **reapers:** Garlic was especially associated with peasant diets. Some have even suggested that Maecenas's joke was a playful response to Alfius's praise of country fare in *Epodes* 2.

4. **Canidia:** A witch who will feature prominently in *Epodes* 5 and 17 (as well as *Satires* 1.8). On Canidia see especially Oliensis (1991) and Paule (2017).

5. **Medea:** The mythological princess from the eastern kingdom of Colchis who helped the hero Jason capture the Golden Fleece and bring it back to Greece. She became the archetypal witch, and Horace highlights two famous instances of her deadly magic. First, she spread a potion on Jason's flesh that gave him the strength to yoke and plow with fire-breathing bulls, sow in the plowed soil a dragon's teeth, and fight the men sprung from the teeth. Second, when Jason abandoned her for another bride, Creusa, Medea killed the bride with a poisoned cloak she sent as a gift. She escaped punishment by flying away on a chariot drawn by winged serpents.

6. **leader . . . Argonauts:** Jason was the leader of the expedition of the Argonauts, whose primary heroic asset was his beauty, particularly in Apollonius's *Argonautica*.

nec tantus umquam siderum insedit vapor   15
    siticulosae Apuliae,
nec munus umeris efficacis Herculis
    inarsit aestuosius.
at si quid umquam tale concupiveris,
    iocose Maecenas, precor   20
manum puella savio opponat tuo,
    extrema et in sponda cubet.

The stars[7] have never given off such heat 15
    to plague Apulia[8] with thirst.
The gift on mighty Hercules's shoulders
    blistered him no more scorchingly.[9]
If ever you again crave some such thing,
    jokester Maecenas, I implore 20
your girl[10] to block your kisses with her hand
    and sleep upon the couch's edge.

---

7. **stars:** This refers to the constellation Canis Major, whose brightest star was Sirius, associated with the pestilential summer heat.
8. **Apulia:** The southern Italian region where Horace was born. It was notorious for drought.
9. **gift . . . more scorchingly:** Hercules was killed by a poisonous robe his wife Deianeira gave him, thinking it was a love charm. Hercules had earlier shot the Centaur Nessus with an arrow dipped in the Hydra's venom, which in turn rendered Nessus's blood highly toxic. As he was dying, he persuaded Deianeira that his blood could be used as a charm that would keep Hercules faithful, and she applied it to the cloak before giving it to her husband.
10. **girl:** This refers most likely to the prostitutes that frequented symposia rather than to Maecenas's wife, Terentia, as some have suggested.

EPODES 4

Lupis et agnis quanta sortito obtigit,
    tecum mihi discordia est,
Hibericis peruste funibus latus
    et crura dura compede.
licet superbus ambules pecunia,   5
    fortuna non mutat genus.
videsne, Sacram metiente te viam
    cum bis trium ulnarum toga,
ut ora vertat huc et huc euntium
    liberrima indignatio?   10
"sectus flagellis hic triumviralibus
    praeconis ad fastidium

EPODES 4[1]

The discord chance has brought to wolves[2] and lambs—
    that is how great mine is with you,
who on your flank are scarred by Spanish whips,[3]
    and on your legs by rigid shackles.
Although you strut around puffed up by wealth,   5
    good fortune does not change your birth.
While walking on the Sacred Way,[4] your toga
    nine arm-spans wide,[5] do you not see
how as the people come and go they wear
    looks of the freest indignation?   10
"He,[6] whom the scourges of triumvirs[7] slashed
    until it made the crier[8] queasy,

---

1. **Epodes 4** (*Iambic Strophe*): In this poem Horace attacks a wealthy freed slave whom he—and, as he argues, everyone else—sees as a nouveau riche and ambitious social upstart. The poem is an exercise in the *liberrima indignatio* (freest indignation, line 10) that often stimulates the iambicist and gives rise to his verse. "Freedom" (*libertas*) in Rome encompassed freedom of speech, which Horace wields in the poem as a means not only to disparage his enemy but also to shore up his own freeborn social position. The fact that Horace's father was himself a freedman, however, has led some to suggest there are potentially uncomfortable parallels between Horace and the upstart.
2. **wolves**: The wolf was a frequent symbol for the iambic poet, for which see Miralles (1983) and Hawkins (2014), as well as the introductory note to *Epodes* 6.
3. **Spanish whips**: The signs of physical abuse on the upstart's body identify him as formerly enslaved.
4. **Sacred Way**: One of the major thoroughfares in ancient Rome; it ran through the Forum.
5. **toga / nine arm-spans wide**: The man's toga marks him as having achieved Roman citizenship, but the enormous width of the fabric is an ostentatious display of his newly acquired wealth.
6. **He**: From this point on, Horace purports to record the gossip of one of the dismayed passers-by.
7. **scourges of triumvirs**: The triumvirs here are judicial officials charged with the punishment of low-status individuals such as slaves.
8. **crier**: The *praeco* (crier) would repeatedly yell out the crimes of the individual being punished.

arat Falerni mille fundi iugera
    et Appiam mannis terit,
sedilibusque magnus in primis eques   15
    Othone contempto sedet.
quid attinet tot ora navium gravi
    rostrata duci pondere
contra latrones atque servilem manum
    hoc, hoc tribuno militum?"   20

plows a Falernian farm[9] (a thousand acres!)
    and trots the Appian with ponies,[10]
and as a grand equestrian he sits   15
    up near the front, despising Otho.[11]
What does it matter that so many ships,
    their faces beaked with heavy weight,
are led out versus thieves and gangs of slaves[12]
    if he—he!—is a soldiers' tribune?"[13]   20

---

9. **Falernian farm:** The Falernian region in Campania was renowned for its superior wine.

10. **Appian with ponies:** The Appian was the main street into and out of Rome via the south; it is the road the upstart would have taken to his Falernian estate. The ponies (*mannis*), as Watson (2003) points out, "were employed in particular by the elegant to draw their carriages, a task more usually performed by the humble mule."

11. **despising Otho:** The law of Lucius Roscius Otho (called the Roscian Law) passed in 67 B.C.E. reserved the first fourteen rows of seats in the theater for men of equestrian rank. The upstart's freed status should normally have barred him from acquiring equestrian rank.

12. **thieves and gangs of slaves:** A reference most likely to Octavian's defeat of the navy of Sextus Pompey in the Sicilian War of 37–36 B.C.E. Horace's suggestion that Pompey's followers were pirates and slaves reflects the propaganda used against him, for which see Watson (2003).

13. **soldiers' tribune:** An army officer that ranked between a centurion and a legate. This rank often served as a stepping-stone to senatorial status. Horace also held the position of *tribunus militum* (tribune of the soldiers), as he tells us at *Satires* 1.6.48.

EPODES 5

"At, o deorum quidquid in caelo regit
        terras et humanum genus,
quid iste fert tumultus? aut quid omnium
        vultus in unum me truces?
per liberos te, si vocata partubus   5
        Lucina veris adfuit,
per hoc inane purpurae decus precor,
        per improbaturum haec Iovem,
quid ut noverca me intueris aut uti
        petita ferro belua?"   10
ut haec trementi questus ore constitit
        insignibus raptis puer,

Alto-long (Child)
- high stakes (Child)
\ see footnote

— Maybe preys on
anxieties of the day
(mortality of women)

Epodes 57

EP.

EPODES 5[1]

"But[2]—O whatever gods there are in heaven
  that rule the earth and human race—
what does that uproar mean? What everyone's
  ferocious looks toward me alone?
By your own children, if Lucina[3] was   5
  invoked and oversaw true births,[4]
I beg you, by this useless purple trim,[5]
  by Jove, who will condemn these things—
why stare at me just like a stepmother[6]
  or wild beast threatened with a sword?"   10
The boy made these complaints with trembling mouth
  and then stood still, his emblems seized.[7]

---

1. **Epodes 5** (*Iambic Strophe*): After briefly introducing us to the witch Canidia in
Epodes 3.8, Horace now presents a long epode, which Mankin (1995) rightly calls
"one of the most mysterious poems in Latin." In an effort to regain the affection of
her beloved Varus (who may or may not be her husband), she and her fellow witches
decide to brew a love potion out of the entrails of a sacrificed citizen boy, whom
they have kidnapped and will force to starve to death by burying him up to his chin
and placing unreachable food before his eyes. Canidia's use of such "sympathetic
magic" will transform the boy's hunger into erotic desire. The boy has recourse only
to curses, which, like magic, feature prominently in iambic poetry. Love magic
was practiced in Rome, as evidenced, for example, by surviving curse tablets and
spells found among the *Magical Papyri*. For the abundant evidence for love magic in
relation to the epode, see Watson (2003, 176–82).
2. **But:** The action begins *in medias res*, with the already kidnapped boy confusedly
trying to ascertain and sway the terrifying actions of the witches. He is the speaker of
the first ten lines.
3. **Lucina:** The goddess of childbirth.
4. **true births:** The boy insinuates that any children Canidia does have are likely the
result of kidnapping.
5. **purple trim:** The boy is wearing the toga praetexta, which was bordered with
a crimson stripe. This marked him as a citizen youth, which ideally should have
protected him from such violence.
6. **stepmother:** *Novercae* (stepmothers) were considered, at least in literature, to be
dangerous and prone to violence through poison.
7. **emblems seized:** The witches strip the boy of his clothing. The insignia for a citizen
boy would have included not only his toga but also the *bulla*, an amulet worn on a
necklace that contained apotropaic phallic symbols (called *fascina*) meant to ward off
harm.

impube corpus, quale posset impia
    mollire Thracum pectora,
Canidia, brevibus illigata viperis   15
    crinis et incomptum caput,
iubet sepulcris caprificos erutas,
    iubet cupressos funebris
et uncta turpis ova ranae sanguine
    plumamque nocturnae strigis   20
herbasque, quas Iolcos atque Hiberia
    mittit venenorum ferax,
et ossa ab ore rapta ieiunae canis
    flammis aduri Colchicis.
at expedita Sagana per totam domum   25
    spargens Avernalis aquas
horret capillis ut marinus asperis
    echinus aut currens aper.
abacta nulla Veia conscientia
    ligonibus duris humum   30

His prepubescent body could have softened
    even the impious hearts of Thracians.[8]
Canidia,[9] with little vipers bound   15
    around her messy hair and head,
orders that fig-trees rooted up from graves,
    orders that funeral cypresses[10]
and eggs anointed with a foul toad's blood[11]
    and feathers from a nocturnal owl[12]   20
and herbs that Iolcus or Iberia,[13]
    fertile in poisons, sends abroad
and bones seized from a starving bitch's maw[14]
    be set alight in Colchian flames.[15]
Sagana,[16] girt for action, sprinkles water   25
    from Lake Avernus[17] through the house.
Her bristly hair stands on its ends just like
    an urchin or a charging boar.
Veia,[18] impeded by no moral scruples,
    used rigid hoes to hollow out   30

---

8. **Thracians:** These easterners were, to the Roman mind, notoriously fierce.
9. **Canidia:** Her name marks her as both old (*canities* = grey hair) and dog-like (*canis* = dog). Oliensis (1991) connects her name with the dangerous "Dog-Star," Canicula, which was thought to enervate men.
10. **funeral cypresses:** On the connections between cypress trees and funerals, see the note on *Odes* 2.14.23.
11. **foul toad's blood:** The *rana rubeta* is a poisonous toad whose blood was used frequently in love magic.
12. **nocturnal owl:** Technically the screech-owl, who had magical associations with bad omens, death, and darkness. See Stocks (2016, 161–67).
13. **Iolcus or Iberia:** Iolcus was a Thessalian city where Jason lived with Medea, the archetypical witch. Similarly, Iberia here indicates a region near Colchis, the eastern city where Medea grew up.
14. **starving bitch's maw:** The dog's starvation will be magically transmogrified into desire.
15. **Colchian flames:** Colchis was Medea's hometown.
16. **Sagana:** Another witch working as Canidia's accomplice. Her name suggests *saga* (witch).
17. **water from Lake Avernus:** Lake Avernus on the Bay of Naples was thought to be an entrance to the underworld.
18. **Veia:** Yet another witch in attendance.

exhauriebat ingemens laboribus,
    quo posset infossus puer
longo die bis terque mutatae dapis
    inemori spectaculo,
cum promineret ore, quantum exstant aqua   35
    suspensa mento corpora;
exsecta uti medulla et aridum iecur
    amoris esset poculum,
interminato cum semel fixae cibo
    intabuissent pupulae.   40
non defuisse masculae libidinis
    Ariminensem Foliam
et otiosa credidit Neapolis
    et omne vicinum oppidum,
quae sidera excantata voce Thessala   45
    lunamque caelo deripit.
hic irresectum saeva dente livido
    Canidia rodens pollicem
quid dixit aut quid tacuit? "o rebus meis
    non infideles arbitrae,   50

the ground (and groaned from labor as she dug),
  so, buried there, the boy could perish
slowly amid a spectacle of food
  changed two or three times through the day,
his face protruding like a body jutting   35
  from water, propped up by the chin[19]—
all so his excised marrow and dried liver[20]
  might turn into a love elixir
whenever, fixed upon forbidden food,
  his pupils finally atrophy.   40
A woman with a man's desire was there,
  Folia from Ariminum,[21]
according to the talk in idle Naples
  as well as each surrounding town.
With a Thessalian spell she charmed the stars   45
  and moon, then ripped them from the sky.
With her one purple tooth Canidia
  savagely gnawed her unclipped thumb[22]—
What did she say or what keep quiet? "You,
  my deeds' not faithless[23] witnesses,   50

---

19. **like a body . . . chin:** Horace compares the appearance of the boy buried
    neck-deep to swimmers treading water. The image especially evokes the starvation
    of Tantalus in the underworld, who in some accounts was standing in a pool of water
    that reached up to his chin but that receded when he tried to drink.
20. **liver:** The liver was considered the seat of desire and strong emotions, and so it
    will transfer the boy's hunger to Varus.
21. **A woman . . . Ariminum:** Yet another witch who attended the sacrifice.
    Ariminum is modern Rimini on the Adriatic coast. Her "man's desire" identifies her
    as homosexual. The Romans considered female-female sexual acts perverse and the
    women who participated in them masculinized.
22. **One purple tooth . . . unclipped thumb:** Canidia has only one tooth left in
    her mouth, and it is discolored and rotting. Her long thumbnail suggests either her
    general neglect of her appearance or that she deliberately grows it out as a tool for
    clawing and digging or to prevent someone from acquiring her nail-clippings to use
    in magic against her.
23. **not faithless:** That is, "faithful." Such an expression of an affirmative through
    a double negative is known as **litotes.**

Nox et Diana, quae silentium regis
    arcana cum fiunt sacra,
nunc, nunc adeste, nunc in hostilis domos
    iram atque numen vertite!
formidulosis cum latent silvis ferae   55
    dulci sopore languidae,
senem, quod omnes rideant, adulterum
    latrent Suburanae canes
nardo perunctum, quale non perfectius
    meae laborarint manus.   60
quid accidit? cur dira barbarae minus
    venena Medeae valent,
quibus superbam fugit ulta paelicem,
    magni Creontis filiam,
cum palla, tabo munus imbutum, novam   65
    incendio nuptam abstulit?
atqui nec herba nec latens in asperis
    radix fefellit me locis.
indormit unctis omnium cubilibus
    oblivione paelicum.   70

Night and Diana,[24] you who rule the silence
    when secret rituals take place,
now, now lend aid, now at my enemy's home
    direct your anger and your power!
When wild beasts hide inside the fearful woods,   55
    all languorous with pleasant sleep,
may the Subura's dogs bark at the aged
    adulterer (a laughingstock!),
covered with such an unguent that my hands
    could not produce another finer.[25]   60
What's happening? Why aren't barbarian[26]
    Medea's dreadful poisons working?
She fled, having avenged with these her pompous
    rival, the child of mighty Creon,[27]
after the robe, a gift imbued with poison,   65
    had killed the brand new bride with fire.
And yet no herb or root, concealed in rough
    terrain, escaped my observation:
he's sleeping in a bed on which I smeared
    forgetfulness of all my rivals.   70

---

24. **Night and Diana:** Canidia appropriately calls on female, chthonic deities. Diana here indicates her underworld guise of Hecate, the goddess of magic.
25. **Subura's dogs . . . another finer:** The unguent with which Varus has anointed himself to look handsome has been drugged by Canidia, but lines 69–70 suggest she has also spread drugs over his bed as well. It is unclear why exactly Canidia wants the Suburan dogs to bark at Varus, but the most likely explanation is that they will bark when they see him leave his current lodgings (with another woman) to return to her. She calls him an "adulterer," which may indicate that he is her husband or simply that in her mind he belongs to her.
26. **barbarian:** This is a loaded term, both for us and for the Romans. It appears numerous times in Horace and, as in other authors, has both negative ("barbarous" or "barbaric" = "ruthless") and neutral ("barbarian" = "foreign") connotations, which in Horace can (as here) overlap into one another. Despite the continued xenophobic use of the term in English, I have decided to keep it given its importance in Roman thought. On the term's use (particularly in Caesar), see Riggsby (2006, 151).
27. **child of mighty Creon:** Euripides's *Medea* recounts how the sorceress murdered her rival with a poisoned cloak after Jason abandoned her for a new marriage to the daughter of Creon.

a! a! solutus ambulat veneficae
    scientioris carmine.
non usitatis, Vare, potionibus,
    o multa fleturum caput,
ad me recurres, nec vocata mens tua   75
    Marsis redibit vocibus:
maius parabo, maius infundam tibi
    fastidienti poculum,
priusque caelum sidet inferius mari,
    tellure porrecta super,   80
quam non amore sic meo flagres uti
    bitumen atris ignibus."
sub haec puer iam non ut ante mollibus
    lenire verbis impias,
sed dubius unde rumperet silentium   85
    misit Thyesteas preces:
"venena magnum non fas nefasque, non valent
    convertere humanam vicem;
diris agam vos; dira detestatio
    nulla expiatur victima: 90
quin, ubi perire iussus exspiravero,
    nocturnus occurram Furor
petamque vultus umbra curvis unguibus,
    quae vis deorum est manium,
et inquietis adsidens praecordiis   95
    pavore somnos auferam:

Ah! Ah! He walks, freed by the incantation
    of some more talented enchantress.
It won't be from these common potions, Varus
    that you'll come rushing back to me—
you'll weep so many tears! Your mind will not   75
    return till called by Marsian spells.[28]
I'll make a greater, pour for you a greater
    elixir to offset your loathing.
Heaven will sooner sink below the sea,
    while up above extends the earth,[29]   80
than you will cease to burn with love for me
    like pitch alight with flames of black."
The boy no longer tried to use soft words
    to mollify the impious women,
but, not sure how he ought to break his silence,   85
    he hurled out curses of Thyestes.[30]
"Poisons can overturn what's right and wrong,
    but they cannot stop human vengeance.
With curses I will hound you. Let no victim
    expiate this, my dreadful curse.   90
And when I breathe my last, compelled to die,
    I'll meet you as a nocturnal Fury.[31]
A ghost, I'll strike your faces with hooked talons.
    The spirits of the dead[32] can do this.
And perching in your terror-stricken heart,   95
    I'll drive away your sleep with dread.

---

28. **Marsian spells:** The Marsians were an Italian people thought to excel at magic.
29. **Heaven . . . earth:** Canidia utters an **adynaton** to express how effective her new spell will be.
30. **curses of Thyestes:** In mythology Thyestes, after being fed his own children by his brother Atreus, famously cursed his brother and his whole line.
31. **nocturnal Fury:** Furies were chthonic deities (usually female) of vengeance with birdlike qualities such as wings and talons.
32. **The spirits of dead:** The *di manes* (shades of the dead) were propitiated and honored with sacrifices and frequently invoked in curses.

vos turba vicatim hinc et hinc saxis petens
contundet obscaenas anus;
post insepulta membra different lupi
et Esquilinae alites;   100
neque hoc parentes heu mihi superstites
effugerit spectaculum."

Hammering you with stones through every street,
　　　a crowd will thrash you ghastly crones.
Then wolves will scatter your unburied limbs—
　　　Esquiline birds[33] will join in, too.　　　　　　　100
My parents, who (alas!) are my survivors,
　　　will not avoid this spectacle."

---

33. **Esquiline birds:** The Esquiline was one of the famous seven hills of Rome,
　　famous for graveyards, especially of the poor. The horror-inducing idea of one's
　　body becoming prey to animals owing to burial being refused goes back to the very
　　opening lines of the *Iliad*.

EPODES 6

Quid immerentis hospites vexas canis
    ignavus adversum lupos?
quin huc inanis, si potes, vertis minas,
    et me remorsurum petis?
nam qualis aut Molossus aut fulvus Lacon,   5
    amica vis pastoribus,
agam per altas aure sublata nives,
    quaecumque praecedet fera:
tu cum timenda voce complesti nemus,
    proiectum odoraris cibum.   10
cave, cave: namque in malos asperrimus
    parata tollo cornua,
qualis Lycambae spretus infido gener,
    aut acer hostis Bupalo.
an si quis atro dente me petiverit,   15
    inultus ut flebo puer?

EPODES 6[1]

Why like a dog harass the blameless[2] guests
    but cower when you're facing wolves?
Why don't you, if you dare, turn idle threats
    toward me and strike one who'll bite back?
For, just like a Molossian hound or tawny   5
    Spartan[3] (a friendly troop to shepherds),
my ears pricked up, I'll chase across deep snow
    whatever beast is rushing off.
But once your timid voice has filled the grove,
    you sniff for food thrown out to you.[4]   10
Beware, beware:[5] to counter evil men
    I raise my ready horns most harshly,
just like the bridegroom scorned by false Lycambes[6]
    or Bupalus's ruthless foe.[7]
Will I, if someone with his black tooth strikes me,   15
    weep like a boy who's unavenged?[8]

---

1. *Epodes* 6 (*Iambic Strophe*): An **invective** against a nameless enemy who attacks the undeserving. Horace pointedly compares himself to a wolf or dog, **metaphors** often used to describe iambic poets, for which see Miralles (1983) and Hawkins (2014). Some scholars have suggested that Horace's canine addressee is another iambic poet who lacks Horace's vituperative bite. Horace here explicitly aligns himself with the harsh, **invective** iambic tradition exemplified by Archilochus and Hipponax, each of whom according to legend drove their targets to suicide.
2. **blameless guests**: A *hospes* (pl. *hospites*) can be either a "stranger" or "guest." I prefer the latter, which lends the poem a sympotic atmosphere.
3. **Molossian . . . Spartan**: Two dog breeds used frequently for hunting.
4. **food thrown out to you**: Horace suggests that his target is like a guard-dog easily quieted with food, which has led some scholars to suggest he is a professional slanderer.
5. **Beware, beware**: Evokes the familiar injunction *cave canem,* "beware the dog," but at this point Horace drops the canine **metaphor** and becomes instead a bull ready to attack.
6. **bridegroom . . . Lycambes**: Archilochus was famous for attacking Lycambes, who engaged his daughter Neobule to Archilochus and then broke the agreement. Archilochus was thought to have attacked him so viciously that both he and Neobule committed suicide.
7. **Bupalus's ruthless foe**: The archaic Greek iambic poet Hipponax attacked the sculptor Bupalus (who had made an unflattering rendering of the artist). Bupalus was also rumored to have killed himself.
8. **boy who's unavenged**: This strongly recalls the boy from *Epodes* 5.

EPODES 7

Quo, quo scelesti ruitis? aut cur dexteris
      aptantur enses conditi?
parumne campis atque Neptuno super
      fusum est Latini sanguinis,
non, ut superbas invidae Carthaginis   5
      Romanus arces ureret,
intactus aut Britannus ut descenderet
      sacra catenatus via,
sed ut secundum vota Parthorum sua
      urbs haec periret dextera?   10
neque hic lupis mos nec fuit leonibus
      numquam nisi in dispar feris.
furorne caecus, an rapit vis acrior,
      an culpa? responsum date!
tacent et albus ora pallor inficit   15
      mentesque perculsae stupent.

EPODES 7[1]

Where, where[2] are you depraved men rushing? Why
    do your right hands hold swords just sheathed?
Upon the fields and over Neptune[3] has
    too little Latin blood been spilled?
Not so the Roman might ignite the pompous[4]   5
    citadels of resentful Carthage[5]
nor so the undefeated Briton[6] might
    descend the Sacred Way in chains,[7]
but so, fulfilling Parthians' prayers,[8] this city
    might perish by its own right hand!   10
Neither do wolves nor lions have this custom—
    they're only brutal toward unlike.
Does blind rage or a stronger force possess you?
    Or is it guilt? Give me an answer!
They do not speak, and pallor drains their faces.   15
    Their minds are struck and stupefied.

---

1. *Epodes* 7 (*Iambic Strophe*): Another poem dealing with the crisis of civil war, in which Horace diagnoses current civic turmoil as stemming from the very foundation of Rome, wherein Romulus murdered his own brother, an act of fratricide that was the prime example and cause of the Roman tendency toward internecine strife. Horace adopts, as in *Epodes* 16, the stance of a public bard with the moral authority to exhort directly the citizen population of Rome in the midst of their rush to renewed war. The dramatic date of the poem is much contested; war was resumed repeatedly during this period, and Horace offers no datable detail. For an overview of possible dates, see Watson (2003).
2. **Where, where:** The **rhetorical questions** and **anaphora** heighten Horace's exasperation here.
3. **Neptune:** The god stands **metonymically** for the sea. Horace's reference here is to naval battle.
4. **pompous:** *Superbus* when applied to buildings or architectural structures can mean "grand," but when applied to people suggests "pompous." Here it explicitly describes Carthage's citadels but implicitly, as a **transferred epithet**, the Carthaginians themselves.
5. **Carthage:** Carthage was destroyed in 146 B.C.E.
6. **undefeated Briton:** Britain was still unconquered.
7. **the Sacred Way . . . chains:** i.e., in a triumphal parade.
8. **Parthians' prayers:** Tensions with Parthia were especially high during this time owing to the capture of the Roman standards at the Battle of Carrhae in 53 B.C.E.

sic est: acerba fata Romanos agunt
　　scelusque fraternae necis,
ut immerentis fluxit in terram Remi
　　sacer nepotibus cruor.　　　　　　20

And so it is: harsh fates drive on the Romans,
    the crime of slaughtering a brother,
when into earth there flowed the blood of blameless
    Remus, a curse for his descendants.   20

Rome was farded on
a man killing his brother

EPODES 8

Rogare longo putidam te saeculo
    viris quid enervet meas,
cum sit tibi dens ater et rugis vetus
    frontem senectus exaret,
hietque turpis inter aridas natis   5
      podex velut crudae bovis?
sed incitat me pectus et mammae putres,
    equina quales ubera,
venterque mollis et femur tumentibus
    exile suris additum.   10
esto beata, funus atque imagines
    ducant triumphales tuum,
nec sit marita, quae rotundioribus
    onusta bacis ambulet.

EPODES 8[1]

Do you, half-rotten from extreme old age,
    dare ask what saps my potency?
When your one tooth[2] is black, and elderly
    old age ploughs up your brow with wrinkles,
and between your withered rump a <u>nasty anus</u>[3]   5
    gapes open like a bloated cow's!
Yes, I am turned on by your chest with breasts
    that sag like udders of a mare
and by your flabby gut and skinny thighs
    fastened on top of swollen calves.   10
You may be rich and have triumphal masks[4]
    to lead your funeral parade,
nor is there any wife whom rounder pearls
    weigh down as she sashays along.

---

1. **Epodes** 8 (*Iambic Strophe*): This is one of Horace's coarsest poems, forming an **invective** against an unnamed woman who seems to have accused Horace of sexual impotence. He retaliates by attacking her with a variety of long-standing misogynistic insults: hypersexuality, old age, animal traits, and a body that elicits disgust in the male viewer. **Invective** and shame, two modes strongly associated with epodic poetry, thus become the means by which a man can reassert his virility and sexual dominance over women and other inferiors.

2. **one tooth:** Horace uses the singular *dens* (tooth) here either as collectively referring to all of her teeth or to imply that a lone, rotted tooth remains in her mouth.

3. **nasty anus:** In the Latin, the adjective "nasty" (*turpis*) is separated from its noun, "anus" (*podex*), in **hyperbaton**. This creates a verbal picture of just how extensive the gaping has become, and the insult is meant to imply that she practices frequent anal intercourse. Gowers (2016) offers the novel suggestion that the focus on the anus marks Horace's target not as a woman but a *cinaedus*, a male who submitted to anal penetration. The feminine adjectives *putidam* (1) and *beata* (11) would therefore be ironic, and this would become a poem not about female sexual license but male degradation.

4. **triumphal masks:** These mark her as a woman of aristocratic status. Elite Romans displayed wax masks (*imagines*) with likenesses of their ancestors in their atria, which were brought out and worn in funeral processions. These *imagines* are triumphal because her ancestors had celebrated military triumphs. Her elite standing places her above Horace in the social hierarchy, while her gender places her below him.

quid quod libelli Stoici inter sericos   15
    iacere pulvillos amant?
illiterati num minus nervi rigent
    minusve languet fascinum?
quod ut superbo provoces ab inguine,
    ore allaborandum est tibi.   20

So what if Stoic booklets love to lie   15
    upon your pillows made of silk?
Isn't a cock that cannot read no less
    erect or phallus no less floppy?[5]
But to arouse it from my pompous groin
    you'll have to work it with your mouth.[6]   20

---

5. **cock . . . less floppy:** Commentators have spilled much ink trying to sort out the meaning of these lines, but they no doubt suggest that the woman's learnedness, unlike her looks, does not factor into whether or not the speaker's penis is erect (*rigent*) or flaccid (*languet*).

6. **work it with your mouth:** Fellatio was considered a degrading and submissive act throughout Greco-Roman antiquity.

EPODES 9

Quando repostum Caecubum ad festas dapes
    victore laetus Caesare
tecum sub alta—sic Iovi gratum—domo,
    beate Maecenas, bibam
sonante mixtum tibiis carmen lyra,   5
    hac Dorium, illis barbarum,
ut nuper, actus cum freto Neptunius
    dux fugit ustis navibus,
minatus Vrbi vincla, quae detraxerat
    servis amicus perfidis?   10

EPODES 9[1]

When will I, joyous in Caesar's triumph,
　　　drink the Caecuban[2] saved for festive
banquets[3] with you inside your lofty home,
　　　as pleases Jove, happy Maecenas,
the lyre ringing out a Dorian song,　　　　　　　　　5
　　　mixed with the flutes' barbarian one?[4]
As recently,[5] when Neptune's leader,[6] driven
　　　from sea, took flight in burnt-up ships—
he'd terrorized the City with the chains
　　　he took from faithless slaves, their friend.[7]　　　10

---

1. *Epodes* 9 (*Iambic Strophe*): This highly disputed companion piece to *Epodes* 1 is likewise addressed to Maecenas and concerns the Battle of Actium. The two chief matters of controversy are where and when its drama unfolds. The likeliest scenario, as Watson (2003) endorses, is that it takes place near Actium during various phases of the campaign, "a series of highly-colored vignettes which review from the perspective of a participant on the Caesarian side crucial events preceding, during, and following Actium." Woodman (2017) has recently placed the action on board a ship just after the battle. It reflects, moreover, Octavian's propaganda depicting Cleopatra as a femme fatale who had enthralled Roman soldiers to her cause. Like the Cleopatra Ode (*Odes* 1.37), Horace couples Actian victory with an imminent celebratory symposium, but here drinking also more immediately serves to allay anxiety over an outcome that is not yet completely resolved.
2. **Caecuban**: A premiere Italian wine.
3. **banquets**: *Dapes* were normally banquets offered to the gods in exchange for a fulfilled prayer.
4. **lyre . . . barbarian**: As Watson (2003) suggests, this probably refers to musical "modes." Besides the Greek Dorian mode played on the lyre, there were six Eastern "barbarian" modes, one of which is taken up by the tibia, a flute similar to an oboe. For the term "barbarian," see note at *Epodes* 5.61.
5. **As recently**: Horace looks back to an even earlier time of drinking, when Octavian defeated Sextus Pompey at sea in 36 B.C.E.
6. **Neptune's leader**: Horace's phrase "Neptune's leader" probably ironically recalls Sextus's boast (recorded by Appian in *Bellum Civile* 5.100) that he was successful in so many sea battles because he was the son of Neptune.
7. **faithless slaves, their friend**: For Sextus Pompey's enlisting of slaves into his army, see the note on *Epodes* 4.19.

Romanus, eheu,—posteri negabitis—
  emancipatus feminae
fert vallum et arma miles et spadonibus
  servire rugosis potest,
interque signa turpe militaria   15
  sol aspicit conopium.
at huc frementis verterunt bis mille equos
  Galli, canentes Caesarem,
hostiliumque navium portu latent
  puppes sinistrorsum citae.   20
io Triumphe, tu moraris aureos
  currus et intactas boves?
io Triumphe, nec Iugurthino parem
  bello reportasti ducem,

A Roman,[8] woe!—you future ages will
    deny it—servile to a woman,[9]
carries the stake and weapons[10] as a soldier,
    able to slave for wrinkled eunuchs.[11]
The sun beholds the foul mosquito net   15
    amid our military standards.
But to our side two thousand Galatians turned
    their groaning horses, chanting "Caesar!"[12]
And in the port the sterns of hostile ships
    lie hidden, driven to the left.[13]   20
Hail, Triumph![14] Are you holding back the golden
    chariots and unbroken bulls?
Hail, Triumph! That commander you brought back
    from Jugurtha's war was not his match;[15]

---

8. **Roman**: This refers either to Antony himself or as a collective singular to his men.

9. **servile to a woman**: The woman is Cleopatra. In general, Augustan writers do not name her but refer to her simply as the "woman." The word *emancipatus,* translated "servile," suggests that Antony voluntarily gave up his freedom and enslaved himself to Cleopatra.

10. **stake and weapons**: Two standard pieces of equipment carried by Roman soldiers. The stake would have been used in the construction of palisades.

11. **wrinkled**: As Mankin (1995) notes, citing Terence's *Eunuch* 357, eunuchs were thought to look like old women.

12. **two thousand Galatians . . . Caesar**: Prior to the battle two thousand Galatian cavalry deserted to Octavian. Galatia was a region in Asia Minor (modern Turkey).

13. **in the port . . . to the left**: A reference to the retreat of much of Antony's navy into the Ambracian Gulf east of Actium prior to the battle. It has been debated what "sterns . . . driven to the left" means exactly, but the most likely explanation is that the words suggest retreat stern-first into port. For an overview, see the note here of Watson (2003).

14. **Hail, Triumph**: Horace turns optimistically to Octavian's future triumph. As Watson (2003) notes, triumphs for civil wars were not permitted, so the victory would ostensibly be against Cleopatra rather than Antony. *Io Triumphe* was the ritual cry voiced during the triumph, but here "Triumph" is addressed as a god and is the second-person addressee of the next three couplets.

15. **That commander . . . match**: Marius, who defeated the Numidian king Jugurtha in 106 b.c.e. He celebrated a triumph for this victory during which Jugurtha was paraded through the streets of Rome. Horace implies that he pales in comparison with Octavian.

neque Africanum, cui super Carthaginem   25
    virtus sepulcrum condidit.
terra marique victus hostis Punico
    lugubre mutavit sagum.
aut ille centum nobilem Cretam urbibus
    ventis iturus non suis,   30
exercitatas aut petit Syrtis Noto,
    aut fertur incerto mari.
capaciores adfer huc, puer, scyphos
    et Chia vina aut Lesbia:
vel quod fluentem nauseam coerceat   35
    metire nobis Caecubum:
curam metumque Caesaris rerum iuvat
    dulci Lyaeo solvere.

neither was Africanus—he whose virtue   25
    set up a tombstone over Carthage.[16]
Beaten on land and sea, the foe has swapped
    a crimson cloak for one of mourning.[17]
He heads to Crete, famed for its hundred cities,
    with winds that do not favor him,   30
or he seeks out the Syrtes, tossed by Notus,[18]
    or is conveyed on sea unknown.
Bring here, slave boy, the more capacious cups
    and Chian wines or Lesbian.[19]
Or, so that it can curb our flowing nausea,[20]   35
    pour out Caecuban wine for us.[21]
It's pleasing to unloose distress and fear
    for Caesar's works with sweet Lyaeus.[22]

---

16. **Africanus ... Carthage**: This refers either to Publius Cornelius Scipio Africanus, who defeated Hannibal in 202 B.C.E., or (more likely) to Scipio Aemilianus Africanus, who razed Carthage in 146 B.C.E., turning it, as Horace suggests, into an immense tombstone. The word "virtue" points not only to this man's military virtue but also to the famed Stoicism (in which virtue was especially prized) of the Scipios.

17. **crimson ... mourning**: Generals wore a scarlet-colored cloak, which Antony now symbolically changes for the dark one worn by common soldiers.

18. **Syrtes, tossed by Notus**: The Syrtes were sandbanks off the coast of Libya. They were dangerously stormy, and Notus (the south wind) was proverbially associated with storms.

19. **Chian wines, or Lesbian**: Two fine Greek wines.

20. **flowing nausea**: A reference most likely to seasickness, indicating their presence aboard ship in the midst of the battle.

21. **Caecuban**: There is disagreement about whether this Caecuban is different or the same as the one mentioned in the first line.

22. **to unloose ... Lyaeus**: Horace puns with *solvere* (to unloose) on Bacchus's cult name of Lyaeus (the loosener). Lyaeus here stands **metonymically** for wine.

EPODES 10

Mala soluta navis exit alite,
     ferens olentem Maevium:
ut <u>horridis</u> utrumque verberes latus,
     Auster, memento <u>fluctibus</u>.
niger rudentis Eurus inverso mari   5
     fractosque remos differat;
insurgat Aquilo, quantus altis montibus
     frangit trementis ilices;
nec sidus atra nocte amicum appareat,
     qua tristis Orion cadit;   10
quietiore nec feratur aequore
     quam Graia victorum manus,
cum Pallas usto vertit iram ab Ilio
     in impiam Aiacis ratem!

EPODES 10[1]

The ship, unmoored, departs with evil omen,
　　carrying stinking Maevius.
Do not forget to pummel both its sides,
　　Auster,[2] with <u>horrifying waves</u>.[3]
May gloomy Eurus[4] overturn the sea　　　　　　　5
　　and strew the halyards and snapped oars.
May Aquilo[5] swell up as when he breaks
　　quivering oaks on lofty mountains;
may no kind star appear on that dark night
　　when sorrowful Orion sets.[6]　　　　　　　10
Let him be borne upon a sea no calmer
　　than was the crew of conquering Greeks[7]
when Pallas[8] turned her anger from burnt Troy
　　to the unholy[9] ship of Ajax!

---

1. ***Epodes* 10** (*Iambic Strophe*): An elaborate curse against a certain Maevius as he sails away on a journey. The poem reverses the standard features of a **propempticon**, which offers prayers and wishes of safety for the one departing. Such curses suit the vituperative nature of iambic poetry. It is not clear what Maevius has done to warrant such curses—Horace specifies only that he is smelly. Vergil in *Eclogues* 3 mentions that a man of the same name wrote bad poetry, leading some to suggest that Horace is attacking an inferior poet. Others, however, have proposed that Maevius's infraction is sexual.
2. **Auster:** The south wind.
3. **horrifying waves:** The **hyperbaton** mirrors the crashing of the waves on either side of the ship.
4. **Eurus:** The east wind.
5. **Aquilo:** The north wind.
6. **sorrowful Orion sets:** As Watson (2003) notes, the constellation Orion brings sorrow to sailors by signaling the stormy season that follows its morning rising on November 7.
7. **crew of conquering Greeks:** After the Trojan War, the Greek victors struggled on the sea as they returned home because of the rape of Cassandra by the lesser Ajax, which angered the goddess Minerva.
8. **Pallas:** That is, Minerva, the Roman name for Athena.
9. **unholy:** A **transferred epithet**. Ajax's impiety arose not so much from the rape (an all too common fate for war captives) than from the fact that he dragged Cassandra from Minerva's altar, where she was a suppliant. This Ajax is the son of Oileus (i.e., the "lesser" Ajax), not the more famous son of Telamon (the "greater" Ajax).

o quantus instat navitis sudor tuis   15
    tibique pallor luteus
et illa non virilis eiulatio,
    preces et aversum ad Iovem,
Ionius udo cum remugiens sinus
    Noto carinam ruperit!   20
opima quodsi praeda curvo litore
    porrecta mergos iuverit,
libidinosus immolabitur caper
    et agna Tempestatibus.

Oh what a sweat is coming for your crew—   15
      for you there comes a yellow pallor[10]
and that unmanly way you wail aloud
      and prayers to Jove (who'll turn his back),
when the Ionian sea,[11] howling with drizzly
      Notus,[12] has ripped the keel apart!   20
But if rich plunder,[13] stretched upon the curving
      seashore, brings pleasure to the gulls,
a lusty goat and lamb will be struck down
      to thank the goddesses of storms.

---

10. **yellow pallor**: Draining of color regularly indicates fear, which as Watson (2003) explains, would create a yellow color on someone with a dark, Mediterranean complexion.
11. **Ionian sea**: The Ionian Sea is south of the Adriatic, between the bottom of the Italian "boot" and the west of Greece. This suggests that Maevius is sailing from Italy to Greece.
12. **drizzly Notus**: A proverbially rainy south wind.
13. **rich plunder**: This most likely indicates Maevius's lifeless corpse.

EPODES 11

Petti, nihil me sicut antea iuvat
     scribere versiculos amore percussum gravi,
amore, qui me praeter omnis expetit
     mollibus in pueris aut in puellis urere.
hic tertius December, ex quo destiti   5
     Inachia furere, silvis honorem decutit.
heu me, per Vrbem—nam pudet tanti mali—
     fabula quanta fui! conviviorum et paenitet,
in quis amantem languor et silentium
     arguit et latere petitus imo spiritus.   10
"contrane lucrum nil valere candidum
     pauperis ingenium?" querebar applorans tibi,
simul calentis inverecundus deus
     fervidiore mero arcana promorat loco.

EPODES 11[1]

Pettius,[2] it's not pleasing (as before)[3]
>   for me to write slight verse when struck by weighty love,
by love, which forces me beyond all others
>   to be consumed with passion for soft boys or girls.[4]
December shakes the beauty from the forests[5]—   5
>   the third since I stopped raging for Inachia.
Poor me! Such scandal shames me—what a story
>   I was through all the city! I regret the banquets
at which my indolence and quietness
>   and sighs from my lungs' depths exposed me as a lover. 10
"Up against wealth[6] a poor man's dazzling genius
>   is useless!" That is what I moaned to you through tears
after the shameless god[7] dislodged my secrets
>   and I was set alight by full-strength wine too fiery.

---

1. **Epodes** 11 (*Third Archilochian*): This poem marks a transition in the *Epodes* from the iambic strophes of poems 1–10 to a burst of metrical variety in the final seven poems. Horace's subject matter in this poem also turns toward the erotic, with Horace taking up the role of a serial lover, blurring the generic distinction between epodic and elegiac love poetry. We see Horace in these last poems, in the words of Bather and Stocks (2016) 12, "test[ing] the limits of the genre's flexibility." In this epode Horace juxtaposes two love affairs, one that took place in the past with a woman named Inachia, and one currently underway with a young man, Lyciscus. A good introduction to the **topoi** of love poetry is Hejduk (2008) 3–23.
2. **Pettius:** This addressee is otherwise unknown.
3. **as before:** The language leaves it unclear whether poetry did or did not offer an effective remedy for lovesickness before, and I have attempted to maintain the ambiguity in the translation.
4. **soft boys or girls:** Softness was normally an attribute of women, but it is also regularly applied to the youthful objects of pederastic desire.
5. **shakes the beauty from the forests:** That is, the leaves are falling from the trees in December. This is the third December since Horace was in love with Inachia.
6. **against wealth:** Horace suggests there was a rich rival for Inachia's affections. This rich rival is a **stock figure** of elegiac poetry, and the typically impoverished lover hopes to prevail over him through gifts of poetry rather than cash.
7. **shameless god:** Bacchus, meant here as **metonymy** for wine.

"quodsi meis inaestuet praecordiis   15
    libera bilis, ut haec ingrata ventis dividat
fomenta vulnus nil malum levantia,
    desinet imparibus certare summotus pudor."
ubi haec severus te palam laudaveram,
    iussus abire domum ferebar incerto pede   20
ad non amicos heu mihi postis et heu
    limina dura, quibus lumbos et infregi latus.

nunc gloriantis quamlibet mulierculam
    vincere mollitie amor Lycisci me tenet,
unde expedire non amicorum queant   25
    libera consilia nec contumeliae graves,
sed alius ardor aut puellae candidae
    aut teretis pueri longam renodantis comam.

"But if there boils inside my guts enough   15
      free-flowing bile[8] to cast upon the wind these useless
dressings[9] that don't assuage the evil wound,
      I'll end such shame and cease to vie with my unequals."[10]
When to your face I'd sternly praised this course,
      ordered to go back home, I'd rush on wobbly feet   20
to her unfriendly doorposts (woe is me!)
      and (woe!) harsh thresholds, where I broke my
            groin and flank.[11]
Love for Lyciscus now possesses me—
      he boasts his softness outdoes any measly woman's.[12]
My friends' outspoken counsels and severe   25
      reproaches cannot disentangle me from him—
another passion could—one for a dazzling
      girl or a shapely boy (un)binding his long hair.[13]

---

8. **free-flowing bile:** That is, anger, thought to be produced by excessive bile from the liver.

9. **useless dressings:** *Fomenta* are fomentations, poultices, or bandages used to treat and dress a wound (in this case, an erotic wound). It is not clear what exactly these "dressings" are, but they prove ineffective alleviations for love. Watson (2003) suggests they indicate poetry (a traditional assuagement of love), but others suggest wine or symposia.

10. **But if there boils . . . with my unequals:** The thought of these lines is unclear, particularly with regard to what Horace means by *pudor* (shame), a difficult word to pin down. Watson (2003) argues that it must refer here "to the shameful behavior in which Horace indulges to console himself for lack of good fortune in love." The lack of clarity in Horace's words leads Mankin (1995) to suggest that "H.'s tirade was a drunken babble."

11. **unfriendly doorposts . . . groin and flank:** Horace takes up position outside the beloved's threshold as an elegiac *exclusus amator* (locked-out lover). We can imagine him singing there a **paraclausithyron** (a song in front of a closed door), typical of lovers in elegy. Some have seen in Horace's references to his "groin" and "flank" a possible allusion to some sort of lewd act.

12. **measly woman's:** The Latin term *muliercula* is highly derisive, a diminutive of the already contemptuous *mulier* (woman).

13. **(un)binding . . . hair:** The Latin term *renodantis* is ambiguous, meaning either to "tie back" or to "untie." Oliensis (2002) 100 nicely observes, "Horace both loosens the grip of Lyciscus and readies himself to enter another erotic nexus—a double movement well captured by the ambiguity of *renodantis* (knotting back/unknotting)."

EPODES 12

Quid tibi vis, mulier nigris dignissima barris?
        munera quid mihi quidve tabellas
mittis nec firmo iuveni neque naris obesae?
        namque sagacius unus odoror,
polypus an gravis hirsutis cubet hircus in alis,   5
        quam canis acer ubi lateat sus.
qui sudor vietis et quam malus undique membris
        crescit odor, cum pene soluto
indomitam properat rabiem sedare; neque illi
        iam manet umida creta colorque   10
stercore fucatus crocodili, iamque subando
        tenta cubilia tectaque rumpit!
vel mea cum saevis agitat fastidia verbis:
        "Inachia langues minus ac me;

EPODES 12[1]

What do you want, you woman whom dark elephants
      would suit?[2] Why send me gifts, and why send tablets?
I'm not a firm young man, nor is my nose impaired.
      For I alone sniff out a rancid polyp[3]
or goat that skulks in hairy armpits[4] more adeptly   5
      than a sharp-nosed dog the hideout of a sow.
Oh what a sweat and awful stench arise all over
      her wrinkled limbs when with my flaccid dick
she races to assuage her feral lust. Her runny
      chalk doesn't stay in place, nor does the blush   10
she feigns with shit from crocodiles.[5] Now in her heat
      she busts the straining bed and canopy!
Or else she censures my disgust with ruthless words:
      "When with Inachia you're not this limp.

---

1. **Epodes 12** (*Alcmanic Strophe*): This poem forms something of a companion piece to *Epodes* 8, also a misogynistic **invective** addressed to an older woman (perhaps the same woman) whom Horace accuses of stirring his erotic revulsion and thus preventing him from achieving an erection. Some think Horace casts himself as a male prostitute or gigolo, but impotence and enervation are motifs that Horace introduces as a feature of his iambic **persona** as early as *Epodes* 1, where he is "soft" (*mollis*) and "not very firm" (*firmus parum*). Horace's failure to achieve virility in this most masculine of genres potentially blunts the force of his iambic bite. On impotence in the *Epodes* see especially Fitzgerald (1988) and Oliensis (1991). For the novel suggestion that *Epodes* 12 is directed not toward a woman at all but toward a *cinaedus*, an effeminate male, see Gowers (2016).

2. **woman . . . elephants would suit**: *Mulier* is a more derogatory term for "woman" than *femina*. See note on *Epodes* 11.24. The reference to elephants is clearly obscene but difficult to decipher. As Watson (2003) notes, there are two possibilities: (a) "it would take an elephant-sized penis to satisfy [her lust]" or (b) her vagina is so stretched from frequent intercourse "that it would take an elephant's organ to achieve a snug fit."

3. **rancid polyp**: Horace probably has in mind the proverbially bad odor of sea creatures.

4. **hairy armpits**: Women in the Greco-Roman worlds typically practiced depilation.

5. **runny chalk . . . shit from crocodiles**: The woman employs make-up to make herself more attractive. Both items, as commentators point out, would have had a foul smell. The chalk would have been used to whiten the face, whereas the crocodile dung would have been applied as a rouge.

Inachiam ter nocte potes, mihi semper ad unum   15
    mollis opus. pereat male, quae te
Lesbia quaerenti taurum monstravit inertem,
    cum mihi Cous adesset Amyntas,
cuius in indomito constantior inguine nervus
    quam nova collibus arbor inhaeret.   20
muricibus Tyriis iteratae vellera lanae
    cui properabantur? tibi nempe,
ne foret aequalis inter conviva, magis quem
    diligeret mulier sua quam te.
o ego non felix, quam tu fugis ut pavet acris   25
    agna lupos capreaeque leones!"

Three times a night you screw Inachia—with me   15
    too soft for even once! Curse Lesbia,[6]
who, when I sought a bull, suggested limp-dicked you.
    Coan Amyntas[7] could have been all mine!
Upon his undefeated groin the shaft stands stiffer
    than a young sapling clinging to the hillsides.   20
For whom was woolen fleece, twice dipped in Tyrian purple,[8]
    acquired in a hurry? You, of course,
so that among your friends there'd be no dinner guest
    whose woman loves him more than I do you.
O wretched me! You flee me like a lamb afraid   25
    of sharp-nosed wolves or deer afraid of lions!"

---

6. **Lesbia**: Watson (2003) suggests this is a madam, thus adding to the picture of the
poem's narrator as a gigolo, but Horace has already mentioned Inachia as a love
interest in the previous poem. One cannot help but think of the Lesbia made famous
by the Roman poet Catullus, active in the mid-first century B.C.E.
7. **Coan Amyntas**: A younger rival from the Greek island of Kos. Watson (2003)
suggests Horace is punning on the Latin verb *coire,* which means "to copulate."
8. **woolen fleece . . . Tyrian purple**: Cloth dyed with costly purple dye derived from
Tyrian shellfish.

EPODES 13

Horrida tempestas caelum contraxit et imbres
      nivesque deducunt Iovem; nunc mare, nunc silvae
Threicio Aquilone sonant: rapiamus, amici,
      occasionem de die, dumque virent genua
et decet, obducta solvatur fronte senectus.   5
      tu vina Torquato move consule pressa meo:
cetera mitte loqui: deus haec fortasse benigna
      reducet in sedem vice. nunc et Achaemenio
perfundi nardo iuvat et fide Cyllenea
      levare diris pectora sollicitudinibus;   10
nobilis ut grandi cecinit Centaurus alumno:
      "invicte, mortalis dea nate puer Thetide,
te manet Assaraci tellus, quam frigida pravi
      findunt Scamandri flumina lubricus et Simois;

EPODES 13[1]

A horrifying storm has shrunk the sky, and rain
        and blizzards draw down Jupiter.[2] Now sea, now woods
resound with Thracian Aquilo.[3] Friends, let us seize
        the day's occasion. While our knees still have their youth
and it is right, let's cast old age from our dark brow.   5
        You,[4] fetch a wine from my Torquatus' consulship.[5]
Dismiss all other talk: a god, perhaps, with kindly
        reversal will set this aright. Now it is pleasing
to pour on Persian balsam and with Mercury's lyre
        to ease our hearts of terrible anxieties—   10
just as the noble Centaur sang to his grown pupil:[6]
        "Invincible boy, you mortal son of godly Thetis,
The land of Assaracus[7] waits for you. The coiled
        Scamander's icy flows and gliding Simois cleave it.

---

1. *Epodes* 13 (*Second Archilochian*): A storm is raging outside, which prompts Horace to call his companions to a symposium inside. The storm and the "terrible anxieties" accompanying it have been read as references to the turmoil of civil war, and Horace offers friendship as the proper antidote to such enmity. Both the Battle of Philippi (42 B.C.E.) and the Battle of Actium (31 B.C.E.) have been proposed as the particular occasion for the epode, but this remains unresolved. The mythological exemplum of Achilles about to depart for Troy certainly suggests a martial context.
2. **Jupiter:** Normally Jupiter is the one who sends down storms, not the one sent down by them. Here he is employed **metonymically** for weather in general.
3. **Thracian Aquilo:** The north wind, Aquilo, was thought to arise in Thrace and was associated with winter storms.
4. **You:** Horace moves from addressing the whole group of friends to an unnamed individual.
5. **my Torquatus' consulship:** L. Manlius Torquatus was consul in the year of Horace's birth, i.e., 65 B.C.E.
6. **noble Centaur . . . grown pupil:** The Centaur Chiron, who possessed wisdom as well as the skill of prophecy, was the tutor of the hero Achilles. Horace introduces the exemplum with **interlocking word order:** A (noble) B (grown) A (Centaur), B (pupil).
7. **The land of Assaracus:** Troy, where Assaracus was an early king. Its principle rivers were the Scamander and the Simois.

unde tibi reditum certo subtemine Parcae   15
    rupere, nec mater domum caerula te revehet.

illic omne malum vino cantuque levato,
    deformis aegrimoniae dulcibus alloquiis."

The fates with their sure thread have sundered your return[8]   15
    from there. Your sea-blue mother will not bring
      you home.
While you are there ease every ill with wine and song,
    the sweet alleviations of unsightly anguish."

---

8. **return:** The Latin *reditus* suggests the Greek *nostos* (homecoming), a theme with
which the Greek epics, such as the *Odyssey*, were preoccupied. Achilles was famously
given a choice: live long with no glory or fight and die young, achieving glory but
forfeiting his *nostos*.

EPODES 14

Mollis inertia cur tantam diffuderit imis
      oblivionem sensibus,
pocula Lethaeos ut si ducentia somnos
      arente fauce traxerim,
candide Maecenas, occidis saepe rogando: 5
      deus, deus nam me vetat
inceptos, olim promissum carmen, iambos
      ad umbilicum adducere.
non aliter Samio dicunt arsisse Bathyllo
      Anacreonta Teium,   10

EPODES 14[1]

Why has soft indolence[2] poured out upon my inmost
    senses so much forgetfulness?
It is as if with my parched throat I've drained down goblets
    that bring about Lethean slumbers.[3]
Kindly Maecenas, you are killing me with questions.   5
    A god,[4] yes, god prohibits me
to bring the iambs I've begun, the song that I
    once promised, to the final draft.[5]
Like this, they say, Anacreon of Teos[6] burned
    for Bathyllus, the Samian.   10

---

1. **Epodes 14** (*First Pythiambic*): As Horace approaches the end of his epode collection, Maecenas seems to be complaining about it taking too long. Horace explains that it is love for a woman named Phryne that is preventing him from finishing, as well as his "soft indolence." This "indolence" is related to the sexual impotence of poems 8 and 12, where his lack of virility led to an inability to achieve erection. Sexual and artistic failure are thus linked.
2. **soft indolence**: The word *inertia* can mean a kind of indolent lethargy, but it also suggests sexual impotence. Compare *Epodes* 12.17, where the old woman explicitly accuses him of being sexually *inertem* (impotent), translated there "limp-dicked." It furthermore frequently suggests *in+ars,* i.e., "without art," adding a further nuance that Horace's indolence has directly affected his ability to make art.
3. **Lethean slumbers**: Lethe was the river in the underworld associated with forgetfulness.
4. **A god**: It is common in *recusationes* for poets to assign their inability to complete a poetic task to the intervention of a god. It is not clear to which god this refers, but Cupid/Amor would work well.
5. **final draft**: Literally "the umbilicus." An *umbilicus* was part of a finished scroll, either the rod the papyrus was wrapped around or a knob attached to the rod.
6. **Anacreon of Teos**: A Greek lyric poet of the sixth/fifth century B.C.E., who wrote frequently about erotic themes. It is not immediately clear why Horace suggests he writes in an imperfect meter—the Latin could also indicate meter that's not overly complicated or "elaborate."

qui persaepe cava testudine flevit amorem
    non elaboratum ad pedem.
ureris ipse miser: quodsi non pulchrior ignis
    accendit obsessam Ilion,
gaude sorte tua; me libertina, nec uno   15
    contenta, Phryne macerat.

How often on a hollow lyre he bewailed
    his love in unperfected meters.
You burn too, wretch. But if the flame that torched sieged Troy[7]
    was no more beautiful than yours,
relish your luck. A freedwoman[8] no single man   15
    can sate, named Phryne, makes me stew.

---

7. **flame . . . Troy**: Helen, whose beauty caused the Trojan War. Maecenas should count
himself lucky, Horace states, if his beloved is beautiful like Helen.

8. **freedwoman . . . Phryne**: Her name and status suggest she is a prostitute. Phryne
was a famous Greek courtesan, the supposed model for Praxiteles's Aphrodite of
Cnidus.

EPODES 15

Nox erat et caelo fulgebat luna sereno
    inter minora sidera,
cum tu magnorum numen laesura deorum
    in verba iurabas mea,
artius atque hedera procera adstringitur ilex,   5
    lentis adhaerens bracchiis,
dum pecori lupus et nautis infestus Orion
    turbaret hibernum mare,
intonsosque agitaret Apollinis aura capillos,
    fore hunc amorem mutuum.   10
o dolitura mea multum virtute Neaera!
    nam si quid in Flacco viri est,
non feret adsiduas potiori te dare noctes,
    et quaeret iratus parem,
nec semel offensae cedet constantia formae,   15
    si certus intrarit dolor.
et tu, quicumque es felicior atque meo nunc
    superbus incedis malo,
sis pecore et multa dives tellure licebit,
    tibique Pactolus fluat   20

EPODES 15[1]

It was the night and in a cloudless sky the moon
      gleamed in the midst of lesser stars,
when you (wronging the power of the mighty gods)
      repeated oaths at my dictation,
your pliant arms embracing me more tightly than   5
      a lofty oak enwrapped by ivy.
As long as wolves vex livestock and Orion sailors
      when he stirs up the wintry sea,
as long as wind blows through Apollo's uncut locks,[2]
      we'd have, you swore, a mutual love.   10
Neaera, how my manliness[3] will make you suffer!
      For Flaccus, if he's man at all,
won't stand your giving to his rival all your nights,
      and in his rage he'll seek an equal.[4]
Nor will his firmness yield to your now hated beauty   15
      if stubborn grief should pierce him through.
And you,[5] who strut around, now luckier than I
      and proud because of my bad luck:
Though you are rich in herds and own a lot of land
      and though Pactolus[6] flows for you   20

---

1. *Epodes* 15 (*First Pythiambic*): Horace laments the inconstant love of Neaera. The faithless female, the rival, the love triangle, and the focus on erotic power dynamics all create significant overlap with elegiac love poetry, continuing a blurring of genres seen already, for example, in *Epodes* 11 and 14. The name Neaera has strong links to prostitution (cf. Demosthenes's *Against Neaera*), so Horace demands sexual constancy from a woman whose profession precludes it. Horace's fragile masculinity is once again a key concern, with the poem's central lines revolving around the question of his "manliness," an attribute that his emphatically stated name Flaccus (Floppy) calls into question.
2. **Apollo's uncut locks:** Apollo's hair was eternally youthful and long.
3. **manliness:** The word *virtus* means both "manliness" and "virtue," but the former meaning prevails here.
4. **an equal:** That is, someone who reciprocates his love—a nearly impossible ideal in Roman love poetry.
5. **you:** Horace now addresses the rival.
6. **Pactolus:** A Lydian river famous for its gold deposits, proverbially associated with wealth.

nec te Pythagorae fallant arcana renati,
        formaque vincas Nirea,
heu heu translatos alio maerebis amores:
        ast ego vicissim risero.

and riddles of reborn Pythagoras[7] don't stump you
    and you top Nireus[8] in beauty—
woe! woe! you'll weep when her love transfers to another.
    But I in turn will have a laugh.

---

7. **riddles of reborn Pythagoras**: The rival understands the obscure teachings of the philosopher Pythagoras, who espoused the doctrine of reincarnation.

8. **Nireus**: A young Greek warrior whom Homer lauds for his beauty.

EPODES 16

Altera iam teritur bellis civilibus aetas,
      suis et ipsa Roma viribus ruit:
quam neque finitimi valuerunt perdere Marsi
      minacis aut Etrusca Porsenae manus,
aemula nec virtus Capuae nec Spartacus acer   5
      novisque rebus infidelis Allobrox
nec fera caerulea domuit Germania pube
      parentibusque abominatus Hannibal,
impia perdemus devoti sanguinis aetas,
      ferisque rursus occupabitur solum.   10
barbarus heu cineres insistet victor et Vrbem
      eques sonante verberabit ungula,

EPODES 16[1]

Another age is now worn down by civil war,
    and Rome itself caves in through its own strength.
The Marsi[2] on its borders could not ravage it,
    Nor threatening Porsena's Etruscan throng,[3]
nor Capua's rival virtue,[4] nor fierce Spartacus,[5]   5
    nor the Allobrogian, faithless in revolt.[6]
Wild Germany with its blue-eyed youth did not subdue it,[7]
    nor Hannibal,[8] that hateful plague to parents.
We, impious age whose blood is damned, will be its ruin,
    and beasts once more will occupy the land.   10
A barbarian[9] victor (woe!) will tramp its ash and flog
    the city with a ringing hoof on horseback.

---

1. **Epodes 16** (*Second Pythiambic*): In this famous but highly disputed poem, Horace assumes the role of a *vates,* a poet-prophet (bard), advising the Romans on how to escape the evils of civil war. His solution, presented as if in an assembly, is an impossible one: escape to the legendary and paradisiacal Isles of the Blessed, where the miraculous Golden Age still thrives. The idea of inherited guilt runs through the poem, further giving the Roman context the flavor of Greek myth, where wrongdoing frequently passes from one generation to the next. Some have seen the epode as a pessimistic corrective to Vergil's *Eclogues* 4, where the Golden Age is poised to make an imminent return to Italy.
2. **The Marsi**: A reference to the Social War of 91–88 B.C.E., presented as a kind of precursor to the current civil upheaval. The Marsi were proverbially militaristic and hardy.
3. **threatening . . . throng**: Lars Porsena was a mythical Etruscan king from Rome's early monarchical period. He led his army against Rome in an attempt to reclaim the throne for Tarquinius Suberbus.
4. **Capua's rival virtue**: Capua sided with Hannibal during the Second Punic War of 218–201 B.C.E. The word *virtus* (translated "virtue" here) also means "manliness," a sense that comes to the fore in line 39.
5. **fierce Spartacus**: A Thracian gladiator who led a slave revolt in Italy in 73–71 B.C.E. and was defeated by Crassus.
6. **the Allobrogian . . . revolt**: The Allobroges were a tribe in southern Gaul. Catiline had tried to win them over to him in his conspiracy of 63 B.C.E., but Allobrogian ambassadors revealed it to the consul Cicero. In 61 B.C.E. they themselves launched an unsuccessful rebellion.
7. **Germany . . . subdue it**: Two Germanic tribes, the Cimbri and the Teutones, invaded Rome and were defeated in 105 B.C.E. at Arausio in France. Though victorious, the Roman troops suffered enormous losses.
8. **Hannibal**: The Carthaginian general who invaded Italy in the Second Punic War.
9. **barbarian**: See note at *Epodes* 5.61.

quaeque carent ventis et solibus ossa Quirini,
    nefas videre! dissipabit insolens.
forte quid expediat communiter aut melior pars   15
    malis carere quaeritis laboribus.
nulla sit hac potior sententia, Phocaeorum
    velut profugit exsecrata civitas
agros atque Lares patrios, habitandaque fana
    apris reliquit et rapacibus lupis,   20
ire pedes quocumque ferent, quocumque per undas
    Notus vocabit aut protervus Africus.
sic placet? an melius quis habet suadere? secunda
    ratem occupare quid moramur alite?
sed iuremus in haec: simul imis saxa renarint   25
    vadis levata, ne redire sit nefas;
neu conversa domum pigeat dare lintea, quando
    Padus Matina laverit cacumina,
in mare seu celsus procurrerit Appenninus,
    novaque monstra iunxerit libidine   30
mirus amor, iuvet ut tigris subsidere cervis,
    adulteretur et columba miluo,

Quirinus' bones,[10] which now are safe from wind and sun—
    A sin to see! In arrogance he'll strew them!
Perhaps you (or the better part[11]) ask all together   15
    what can release you from these wretched labors.
May this proposal be thought best: as the Phocaean
    state[12] swore an oath with curses and then fled
ancestral fields and Lares,[13] giving up the shrines
    to boars and greedy wolves to occupy,   20
let's go wherever feet will lead, through waves wherever
    Notus or raging Africus[14] will call.
Do you approve? Is there a better plan? The omens
    bring luck—why do we wait to board the ship?
Let's swear these oaths: only when rocks rise from the depths, 25
    grown light, will homecoming not be a sin.
May it disgust us to set sail back home until
    the Padus bathes the summit of Matinus[15]
or the high Apennines[16] fall down beneath the sea
    and shocking love makes monstrous combinations   30
with novel lust, so tigers thrill to mate with deer,
    the dove commits adultery[17] with the kite,

---

10. **Quirinus' bones**: Quirinus was the cult name of Romulus, the founder of Rome, whose bones were allegedly buried in the forum and were assigned an apotropaic function.
11. **the better part**: Here and in line 37 Horace exposes a marked elitism. If the entire city will not go, at least the better part will.
12. **Phocaean state**: The Phocaeans were Ionian Greeks who, according to Herodotus (1.165), surrendered their city to the Persians. They cursed anyone who would return before a lump of iron they dropped into the sea should float back up again. Horace clearly alludes to this curse in lines 25–26.
13. **Lares**: The Roman household gods, here attributed to the Greek Phocaeans. The Lares here perhaps stand **metonymically** for their houses.
14. **Notus ... Africus**: The south and southwest winds, respectively.
15. **Padus ... Matinus**: The Padus is the Po River in Northern Italy, and Matinus a mountain in the Southern Italian region of Apulia. This is one of several **adynata** running through this section of the poem that underline the impossibility of return.
16. **Apennines**: A mountain range in central Italy, far from the sea.
17. **dove ... adultery**: Doves were proverbially faithful to their mates.

credula nec ravos timeant armenta leones,
　　ametque salsa levis hircus aequora.
haec et quae poterunt reditus abscindere dulcis　　　　35
　　eamus omnis exsecrata civitas,
aut pars indocili melior grege; mollis et exspes
　　inominata perpremat cubilia!
vos quibus est virtus, muliebrem tollite luctum,
　　Etrusca praeter et volate litora.　　　　40
nos manet Oceanus circumvagus: arva, beata
　　petamus arva, divites et insulas,
reddit ubi Cererem tellus inarata quotannis
　　et imputata floret usque vinea,
germinat et numquam fallentis termes olivae,　　　　45
　　suamque pulla ficus ornat arborem,
mella cava manant ex ilice, montibus altis
　　levis crepante lympha desilit pede.
illic iniussae veniunt ad mulctra capellae,
　　refertque tenta grex amicus ubera;　　　　50
nec vespertinus circumgemit ursus ovile,
　　nec intumescit alta viperis humus:
pluraque felices mirabimur; ut neque largis
　　aquosus Eurus arva radat imbribus,
pinguia nec siccis urantur semina glaebis,　　　　55
　　utrumque rege temperante caelitum.
non huc Argoo contendit remige pinus,
　　neque impudica Colchis intulit pedem;

gullible cattle have no fear of tawny lions,
      and hairy goats, now sleek, love salty water.
After we've sworn these oaths with curses that cut off   35
      our sweet return, let's go, the state in full—
or that part better than the ignorant herd. The soft
      and desolate can sprawl on ill-starred beds!
You who have manliness, discard your female sorrow
      and take wing out beyond Etruscan shores.[18]   40
Encircling Ocean[19] waits for us. Let's seek the fields,
      the blessed fields and islands full of bounty,
where every year the earth, unplowed, produces Ceres[20]
      and vines are ever blooming, though not pruned,
where olive boughs do not deceive but bud and sprout,   45
      and ripened figs embellish their own tree,
where honey seeps from hollow oaks and water gently
      leaps from the lofty peaks with splashing feet.
There, goats come of their own accord to milking pails;
      the friendly flock brings back distended udders.   50
There's no bear growling round the sheepfold in the evening,
      nor does the ground swell up on high with snakes.
We, happy, will behold more marvels: how wet Eurus
      does not erode the fields with too much rain,
how plump seeds never bake in arid clods of earth—   55
      because the king of gods tempers them both.
The pine tree did not guide the Argo's rowers[21] here,
      nor did the shameless Colchian[22] ever reach it.

---

18. **Etruscan shores**: Italy
19. **Encircling Ocean**: An allusion to the Homeric idea that the earth was a flat disk surrounded by the Ocean.
20. **Ceres**: The goddess here stands **metonymically** for grain. Spontaneous agricultural production was a longstanding feature of the Golden Age.
21. **pine tree . . . Argo's rowers**: The pine stands **metonymically** for the ship itself. Sailing was not practiced during the Golden Age, the end of which was thought to coincide with the launch of Argo, the first ship, and thus the age of heroes.
22. **shameless Colchian**: Medea. According to some traditions, however, Medea and Achilles were married in the Isles of the Blessed.

non huc Sidonii torserunt cornua nautae
  laboriosa nec cohors Vlixei: 60
nulla nocent pecori contagia, nullius astri
  gregem aestuosa torret impotentia.
Iuppiter illa piae secrevit litora genti,
  ut inquinavit aere tempus aureum;
aere, dehinc ferro duravit saecula, quorum   65
  piis secunda vate me datur fuga.

Sidonian sailors[23] never turned their yardarms here,
        nor did Odysseus' comrades, racked with labors.   60
There aren't diseases that can harm the flock, no star's
        boiling intensity inflames the herd.
Jupiter marked those shores out for a pious race
        back when he dulled the time of gold with bronze.[24]
With bronze, then iron he made the ages hard. The pious,   65
        if I'm their bard,[25] can luckily escape them.

23. **Sidonian sailors**: Sidon was in Phoenicia, renowned for its skill in sailing.
24. **time of gold with bronze**: The ages traditionally run from gold to silver,
    bronze, and iron. Horace, however, omits the Silver Age.
25. **bard**: See note on *Odes* 1.1.35.

EPODES 17

Iam iam efficaci do manus scientiae,
supplex et oro regna per Proserpinae,
per et Dianae non movenda numina,
per atque libros carminum valentium
refixa caelo devocare sidera,   5
Canidia, parce vocibus tandem sacris,
citumque retro solve, solve turbinem.
movit nepotem Telephus Nereium,
in quem superbus ordinarat agmina
Mysorum et in quem tela acuta torserat: 10
unxere matres Iliae addictum feris
alitibus atque canibus homicidam Hectorem,

EPODES 17[1]

"Now, now I yield my hands[2] to proven knowledge
and plead, a suppliant, by Proserpina's realm[3]
and by Diana's power (not for rousing)
and by[4] the books of incantations able
to pluck stars from the sky and call them down,   5
Canidia, now stop these cursed charms
and back, turn back the top[5] you set to spin.
Telephus roused to pity Nereus' grandson,[6]
against whom pompously he'd lined his troops
of Mysians and aimed sharp-pointed spears.   10
Troy's mothers oiled man-slaying[7] Hector's corpse,
which had been left to savage birds and dogs,

---

1. ***Epodes* 17** (*Iambic Trimeter*): This final poem of the *Epodes* presents a second
encounter with the witch Canidia, with the narrator himself replacing the boy of
Epodes 5 as the victim of her magic. Her assault, which has left him hovering on the
verge of death, is seemingly in retaliation for the narrator's divulgence of the magical
mystery rites in which she takes part (rites described also by Priapus in *Satires* 1.8),
and Horace begs her for release in a mock-prayer. The poem pits the male iambicist
against the female witch and suggests, once more, that the first lacks the potency
required to vanquish those over whom he should maintain supremacy. Horace gives
Canidia the collection's closing words, but in the last line she hints at the possibility
that her magic just may fail against him. The collection thus ends on an open-ended
note, leaving it ultimately to the reader to decide how the showdown will play
out. The poem, uniquely in the *Epodes,* is not in an epodic meter—it is instead in
continuous iambic trimeter.
2. **I yield my hands**: Horace assumes the posture of surrender as well as supplication.
3. **plead . . . Proserpina's realm**: Horace introduces here the heavy "p" **alliteration**
that runs through the poem, which is often used to express disdain. Even as Horace
pleads for release, he cannot help but show his scorn. I have tried to replicate this as
much as English will allow.
4. **by . . . by . . . by**: The triple **anaphora** is characteristic of prayers and religious
language.
5. **top**: Magic frequently involved the use of spinning objects.
6. **Telephus . . . Nereus' grandson**: Horace gives several mythological examples of
suppliants moving victors to pity. Nereus's grandson is Achilles, who attacked Mysia,
where Telephus was king, on his way to the Trojan War. Achilles wounded him in the
thigh but, after Telephus pled with him, healed him with scrapings from his spear.
7. **man-slaying**: Horace's *homicidiam* translates ἀνδροφόνος (man-slayer), one of
Homer's most frequent **epithets** for Hector. The mothers of Troy anointed his body
in preparation for burial.

postquam relictis moenibus rex procidit
heu pervicacis ad pedes Achillei:
saetosa duris exuere pellibus   15
laboriosi remiges Vlixei
volente Circa membra; tunc mens et sonus
relapsus atque notus in vultus honor.
dedi satis superque poenarum tibi,
amata nautis multum et institoribus: 20
fugit iuventas et verecundus color
relinquor ossa pelle amicta lurida;
tuis capillus albus est odoribus;
nullum ab labore me reclinat otium;
urget diem nox et dies noctem, neque est   25
levare tenta spiritu praecordia.
ergo negatum vincor ut credam miser,
Sabella pectus increpare carmina
caputque Marsa dissilire nenia.
quid amplius vis? o mare et terra, ardeo   30
quantum neque atro delibutus Hercules
Nessi cruore nec Sicana fervida
virens in Aetna flamma: tu, donec cinis

after the king went from the walls and fell
(woe!) at the feet of obstinate Achilles.[8]
The rowers of Odysseus, racked with labors,[9]   15
cast off their hardened pelts from bristly limbs
as soon as Circe willed.[10] Then mind and speech
returned—so too their faces' wonted beauty.
I've paid the price enough and more to you,
beloved so much by sailors and street vendors.[11]   20
My youth and ruddy glow have fled away.
I'm left just bones wrapped in a sallow pelt.
My hair is white due to your stinking unguents.
No respite from my labor lets me rest—
night follows day and day the night.[12] And I   25
can't soothe the tightness in my chest by breathing.
Wretched, I'm must admit what I denied:
that Samnite incantations *can* faze hearts
and Marsian spells *can* split a head in two.[13]
You want what more? O sea and land, I burn   30
hotter than Hercules besmeared with Nessus'
black blood[14] and hotter than Sicilian flames
that swell in Aetna's fires.[15] Will you, until

---

8. **fell . . . Achilles:** Priam's famous supplication of Achilles, which results in the
ransoming of Hector's body, is described in *Iliad* 24.
9. **racked with labors:** It is unclear in Horace's Latin whether *laboriosi* modifies
Odysseus or his rowers, and I have tried to maintain the ambiguity.
10. **as soon as Circe willed:** Like Canidia, Circe is a female witch whose spells
attack men. She turned Odysseus's crew into swine but reversed her spell when
Odysseus overpowered and sexually outmaneuvered her—although Horace makes it
seem like a case of persuasion.
11. **sailors and street vendors:** Horace accuses Canidia of low-class prostitution.
12. **No respite . . . night:** Canidia's spells have caused him insomnia.
13. **split a head in two:** I.e., cause severe headache.
14. **Hercules . . . black blood:** Nessus was a centaur Hercules shot with an arrow
poisoned in the Hydra's blood. As he died, Nessus gave Hercules's wife Deianeira
some of his poisoned blood to use as a love potion. She later gave Hercules a shirt
steeped in the blood, which caused the hero's skin to burn in an agonizing death.
15. **Aetna's fires:** Aetna is a volcano on the island of Sicily. Vulcan was often
thought to have his workshop here.

iniuriosis aridus ventis ferar,
cales venenis officina Colchicis?   35
quae finis aut quod me manet stipendium?
effare: iussas cum fide poenas luam,
paratus expiare, seu poposceris
centum iuvencos sive mendaci lyra
voles sonari, tu pudica, tu proba   40
perambulabis astra sidus aureum.
infamis Helenae Castor offensus vicem
fraterque magni Castoris, victi prece,
adempta vati reddidere lumina:
et tu, potes nam, solve me dementia,   45
o nec paternis obsoleta sordibus,
neque in sepulcris pauperum prudens anus
novendialis dissipare pulveres.
tibi hospitale pectus et purae manus,
tuusque venter Pactumeius, et tuo   50
cruore rubros obstetrix pannos lavit,
utcumque fortis exsilis puerpera.

I'm borne on noxious winds as dried-out ash,
keep burning like a lab of Colchian poison?[16]   35
What end or punishment awaits for me?
Tell me—I'll truly pay the price you bid.
I'm ready to atone, if you'll demand
a hundred calves[17] or wish to be extolled
with feigning lyre: 'You pure, you upright lady,[18]   40
a golden star, you'll tour the constellations.'[19]
Castor and mighty Castor's brother, angry
for Helen's sake[20] but conquered by entreaty,
gave back the bard[21] the eyes they'd snatched away.
And you (you can!), release me from my madness—   45
you're not low-class and born from vulgar parents,[22]
you're no old hag who skillfully can strew
nine-day-old ashes in the tombs of paupers.[23]
Your heart is kind to guests, your hands unsullied.[24]
And Pactumeius is your progeny.   50
The midwife scrubbed *your* blood from putrid rags,
however nimbly you hopped up postpartum."[25]

---

16. **Colchian poison:** Allusion to Medea, the famous witch from Colchis on the
    Black Sea. I punctuate this as a question, following Mankin (1995).
17. **a hundred calves:** A sacrifice of this size was known as a "hecatomb." This was
    an outlandishly large sacrifice for the "divine" Canidia.
18. **You pure, you upright lady:** The repeated use of the second-person singular
    "you" (**Du-Stil**) parodies the style of prayers. Horace's use of disdainful "p"
    alliteration undercuts the mock praise his "falsifying lyre" here offers.
19. **tour the constellations:** Horace mockingly foretells Canidia's deification.
20. **for Helen's sake:** Helen was the sister of Castor and Pollux.
21. **the bard:** The lyric poet Stesichorus, whom, according to legend, Castor and Pollux
    blinded for defaming Helen in his verses. After he recanted, they returned his sight.
22. **not low-class . . . parents:** Horace issues a series of sarcastic denials and thereby
    suggests that all of these things are in fact true. He first denies that Canidia is low-born.
23. **old hag . . . tombs of paupers:** Horace hints that Canidia pillages the tombs of
    the recently deceased poor to acquire bones for use in her magic rites.
24. **kind to guests . . . unsullied:** He accuses her of killing her own guests, an act
    of extreme religious sacrilege.
25. **Pactumeius . . . postpartum:** Canidia has falsely pretended to have given birth to a
    child she stole, presumably for use in her magic or to pass off as her husband's heir.

        "quid obseratis auribus fundis preces?
non saxa nudis surdiora navitis
Neptunus alto tundit hibernus salo.   55
inultus ut tu riseris Cotyttia
vulgata, sacrum liberi Cupidinis,
et Esquilini pontifex venefici
inpune ut Vrbem nomine impleris meo?
quid proderit ditasse Paelignas anus   60
velociusve miscuisse toxicum?
sed tardiora fata te votis manent:
ingrata misero vita ducenda est in hoc,
novis ut usque suppetas laboribus.
optat quietem Pelopis infidi pater,   65
egens benignae Tantalus semper dapis,
optat Prometheus obligatus aliti,
optat supremo collocare Sisyphus
in monte saxum; sed vetant leges Iovis.
voles modo altis desilire turribus,   70

"Why pour these prayers into my plugged-up ears?
To naked seamen rocks are just as deaf,
which wintry Neptune strikes upon the deep.   55
Shall you, unpunished, mock and tell Cotyto's
mysteries, rite of unrestricted Cupid?[26]
As chief priest of the magic Esquiline,[27]
you'll fill the city with my name scot-free?
What use was it to pay Pelignian[28]   60
old hags or brew a faster-acting toxin?
But death that's slower than you'd like awaits.
A wretch, you'll live your thankless life for this:
ever to be at hand for novel labors.
Unfaithful Pelops' father longs for peace—   65
Tantalus who forever lacks rich feasts.
Chained for the bird,[29] Prometheus longs for peace.
Sisyphus longs to set the rock upon
the mountain's peak, but Jove's decrees forbid.[30]
Now you will want to leap from lofty towers,   70

---

26. **Cotyto's mysteries. . . . Cupid**: Cotyto was a Thracian goddess associated
with magic. The divulgence of such mystery rites was considered a grave impiety.
Because of their secrecy, such rites were often associated by outsiders with
unrestrained sexuality, a link Canidia freely admits, as Cupid stands **metonymically**
for sex here.

27. **chief priest . . . Esquiline**: In *Satires* 1.8, Canidia's magical ceremonies take
place on the Esquiline Hill. It is unclear what she means by accusing Horace of being
the Esquiline's *pontifex* (chief priest), but two suggestions have been made: (a) she
sees him as an opposing sorcerer or (b) he has taken up the role of moral censor in
order to condemn her rites.

28. **Pelignian**: A Samnite tribe.

29. **Chained for the bird**: Because he stole fire from the gods to give to humans,
Prometheus was chained to a rock and his regenerating liver was constantly
devoured by an eagle. Horace places his punishment in the Underworld, though
normally it is located in the Caucasus mountains.

30. **Unfaithful Pelops' . . . decrees forbid**: Canidia sees herself in the role of
punishing a great sinner such as Tantalus (the father of Pelops who attempted to
feed his son to the gods), Prometheus (who stole fire for mankind), or Sisyphus (who
tried, e.g., to cheat death).

modo ense pectus Norico recludere,
frustraque vincla gutturi innectes tuo,
fastidiosa tristis aegrimonia.
vectabor umeris tunc ego inimicis eques,
meaeque terra cedet insolentiae.   75
an quae movere cereas imagines,
ut ipse nosti curiosus, et polo
deripere lunam vocibus possim meis,
possim crematos excitare mortuos
desiderique temperare pocula,   80
plorem artis in te nil agentis exitus?"

now use a Noric sword[31] to slice your chest.
You'll tie a noose around your neck in vain,[32]
while heavy-hearted with oppressive anguish.
And then I'll ride astride[33] your hated shoulders,
and earth shall yield to my effrontery.   75
But since I *can* rouse dolls made out of wax—
as you yourself, a meddler, know—and can
pull down the moon from heaven with my charms
and can reanimate cremated dead
and mix up potions that produce desire,   80
I'll weep my art won't work on you at last?[34]

---

31. **Noric sword**: The province of Noricum produced fine iron.
32. **noose . . . in vain**: The iambicists Archilochus and Hipponax were thought to
    have driven their victims to suicide in this way, but Horace will have no such recourse
    from Canidia.
33. **ride astride**: She imagines herself as an *eques* (equestrian) riding atop her
    victim as though on horseback.
34. **I'll weep . . . at last**: Canidia suggests that, since her magical art has already
    proven itself effective, she will not be unable to influence Horace too. The final
    word *exitus,* translated here "at last," signals the close of the *Epodes,* balancing the
    collection's first word *ibis,* "you will go/embark."

ODES 1

ODES 1.1

Maecenas atavis edite regibus,
o et praesidium et dulce decus meum,
sunt quos curriculo pulverem Olympicum
collegisse iuvat, metaque fervidis
evitata rotis palmaque nobilis   5
terrarum dominos evehit ad deos;
hunc, si mobilium turba Quiritium
certat tergeminis tollere honoribus;

ODES 1.1[1]

Maecenas, born of regal ancestors,
O my protection and my sweet adornment,
some with a chariot delight to stir
Olympic dust and to avoid the turning
post with their burning wheels. The noble palm   5
uplifts them to the gods, lords of the lands.[2]
One man delights if the fickle Roman mob
competes to raise him up with triple honors,[3]

---

1. *Odes* 1.1 (*First Asclepiadean*): This opening poem takes the form of a **priamel**, a
list of rejected foils punctuated by the preferred alternative. Horace repudiates the
lifestyles that make up the **priamel** to varying degrees; whereas the discontented
merchant will largely remain an object of censure, for example, the idler who spends
part of his day relaxing with wine will have much in common with facets of Horace's
lyric **persona**. This catalog foreshadows many features of the poems to come and
marks their author as a complicated personality. Throughout the first book my notes
are indebted to the commentaries of Nisbet and Hubbard (1970), Garrison (1991), and
Mayer (2012). West (1995) also offers a helpful reading of each poem.
2. **lords of the lands**: The Latin leaves it ambiguous whether the athletes or the gods are
the "lords of the land." I have tried to keep the ambiguity.
3. **triple honors**: Interpretations of this vary. Some suggest this means three rounds
of public applause, others the three offices (a more concrete meaning of *honor*) of
aedile, praetor, and consul.

illum, si proprio condidit horreo
quidquid de Libycis verritur areis.   10
gaudentem patrios findere sarculo
agros Attalicis condicionibus
numquam demoveas ut trabe Cypria
<u>Myrtoum</u> pavidus nauta secet <u>mare</u>.
luctantem Icariis fluctibus Africum   15
mercator metuens otium et oppidi
laudat rura sui; mox reficit ratis
quassas, indocilis pauperiem pati.
est qui nec veteris pocula Massici
nec partem solido demere de die   20
spernit, nunc viridi membra sub arbuto
stratus, nunc ad aquae lene caput sacrae.
multos castra iuvant et lituo tubae
permixtus sonitus bellaque matribus
detestata. manet sub Iove frigido   25
venator tenerae coniugis immemor,
seu visa est catulis cerva fidelibus,

another if he's stored in his own barn
all that is swept from Libyan threshing-floors.[4]   10
The man who loves to cleave paternal fields
by hoe—not with the wealth of Attalus[5]
could you move him to split the sea of Myrto[6]
with a Cyprian ship-beam[7] as a frightened sailor.
The trader, terrified when Africus[8]   15
wrestles Icarian waves,[9] extols his own
town's ease and farms—but soon rebuilds his broken
fleet since he can't put up with poverty.
Another won't refuse cups of aged Massic[10]
nor to take time out of his busy day   20
to stretch his limbs, now under green arbutus,
now near a gentle source of sacred water.[11]
Many the camp delights, the mingled noise
of horn and trumpet, and the wars that mothers
detest. There waits beneath the frigid sky   25
a hunter heedless of his tender wife,
whether his faithful dogs have seen a deer

---

4. **Libyan threshing-floors:** Libya in northern Africa was a major producer of grain for Rome.
5. **Attalus:** A fantastically wealthy king of Pergamon in Asia Minor.
6. **the Sea of Myrto:** The Myrtoan sea was a famously stormy stretch of the Mediterranean running between the Peloponnese and the Cyclades. The **hyperbaton** between *Myrtoum* ("Myrtoan") and *mare* ("sea") nicely recreates the frightened sailor's "splitting" of it.
7. **Cyprian ship-beam:** Cyprus was an island in the eastern Mediterranean known for its shipbuilding. Horace's geographical terms in the opening poem span the Mediterranean basin.
8. **Africus:** The proverbially stormy southwest wind.
9. **Icarian waves:** The Icarian sea was where Icarus fell to his death when he flew too close to the sun on waxen wings. Icarus's flight challenged the limits imposed on mankind by the gods, and the trader exhibits a similarly doomed impiety.
10. **Massic:** A fine Italian wine from Campania.
11. **green arbutus . . . water:** The tree and water lend this the atmosphere of a *locus amoenus*, introducing an important motif of the odes.

seu rupit <u>teretes</u> **Marsus aper** <u>plagas</u>.
me doctarum hederae praemia frontium
dis miscent superis, me gelidum nemus   30
nympharumque leves cum Satyris chori
secernunt populo, si neque tibias
Euterpe cohibet nec Polyhymnia
Lesboum refugit tendere barbiton.
quodsi me lyricis vatibus inseres,   35
sublimi feriam sidera vertice.

or a **Marsian boar** has burst the close-mesh nets.[12]
But me the ivy prize of learned brows
mingles with gods above. The chilly grove   30
and sprightly dances of the nymphs and satyrs
remove me from the people, if Euterpe
does not withhold the flute nor Polyhymnia[13]
refuse to tune the Lesbian barbiton.[14]
If you will place me with the lyric bards,[15]   35
I'll strike the stars with my exalted head.

---

12. **Marsian boar . . . nets:** Horace again uses **hyperbaton** to create a word
    picture. The "Marsian boar" (*Marsus aper*) is caught within and breaks apart the
    "tightly woven nets" (*teretes plagas*). The label "Marsian" is a **transferred epithet**
    more properly describing the hunter. The Marsi were a proverbially rugged Italian
    people.
13. **Euterpe . . . Polyhymnia:** Euterpe and Polyhymnia are two of the nine Muses,
    whose aid it is customary to invoke in opening or dedicatory poems.
14. **flute . . . barbiton:** The tibia/flute was a wind instrument usually made out
    of reed, and the barbiton was a stringed instrument similar to a lyre. Lyric poetry
    originally was accompanied by music, and Horace maintains this impression in his
    Odes. The barbiton is "Lesbian" in honor of Sappho and Alcaeus, both of Lesbos and
    preeminent lyric poets of archaic Greece.
15. **lyric bards:** The canon of nine lyric poets had already been set during the
    Hellenistic period. These include Alcaeus, Alcman, Anacreon, Bacchylides, Ibycus,
    Pindar, Sappho, Simonides, and Stesichorus. *Vates* (bard) was a key term for
    Augustan poets and suggested divinely inspired, authoritative speech.

ODES 1.2

Iam satis terris nivis atque dirae
grandinis misit Pater et rubente
dextera sacras iaculatus arces
      terruit urbem,

terruit gentis, grave ne rediret   5
saeculum Pyrrhae nova monstra questae,
omne cum Proteus pecus egit altos
      visere montis,

piscium et summa genus haesit ulmo
nota quae sedes fuerat columbis,   10
et superiecto pavidae natarunt
      aequore dammae.

vidimus flavum Tiberim retortis
litore Etrusco violenter undis
ire deiectum monumenta regis   15
      templaque Vestae,

ODES 1.2[1]

Now has the Father[2] sent sufficient snow
and dreadful hail to earth, and with his red
right hand[3] he's struck the holy citadels,
     making the city,

making the nations fear that Pyrrha's grievous   5
age comes again.[4] She wept at strange new wonders[5]
while Proteus guided his whole flock[6] to see
     towering mountains,

and fish were clinging to the elm tree's top,
which once had been the wonted home for doves,   10
and in the overflowing sea swam deer
     quaking with terror.

We've seen[7] the tawny Tiber wildly twist
his wave back from the Tuscan shore[8] and rush
up to the king's memorial and Vesta's   15
     temple[9] to raze them,

---

1. **Odes 1.2** (*Sapphic Strophe*): In this second ode, Horace adopts the voice of a public
   spokesperson diagnosing the city's precarious situation and offering as solutions piety
   and Augustus's almost divine leadership. He interprets the bad weather of the opening
   stanza as a sign that Jupiter is on the verge of destroying the current impious age just as
   he did previously in the great flood, a fear strengthened by a recent flood of the Tiber.
   In the poem's second half the speaker calls for help from a series of gods important to
   Rome: Apollo, Venus, Mars, and finally Mercury, whose earthly incarnation is Augustus.
2. **Father**: Jupiter.
3. **red right hand**: His hand is red from casting fiery thunderbolts.
4. **Pyrrha's . . . comes again**: Pyrrha, along with her husband Deucalion, survived the
   great flood Jupiter sent against early man. They repopulated the lands by throwing
   stones behind them, which then transformed to people.
5. **strange new wonders**: I.e., the topsy-turvy world created by the flood.
6. **Proteus . . . flock**: Proteus was a sea-god whose "flock" consisted of seals.
7. **We've seen**: The Tiber flooded regularly, and it's not clear precisely which
   occurrence Horace has in mind here.
8. **Tuscan shore**: The reference is not entirely clear, but most commentators nowadays
   take this as a reference to the Tiber's western bank near the Janiculum Hill.
9. **king's . . . Vesta's temple**: The early king Numa was credited with the building of the
   Regia, where the Pontifex Maximus lived, and the temple of Vesta, both of which are
   located in the Roman Forum.

Iliae dum se nimium querenti
iactat ultorem, vagus et sinistra
labitur ripa Iove non probante u-
            xorius amnis.   20

audiet civis acuisse ferrum
quo graves Persae melius perirent,
audiet pugnas vitio parentum
            rara iuventus.

quem vocet divum populus ruentis   25
imperi rebus? prece qua fatigent
virgines sanctae minus audientem
            carmina Vestam?

cui dabit partis scelus expiandi
Iuppiter? tandem venias precamur   30
nube candentis umeros amictus,
            augur Apollo,

sive tu mavis, Erycina ridens,
quam Iocus circum volat et Cupido;

while boasting he was Ilia's avenger[10]—
the girl who wept too much. Though Jove did not
approve, he glided past his eastern bank, u-
    xorious river.   20

The youth will hear how citizens made sharp
the sword with which the Persians should have perished,[11]
hear of the battles[12] of their parents, by whose
    crime they are fewer.[13]

The people should invoke which god to help   25
the toppling empire's fortunes? With what prayer
should sacred virgins[14] beg (though she hears not)
    Vesta with chanting?

To whom will Jupiter allot the task
of expiating crime? Now come, we pray,   30
your gleaming shoulders covered in a cloud,
    augur Apollo,[15]

or you, if you would rather, smiling Venus,[16]
around whom Jollity and Cupid flutter,

---

10. **Ilia's avenger:** Ilia was another name for Rhea Silvia, who was raped by the
god Mars and gave birth to Romulus and Remus. She was thereupon thrown into
the Tiber in a kind of quasi-marriage. Horace thus suggests the flood was the Tiber's
retaliation for the treatment of his "wife."
11. **Persians . . . perished:** Here this indicates the Parthians, against whom Crassus
suffered a defeat in 53 B.C.E. Augustus would recover the captured Roman standards
diplomatically in 20 B.C.E.
12. **battles:** That is, the battles of the civil wars.
13. **fewer:** The civil wars caused a decrease in population that Augustus's moral
reforms, with their emphasis on childbearing, would aim to correct.
14. **sacred virgins:** The Vestal Virgins, who were tasked with securing via prayer
and their own inviolable persons the public safety of Rome.
15. **augur Apollo:** Apollo was a god of prophecy. Augustus credited him with his
victory at Actium in 31 B.C.E.
16. **smiling Venus:** Aphrodite's chief Homeric **epithet** is "laughter-loving," but
Horace has Venus's Homeric guise in mind less than her important role in Roman
cult as *genetrix* (mother) to the Romans via Aeneas and his descendants, including
Julius Caesar and Augustus.

sive neglectum genus et nepotes   35
    respicis auctor,

heu nimis longo satiate ludo,
quem iuvat clamor galeaeque leves,
acer et Mauri peditis cruentum
    voltus in hostem;   40

sive mutata iuvenem figura
ales in terris imitaris almae
filius Maiae patiens vocari
    Caesaris ultor:

serus in caelum redeas diuque   45
laetus intersis populo Quirini,
neve te nostris vitiis iniquum
    ocior aura

tollat; hic magnos potius triumphos,
hic ames dici pater atque princeps,   50
neu sinas Medos equitare inultos
    te duce, Caesar.

or you,[17] our founder, if you prize your scorned   35
    race and descendants,

if (woe!) you're sated by your drawn-out game,
you who delight in shouts and polished helmets
and the Marsian soldier's ruthless look[18] against his
    bloody opponent.   40

Or you, if, shape transformed, you imitate
a youth upon the lands,[19] O winged son
of kindly Maia, you who let us call you
    Caesar's avenger.[20]

May you go back to heaven late, and gladly   45
remain at length among Quirinus' people,[21]
And may no breeze, although you hate our crimes,
    come to uplift you

too quickly. Here enjoy your mighty triumphs,
and here enjoy the names Father and Princeps,[22]   50
and don't let Medes[23] ride unavenged while you are
    leading us, Caesar.

---

17. **or you:** Mars, the ancestor of the Romans through Romulus and Remus. He is the god addressed through the next stanza.
18. **Marsian . . . look:** The Italian Marsi were considered especially fierce soldiers.
19. **you imitate . . . the lands:** Mercury, whose earthly incarnation Horace here suggests is Augustus.
20. **Caesar's avenger:** A reference to the defeat of Brutus and Cassius in retaliation for the assassination of Julius Caesar. Augustus treated this defeat as a mark of filial piety toward his adoptive father.
21. **Quirinus' people:** The Romans. Quirinus was the cult name of Romulus.
22. **Father and Princeps:** The title of "father" would not officially be granted to Augustus until 2 B.C.E. *Princeps* (chief or first citizen) was Augustus's preferred, unofficial title, marking him not as a king or monarch but a first among equals. I have chosen to leave it untranslated.
23. **Medes:** I.e., Parthians.

***ODES* 1.3**

     Sic te diva potens Cypri,
sic fratres Helenae, lucida sidera,
     ventorumque regat pater
obstrictis aliis praeter Iapyga,

     navis, quae tibi creditum   5
debes Vergilium, finibus Atticis
     reddas incolumem precor,
et serves animae dimidium meae.

     illi robur et aes triplex
circa pectus erat, qui fragilem truci   10
     commisit pelago ratem
primus, nec timuit praecipitem Africum

ODES 1.3[1]

>   May she, the goddess who rules Cyprus,[2]
>   May Helen's brothers, shining constellation,[3]
>   direct you, and the lord of winds[4]
>   with all of them confined apart from Iapyx[5]—

>   O ship, indebted to pay back   5
>   Vergil, entrusted to you.[6] Bring him safe,
>   to Attic borders[7] and, I beg,
>   preserve unharmed my spirit's other half.

>   That man had oak and triple bronze[8]
>   encircling his heart, whoever trusted   10
>   a fragile raft to savage ocean
>   first,[9] unafraid of headlong Africus[10]

---

1. **Odes 1.3** (*Second Asclepiadean*): A **prompempticon** addressed to a ship carrying Horace's friend, the great poet Vergil, to Greece. After praying to various gods to keep the ship safe, Horace moralizes about the audacity and impiety of human beings, exemplified by sailing and the crossing of other natural barriers put in place by divine providence. The theme of human daring, and the ambivalent assessment of it, goes back to early Greek literature. An especially striking literary forerunner is the "Hymn to Man" in Sophocles's *Antigone*. Some have read the ode allegorically as illustrating either the danger of Vergil's epic task—ships were often a **metaphor** for poetry, as in *Odes* 4.15.1-4—or the current dangers of civil war facing the "ship of state" (cf. *Odes* 1.14).
2. **goddess . . . Cyprus**: Venus. Her birth from the sea made her a suitable protector of sailors.
3. **Helen's . . . constellation**: Castor and Pollux. They formed the constellation Gemini as well as appearing to sailors in the guise of "St. Elmo's Fire." The latter was viewed by sailors as a propitious sign.
4. **lord of Winds**: Aeolus, who in myth kept the winds locked inside a vast cavern.
5. **Iapyx**: The west-northwest wind—it would have been favorable to those sailing from Brundisium in Italy to Greece.
6. **pay back . . . entrusted to you**: Horace employs here the language of finance and trade.
7. **Attic borders**: Attica was the Greek region in which Athens was located.
8. **triple bronze**: That is, three layers of bronze
9. **trusted . . . first**: Sailing was one of the various human arts that traditionally marked the end of the Golden Age. The Argo was often considered the first ship, but Horace does not seem to have anything so specific in mind.
10. **Africus**: The stormy southwest wind.

decertantem Aquilonibus
nec tristis Hyadas nec rabiem Noti,
    quo non arbiter Hadriae   15
maior, tollere seu ponere vult freta.

    quem mortis timuit gradum
qui siccis oculis monstra natantia,
    qui vidit mare turbidum et
infamis scopulos Acroceraunia?   20

    nequiquam deus abscidit
prudens Oceano dissociabili
    terras, si tamen impiae
non tangenda rates transiliunt vada.

    audax omnia perpeti   25
gens humana ruit per vetitum nefas.
    audax Iapeti genus
ignem fraude mala gentibus intulit.

    post ignem aetheria domo
subductum macies et nova febrium   30
    terris incubuit cohors,
semotique prius tarda necessitas

fighting it out with Aquilos[11]
or stormy Hyades[12] or raging Notus[13]—
   the Adriatic's[14] greatest master,   15
whether he wants to raise or quell the sea.

What step of death alarmed that man,
who gazed dry-eyed upon the swimming monsters,
   who gazed upon the swollen sea and
Acroceraunia, the ill-famed cliffs?[15]   20

To no avail[16] the prudent god
used Ocean to divide and split apart
   the lands, if nonetheless unholy
ships overleap the depths one should not touch.

Daring to take up everything,   25
the human race speeds through forbidden sin.
   The daring son of Iapetus[17]
gave fire to nations through an evil trick.

Once fire was stolen from its home
in heaven, famine and a brand new host   30
   of fevers lay upon the lands,
and death's necessity, before remote

---

11. **Aquilos:** The Aquilos were the north winds.
12. **Hyades:** A group of stars in the constellation Taurus connected to rain.
13. **Notus:** The south wind.
14. **Adriatic's:** The Adriatic is the sea to the east of Italy.
15. **Acroceraunia . . . cliffs:** Either the Ceraunian mountain range in modern Albanian or, more specifically, the Cape of Gjuhëz.
16. **To no avail:** Horace often employs the middle of an ode as a **pivot** to develop another, related idea.
17. **son of Iapetus:** Prometheus, who stole fire for mankind by hiding it in a fennel stalk. In retaliation for this gift, Jupiter afflicted humans with disease and death (usually through the acquisition of Pandora, the first mortal woman). Commentators object that Prometheus is not an entirely suitable parallel for the audacity of the *human* race because he is in fact a god, but the myth does illustrate how every seeming human achievement (i.e., fire) brings with it the potential for suffering.

           leti corripuit gradum.
expertus vacuum Daedalus aera
           pennis non homini datis: 35
perrupit Acheronta Herculeus labor.

           nil mortalibus ardui est:
caelum ipsum petimus stultitia neque
           per nostrum patimur scelus
iracunda Iovem ponere fulmina.   40

and long-drawn-out, quickened its pace.
Daedalus[18] made a trial of empty air
    on wings not granted to a human;   35
Hercules' labor broke through Acheron.[19]

    Nothing is too steep for mortals—
Heaven itself we storm[20] in folly, nor
    through our misdeeds do we permit
Jupiter to put down his angry bolts.   40

18. **Daedalus**: The master craftsman of myth who made wings sealed together
with wax for himself and his son, Icarus. The latter flew too high, melting the wax,
and plunged to his death in the sea.
19. **Hercules' . . . Acheron**. Hercules performed a series of twelve labors, the last
of which was to steal Cerberus from the Underworld. Acheron, one of the rivers of
Hell, stands for the Underworld via **synecdoche.**
20. **Heaven . . . storm**: An allusion to the myth of the Giants, who tried to ascend
to heaven. Jupiter (i.e., Jove) struck them with his thunderbolt, then imprisoned
them in Tartarus.

ODES 1.4

Solvitur acris hiems grata vice veris et Favoni,

      trahuntque siccas machinae carinas,
ac neque iam stabulis gaudet pecus aut arator igni,
      nec prata canis albicant pruinis.

iam Cytherea choros ducit Venus imminente Luna,   5
      iunctaeque Nymphis Gratiae decentes
alterno terram quatiunt pede, dum gravis Cyclopum
      Vulcanus ardens visit officinas.

nunc decet aut viridi nitidum caput impedire myrto
      aut flore terrae quem ferunt solutae;   10
nunc et in umbrosis Fauno decet immolare lucis,
      seu poscat agna sive malit haedo.

pallida Mors aequo pulsat pede pauperum tabernas
      regumque turris. o beate Sesti,

ODES 1.4[1]

Sharp winter thaws as spring and Zephyr[2] take their
    welcome turn,
        and winches haul back down the dried-out keels.
No longer[3] does the herd take joy in stalls or plowman fire,
        nor are the meadows white with hoary frost.

Now Cytherean Venus[4] leads the dances, moon on high,   5
        and lovely Graces intertwined with nymphs
convulse the earth with alternating feet, while burning Vulcan
        sees to the heavy workshops of Cyclopes.[5]

Now it is right to bind one's gleaming head with verdant myrtle
        or with whatever flower earth brings forth.   10
Now too it's right in shady groves to sacrifice to Faunus,[6]
        whether he wants a lamb or else a goat.

Pale death with her impartial foot pounds[7] huts of paupers
        and kingly towers. Happy Sestius,[8]

---

1. **Odes 1.4** (*Fourth Archilochean*): This ode takes up one of Horace's favorite themes: the similarities and differences between the cycles of nature and human life. Each season brings its particular pleasures that we ought to embrace as well as hardships that we must endure. Horace reminds us of death and its inevitability in order that we, no matter our current season or time of life, will aim to live more fully in the present. The description of Venus dancing with nymphs and graces no doubt influenced Botticelli's *Primavera*.
2. **Zephyr:** The warm spring wind.
3. **No longer:** Horace incorporates numerous temporal adverbs throughout the poem to illustrate the movement of time, for which see Ancona (1994, 45–52).
4. **Cytherean Venus:** Venus was traditionally associated with the island Cythera.
5. **Cyclopes:** The most famous Cyclops was Polyphemus, from Homer's *Odyssey*, but the other well-known Cyclopes were those who worked in Vulcan's workshops and manufactured the various accouterments of gods—in particular, the lightning bolts of Jupiter.
6. **Faunus:** A native Italian god often identified with Pan.
7. **impartial foot pounds:** As Horace's words here suggest, the Romans tended to kick on doors with their feet rather than knock on them with their hands.
8. **Happy Sestius:** For *beatus* (happy), see the note on *Epodes* 2.1. The addressee is Lucius Sestius, who had a successful political career, becoming suffect consul in 23 B.C.E., the year *Odes* 1–3 were published.

vitae summa brevis spem nos vetat incohare longam.   15
        iam te premet nox fabulaeque Manes

et domus exilis Plutonia; quo simul mearis,

        nec regna vini sortiere talis,
nec tenerum Lycidan mirabere, quo calet iuventus
        nunc omnis et mox virgines tepebunt.   20

the short extent of life keeps us from taking up long hope.   15
    Night will oppress you soon, the fabled Shades,

and Pluto's meager house,[9] where you, as soon as you've arrived,
    won't win by dice dominion over wine[10]
nor marvel at young Lycidas,[11] for whom now all the youth
    are hot and soon the virgins will grow warm.   20

---

9. **Pluto's meager house:** The Underworld, where Pluto was king.
10. **dominion over wine:** At a symposium, the "symposiarch" was chosen through a role of the dice. He decided how and when the guests would drink.
11. **Lycidas:** A boy now the appropriate age to be the *eromenos* (beloved) of an older man in a pederastic relationship. He is, however, on the cusp of aging out of this role.

ODES 1.5

Quis multa gracilis te puer in rosa
perfusus liquidis urget odoribus
      grato, Pyrrha, sub antro?
           cui flavam religas comam,

simplex munditiis? heu quotiens fidem   5
mutatosque deos flebit et aspera
      nigris aequora ventis
           emirabitur insolens,

qui nunc te fruitur credulus aurea,
qui semper vacuam, semper amabilem   10

ODES 1.5[1]

What slender boy suffused with liquid perfumes
is pressing you down into many roses,
    Pyrrha,[2] beneath a pleasant grotto?[3]
        For whom do you bind your blonde hair

in simple elegance?[4] Alas—how often   5
he'll weep of loyalty and altered gods,
    and at the seas, harsh with dark winds,
        he'll wonder in naïve surprise,

who now enjoys you, trusting that you're golden,
who hopes you'll be forever free, forever   10

---

1. *Odes* 1.5 (*Fourth Asclepiadean*): The so-called Pyrrha Ode, perhaps Horace's most translated (and yet most untranslatable) poem. Horace here contrasts his own experienced detachment from eroticism with an unnamed boy's youthful naïveté and idealism. In general, the Horatian lyric **persona** observes and advises others on love and sex but tries (at times unsuccessfully) to keep himself removed from this sphere.
2. **Pyrrha:** Her name, from the Greek πῦρ (fire), is suggestive of a fiery temperament. Her status is unclear, though she is perhaps best thought of as a *meretrix*, a "prostitute" or (more euphemistically) "courtesan."
3. **What slender boy . . . pleasant grotto:** These opening lines are famously impossible to translate owing to the complexly **chiastic** word order (ABCBA). Horace brilliantly creates a picture of the couple's embrace by placing *gracilis puer* (slender boy) around *te* (you) and placing them both within *multa rosa* (many roses). Her name *Pyrrha*, moreover, is placed inside the *grato antro* (pleasant grotto), creating another word picture mimicking her position in the cave. This simply cannot be replicated in English word order.
4. **simple elegance:** *Simplex munditiis* is another difficult phrase to translate and constitutes a Horatian **callida iunctura** or "clever joining" of words. Literally it means "simple in elegance" and suggests Pyrrha's oxymoronic combination of simplicity and refinement. *Munditia* is a key word of Horatian ethics and aesthetics, indicating a midpoint between the extremes of too little and too much adornment. Her simple bun is no doubt akin to the *nodus* style that the women of Augustus's family popularized.

> sperat, nescius aurae
>   fallacis! miseri, quibus

intemptata nites. me tabula sacer
votiva paries indicat uvida
   suspendisse potenti   15
      vestimenta maris deo.

        lovable, not aware the breeze
               deceives. O wretched men for whom

    you shine untested. As for me, a holy
    wall with a votive tablet shows that I
        have hung up my still dripping clothes[5]   15
            to the deity[6] who rules the sea.

---

5. **votive tablet . . . dripping clothes**: Horace's votive tablet and wet clothes are thank-offerings for having survived similarly treacherous erotic tempests.

6. **deity**: The god of the sea would be Neptune, an odd choice for the erotic context. Some critics emend the final *deo* (god) to *deae* (goddess), which could more suitably refer to Venus, the goddess of love, who was born from the sea. I have tried to keep the god's gender ambiguous with "deity."

ODES 1.6

Scriberis Vario fortis et hostium
victor Maeonii carminis alite,
quam rem cumque ferox navibus aut equis
      miles te duce gesserit:

nos, Agrippa, neque haec dicere nec gravem   5
Pelidae stomachum cedere nescii
nec cursus duplicis per mare Vlixei
      nec saevam Pelopis domum

conamur, tenues grandia, dum pudor
imbellisque lyrae Musa potens vetat   10
laudes egregii Caesaris et tuas
      culpa deterere ingeni.

ODES 1.6[1]

You'll be described as brave, a vanquisher
of foes, by Varius,[2] the Lydian songbird[3]—
whatever feat the ruthless soldier waged
    on ship or horse with you as leader.

I do not try to tell these things, Agrippa,   5
nor obstinate Achilles' heavy spleen,[4]
nor the path of devious Odysseus
    at sea,[5] nor Pelops' brutal house[6]—

too slim for such big themes—as long as shame
and the Muse who governs the unwarlike lyre   10
keep me from marring splendid Caesar's praises,
    and yours, with my imperfect talent.

---

1. **Odes 1.6** (*Third Asclepiadean*): In this **recusatio**, Horace denies that he is capable of
singing the epic praises of Augustus and Agrippa, the latter of whom is his addressee.
As Augustus's victorious general at Actium, he was hugely instrumental in the rise of
the principate. In 21 B.C.E. he would marry Augustus's daughter Julia, with whom he
would have five children. It is unlikely that Horace was formally requested to write
such a poem; rather, he uses the ode as an opportunity to lay out at this early stage
the smaller and lighter scope of his lyric project. The **recusatio**, moreover, allows
Horace to balance his refusal with **encomium** of both men.
2. **Varius:** Lucius Varius Rufus, Horace's fellow poet, whom Horace mentions in *Satires*
1.6 as one of the friends (the other being Vergil) who introduced him to Maecenas. In
addition to epic, he wrote tragedy and an **encomium** of Augustus.
3. **Lydian songbird:** A singer of epic. "Lydian" alludes to Homer, thought to have been
from Maeonia/Lydia. It was not unusual for poets to be compared to birds—see
Odes 4.2.25, where Horace refers to Pindar as the "swan of Dirce."
4. **Achilles' heavy spleen:** The subject of Homer's *Iliad*. The anatomical "spleen"
(literally, "stomach") almost comically deflates the hero's Homeric "wrath." Some
have suggested that Horace is displaying what a terrible epic poet he would be!
5. **path . . . at sea:** The subject of Homer's *Odyssey*. Horace's *duplex* (devious)
points to the hero's ability to lie, often more positively assessed as "wiliness" or
"resourcefulness." This trait, however, had taken on a more sinister aspect in the
hero's post-Homeric legacy, particularly on the tragic stage.
6. **Pelops' brutal house:** One of the most famous houses of Greek myth, afflicted
with suffering inherited through several generations (Tantalus, Pelops, Atreus
and Thyestes, Menalaus and Agamemnon). Although Horace cites this myth as a
suitable theme for epic, it was especially popular for tragedy. Varius himself wrote an
acclaimed tragedy called *Thyestes* that does not survive.

quis Martem tunica tectum adamantina
digne scripserit aut pulvere Troico
nigrum Merionen aut ope Palladis   15
    Tydiden superis parem?

nos convivia, nos proelia virginum
sectis in iuvenes unguibus acrium
cantamus, vacui sive quid urimur
    non praeter solitum leves.   20

Who worthily can write of steel-clad Mars,
Meriones turned black by Trojan dust,[7]
or Diomedes, who with help from Pallas   15
    became the equal of the gods?[8]

I sing of feasts, of battles virgins wage,
their fingernails filed sharp, against young men.
Whether I'm unattached or hot with love,
    it is my custom to be light.   20

---

7. **Meriones**: A Greek warrior who fought in the Trojan War.
8. **Diomedes . . . gods**: In *Iliad* 5 the Greek warrior Diomedes goes on a massive killing spree with the help of Athena.

ODES 1.7

Laudabunt alii claram Rhodon aut Mytilenen
      aut Epheson bimarisve Corinthi
moenia vel Baccho Thebas vel Apolline Delphos
      insignis aut Thessala Tempe:

sunt quibus unum opus est intactae Palladis urbem   5
      carmine perpetuo celebrare et
undique decerptam fronti praeponere olivam:
      plurimus in Iunonis honorem

aptum dicet equis Argos ditesque Mycenas:
      me nec tam patiens Lacedaemon   10
nec tam Larisae percussit campus opimae,
      quam domus Albuneae resonantis

et praeceps Anio ac Tiburni lucus et uda
      mobilibus pomaria rivis.

ODES 1.7[1]

Others will praise[2] distinguished Rhodes or Mytilene
    or Ephesus or two-sea'd Corinth's walls,
or Thebes, which Bacchus has made eminent, or Delphi,
    famed for Apollo, or Thessalian Tempe.[3]

For some their only task is honoring the city   5
    of virgin Pallas[4] in unceasing song[5] and
putting upon their brow the olive widely plucked.[6]
    Many a one will tell in Juno's honor

of Argos fit for horses or of rich Mycenae.
    But as for me, unyielding Lacedaemon[7]   10
or rich Larisa's plain[8] do not strike me as much
    as echoing Albunea's abode,[9]

cascading Anio, the thicket of Tiburnus,[10]
    and orchards drenched by quickly moving brooks.

---

1. *Odes* **1.7** (*Alcmanic Strophe*): The structure of this ode has been described as "rambling" or "problematic," but through it runs the idea that one must embrace the light, private pleasures that life affords. Horace first offers a *recusatio* expressing preference for unwarlike Italian landscapes that evoke the private, nonepic world of lyric. He then **pivots** in the poem's middle to advise his addressee, Plancus, on the need to balance his public, martial activities with sympotic levity, the latter of which provides an antidote to the anxiety caused by the former.
2. **Others will praise:** Horace opens the poem with a **priamel.**
3. **Rhodes . . . Thessalian Tempe:** A list of locales in Greece and Asia Minor. Corinth is "two-sea'd" because it sits on the isthmus between the Saronic Gulf and the Gulf of Corinth. Thebes was the birthplace of Bacchus, whereas Delphi and Tempe, a valley in Thessaly, were sacred to Apollo.
4. **city of virgin Pallas:** Athens.
5. **unceasing song:** That is, epic.
6. **widely plucked:** That is, from a number of different literary genres. It could also suggest the frequency with which epic, unlike lyric, has been taken up as a topic of poetry.
7. **Lacedaemon:** Sparta.
8. **Larisa's plain:** A city in Thessaly.
9. **echoing Albunea's abode:** Tibur, where Albunea was a sibyl. The adjective "echoing" is a **transferred epithet.**
10. **Anio . . . Tiburnus:** Anio is a river that flows through Tibur. Tiburnus was one of the three brothers who founded Tibur.

albus ut obscuro deterget nubila caelo   15
  saepe Notus neque parturit imbris

perpetuo, sic tu sapiens finire memento
  tristitiam vitaeque labores
molli, Plance, mero, seu te fulgentia signis
  castra tenent seu densa tenebit   20

Tiburis umbra tui. Teucer Salamina patremque
  cum fugeret, tamen uda Lyaeo
tempora populea fertur vinxisse corona,
  sic tristis affatus amicos:

"quo nos cumque feret melior fortuna parente,   25
  ibimus, o socii comitesque.
nil desperandum Teucro duce et auspice Teucro.
  certus enim promisit Apollo

ambiguam tellure nova Salamina futuram.
  o fortes peioraque passi   30
mecum saepe viri, nunc vino pellite curas;
  cras ingens iterabimus aequor."

Just as the shining Notus[11] often wipes away   15
    clouds from the sky and does not bring the rain

unceasingly, so you should sensibly remember
    to put an end to sadness and life's toils,
Plancus,[12] with mellow full-strength wine, whether the camp
    that gleams with standards holds you or the dense   20

shade of your Tibur. Teucer,[13] when he fled his father
    and Salamis, still—it is said—encircled
his temples with a poplar garland drenched with Bacchus[14]
    and spoke these words to his despairing friends:

"Wherever fortune—gentler than my father—brings us,   25
    there we will go, my allies and companions.
Do not despair while Teucer leads and Teucer guards you.
    Infallible Apollo[15] promised that

in a new land there'd be a different Salamis.
    You men who've bravely weathered even worse   30
with me so often, now drive off your cares with wine.
    Tomorrow we resume the mighty sea."

---

11. **Notus:** The south wind.
12. **Plancus:** Lucius Munatius Plancus, who was consul in 42 B.C.E. He had been
    an ally of Antony but deserted to Octavian prior to Actium. Many have suggested
    that the thought of the ode is directly related to his political travails, but there is no
    agreement as to how. For detailed proposals, see Nisbet and Hubbard's commentary
    (1970) as well as Moles (2002). Like Horace, he has a personal connection to
    Tibur—it was his birthplace.
13. **Teucer:** Horace now launches into the mythological exemplum of Teucer, the
    son of Telemon, who ruled Salamis, and half-brother of Ajax. Ajax and Teucer fought
    alongside one another on the Greek side at Troy. After Ajax committed suicide, their
    father banned Teucer from Salamis for leaving the death unavenged, after which he
    founded a new "Salamis" on the island of Cyprus.
14. **Bacchus:** Metonymy for wine.
15. **Infallible Apollo:** Apollo had produced an oracle promising Teucer a new
    Salamis.

ODES 1.8

Lydia, dic, per omnis
te deos oro, Sybarin cur properes amando
     perdere, cur apricum
oderit campum, patiens pulveris atque solis,

cur neque militaris   5
inter aequalis equitet, Gallica nec lupatis
     temperet ora frenis?
cur timet flavum Tiberim tangere? Cur olivum

sanguine viperino
cautius vitat neque iam livida gestat armis   10
     bracchia, saepe disco,
saepe trans finem iaculo nobilis expedito?

quid latet, ut marinae
filium dicunt Thetidis sub lacrimosa Troiae
     funera, ne virilis   15
cultus in caedem et Lycias proriperet catervas?

ODES 1.8[1]

Lydia, tell—by all the gods
I beg of you—why do you rush to wreck Sybaris
    by loving him? Why does he shun
the sunny field,[2] though tolerant of dirt and sun?

    And why among his military   5
fellows does he not ride, or bridle Gallic muzzles[3]
    by using bits with jagged teeth?
Why does he fear to touch the tawny Tiber?[4] Why

    does he shun oil[5] more cautiously
than viper's blood, no longer sporting arms all bruised   10
    by weapons, though renowned for often
throwing the javelin and discus past the line?

    Why does he hide just like the son
of briny Thetis[6] (as they say) before Troy's tearful
    destruction, lest his manly dress   15
drag him amid the slaughter and the Lycian throngs?[7]

---

1. **Odes 1.8** (*Second Sapphic Strophe*): Like the Pyrrha of *Odes* 1.5, Lydia (whose name is also Greek) is ruining her elite young lover with desire. In both poems, Horace plays the outside observer to the love affairs of others. This ode explores in particular the emasculating effects of *amor*, ending with the mythological exemplum of Achilles, who, in order to avoid the Trojan War, hid on the island of Skyros in the court of king Lycomedes, disguised as a girl. While there he had an affair with the princess Deidamia, with whom he fathered Neoptolemus. Odysseus successfully sought him out by offering the island's young women presents, among which was a set of armor that the young warrior could not refuse, revealing himself.
2. **the sunny field:** The Campus Martius, where military practice would have taken place.
3. **Gallic muzzles:** That is, the muzzles of Gallic horses.
4. **tawny Tiber:** To swim after exercise.
5. **oil:** Olive oil was applied before exercise.
6. **the son . . . Thetis:** Achilles. Thetis was a sea-nymph.
7. **Lycian throngs:** Lycia, in the south of Asia Minor, was a Trojan ally.

ODES 1.9

Vides ut alta stet nive candidum
Soracte nec iam sustineant onus
    silvae laborantes, geluque
        flumina constiterint acuto?

dissolve frigus ligna super foco   5
large reponens atque benignius
    deprome quadrimum Sabina,
        o Thaliarche, merum diota:

permitte divis cetera, qui simul
stravere ventos aequore fervido   10
    deproeliantis, nec cupressi
        nec veteres agitantur orni.

quid sit futurum cras fuge quaerere et
quem Fors dierum cumque dabit lucro

ODES 1.9[1]

Do you see how beneath deep snow stands white
Soracte,[2] how the straining woods can prop
    their burden up no more and how the piercing
        ice has now made the rivers' flows stand still?

Dissolve the cold. Unsparingly replace   5
the logs upon the hearth and without stint
    draw out the full-strength wine now four-years-old,
        O Thaliarchus,[3] from its Sabine jar.[4]

Leave to the gods all else.[5] As soon as they
have calmed the winds that on the boiling sea   10
    contend in battle, neither cypress trees
        nor ancient ash are driven to and fro.

Abstain from asking what will be tomorrow
and count as gain whatever days your luck

---

1. **Odes 1.9** (*Alcaic Strophe*): The so-called Soracte Ode, based on an extant fragment of Alcaeus (*GL* I 338), is one of Horace's most loved but also debated poems. Like *Odes* 1.4, it takes up the theme of the seasonal cycles of the year and of human life. In the first half Horace urges his addressee, Thaliarchus, to join him in taking advantage of the pleasures afforded by the wintertime (which some interpret as a **metaphor** for old age). In the second, he exhorts Thaliarchus, who is in the "springtime" of his life, not to avoid the pleasures suitable to youth.
2. **Soracte:** A mountain twenty miles north of Rome that would likely have been visible from Horace's Sabine estate.
3. **Thaliarchus:** Horace's otherwise unknown addressee. His Greek name suggests "master of the festivity." Some have suggested that he is the symposiarch at Horace's drinking party, though no other members seem to be present. Others argue that he is Horace's pederastic *eromenos* (youthful male beloved) or slave.
4. **Sabine jar:** Yet another detail placing the action on Horace's Sabine estate. The word *diota* is a Latin transliteration of a Greek word for a jar with two handles. The Italian wine stored in a Greek jar creates a nice antithesis that perhaps evokes Horace's Latin words written in a Greek meter.
5. **Leave ... all else:** A new (but unclearly provenanced) papyrus discovered in 2014 reveals that these lines are indebted to the third stanza of Sappho's "Brothers Poem:" τὰ δ' ἄλλα / πάντα δαιμόνεσσιν ἐπιτρόπωμεν / εὐδίαι γὰρ ἐκ μεγάλαν ἀήταν / αἶψα πέλονται. (For the rest, / let's simply leave it to the gods: / great stormy blasts go by and soon / give way to calm [trans. Christopher Pelling]). On Horace's use of Sappho here, see Phillips (2014).

                    appone, nec dulcis amores   15
                        sperne puer neque tu choreas,

donec virenti canities abest
morosa. nunc et campus et areae
            lenesque sub noctem susurri
                    composita repetantur hora,   20

nunc et latentis proditor intimo
gratus puellae risus ab angulo
            pignusque dereptum lacertis
                    aut digito male pertinaci.

will grant. Nor while you're still a boy avoid   15
    delightful love affairs and choral dances,

as long as you are green with youth and free
of crotchety white hair. Let now the plain
    and squares be sought, and, just before the night,
        soft whispers at an hour prearranged,   20

now too a girl's sweet laughter, which betrays
her hiding place inside a secret corner,
    and a memento ripped off of her arm
        or from her finger,[6] fruitlessly resisting.

---

6. **arm . . . finger**: A bracelet and a ring.

ODES 1.10

Mercuri, facunde nepos Atlantis,
qui feros cultus hominum recentum
voce formasti catus et decorae
      more palaestrae,

te canam, magni Iovis et deorum   5
nuntium curvaeque lyrae parentem,
callidum quidquid placuit iocoso
      condere furto.

te, boves olim nisi reddidisses
per dolum amotas, puerum minaci   10
voce dum terret, viduus pharetra
      risit Apollo.

quin et Atridas duce te superbos
Ilio dives Priamus relicto
Thessalosque ignis et iniqua Troiae   15
      castra fefellit.

ODES 1.10[1]

Mercury, Atlas's smooth-spoken grandson,[2]
who wisely shaped new humans' brutish ways
through language and the institution of
    beautiful wrestling,[3]

of you I'll sing, the messenger of mighty   5
Jove and the gods, the curving lyre's inventor,[4]
who cleverly with playful theft[5] can hide
    that which has pleased you.

Once,[6] when Apollo frightened you, a child,
with threatening voice if you did not return   10
the cattle filched through trickery, he laughed,
    robbed of his quiver.

With you as leader, wealthy Priam[7] left
Ilium, hidden from the pompous sons
of Atreus, Thessalian fires, and camps   15
    hostile to Trojans.

---

1. *Odes* 1.10 (*Sapphic Strophe*): This is the first time Horace repeats a meter in the first book, marking the end of what scholars describe as the "Parade Odes," in which Horace shows off his metrical versatility. The ode is a **hymn** to the god Mercury and follows the conventional formula for addressing a deity. The deity is named, his attributes are described, his famous tales and exploits are mentioned, and the god is repeatedly addressed using **Du-Stil**. Mercury holds a particularly prominent place in Horace's *Odes* (cf. 2.17.29, 2.7.13, as well as *Satires* 2.6.5), as is suitable given his role as the inventor of the lyre and thus lyric poetry.
2. **Atlas's smooth-spoken grandson**: Mercury was the son of Maia, the daughter of the Titan Atlas.
3. **language . . . wrestling**: Horace credits Mercury here with the civilizing inventions of language and wrestling. As Mayer (2012) notes, an inscription on a statue base (from the early imperial period) echoes this: *sermonem docui mortales atque palaestram* (I taught mortals speech and wrestling) (*CIL* vi 520).
4. **lyre's inventor**: The *Homeric Hymn to Hermes* describes how Hermes/Mercury, while still a child, invented the lyre using a tortoise shell.
5. **playful theft**: Mercury was a god of trickery and thus of thieves.
6. **Once**: Horace recounts another story from the *Homeric Hymn to Hermes*, in which the young god stole Apollo's cattle on the very day of his birth.
7. **wealthy Priam**: In *Iliad* 24, Hermes/Mercury escorts Priam out of the city and to the Greek camps in order to ransom his son Hector's body from Achilles.

tu pias laetis animas reponis
sedibus virgaque levem coerces
aurea turbam, superis deorum
    gratus et imis.   20

You settle pious souls within the joyous
realms,[8] and you keep the weightless horde confined
with your gold staff. You gratify the gods
                    upper and lower.   20

---

8. **settle . . . realms**: Mercury was the psychopomp, the escort of souls to and from the
Underworld.

ODES 1.11

Tu ne quaesieris, scire nefas, quem mihi, quem tibi
finem di dederint, Leuconoe, nec Babylonios
temptaris numeros. ut melius, quicquid erit, pati,
seu pluris hiemes seu tribuit Iuppiter ultimam,
quae nunc oppositis debilitat pumicibus mare   5
Tyrrhenum: sapias, vina liques, et spatio brevi
spem longam reseces. dum loquimur, fugerit invida
aetas: carpe diem, quam minimum credula postero.

ODES 1.11[1]

You should not seek—knowing is sin—what end for me or you
the gods have set, Leuconoe,[2] nor study Babylonian
astrology.[3] It's better just to endure whatever happens,
if Jove allots even more winters or this final one,
which even now on the opposing cliffs wears out the sea   5
of Tuscany.[4] Be wise, filter the wine. Prune back long hope
to fit life's narrow span. While we are speaking, jealous time
has fled. Harvest the day.[5] Don't count at all upon tomorrow.

---

1. *Odes* 1.11 (*Fifth Asclepiadean*): This is one of Horace's best-loved poems, in which he coins the enduring tag *carpe diem*. Horace here urges us to glean the most enjoyment from our short human lives by taking pleasure from each present moment and not directing anxious attention to the unpredictable future. A nice metrical feature of the poem is the preponderance of choriambs (—◡◡—), dum-diddy-dum (cf. the English phrase "over the hill"), with three present in each line of Latin. I have incorporated one choriamb into each line of the translation; thus, for example, the choriamb *scire nefas* becomes "knowing in sin" and *carpe diem* becomes "harvest the day."

2. **Leuconoe**: A Greek woman's name. Some think the goal is seduction, but by directing his ethical advice to this female, nonelite addressee, Horace implies that anyone, regardless of gender, status, or nationality, can *carpe diem*—the only requirement is a short human life. The meaning of her name has been debated. Most interestingly, Clay (2015) connects it to the Greek words "white" (λευκόιον) and "mind" (νοῦς) and argues that her name suggests "the girl whose thoughts are dominated by winter and death." At the same time, the name may allude to the Greek word for the snowdrop flower (λευκόιον), which, as Clay points out, "is the first to bloom when winter begins to give way to spring."

3. **astrology**: Developed in Babylonia, astrology was considered by the Romans an exotic—though popular—eastern import.

4. **sea of Tuscany**: The Tyrrhenian sea, on the western coast of Italy.

5. **Harvest the day**: *Carpe diem* is popularly translated as "seize the day," but this does disservice to Horace's image. *Carpe* means to "pluck" or "harvest" the day as if it were ripe fruit.

ODES 1.12

Quem virum aut heroa lyra vel acri
tibia sumis celebrare, Clio?
quem deum? cuius recinet iocosa
      nomen imago

aut in umbrosis Heliconis oris   5
aut super Pindo gelidove in Haemo,
unde vocalem temere insecutae
      Orphea silvae

arte materna rapidos morantem
fluminum lapsus celerisque ventos,   10
blandum et auritas fidibus canoris
      ducere quercus?

quid prius dicam solitis parentis
laudibus, qui res hominum ac deorum,
qui mare et terras variisque mundum   15
      temperat horis?

ODES 1.12[1]

What man or hero, Clio,[2] do you choose
to honor on the lyre or shrill pipe?[3]
What god?[4] Whose name, as it reverberates, will
    playfully echo

upon the shady slopes of Helicon   5
or Pindus' summit or on frigid Haemus?[5]
This was the place where forests blindly followed
    Orpheus singing

and slowing with his mother's art the swift
courses of rivers and the rapid winds.   10
He charmed the ears of oaks and led them as he
    sounded his lyre.[6]

What should I sing before the Father's[7] ancient
praises, who guides the works of men and gods,
who guides through fluctuating seasons ocean,   15
    land, and the heavens?

---

1. *Odes* 1.12 (*Sapphic Strophe*): A long ode rehearsing multiple episodes from Roman history and ending in **encomium** of Augustus, with strong echoes from Pindaric victory odes. The poem consists of a lengthy **priamel** wherein Horace considers whom he should take up as the object of his lyric praise. In the opening lines Horace puts forth three possible topics: a man, hero, or god. He then proceeds **chiastically** to move through a list of gods, heroes, and men, all of whom operate as foils for the final figure of Augustus. The relationship between Augustus and Jupiter is especially prominent in the poem's close.

2. **Clio**: One of the Muses, often associated with history.

3. **pipe**: The tibia was a reed pipe used to accompany choral lyric songs.

4. **man . . . hero . . . god**: Horace here adapts the opening lines of Pindar's *Olympians* 2: "What god, what hero, what man will we sing of?"

5. **Helicon . . . Pindus' . . . Haemus**: Three mountains meant to evoke poetic haunts. Helicon in Greece was home to the Muses, whereas Haemus in Thrace was associated with the mythical musician Orpheus. The particular relationship between Pindus, in northern Greece, and poetry is unclear.

6. **charmed . . . lyre**: Orpheus was the son of the Muse Calliope. According to myth, his song had the power to mesmerize and control nature.

7. **Father**: Jupiter.

unde nil maius generatur ipso,
nec viget quicquam simile aut secundum:
proximos illi tamen occupavit
    Pallas honores.   20

proeliis audax, neque te silebo,
Liber, et saevis inimica Virgo
beluis, nec te, metuende certa
    Phoebe sagitta.

dicam et Alciden puerosque Ledae,   25
hunc equis, illum superare pugnis
nobilem; quorum simul alba nautis
    stella refulsit,

defluit saxis agitatus umor,
concidunt venti fugiuntque nubes,   30
et minax, †quia sic voluere, ponto
    unda recumbit.

Romulum post hos prius an quietum
Pompili regnum memorem, an superbos
Tarquini fascis, dubito, an Catonis   35
    nobile letum.

He brings forth nothing greater than himself,
and there is nothing similar or second.
And yet the place of honor next to him
        Pallas possesses,   20

the bold in battle. I will not omit
you, Liber, nor the virgin foe of ruthless
wild beasts, nor, Phoebus,[8] you, who with your surefire
        arrow are dreadful.

I'll sing of Hercules and Leda's sons[9]—   25
one of them famed for conquering with horses,
one with his fists. As soon as their star gleams
        brightly for sailors,

the storm-tossed water flows down from the cliffs,
the winds diminish, and the clouds take flight;   30
the threatening wave, because they've willed it so,
        sinks on the ocean.

I am unsure if after these I'll mention
Romulus first or Numa's[10] peaceful reign
or Tarquin's pompous fasces[11] or the famed   35
        passing of Cato.[12]

---

8. **Pallas ... Liber ... Phoebus:** Minerva, Bacchus, and Apollo.
9. **Leda's sons:** Castor and Pollux (the Dioscuri). Castor was associated with horses, Pollux with boxing. The brothers also act as the patron saints of sailors, particularly in their guise as St. Elmo's Fire.
10. **Romulus ... Numa:** Romulus was the legendary founder and first king of Rome. Numa was his successor, associated with peace and the institution of Roman religious traditions.
11. **Tarquin's pompous fasces:** Tarquin the Proud or Pompous (Tarquinius Superbus) was the final king of Rome, expelled after his son Sextus raped Lucretia. The word "pompous" is a **transferred epithet** applied to the fasces, the bundles of rods and axes that lictors carried to symbolize Roman power and authority.
12. **Cato:** Marcus Porcius Cato, who in 46 B.C.E. committed suicide rather than live under Julius Caesar's dictatorship.

Regulum et Scauros animaeque magnae
prodigum Paulum superante Poeno
gratus insigni referam Camena
      Fabriciumque.   40

hunc et incomptis Curium capillis
utilem bello tulit et Camillum
saeva paupertas et avitus apto
      cum lare fundus.

crescit occulto velut arbor aevo   45
fama Marcelli; micat inter omnis
Iulium sidus, velut inter ignis
      luna minores.

gentis humanae pater atque custos,
orte Saturno, tibi cura magni   50
Caesaris fatis data: tu secundo
      Caesare regnes.

With glorifying Muse I'll gladly mention
Regulus and the Scauri, Paulus (who
gave his great soul when Hannibal prevailed)[13]—
    also Fabricius.[14]   40

This man[15] and long-haired Curius and Camillus[16]
were good in war because fierce poverty
and an ancestral farm with fitting home
    raised them to be so.

Marcellus' fame[17] increases like a tree   45
through time unseen. The Julian star[18] outshines
the rest just like the moon among the lesser
    heavenly fires.

Father and champion of the human race,
offspring of Saturn,[19] fate has granted you   50
the care of mighty Caesar. May you rule,
    him as your second.

---

13. **Regulus, Scauri, Paulus:** Marcus Atilius Regulus was a Roman general in the First Punic War (for whom see the notes to *Odes* 3.5). The most famous Scaurus was Marcus Aemilius Scaurus, who was consul in 115 B.C.E. and was often praised as an exemplar of old-fashioned Roman values. Lucius Aemilius Paulus was consul in 219 and 216 B.C.E. and died while opposing the Carthaginian general Hannibal at the Battle of Cannae in 216 B.C.E.
14. **Fabricius:** Gaius Fabricius Luscinus was consul in 282 and 278 B.C.E. as well as censor in 275 B.C.E. He was also a frequent exemplar for old-fashioned Roman austerity.
15. **This man:** That is, Fabricius.
16. **Curius and Camillus:** Manius Curius Dentatus was consul in 290, 284, 275, and 274 as well as censor in 272 B.C.E. As general, he triumphed over the Samnites in 290 B.C.E. Marcus Furius Camillus was censor in 403 B.C.E. and held the dictatorship five times and was tribune six times. He was given the title "Second Founder of Rome" after repelling the Gauls in 390 B.C.E.
17. **Marcellus' fame:** Marcus Claudius Marcellus was consul multiple times (222, 215, 214, 210, and 208 B.C.E.) and a noted general.
18. **Julian star:** Probably an allusion to the comet that appeared after Julius Caesar's assassination in 44 B.C.E., which was taken as evidence for his deification. As Pandey (2013, 426–27) points out, however, the star is markedly placed not in the section on gods but in the one on mortals, "delicately circumscribing Augustus' unprecedented but nevertheless mortal power."
19. **offspring of Saturn:** Jupiter.

ille seu Parthos Latio imminentis
egerit iusto domitos triumpho,
sive subiectos Orientis orae   55
    Seras et Indos,

te minor laetum reget aequus orbem;
tu gravi curru quaties Olympum,
tu parum castis inimica mittes
    fulmina lucis.   60

Whether he leads the conquered Parthians[20]
(now threatening Latium) in a rightful triumph
or, from the eastern shore, the subjugated   55
    Chinese and Indians,[21]

your junior, he will rule a happy world.
You'll shake Olympus in your heavy chariot;
you will propel against polluted groves
    odious lightning.   60

---

20. **Parthians:** See the note on *Odes* 1.2.23.
21. **Chinese and Indians:** Mayer (2012) calls this "encomiastic fantasy" given the
extreme unlikelihood of such a campaign.

ODES 1.13

    Cum tu, Lydia, Telephi
cervicem roseam, cerea Telephi
      laudas bracchia, vae meum
fervens difficili bile tumet iecur.

    tum nec mens mihi nec color   5
certa sede manet, umor et in genas
      furtim labitur, arguens
quam lentis penitus macerer ignibus.

    uror, seu tibi candidos
turparunt umeros immodicae mero   10
      rixae, sive puer furens
impressit memorem dente labris notam.

    non, si me satis audias,
speres perpetuum dulcia barbare
      laedentem oscula quae Venus   15
quinta parte sui nectaris imbuit.

    felices ter et amplius
quos irrupta tenet copula nec malis
      divulsus querimoniis
suprema citius solvet amor die.   20

ODES 1.13[1]

Whenever, Lydia, you praise,
the rosy neck of Telephus, the waxy
    forearms of Telephus—alas!—
my boiling liver swells with stubborn bile.[2]

Then not my mind nor my complexion[3]   5
remain in their fixed place, and on my cheeks
    a tear slips secretly, revealing
how deeply I am steeped in sluggish fires.

I burn, whether your gleaming shoulders
are bruised from fights that full-strength wine has made   10
    extreme, or if the raging boy
has marked your lips with teeth as a memento.

You'd not expect, if you should heed me,
him to be constant, who barbarically[4]
    does harm to your sweet mouth, which Venus   15
has steeped with a fifth part of her own nectar.[5]

Thrice blessed and even more are those
whom an unbroken bond holds fast, whom love,
    not torn apart by base complaints,
will split no sooner than the final day.   20

---

1. **Odes 1.13** (*Second Asclepiadean*): The Horatian **persona** here is struck with jealousy when hearing Lydia praise the beauty of her lover, Telephus. It is hard to determine the nature of the relationship between the narrator and Lydia, i.e., whether they were previously or are potentially a romantic pairing. Whereas the **persona** seems to denounce and hold himself up as an alternative to the violence on which Lydia's relationship with Telephus is centered, he nevertheless himself displays a propensity toward jealous rage.
2. **liver . . . bile:** In ancient physiognomy, the liver was the seat of a range of emotions, including anger.
3. **complexion:** Paleness was a traditional symptom of erotic love.
4. **barbarically:** See note at *Epodes* 5.61.
5. **steeped . . . nectar:** The meaning of these lines is debated, but most commentators now suggest he means a 1:5 dilution of Venus's nectar, which would still be extremely sweet.

ODES 1.14

O navis, referent in mare te novi
fluctus! o quid agis? fortiter occupa
    portum! nonne vides ut
        nudum remigio latus,

et malus celeri saucius Africo,   5
antennaeque gemant, ac sine funibus
    vix durare carinae
        possint imperiosius

aequor? non tibi sunt integra lintea,
non di quos iterum pressa voces malo.   10
    quamvis Pontica pinus,
        silvae filia nobilis,

iactes et genus et nomen inutile,
nil pictis timidus navita puppibus
    fidit. tu, nisi ventis   15
        debes ludibrium, cave.

ODES 1.14[1]

O ship, new waves will carry you back out
to sea! What are you doing? Bravely make
     for port! Do you not see just how
        your side is stripped of all its oars,

how headlong Africus[2] has snapped your mast,   5
and how your yardarms groan and, without ropes,[3]
     your keel is scarcely capable
        of lasting on the domineering

ocean? You have no sails that are not ripped
nor gods to call when pressed again by trouble.   10
     Although you're made of Pontic pine,[4]
        the daughter of a noble forest,

and boast a family and name now useless,
the frightened mariner does not put trust
     in painted sterns.[5] Unless you owe   15
        a plaything to the winds, beware.

---

1. **Odes 1.14** (*Fourth Asclepiadean*): Many, starting already in antiquity, have read this poem, addressed to a damaged ship, as an allegory of the "ship of state." The specific referents of the allegory, however, have been much debated, i.e., whether the ship refers to a specific political group (such as the followers of Brutus or Sextus Pompey) or the state in general. The ship of state allegory is strongly indebted to the poetry of Alcaeus, particularly fr. 6 and 208 (Campbell). Other theories have been put forth as to what Horace's ship represents, most notably that the ship is a woman. Anderson (1966) suggests the ship is a worn-out prostitute, whereas Knorr (2006) argues that she is a young courtesan involved in a love triangle with the placid Horace and a passionate rival. Yet another theory is that the ship represents poetry, an image familiar, for example, from *Odes* 4.15.3–4. For this interpretation see, for example, Davis (1989) and Zumwalt (1977).
2. **Africus:** The stormy southwest wind.
3. **ropes:** Refers to the helps used to undergird and strengthen the ship.
4. **Pontic pine:** Pontus, near the Black Sea, was a major source of timber.
5. **painted sterns:** That is, the ship's purely decorative assets.

nuper sollicitum quae mihi taedium,
nunc desiderium curaque non levis,
   interfusa nitentis
      vites aequora Cycladas.   20

Lately you made me anxious and annoyed,
but now I long and care for you not slightly,
   so please avoid the waters flowing
      between the shining Cyclades.[6]   20

---

6. **Cyclades:** A group of islands in the Aegean Sea.

ODES 1.15

Pastor cum traheret per freta navibus
Idaeis Helenen perfidus hospitam,
ingrato celeris obruit otio
      ventos, ut caneret fera

Nereus fata: mala ducis avi domum,   5
quam multo repetet Graecia milite,
coniurata tuas rumpere nuptias
      et regnum Priami vetus.

heu, heu, quantus equis, quantus adest viris
sudor! quanta moves funera Dardanae   10
genti! iam galeam Pallas et aegida
      currusque et rabiem parat.

ODES 1.15[1]

The shepherd[2] carried[3] Helen through the sea
on Ida's ships[4]—so faithless to his hostess—
when Nereus[5] with unwelcome calm subdued
    the rapid winds so he could sing

harsh doom: "With evil omen you lead home   5
a woman Greece will claim with many soldiers,
swearing an oath to break apart your marriage
    and Priam's long-established realm.[6]

Alas! Alas! How horses and the men
will sweat! How many deaths you cause the race   10
of Dardanus![7] Now Pallas primes her helmet
    and shield, her chariot and fury.

---

1. **Odes 1.15** (*Third Asclepiadean*): An ode rehearsing in lyric form the events of the Trojan War, material normally found in epic, especially Homer's *Iliad*. The ode consists of a prophecy delivered by the sea-god Nereus as the ship carrying Paris and Helen crosses the sea from Greece to Troy. Some have read this poem, like the last, as an allegory, with Paris and Helen standing in for Antony and Cleopatra, an affair that similarly led to the deaths of many people.
2. **shepherd:** Paris was given to a shepherd to be raised after his mother, Hecuba, dreamed while pregnant that she gave birth to a firebrand. He thereupon became a shepherd himself.
3. **carried:** The verb *traheret* (to pull or carry) is ambivalent here—it can be used for "dragging away" plunder but also for simply "conveying" something or someone. The verb therefore leaves the question of Helen's guilt or victimhood ambiguous. At the same time, however, Horace makes it clear that Paris had violated the rules of hospitality and betrayed not Menelaus his *host*, but Helen, his *hostess*.
4. **Ida's ships:** The timber used to build Paris's ships was grown on Mt. Ida, near Troy.
5. **Nereus:** Father of Thetis and grandfather of Achilles.
6. **Priam's . . . realm:** Priam was the king of Troy.
7. **Dardanus:** Ancient founder of Troy and ancestor of Priam.

nequiquam Veneris praesidio ferox
pectes caesariem grataque feminis
imbelli cithara carmina divides,   15
    nequiquam thalamo gravis

hastas et calami spicula Gnosii
vitabis strepitumque et celerem sequi
Aiacem; tamen heu serus adulteros
    crines pulvere collines.   20

non Laertiaden, exitium tuae
gentis, non Pylium Nestora respicis?
urgent impavidi te Salaminius
    Teucer, te Sthenelus sciens

pugnae, sive opus est imperitare equis,   25
non auriga piger. Merionen quoque
nosces. ecce furit te reperire atrox
    Tydides melior patre,

Made proud in vain by Venus's protection,[8]
you'll comb your tresses and play songs that please
women on your unwarlike cithara.[9]   15
    In vain inside your room you'll flee

the weighty spears, the points of Cretan arrows,
the din of battle, and the swift pursuit
of Ajax.[10] Yet, (alas!) you will at length
    taint your adulterous locks with dirt.[11]   20

Do you not see Laertes' son, your people's
destruction,[12] at your back, nor Pylian Nestor?[13]
Intrepid men pursue you: Salamis's
    Teucer and Sthenelus,[14] who's skilled

in war and, if there's need, at steering horses,   25
no sluggish charioteer. You'll also know
Meriones.[15] Look! Wild to find you, there's
    Tydeus's son,[16] his father's better.

---

8. **Venus's protection**: In *Iliad* 3, Aphrodite rescues Paris from his duel with Menelaus. She favors him since he chose her in the beauty contest with Juno (Hera) and Minerva (Athena).
9. **cithara**: A stringed instrument similar to a lyre.
10. **swift pursuit of Ajax**: This is Ajax the son of Oileus, famed for his running, not Ajax the son of Telamon.
11. **adulterous locks with dirt**: A reference to Paris's future death. He will be killed by the arrow of Philoctetes.
12. **Laertes' son . . . destruction**: Odysseus, who will come up with the plan for the Trojan Horse.
13. Pylian **Nestor**: Nestor, the king of Pylos, was the oldest of the Greek heroes at Troy and famous chiefly for his wise counsel.
14. **Teucer and Sthenelus**: For Teucer, see note on *Odes* 1.7.21. Sthenelus was the charioteer of Diomedes.
15. **Meriones**: Yet another Greek hero who fought at Troy.
16. **Tydeus's son**: Diomedes, who in *Iliad* 5 unleashes a massive killing spree on the Trojans.

quem tu, cervus uti vallis in altera
visum parte lupum graminis immemor,   30
sublimi fugies mollis anhelitu,
      non hoc pollicitus tuae.

iracunda diem proferet Ilio
matronisque Phrygum classis Achillei;
post certas hiemes uret Achaicus   35
      ignis Iliacas domos.

From him, just like a deer that's seen a wolf
across a dale (forgetful of the grass),   30
you'll flee, all soft, with shallow, panting breaths.
    This isn't what you pledged your woman.

Achilles' angry forces will postpone[17]
the day of doom for Troy and Phrygian matrons.
But once a fixed amount of winters[18] passes,   35
    Greek fire will burn the homes of Troy."

---

17. **will postpone:** A reference to Achilles's anger at Agamemnon (the subject of
    the *Iliad*), which leads him to remove his troops from battle and encamp by the ships.
18. **fixed amount of winters:** The Trojan War stretched out for ten years.

ODES 1.16

O matre pulchra filia pulchrior,
quem criminosis cumque voles modum
    pones iambis, sive flamma
        sive mari libet Hadriano.

non Dindymene, non adytis quatit   5
mentem sacerdotum incola Pythiis,
    non Liber aeque, non acuta
        sic geminant Corybantes aera,

tristes ut irae, quas neque Noricus
deterret ensis nec mare naufragum   10
    nec saevus ignis nec tremendo
        Iuppiter ipse ruens tumultu.

ODES 1.16[1]

Daughter more lovely than your lovely mother,[2]
you may impose whatever end you'd like
      upon my harsh invectives. Throw them in fire,
           or, if you want, the Adriatic Sea.[3]

Not Dindymus's goddess[4] nor the dweller   5
in Pythian shrines[5] nor Liber[6] shake the minds
      of priests as much, nor do the Corybantes[7]
           strike on their cymbals quite as piercingly,

as bitter anger, which a Noric sword[8]
cannot avert, nor ship-destroying sea,   10
      nor vicious fire, nor Jupiter himself
           while crashing in a terrifying storm.

---

1. ***Odes* 1.16** (*Alcaic Strophe*): The narrator promises an unnamed girl that he will recant his **invective** iambs against her if she will return his affection. Scholars are unsure what invectives he is referring to—they are not found in his earlier iambic *Epodes*, though it is not necessary to the poem's dramatic fiction that he be referring to any particular poems. It is technically a **palinode**, a poem written to correct or retract an earlier poem, and its most likely model is a palinode of Stesichorus in which he recants the earlier blame he laid on Helen as the cause of the Trojan War. This allusion to the Helen palinode is fitting since in the preceding poem Horace identifies Helen's relationship with Paris as the root of the Trojan conflict.
2. **Daughter . . . mother:** The reference to the addressee's mother is unclear, but it is most likely that the narrator had insulted not just the girl but the girl's mother in his earlier **invectives.**
3. **Adriatic Sea:** The sea to the east of the Italian Peninsula.
4. **Dindymus's goddess:** Dindymus was a Phrygian mountain associated with Cybele, the great mother goddess. Her priests, the Galli, were famous for castrating themselves in an ecstatic frenzy.
5. **dweller . . . shrines:** Apollo, whose priestess at Delphi was known as the Pythia. She entered a trance-like state while delivering oracles from the god.
6. **Liber:** Bacchus, whose followers, the Bacchants or Maenads, worshipped him in a frenzied, ecstatic state.
7. **Corybantes:** Mythical priests of Cybele, but, as Nisbet and Hubbard (1970) point out, they were associated with various ecstatic cults and are often identified with the Curetes, attendants of Rhea. The cymbals they strike were used frequently in ecstatic worship.
8. **Noric sword:** The province of Noricum was a key producer of iron.

fertur Prometheus addere principi
limo coactus particulam undique
    desectam et insani leonis
        vim stomacho apposuisse nostro.   15

irae Thyesten exitio gravi
stravere et altis urbibus ultimae
    stetere causae cur perirent
        funditus imprimeretque muris   20

hostile aratrum exercitus insolens.
compesce mentem: me quoque pectoris
    temptavit in dulci iuventa
        fervor et in celeres iambos

misit furentem: nunc ego mitibus   25
mutare quaero tristia, dum mihi
    fias recantatis amica
        opprobriis animumque reddas.

Prometheus,[9] it is said, when forced to add
to our primeval clay a part cut out
    from all the other animals, affixed   15
        a raging lion's violence to our belly.

Anger it was that laid Thyestes[10] low
in heavy ruin, and it's been the foremost
    reason why lofty cities are destroyed
        from their foundations and a pompous army   20

lodges its hostile plow into the walls.
Check your emotion. Boiling of the chest[11]
    afflicted me as well in my sweet youth
        and sent me raging forth into impulsive

invectives. Now I'm seeking to exchange   25
the bitter for the mild—but only if
    you'll be my girlfriend[12] once I have recanted
        my insults, and return to me your heart.

---

9. **Prometheus:** The mythological deity was sometimes credited with the manufacture of the first humans. Horace's version has no exact parallel, but he seems to suggest that animals were created first, which left behind nothing for men, who therefore had to be assembled from spare parts.
10. **Thyestes:** The brother of Atreus, who seduced his brother's wife. Atreus got vengeance by cooking Thyestes's children and serving them to him.
11. **Boiling of the chest:** That is, anger. As Mayer (2012) points out, the expression "reflects the current medical view that heated blood accounts for anger."
12. **girlfriend:** Horace's Latin can mean either "friend" or "girlfriend."

ODES 1.17

Velox amoenum saepe Lucretilem
mutat Lycaeo Faunus et igneam
     defendit aestatem capellis
          usque meis pluviosque ventos.

impune tutum per nemus arbutos   5
quaerunt latentis et thyma deviae
     olentis uxores mariti,
          nec viridis metuunt colubras

nec Martialis haediliae lupos,
utcumque dulci, Tyndari, fistula   10
     valles et Vsticae cubantis
          levia personuere saxa.

di me tuentur, dis pietas mea
et musa cordi est. hic tibi copia
     manabit ad plenum benigno   15
          ruris honorum opulenta cornu:

ODES 1.17[1]

Swift Faunus[2] often leaves behind Lycaeus,[3]
swapping it for Lucretilis' delights.[4]
    And from my goats he constantly repels
        the fiery summer heat and rainy winds.

As they meander through protected meadows,   5
the consorts of the reeking husband[5] safely
    track down concealed arbutus trees and thyme,
        nor do their little kids have any fear

of green-hued serpents or the wolves of Mars,[6]
whenever, Tyndaris, the pleasant panpipe   10
    echoes across the valleys and the smooth
        boulders on Ustica's[7] reclining hills.

Gods safeguard me. By the gods my piety
and Muse are cherished. Here for you abundance
    will flow profusely from a lavish horn,[8]   15
        rich in the glories of the countryside.

---

1. *Odes* **1.17** (*Alcaic Strophe*): This ode forms an invitation to a woman named Tyndaris
   to join Horace at his rural retreat in the Sabine hills. Horace first describes the divine
   protection his farm enjoys, then outlines the hospitality that Tyndaris can expect to
   receive while there. The farm takes on the features of an idealized *locus amoenus*
   from which the less appealing aspects of erotic love, such as jealousy and brawls, are
   excluded. The name Tyndaris clearly evokes Tyndareus, the father of Helen, thereby
   building on the Helen-sequence begun in 1.15. Helen's love triangle with Paris and
   Menelaus provides a parallel for the one between Horace, Tyndaris, and the jealous
   Cyrus, for which see Nagel (2000).
2. **Faunus:** A rural Italian deity often identified with the Greek Pan. He was particularly
   associated with flocks.
3. **Lycaeus:** A mountain in the Greek region of Arcadia that was associated with Pan.
4. **Lucretilis' delights:** Lucretilis was a hill in the Sabine countryside.
5. **reeking husband:** The billy goat.
6. **wolves of Mars:** Mars was often associated with wolves; for example, his sons
   Romulus and Remus were suckled by a she-wolf as infants.
7. **Ustica:** This location is otherwise unknown.
8. **abundance . . . horn:** Horace's *copia . . . cornu* suggests a cornucopia, an ancient
   symbol of fertility often depicted with various female goddesses, particularly Fortuna.

hic in reducta valle Caniculae
vitabis aestus et fide Teia
    dices laborantis in uno
        Penelopen vitreamque Circen: 20

hic innocentis pocula Lesbii
duces sub umbra, nec Semeleius
    cum Marte confundet Thyoneus
        proelia, nec metues protervum

suspecta Cyrum, ne male dispari   25
incontinentis iniciat manus
    et scindat haerentem coronam
        crinibus immeritamque vestem.

Here in a distant valley you'll avoid
the Dog Star's heat and on a Teian lyre[9]
     you'll sing about Penelope and glassy[10]
         Circe, two women troubled by one man.[11]   20

Here in the shade you'll drink down cups of harmless
Lesbian wine.[12] Thyoneus, the son
     of Semele,[13] won't mix it up in battle
         with Mars, nor will you be afraid that reckless

Cyrus[14] in all his jealousy might lay   25
unbridled hands on you, no match for him,[15]
     and rip to shreds the garland wrapped around
         your hair, together with your blameless clothing.

---

9. **Teian lyre:** The Ionian city of Teos was the home of the Greek lyric poet Anacreon. Tyndaris is therefore, like Horace, a lyric poet, but as the next lines show, her subject matter is Penelope and Circe, the women of Homer's *Odyssey*.

10. **glassy:** The adjective has befuddled commentators, most of whom suggest it evokes the sea. Circe was the daughter of Perse, a daughter of Ocean.

11. **one man:** Odysseus.

12. **harmless Lesbian wine:** Horace calls this highly esteemed wine "harmless" because it was considered less intoxicating than other varieties.

13. **Thyoneus . . . Semele:** A double matronymic for Bacchus. His mother was Semele, and she was called Thyone after her death.

14. **Cyrus:** A jealous, would-be lover of Tyndaris.

15. **no match for him:** That is, she lacks equal physical strength to fight him back.

ODES 1.18

Nullam, Vare, sacra vite prius severis arborem
circa mite solum Tiburis et moenia Catili.
siccis omnia nam dura deus proposuit, neque
mordaces aliter diffugiunt sollicitudines.
quis post vina gravem militiam aut pauperiem crepat?   5
quis non te potius, Bacche pater, teque, decens Venus?
ac ne quis modici transiliat munera Liberi,
Centaurea monet cum Lapithis rixa super mero

debellata, monet Sithoniis non levis Euhius,
cum fas atque nefas exiguo fine libidinum   10
discernunt avidi. non ego te, candide Bassareu,
invitum quatiam, nec variis obsita frondibus
sub divum rapiam. saeva tene cum Berecyntio

ODES 1.18[1]

Varus, you ought to plant no tree before the sacred vine
round the mild soil of Tibur and the walls of Catilus.[2]
The god[3] ordained that for the sober everything be hard,
and gnawing troubles can't disperse in any other way.
Who, after wine, harps on about harsh war or poverty   5
instead of you, O father Bacchus, and, fair Venus, you?
But let nobody overstep the gifts of moderate Liber—
thus warns the Centaurs' quarrel with Lapiths, fought
    while drinking
unwatered wine.[4] Thus Euhius warns, not gentle to Sithonians[5]
when with too fine a line they separated right and wrong,   10
eager for sex. But I'll not shake[6] you, splendid Bassareus,[7]
against your will, nor take into the open what is veiled
by various leaves.[8] Restrain the ruthless tambourines and horn

---

1. *Odes* 1.18 (*Fifth Asclepiadean*): An ode celebrating both the gifts and the dangers of
   Bacchus in his guise as god of wine. The poem addresses first Varus, whose historical
   identity cannot be ascertained, then transitions into an address to the god himself.
   The topic of wine offers Horace an opportunity to develop one of his most recognized
   themes: moderation. Commager (1957) remains the best study of wine in the *Odes*.
2. **Catilus.** One of the legendary founders of Tibur in the Sabine hills. Varus, like
   Horace, seems to have an estate in this area.
3. **The god:** This refers not to Bacchus but to some general "god."
4. **Centaurs' quarrel ... unwatered wine:** The half-horse/half-man Centaurs were
   thought to be especially susceptible to wine's intoxicating effects. At the wedding of
   the Lapith king Pirithous to Hippodamia, the drunken Centaur Eurytus tried to steal
   the bride, whereupon the famous Centauromachy ensued.
5. **Euhius ... Sithonians:** Euhius is another cult name for Bacchus. Here we see
   Bacchus in his harsh guise, though it is not clear what the Sithonians, a Thracian
   tribe, did to elicit his ire. As in the Centauromachy, however, their sin surely
   combined excessive drink and sexual desire.
6. **shake:** Probably a reference to the thyrsus, the ivy-topped staff shaken by
   worshippers of Bacchus.
7. **Bassareus:** Another cult name for Bacchus.
8. **veiled by various leaves:** A reference to the cult's mysterious objects, which were
   meant to be revealed only to initiates.

cornu tympana, quae subsequitur caecus Amor sui
et tollens vacuum plus nimio Gloria verticem   15
arcanique Fides prodiga, perlucidior vitro.

of Berecyntus.[9] Trailing after these come blind self-love
and Glory, elevating far too high her empty head,   15
and Loyalty that gives out secrets, see-through just like glass.

<hr/>

9. **tambourines . . . Berecyntus**: A reference to the musical instruments used in the
ecstatic worship of Cybele, analogous to the intoxication of wine. Berecyntus was a
mountain in Phrygia associated with the goddess.

ODES 1.19

Mater saeva Cupidinum
Thebanaeque iubet me Semelae puer
　　　et lasciva Licentia
finitis animum reddere amoribus.

　　　urit me Glycerae nitor   5
splendentis Pario marmore purius:
　　　urit grata protervitas
et vultus nimium lubricus aspici.

　　　in me tota ruens Venus
Cyprum deseruit, nec patitur Scythas   10
　　　et versis animosum equis
Parthum dicere nec quae nihil attinent.

　　　hic vivum mihi caespitem, hic
verbenas, pueri, ponite turaque
　　　bimi cum patera meri: 15
mactata veniet lenior hostia.

ODES 1.19[1]

The ruthless mother of the Cupids[2]
and son of Theban Semele[3] and wanton
    Licentiousness are bidding me
to start again the love affairs I've finished.

The gleam of Glycera inflames me—   5
she shines more brilliantly than Parian marble.[4]
    Her welcome forwardness inflames me,
and face too slippery to gaze upon.[5]

Venus attacks me at full tilt,
forsaking Cyprus,[6] and won't let me sing[7]   10
    of Scythians or the Parthian, brave
on backward horses[8]—things that do not matter.

Here place fresh turf for me, my slaves,[9]
here leafy twigs and incense and a bowl
    of two-year-old unwatered wine.   15
She'll come more gently with a victim slain.

---

1. *Odes* 1.19 (*Second Asclepiadean*): An ode in which Horace describes how he once
more feels erotic love, although he had previously finished with it. Horace thus
repeats his frequent pose, seen already, for example, in *Odes* 1.5, of being retired from
eroticism. His unwilling return anticipates *Odes* 4.1, where likewise his resistance
makes the force of love all the more powerful.
2. **ruthless mother . . . Cupids:** Venus, here standing **metonymically** for erotic love.
3. **son . . . Semele:** Bacchus, god of wine. This detail, as Mayer (2012) suggests, may
locate the setting at a symposium.
4. **Parian marble:** A marble renowned for its beauty. Horace's erotic gaze has
transformed Glycera into a type of statue. On the gaze in the poem see especially
Sutherland (2003).
5. **too slippery to gaze upon:** This "arresting phrase," as Mayer (2012) states, has
puzzled scholars. As Sutherland (2003, 68) explains, "Glycera's *vultus lubricus* most
resembles the 'slippery path': one's gaze cannot maintain its hold on such a face, and
one may even risk danger by gazing upon it."
6. **Cyprus:** An island sacred to Venus.
7. **won't let me sing:** Venus's dictation of Horace's subject matter gives the poem the
flavor of a ***recusatio***.
8. **brave . . . horses:** The Parthians were famous for feigning retreat, then turning and
shooting.
9. **slaves:** Horace uses the word *pueri* (boys), but this is regularly used to designate slaves.

ODES 1.20

Vile potabis modicis Sabinum
cantharis, Graeca quod ego ipse testa
conditum levi, datus in theatro
        cum tibi plausus,

care Maecenas eques, ut paterni   5
fluminis ripae simul et iocosa
redderet laudes tibi Vaticani
        montis imago.

Caecubum et prelo domitam Caleno
tu bibes uvam: mea nec Falernae   10
temperant vites neque Formiani
        pocula colles.

ODES 1.20[1]

You'll drink a frugal Sabine wine[2] from modest
goblets, which I myself sealed up and stored
in a Greek jar, when in the theater
    you were applauded,[3]

dear knight Maecenas,[4] while the banks of your   5
ancestral river[5] and the mountainside
of Vaticanus[6] with its laughing echo
    doubled your praises.

You can imbibe Caecuban and the grape
tamed by Calenian presses. As for me,   10
neither Falernian vines nor Formian[7] hills
    temper my wine cups.

---

1. **Odes 1.20** (*Sapphic Strophe*): This is one of Horace's invitation poems to Maecenas (see also 3.8 and 3.29). It offers Horace a chance to describe his own moderate style of life, which he invites the grander Maecenas to share. Some have read the poem **metaphorically**, with the wine suggestive of the poem itself. In this reading, the Greek vase is analogous to the Greek meter, and the Sabine (Italian) wine to the Latin words. For this reading, see esp. Putnam (1969).
2. **frugal Sabine wine:** The detail places the future dinner at Horace's Sabine estate, which may have been a gift to him from Maecenas. This was not a region known for excellent wine.
3. **theater . . . applauded:** Maecenas seems to have received a public acclamation in the Theater of Pompey in the Campus Martius. Horace mentions this again in *Odes* 2.17.25 and suggests that it was given upon Maecenas's recovery from an illness.
4. **knight Maecenas:** Maecenas famously retained equestrian rank, never attempting to rise to senatorial status.
5. **ancestral river:** The Tiber, which arises in Etruria. Maecenas traced his ancestry back to Etruscan kings, for which see also the opening of *Odes* 1.1.
6. **mountainside of Vaticanus:** The Janiculum, not the area known today as the Vatican.
7. **Caecuban . . . Calenian . . . Falernian . . . Formian:** The four most prized Italian vintages.

ODES 1.21

Dianam tenerae dicite virgines,
intonsum, pueri, dicite Cynthium
    Latonamque supremo
        dilectam penitus Iovi.

vos laetam fluviis et nemorum coma,   5
quaecumque aut gelido prominet Algido,
    nigris aut Erymanthi
        silvis aut viridis Cragi.

vos Tempe totidem tollite laudibus
natalemque, mares, Delon Apollinis,   10
    insignemque pharetra
        fraternaque umerum lyra.

hic bellum lacrimosum, hic miseram famem
pestemque a populo et principe Caesare in
    Persas atque Britannos   15
        vestra motus aget prece.

ODES 1.21[1]

Sing of Diana, O you tender virgins.
Sing of the long-haired Cynthian,[2] you boys,
    and of Latona deeply loved
        by Jupiter,[3] the most supreme.

You,[4] sing of her whose happiness is streams   5
and leafy groves, whichever overhang
    cold Algidus, and the dark woods
        of Erymanthus or lush Cragos.[5]

You,[6] celebrate with just as many praises
Tempe and Delos,[7] birthplace of Apollo,   10
    whose shoulder is renowned for wearing
        the quiver and his brother's lyre.

Moved by your prayer, he will drive tearful war
and wretched dearth and sickness from our people
    and from our princeps[8] Caesar, leading   15
        them to the Persians and the Britons.[9]

---

1. *Odes* 1.21 (*Fourth Asclepiadean*): A **hymn** to the twin gods Diana and Apollo,
   addressed as though to a double chorus of girls and boys, with the speaker acting as a
   guide or advisor giving them direction. The god Apollo was especially important to
   Augustus, who credited him with his victory at Actium. As John Miller (2009, 265)
   points out, the hymn is something of a precursor to the *Carmen Saeculare* of 17 B.C.E.
2. **long-haired Cynthian**: "Cynthian" was one of the most common cult names of
   Apollo. He was an eternally youthful and long-haired deity.
3. **Latona . . . Jupiter**: Latona (Leto) was the mother of Diana and Apollo. Although
   Horace presents Jupiter's feelings for her as loving, little is known of how Latona
   came to be impregnated by him. Jupiter is a notorious rapist, but Hesiod (*Theogony*
   918) counts her among Jupiter's wives.
4. **You**: The girls' chorus, who will sing of Diana.
5. **Algidus . . . Erymanthus . . . Cragos**: Algidus was an Italian ridge running from
   Tusculum to the Alban hills. Erymanthus was a Peloponnesian mountain range;
   Cragus, a Lycian range.
6. **You**: The boys' chorus, which will sing of Apollo.
7. **Tempe and Delos**: Tempe was a valley in Thessaly; Delos was the Aegean island
   where the twins were born.
8. **princeps**: See the note on 1.2.50.
9. **Persians and Britons**: For the Persians (i.e., the Parthians), see note on *Odes* 1.2.23.
   The Britons were as yet unconquered.

ODES 1.22

Integer vitae scelerisque purus
non eget Mauris iaculis neque arcu
nec venenatis gravida sagittis,
       Fusce, pharetra,

sive per Syrtis iter aestuosas   5
sive facturus per inhospitalem
Caucasum vel quae loca fabulosus
       lambit Hydaspes.

namque me silva lupus in Sabina,
dum meam canto Lalagen et ultra   10
terminum curis vagor expeditis,
       fugit inermem,

quale portentum neque militaris
Daunias latis alit aesculetis

ODES 1.22[1]

Whoever's life is pure and free of crime
requires no Moroccan[2] darts or bow
or quiver loaded down with poison tipped
      arrows, O Fuscus,

whether he'll journey through the fiery Syrtes   5
or Caucasus, which does not welcome guests,
or else those places lapped by the Hydaspes,[3]
      told of in stories.

For while I sang inside the Sabine woods
of my Lalage,[4] strolling carefree past   10
the boundary line, a wolf fled me, although
      I had no weapon.

It was a monster such as neither warlike
Daunia[5] nourishes in its wide forests

---

1. **Odes 1.22** (*Sapphic Strophe*): Horace in this poem evokes two ancient precepts: (a) that the good man need not be afraid (popular especially among Stoic philosophers) and (b) that nothing can harm a lover (common among elegiac love poets). The locales mentioned in the poem run from Horace's Sabine woods to the farthest stretches of the known world, where Horace's love for Lalage, he states, can keep him safe. Scholars disagree about the tone of the poem, though most concur that it contains a dose of humor. Davis (1987) reads the poem as an expression of allegiance to Horace's current lyric poetry and repudiation of the invective manner of the *Epodes*, represented here by the figure of the wolf. For the wolf as a symbol of iambic invective, see Miralles (1983) and Hawkins (2014).
2. **Moroccan**: Ancient Mauretania covered what is now Morocco and northern Algeria. I have used the modern term so as not to confuse the area with the present-day country of Mauretania.
3. **Syrtes . . . Caucasus . . . Hydaspes**: The Syrtes were sandbanks off the coast of northern Africa, but the word also refers to the surrounding desert. The Caucasus was a mountain chain separating Europe and Asia and running from the Black to the Caspian Seas. The Hydapses was a river in northwest Indian, now called the Jhelum.
4. **Lalage**: Her name, from the Greek word *lalein*, means something akin to our "chatterbox."
5. **warlike Daunia**: Daunia is another name for Apulia, the Italian region in which Horace was born and that was famous for wolves. Its legendary founder was Daunus.

nec Iubae tellus generat, leonum   15
    arida nutrix.

pone me pigris ubi nulla campis
arbor aestiva recreatur aura,
quod latus mundi nebulae malusque
    Iuppiter urget;   20

pone sub curru nimium propinqui
solis in terra domibus negata:
dulce ridentem Lalagen amabo,
    dulce loquentem.

nor the terrain of Juba[6] spawns, the arid   15
    wet nurse of lions.

Put me in barren plains where not a single
tree is restored by breezes in the summer,[7]
a district of the world that fog and foul
    Jupiter[8] burdens.   20

Put me down where the chariot of the sun
descends too close to lands denied to homes:[9]
still I will love Lalage sweetly laughing,
    sweetly conversing.[10]

---

6. **terrain of Juba**: Mauretania or Numidia. Juba II was king in Mauretania and then restored by Augustus to the Numidian throne, which had belonged to his father.
7. **barren plains . . . summer**: The arctic north.
8. **Jupiter**: Used **metonymically** for the weather.
9. **lands denied to homes**: The arid, hot south.
10. **sweetly laughing, / sweetly conversing**: An imitation of Catullus and Sappho. Sappho (fr. 31) speaks of a woman "sweetly speaking and laughing pleasantly." In translating and adapting this poem into Latin, Catullus (poem 51) speaks of Lesbia as *dulce ridentem* (sweetly laughing.)

ODES 1.23

Vitas inuleo me similis, Chloe,
quaerenti pavidam montibus aviis
    matrem non sine vano
        aurarum et silvae metu.

nam seu mobilibus veris inhorruit   5
adventus folliis seu virides rubum
    dimovere lacertae,
        et corde et genibus tremit.

atqui non ego te tigris ut aspera
Gaetulusve leo frangere persequor: 10
    tandem desine matrem
        tempestiva sequi viro.

ODES 1.23[1]

You flee me, Chloe,[2] like a little deer
seeking its timid mother on the trackless
      mountainsides, not without an empty
          terror of breezes and the woods.

For whether spring, as it approaches, shakes   5
the rustling foliage or green-hued lizards
      have pushed apart the prickly shrubs,
          she trembles in her heart and knees.

But I don't chase you like a ruthless tiger
or lion of Gaetulia[3] to crush you.   10
      Finally cease to trail your mother—
          you are in season[4] for a man.[5]

---

1. ***Odes* 1.23** (*Fourth Asclepiadean*): Horace compares his young female addressee,
Chloe, to a fawn whose fears are, according to the male speaker, groundless. The
comparison of women to animals is frequently repeated—cf., for example, *Epodes* 8,
where the comparisons are hardly flattering, and *Odes* 2.5, where a girl is compared
to a heifer. The theme of seasons and their relation to human life is again prominent
in this poem, with the onset of puberty signaling (according to the speaker, at least)
readiness for sexuality.
2. **Chloe:** The Greek name suggests a young shoot of grass.
3. **lion of Gaetulia:** Gaetulia was a region of northern Africa.
4. **in season:** The Latin *tempestiva* can describe fruits ready to be plucked or people that
are in their prime.
5. **man:** The Latin *vir* can denote either a "man" in general or a "husband" in particular.

ODES 1.24

Quis desiderio sit pudor aut modus
tam cari capitis? praecipe lugubris
cantus, Melpomene, cui liquidam pater
    vocem cum cithara dedit.

ergo Quintilium perpetuus sopor   5
urget! cui Pudor et Iustitiae soror,
incorrupta Fides, nudaque Veritas
    quando ullum inveniet parem?

multis ille bonis flebilis occidit,
nulli flebilior quam tibi, Vergili.   10
tu frustra pius heu non ita creditum
    poscis Quintilium deos.

ODES 1.24[1]

What restraint[2] or limit should be placed
on mourning one so dear? Teach me a song
of grief, Melpomene.[3] Your father gave you
    a flowing voice and cithara.[4]

It seems an everlasting sleep weighs down   5
Quintilius. At what time will Restraint
and uncorrupted Faith, sister of Justice,
    and naked Truth reveal his equal?

His dying has made many good men weep,
but, Vergil, none has wept him more than you.   10
Pious in vain,[5] you beg the gods return
    Quintilius, not entrusted thus.[6]

---

1. *Odes* 1.24 (*Third Asclepiadean*): A **dirge** for Quintilius Varus, addressed to his friend, the famous poet Vergil. At *Ars Poetica* 438–39 Horace credits Varus with being an astute literary critic. The poem engages with the important Horatian themes of death and moderation, but whereas elsewhere he often exhorts his addressee to remember his own death and live accordingly, he here advises Vergil on how to go on living after the death of a loved one.
2. **restraint**: This translates the difficult Latin word *pudor*, repeated again in line 6. The word has many connotations, including, for example, "shame," "a sense of propriety or restraint," "modesty/chastity," and "self-respect." Nisbet and Hubbard (1970) connect its use here to the Greek *aidos*, which they gloss as the "fear of going too far."
3. **Melpomene**: One of the Muses, who were the daughters of Zeus and Mnemosyne (Memory).
4. **cithara**: A stringed instrument similar to a lyre.
5. **Pious in vain**: The presence of the word *pius* (pious) in a poem to Vergil is very pointed, since his Aeneas's most famous attributes is *pietas* (piety.)
6. **not entrusted thus**: An unclear phrase with two possible meanings, as explained by Mayer (2012): "It might mean that Quintilius was not entrusted by the gods to Virgil as a friend to keep forever or . . . that Virgil had in circumstances unspecified (a journey perhaps . . . or during a serious illness) entrusted Quinilius to the care of the gods."

quid si Threicio blandius Orpheo
auditam moderere arboribus fidem,
num vanae redeat sanguis imagini,   15
    quam virga semel horrida,

non lenis precibus fata recludere,
nigro compulerit Mercurius gregi?
durum: sed levius fit patientia
    quidquid corrigere est nefas.   20

What if more charmingly than Thracian Orpheus[7]
you played your lyre to the listening trees—
could blood return now to his empty ghost,   15
    which Mercury,[8] who's not disposed

to undo death with tears, has led forever
with his dread staff down to the murky herd?
It's difficult. But fortitude makes lighter
    whatever it's a sin to fix.[9]   20

---

7. **Thracian Orpheus**: Orpheus's song had the ability to charm trees, but he also used
   it to persuade Pluto and Proserpina to give back his deceased wife, Eurydice, to him.
   He ultimately failed, however, to restore her to life. Instructed not to look back at her
   until they exited the underworld, he could not refrain from stealing a glimpse. Vergil
   tells this story in his *Georgics*, and Horace may be nodding to this poem here.
8. **Mercury**: The god is described here in his role as the psychopomp, the guide of souls
   to and from the underworld.
9. **to fix**: The word *corrigere* (to fix) is used elsewhere to describe the "fixing" or
   "editing" of literary faults. This is in fact, as Putnam (1992–93, 134) points out, the
   word Horace puts in the mouth of Quintilius Varus at *Ars Poetica* 338. If one recites
   a work to him, Horace's says, his response will be *corrige*, "fix it." The word perhaps
   inserts a bit of good-natured humor into the poem.

ODES 1.25

Parcius iunctas quatiunt fenestras
iactibus crebris iuvenes protervi,
nec tibi somnos adimunt, amatque
      ianua limen,

quae prius multum facilis movebat   5
cardines; audis minus et minus iam
"me tuo longas pereunte noctes,
      Lydia, dormis?"

invicem moechos anus arrogantis
flebis in solo levis angiportu,   10
Thracio bacchante magis sub inter-
      lunia vento,

cum tibi flagrans amor et libido,
quae solet matres furiare equorum,
saeviet circa iecur ulcerosum,   15
      non sine questu

ODES 1.25[1]

Less frequently do forward young men shake
your shuttered windows with repeated blows,
and they no longer steal your sleep. The door
    clings to the threshold,

which so obligingly before would move   5
its hinges.[2] Less and less now are you hearing,
"Do I despair through lengthy nights, while you,
    Lydia, slumber?"

In turn, a worthless crone, you will lament
your pompous lovers in a lonely alley[3]   10
while even more on moonless nights the wind
    raves like a Bacchant.[4]

Then, setting you aflame, the love and passion
accustomed to drive horses' mothers mad[5]
will rage around your ulcer-ridden liver[6]—   15
    all while you grumble

---

1. **Odes 1.25** (*Sapphic Strophe*): A variant of the *carpe diem* theme, this is a song both of misogynistic abuse as well as seduction. Horace tries to persuade Lydia, his addressee, to yield to erotic persuasion now before she turns too old and undesirable. It is not clear whether the speaker himself is trying to seduce Lydia or merely offering her an instructive warning.
2. **windows . . . hinges:** The poem opens with a **topos** from love poetry: the **paraclausithyron.**
3. **in a lonely alley:** Horace hints that as Lydia grows older she will turn to prostitution.
4. **Bacchant:** One of the ecstatic followers of Bacchus.
5. **drive . . . mad:** Mares were thought to be particularly susceptible to erotic madness, as described by Vergil in *Georgics* 3.
6. **ulcer-ridden liver:** The liver was considered the seat of powerful emotion.

laeta quod pubes hedera virenti
gaudeat pulla magis atque myrto,
aridas frondis hiemis sodali
    dedicet Euro.   20

since lush young men derive from verdant ivy
more pleasure than they do from dingy myrtle—
the dried-out leaves[7] they dedicate to Eurus,
    winter's companion.   20

---

7. **verdant ivy ... dark-hued myrtle ... dried-out leaves:** The leaves are clearly
symbolic for women of different ages, but scholars differ as to exactly how. The
likeliest scenario, as outlined by Nisbet and Hubbard (1970), is that the ivy = young
women (like leaves in spring); myrtle = older women (late summer); dried-out
leaves = aged women (autumn).

ODES 1.26

Musis amicus tristitiam et metus
tradam protervis in mare Creticum
    portare ventis, quis sub Arcto
        rex gelidae metuatur orae,

quid Tiridaten terreat, unice   5
securus. o quae fontibus integris
    gaudes, apricos necte flores,
        necte meo Lamiae coronam,

Piplea dulcis! nil sine te mei
prosunt honores: hunc fidibus novis,   10
    hunc Lesbio sacrare plectro
        teque tuasque decet sorores.

ODES 1.26[1]

The Muses' friend, I will hand over gloom
and fear to violent winds to carry off
        into the Cretan Sea.[2] Which king of icy
            regions beneath the Bear[3] is causing fear,

what frightens Tiridates[4]—my indifference   5
cannot be matched. O you who take your joy
        in unpolluted springs, weave sun-drenched flowers,
            weave for my Lamia[5] a garland,

sweet Piplean![6] Without you I bestow
useless renown: to venerate this man   10
        with a new lyre and a Lesbian plectrum[7]
            is suitable for you and for your sisters.

---

1. ***Odes* 1.26** (*Alcaic Strophe*): In this short poem addressed to one of the Muses, Horace professes indifference to the political machinations on the empire's edges, choosing instead to concern himself with the private world of lyric friendship.
2. **Cretan Sea**: A stormy stretch of sea, but, as Nisbet and Hubbard (1970) point out, one that was also "a long way from Rome and Horace."
3. **icy region . . . bear**: In the far north. The constellation of the Bear suggests the north generally.
4. **Tiridates**: A Parthian king, exiled to Syria.
5. **Lamia**: Most likely Lucius Aelius Lamia, a member of an elite family from Formiae. Horace also mentions him in *Odes* 1.36 and 3.17 and in *Epistles* 1.14.
6. **sweet Piplian**: Horace singles out one of the Muses. Pipleia was a mountain located in Pieria, the region most strongly associated with the Muses.
7. **Lesbian plectrum**: Lesbos was associated with the lyric poets Alcaeus and Sappho. The plectrum was the stick used to strum the lyre strings.

ODES 1.27

Natis in usum laetitiae scyphis
pugnare Thracum est: tollite barbarum
    morem, verecundumque Bacchum
        sanguineis prohibete rixis.

vino et lucernis Medus acinaces   5
immane quantum discrepat: impium
    lenite clamorem, sodales,
        et cubito remanete presso.

vultis severi me quoque sumere
partem Falerni? dicat Opuntiae   10
    frater Megillae, quo beatus
        vulnere, qua pereat sagitta.

cessat voluntas? non alia bibam
mercede. quae te cumque domat Venus
    non erubescendis adurit   15
        ignibus, ingenuoque semper

ODES 1.27[1]

To fight with goblets meant to bring us joy
is Thracian.[2] Do away with this barbaric[3]
    custom and keep the moderated Bacchus
        removed from arguing that ends in blood.

How greatly does the sabre of the Medes[4]   5
run counter to our wine and lamps: now take
    it easy with your impious shouting, comrades,
        and keep your place, supported by your elbow.[5]

You want me too to have my share of dry
Falernian?[6] Then let Opuntian   10
    Megilla's brother[7] say what wound and arrow[8]
        cause him to pine away so happily.

You are unwilling? I'll not drink on any
different terms. Whichever Venus tames you
    she scorches you with flames that need not make   15
        you blush. It always is a freeborn love[9]

---

1. *Odes* 1.27 (*Alcaic Strophe*): The scene of this ode is a symposium at which the drinking
seems to be getting out of hand. The first third takes up the theme (seen already
in *Odes* 1.18) of moderate versus immoderate drinking. The speaker then turns to
addressing a young man and asking him who is the current object of his erotic desire.
2. **Thracian**: Thracian here generically suggest "barbarians." The Greeks and Romans
often held xenophobic beliefs that "barbarians" were excessive and unrestrained,
particularly in the spheres of drink and sex.
3. **barbaric**: See note at *Epodes* 5.61.
4. **sabre of the Medes**: The Medes here indicate the Parthians. The word *acinaces*
(sabre) seems to be a Persian word that Horace has adopted into Latin.
5. **supported . . . elbow**: The attendees of the symposium would have reclined on a
couch, propping themselves up on their left elbows.
6. **Falernian**: One of the premiere Italian wines.
7. **Opuntian Megilla's brother**: One of Horace's fellow-symposiasts. Opus was a city in
the Greek region of Locris.
8. **arrow**: A reference to Cupid's arrow.
9. **freeborn love**: Most commentators suggest the word *ingenuo* (freeborn) means here
something like "respectable," i.e., not one to be ashamed of. But it remains a striking
word to use in this context, especially given Augustus's moral legislation, with its
focus on curtailing elite female sexuality.

amore peccas. quidquid habes, age,
depone tutis auribus. a! miser,
    quanta laborabas Charybdi,
        digne puer meliore flamma.   20

quae saga, quis te solvere Thessalis
magus venenis, quis poterit deus?
    vix illigatum te triformi
        Pegasus expediet Chimaera.

that makes you trip. Whatever is the case,
entrust it to my faithful ears. Ah, wretch!
How mighty a Charybdis[10] you contend with!
Boy, you are worthy of a better flame.   20

What witch, what warlock with Thessalian poisons,
what god will have the power to release you?
Scarcely will Pegasus untangle you,
wrapped as you are in this triform Chimaera.[11]

---

10. **Charybdis**: This was the monstrous female whirlpool famous from epics such
as the *Odyssey*. She would suck down and devour ships and men.
11. **Perseus . . . Chimaera**: The Chimaera is another monstrous female, with an
amalgam body made up of a lion, goat, and snake. She was defeated by Bellerophon
and his flying horse, Pegasus.

ODES 1.28

Te maris et terrae numeroque carentis harenae
     mensorem cohibent, Archyta,
pulveris exigui prope litus parva Matinum
     munera, nec quicquam tibi prodest

aerias temptasse domos animoque rotundum   5
     percurrisse polum morituro.
occidit et Pelopis genitor, conviva deorum,
     Tithonusque remotus in auras,

et Iovis arcanis Minos admissus, habentque
     Tartara Panthoiden iterum Orco   10

ODES 1.28[1]

You measurer of sea and earth and sand (which can't
    be counted), Archytas,[2] a small
tribute of meager dust confines you near the Matine
    shore.[3] It avails you not at all

to have explored celestial homes and roamed the vaulted   5
    sky with your mind—you, doomed to die.
So too did Pelops' father[4] die, who dined with gods,
    and Tithonus,[5] whisked to the breezes,

and Minos, taught Jove's mysteries.[6] And Tartarus
    holds Panthus' son,[7] cast down again   10

---

1. *Odes* 1.28 (*Alcmanic Strophe*): This is one of Horace's most difficult and debated odes. The chief point of contention is how the poem's two halves cohere. In the first, an unnamed speaker observes how even Archytas, the famed philosopher, could not cheat death and now lies buried under a small plot of dust. In the second, the speaker reveals that he too is dead, having drowned at sea, and remains unburied. He now calls on a passing sailor to give him a basic burial and issues blessings if he does and curses if he does not. The curses connect the poem to the *Epodes*, where curses abound, a connection made even stronger by the poem being written in an epodic meter, Alcmanic strophe (for which see *Epodes* 12).

2. **Archytas**: A fourth-century B.C.E. Pythagorean philosopher from the Italian town of Tarentum, which was part of *Magna Graecia*, the coastal areas of Southern Italy inhabited by Greek colonists. He was an especially famous and successful mathematician.

3. **Matine shore**: The precise location is uncertain, but it is most likely on the coast of Apulia, which lies along the Adriatic.

4. **Pelops' father**: Tantalus. While dining with the gods he fed them his son Pelops, who was later revived. As punishment, Tantalus is one of the sinners eternally tortured in the underworld.

5. **Tithonus**: The lover of the goddess Dawn. He technically did *not* die, since she asked her father Jupiter to grant him eternal life but forgot to ask for eternal youth. He eventually withered away—in some versions becoming a cicada.

6. **Minos ... Jove's mysteries**: Minos was a mythological king in Crete whose laws were supposedly given to him by Jupiter himself.

7. **Tartarus ... Panthus' son**: Tartarus is another name for the underworld. Panthus's son is Euphorbus, whom Menelaus kills in the *Iliad*. The philosopher Pythagoras, to whom Archytas was an adherent, claimed to be Euphorbus's reincarnation. He supposedly proved this by identifying a shield hung in the temple of Hera of Argos that was dedicated by Euphorbus. The idea here is not so much that Euphorbus was mortal but that even Pythagoras was.

demissum, quamvis clipeo Troiana refixo
    tempora testatus nihil ultra

nervos atque cutem morti concesserat atrae,
    iudice te non sordidus auctor
naturae verique. sed omnis una manet nox   15
    et calcanda semel via leti.

dant alios Furiae torvo spectacula Marti;
    exitio est avidum mare nautis;
mixta senum ac iuvenum densentur funera; nullum
    saeva caput Proserpina fugit.   20

me quoque devexi rabidus comes Orionis
    Illyricis Notus obruit undis.
at tu, nauta, vagae ne parce malignus harenae
    ossibus et capiti inhumato

particulam dare: sic, quodcumque minabitur Eurus   25
    fluctibus Hesperiis, Venusinae
plectantur silvae te sospite, multaque merces
    unde potest tibi defluat aequo

to Orcus—though he proved by taking down the shield
    he lived in Trojan times and so

had yielded to dark death his nerves and flesh alone—
    in your view not a trifling expert
of nature and of truth. One night awaits us all;   15
    we tread death's path a single time.

Furies give some to vicious Mars as spectacles;[8]
    the greedy sea brings doom to sailors;
the jumbled corpses[9] of the young and old pile up.
    Brutal Proserpina spurns no head.[10]   20

Notus, the wild companion of Orion's setting,[11]
    drowned me, too, in Illyrian waves.[12]
But, sailor, you—don't greedily refrain from giving
    my tombless bones and head a grain

of roving sand. If done, whatever Eurus threatens   25
    on western waves, may you be spared,
Venusia's forests struck instead.[13] And may great gain
    flow down to you from where it can,

---

8. **Furies ... spectacles**: The Furies were goddesses of vengeance and wrath. Mars stands here in **metonymy** for war. The word *spectacula* (spectacles) suggests a connection between death on the battlefield and death in the arena.

9. **corpses**: A *funus* can mean a funeral procession, a corpse, or just death in general, and scholars/translators have understood this line in all three ways. I follow the dictionary by Lewis and Short (1962), who cite this passage as an instance of the word designating "corpses," which would create a vivid image of dead bodies heaped up indiscriminately.

10. **Proserpina**: Wife of Hades and the queen of the underworld. It was thought that she took a lock of hair from those about to die.

11. **Notus ... Orion's setting**: Notus was the south wind, whose storms are here caused by the setting of Orion in November.

12. **Illyrian waves**: The speaker seems to have been sailing from Italy to Illyria.

13. **Eurus ... struck instead**: The speaker offers a blessing to the sailor if he buries him, asking that anything that Eurus (the east wind) threatens at sea should be suffered not by the sailor but by the forests of Venusia. Venusia was Horace's birthplace in Apulia.

ab Iove Neptunoque sacri custode Tarenti.
    neglegis immeritis nocituram   30
postmodo te natis fraudem committere? fors et
    debita iura vicesque superbae

te maneant ipsum: precibus non linquar inultis,
    teque piacula nulla resolvent.
quamquam festinas, non est mora longa; licebit   35
    iniecto ter pulvere curras.

from kindly Jove and Neptune, holy Tarentum's guard.[14]
      Do you not care that you'll do harm   30
that later will afflict your guiltless heirs? Perhaps
      unpaid rites and a proud requital

await you too. I'll not be left with prayers unanswered,
      and no atonement will release you.
Although you're hurrying, it's not a long delay—   35
      throw dust three times and then be off.

---

14. **holy Tarentum's guard:** Taras, the legendary founder of Tarentum, was the son of Neptune. The city therefore enjoyed his divine favor.

ODES 1.29

Icci, beatis nunc Arabum invides
gazis, et acrem militiam paras
    non ante devictis Sabaeae
        regibus horribilique Medo

nectis catenas? quae tibi virginum   5
sponso necato barbara serviet?
    puer quis ex aula capillis
        ad cyathum statuetur unctis,

doctus sagittas tendere Sericas
arcu paterno? quis neget arduis   10
    pronos relabi posse rivos
        montibus et Tiberim reverti,

cum tu coemptos undique nobilis
libros Panaeti Socraticam et domum
    mutare loricis Hiberis,   15
        pollicitus meliora, tendis?

ODES 1.29[1]

Iccius, do you envy now the happy
wealth of the Arabs?[2] Are you undertaking
    a harsh campaign on Saba's kings,[3] not yet
        subdued? And for the terrifying Mede[4]

do you weave fetters? Which barbarian[5] virgin,   5
her fiancé cut down, will be your slave?
    What boy born in a royal court, his hair
        perfumed, will be set up beside your ladle,[6]

though he was taught to aim with Chinese arrows[7]
upon his father's bow? Who would deny   10
    that downward-rushing rivers could flow backward
        up lofty peaks and Tiber change its course,

when *you* aspire to trade the books of famed
Panaetius,[8] purchased the whole world over,
    as well as Socrates's school,[9] for Spanish   15
        breastplates? You led us to expect much better!

---

1. *Odes* 1.29 (*Alcaic Strophe*): Horace addresses a man named Iccius, also the recipient of *Epistles* 1.12, about whom little else is known for certain. In both the epistle and the ode, he is given to extremes, inconsistent, and eager for wealth. Here, his previous love of philosophy is too easily replaced by a desire for eastern wealth. The tone of Horace's critique has been debated—is it playfully teasing or more severe?

2. **happy wealth of the Arabs:** Arabia was proverbially wealthy. The word *beatis* (happy) is pointed—Iccius falsely believes that such wealth can provide him with happiness.

3. **harsh . . . kings:** In 26 B.C.E., Aelius Gallus led (unsuccessfully) a campaign against the Sabaeans, an Arab group in what is now Yemen.

4. **Mede:** That is, Parthian.

5. **barbarian:** See note at *Epodes* 5.61.

6. **will be set up . . . ladle:** The royal boy will become Iccius's cupbearer—and probably exploited in sexual bondage as a *puer delicatus*, a slave favorite. The Latin word *statuetur* (will be set up) suggests also the idea of a "statue." That is, the boy is one of the artistic and valuable "objects" Iccius hope to acquire.

7. **Chinese arrows:** The boy is highborn, as his imported Chinese arrows indicate.

8. **famed Panaetius:** A second-century B.C.E. Stoic philosopher, credited with introducing the philosophy to Rome.

9. **Socrates's school:** Many different philosophical systems traced themselves back to Socrates, but the mention of Panaetius would suggest Stoicism.

ODES 1.30

O Venus, regina Cnidi Paphique,
sperne dilectam Cypron et vocantis
ture te multo Glycerae decoram
        transfer in aedem.

fervidus tecum puer et solutis   5
Gratiae zonis properentque Nymphae
et parum comis sine te Iuventas
        Mercuriusque.

ODES 1.30[1]

O Venus, queen of Cnidus and of Paphos,
spurn your beloved Cyprus[2] and transfer
yourself to Glycera's fair shrine[3]—with much
        incense she summons.

And may your fiery boy rush forth with you,   5
along with Graces (belts undone) and Nymphs
and Youthfulness, whose charm is lost without you—
        Mercury also.[4]

---

1. *Odes* 1.30 (*Sapphic Strophe*): A short **cletic hymn** to Venus. The speaker asks Venus
   to leave her favored cities and come instead to the house/shrine of a woman named
   Glycera (Sweetie), most likely a prostitute, for whom Venus would be the patron
   goddess.
2. **Cnidus . . . Paphos . . . Cyprus:** Three locales sacred to Venus. Cnidus was a city
   in Asia Minor, where in antiquity one could see the famous Aphrodite statue of
   Praxiteles. Paphos was a city on the southwest coast of the island Cyprus.
3. **shrine:** The word *aedes* can refer to a temple, a shrine, or a house. Horace may be
   suggesting that Glycera has a shrine to Venus within her house or even that the entire
   house, as a locus of prostitution, was something of a shrine to Venus.
4. **Mercury also:** Nisbet and Hubbard (1970) as well as Mayer (2012) suggest that
   Mercury is invoked here as a god of persuasion, which would be useful in seduction.
   The ancient scholiast pseudo-Acro notes that, if Glycera is a prostitute, she may want
   his presence rather as a god of business and financial gain.

ODES 1.31

Quid dedicatum poscit Apollinem
vates? quid orat de patera novum
      fundens liquorem? non opimae
          Sardiniae segetes feraces,

non aestuosae grata Calabriae   5
armenta, non aurum aut ebur Indicum,
      non rura quae Liris quieta
          mordet aqua taciturnus amnis.

premant Calenam falce quibus dedit
Fortuna vitem, dives et aureis   10
      mercator exsiccet culullis
          vina Syra reparata merce,

dis carus ipsis, quippe ter et quater
anno revisens aequor Atlanticum

ODES 1.31[1]

What does the bard[2] request of consecrated
Apollo?[3] What entreat while from the bowl
  he pours new liquid?[4] Not the overflowing
    cornfields of bountiful Sardinia,[5]

and not the pleasant herds of sweltering   5
Calabria,[6] not gold or Indian ivory,
  and not the fields that Liris[7] eats away
    with its unhurried flow, a silent river.

Those to whom Fortune gave Calenian vines[8]
can prune them with a sickle. Let the wealthy   10
  merchant drain dry from golden cups the wines
    that he obtained with Syrian merchandise.[9]

The gods must love him since he goes each year
three or four times to the Atlantic Ocean,[10]

1. *Odes* 1.31 (*Alcaic Strophe*): The speaker of this ode assumes the role of a divinely
 inspired bard (*vates*) considering what is a worthy request to make of the god Apollo.
 The **persona** of the *vates* suggests a public role, but the prayer itself pertains to
 the speaker's private, individual life. The occasion seems to be the festival of the
 Meditrinalia on October 11, when the newly made vintage was presented to the gods.
2. **bard:** For *vates* (bard), see note at *Odes* 1.1.35.
3. **consecrated Apollo:** A reference to the new Temple of Apollo commissioned
 by Augustus and consecrated on October 9, 28 B.C.E. The god here stands
 metonymically for his temple.
4. **new liquid:** That is, the new vintage.
5. **cornfields . . . Sardinia:** The island Sardinia was one of the major sources of grain for
 the Romans.
6. **Calabria:** A region located at the "toe" of the Italian peninsula.
7. **Liris:** A river that ran between Latium and Campania. This was a region known for
 producing fine wine.
8. **Calenian vines:** Calenian was a highly regarded Campanian wine.
9. **Syrian merchandise:** Syria was at the crossroads of several major trade routes that
 crossed the ancient Mediterranean.
10. **Atlantic Ocean:** The merchant's travels take him the full span of the
 Mediterranean, from Syria in the east through to the Atlantic in the west. As Mayer
 (2012) notes, he is probably headed to the Roman province of Baetica, located in
 southern Spain.

impune. me pascunt olivae,   15
    me cichorea levesque malvae.

frui paratis et valido mihi,
Latoe, dones, at, precor, integra
    cum mente, nec turpem senectam
        degere nec cithara carentem.   20

unpunished. As for me, I feed on olives,   15
　　endive, and mallow—easy to digest.

May you grant me to savor what I have
in good health, son of Leto[11]—but, I pray,
　　with mind intact, and let me pass old age
　　　　that's neither frail nor lacks the cithara.[12]   20

---

11. **son of Leto**: Apollo.
12. **cithara**: A stringed instrument similar to the lyre.

ODES 1.32

Poscimur. si quid vacui sub umbra
lusimus tecum, quod et hunc in annum
vivat et pluris, age dic Latinum,
      barbite, carmen,

Lesbio primum modulate civi,   5
qui ferox bello, tamen inter arma
sive iactatam religarat udo
      litore navim,

Liberum et Musas Veneremque et illi
semper haerentem puerum canebat   10
et Lycum nigris oculis nigroque
      crine decorum.

o decus Phoebi et dapibus supremi
grata testudo Iovis, o laborum
dulce lenimen, mihi cumque salve   15
      rite vocanti.

ODES 1.32[1]

We are requested.[2] If beneath the shade
we leisurely have played[3] upon you something
to live this year and more, come sing a Latin
      poem, O lyre,

which first the citizen of Lesbos[4] tuned.   5
Though fierce in war, when he was not in battle
or if he had tied up his storm-tossed ship[5]
      to the wet seashore,

he would sing songs of Liber and the Muses,
of Venus and the boy stuck to her always,[6]   10
of Lycus[7] also, whose dark eyes and dark
      hair made him lovely.

O turtle shell,[8] you charm of Phoebus,[9] welcome
at feasts of highest Jove, O sweet reliever
of labors, hear my call whenever I   15
      summon you duly.

---

1. ***Odes* 1.32** (*Sapphic Strophe*): A **hymn** to his lyre, which he invokes as though a god. West (1995, 153–54) lays out the many elements it has in common with traditional prayers, from the use of the vocative case to the recounting of the lyre's past feats and the request for a benefaction.
2. **We are requested:** If this reading is right, it would suggest the poem is performed by request or even is written on commission—but it is not clear who the requestor or commissioner would be. Another manuscript reading is *poscimus* (we request), which would initiate the prayer to the lyre. Horace's use of the first-person plural "we" suggests his role as a public poet, but by line 15 Horace employs instead the more personal first-person singular.
3. **played:** The word *lusi* suggests playful verse, i.e., non-epic poetry.
4. **citizen of Lesbos:** Alcaeus.
5. **storm-tossed ship:** Two of Alcaeus's fragments (6 and 208) are about a storm-tossed ship. See the introductory note to *Odes* 1.14.
6. **boy stuck to her always:** Cupid.
7. **Lycus:** Unknown from what survives of Alcaeus's verse, but clearly here his pederastic beloved.
8. **turtle shell:** According to myth, the god Mercury invented the lyre using a hollow turtle shell.
9. **charm of Phoebus:** Apollo was associated with the lyre and lyric poetry.

ODES 1.33

Albi, ne doleas plus nimio memor
immitis Glycerae neu miserabilis
decantes elegos, cur tibi iunior
    laesa praeniteat fide,

insignem tenui fronte Lycorida   5
Cyri torret amor, Cyrus in asperam
declinat Pholoen; sed prius Apulis
    iungentur capreae lupis,

quam turpi Pholoe peccet adultero.
sic visum Veneri, cui placet imparis   10
formas atque animos sub iuga aenea
    saevo mittere cum ioco.

ipsum me melior cum peteret Venus,
grata detinuit compede Myrtale
libertina, fretis acrior Hadriae   15
    curvantis Calabros sinus.

ODES 1.33[1]

Albius,[2] do not grieve too much, recalling
harsh Glycera,[3] nor keep on singing wretched
elegies asking why she broke her faith
      and now a younger man[4] outshines you.

Beautiful with her slender brow, Lycoris   5
blazes with love for Cyrus. Cyrus leans
toward bitter Pholoe. But goats would sooner
      mate with Apulian lions than

Pholoe trespass with an ugly lover.
This pleases Venus. She delights in sending   10
conflicting forms and minds beneath her yoke[5]
      of bronze. It is her savage joke.

When a nobler Venus sought out me myself,
Myrtale held me in her pleasant shackle—
freedwoman fiercer than the Adriatic,   15
      which hollows out Calabrian bays.[6]

---

1. *Odes* 1.33 (*Third Asclepiadean*): The speaker of this ode argues for restraint when it comes to the kind of lament familiar from erotic elegy, in which a lover bemoans his mistress's failure to reciprocate his affection.
2. **Albius:** This may be the elegiac poet Albius Tibullus, whose poetry still survives. Horace addresses him in *Epistles* 1.4 as well.
3. **harsh Glycera:** The name Glycera means something like "sweetie pie," which forms a *callida iunctura* with "harsh."
4. **younger man:** The rival was a **stock figure** of elegiac poetry.
5. **beneath her yoke:** Suggests "subjugation" (literally sending someone "beneath a yoke"). Horace presents erotic love as a kind of domination, a view in line with that of the elegists, who frequently develop the **metaphor** of *servitium amoris*.
6. **Adriatic . . . Calabrian bays:** Horace has in mind here the Gulf of Tarentum, which carves out the "heel" of Italy.

ODES 1.34

Parcus deorum cultor et infrequens
insanientis dum sapientiae
      consultus erro, nunc retrorsum
         vela dare atque iterare cursus

cogor relictos: namque Diespiter,   5
igni corusco nubila dividens
      plerumque, per purum tonantis
         egit equos volucremque currum,

quo bruta tellus et vaga flumina,
quo Styx et invisi horrida Taenari   10
      sedes Atlanteusque finis
         concutitur. valet ima summis

mutare et insignem attenuat deus,
obscura promens; hinc apicem rapax
      fortuna cum stridore acuto   15
         sustulit, hic posuisse gaudet.

ODES 1.34[1]

I was a scarce, infrequent worshipper
of gods, while I was erring as an expert
      in an insane philosophy.[2] Now I
           am forced to set sail backward and repeat

the course I left behind. For Jupiter—   5
who breaks through rain-clouds with his flashing fire,
      most of the time—propelled his thundering steeds
           and flying chariot through a clear blue sky.

At this the heavy earth and rambling rivers,
at this the Styx and horrid home of loathed   10
      Taenarus and the boundary of Atlas[3]
           convulsed. God[4] has the power to exchange

the lofty and the low. He shrinks the grand,
brings the obscure to view. From this man greedy
      Fortune with high-pitched shrieking takes away   15
           the crown, gleeful to place it on another.

---

1. **Odes** 1.34 (*Alcaic Strophe*): This ode has often been read as a recantation of
Epicureanism, a philosophy that denied the gods' involvement in human affairs and
celestial phenomena. The speaker says he was proven wrong by thunder on a clear
day, which he took as proof of Jupiter's involvement in the world of nature. Others,
for example Fain (2006), see here a reference to the instable world of Roman politics
and military affairs. Perhaps the most profound imitation of this poem is Seamus
Heaney's "Anything Can Happen," a meditation on September 11, 2001.
2. **philosophy**: The Latin word *sapientia* (wisdom) suggests not just the abstract quality
but the more concrete idea of "philosophy" or even "philosophical school."
3. **Styx . . . Taenarus . . . boundary of Atlas**: The Styx was the best known river in
the underworld. Taenarus, in the Peloponnese, was thought to have an entrance to
Hades. Atlas was the Titan who held up the heavens far in the west.
4. **God**: The word *deus* (god) here could refer specifically to Jupiter or generally to
"God" or "divine power."

ODES 1.35

O diva, gratum quae regis Antium,
praesens vel imo tollere de gradu
      mortale corpus vel superbos
          vertere funeribus triumphos,

te pauper ambit sollicita prece   5
ruris colonus, te dominam aequoris
      quicumque Bithyna lacessit
          Carpathium pelagus carina.

te Dacus asper, te profugi Scythae,
urbesque gentesque et Latium ferox   10
      regumque matres barbarorum et
          purpurei metuunt tyranni,

iniurioso ne pede proruas
stantem columnam, neu populus frequens
      ad arma cessantis, ad arma   15
          concitet imperiumque frangat.

ODES 1.35[1]

You, goddess, who rule charming Antium,[2]
ready to lift up from the lowest rung
    a mortal body or transform triumphal
        processions into funeral parades,

to you the needy rustic farmer prays   5
with anxious plea; to you, the ocean's mistress,
    he prays, whoever harries the Carpathian
        sea with a vessel from Bithynia.[3]

You the harsh Dacian fears; you, fleeing Scythians.[4]
Cities and nations, even warlike Latium,   10
    the mothers of barbarian[5] kings, and tyrants
        bedecked in purple are afraid that you

might topple over with your deadly foot
the standing pillar, that the thronging crowd
    might instigate the hesitant to arms,   15
        to arms,[6] and crash to pieces their dominion.

---

1. *Odes* 1.35 (*Alcaic Strophe*): A lengthy and difficult **hymn** to the goddess Fortuna (whom Horace never names but who is mentioned at the end of the previous ode). She is the principal of chance that can bring blessings or destruction to individuals and states (both the rulers and the ruled). In the concluding stanzas we learn that the prayer is designed to make two requests: (a) Fortune's favor for Augustus as he prepares to strike against foreign foes and (b) Fortune's aid in redirecting violence away from internal civil war and toward exterior expansion.
2. **Antium:** Modern Anzio, on the coast of Latium.
3. **Carpathian . . . Bithynia:** The Carpathian sea consists of the waters surrounding the island Carpathos in the southeastern Aegean. Bithynia, in the northern part of Asia Minor, was a major producer of the timber used to build boats.
4. **Dacian . . . Scythian:** The Dacians lived to the west of the Black Sea, the Scythians north of the Black Sea.
5. **barbarian:** See note at *Epodes* 5.61.
6. **to arms, to arms:** The repetition mimics the mob's cry as they go to overthrow the powerful.

te semper anteit saeva Necessitas,
clavos trabalis et cuneos manu
      gestans aena, nec severus
          uncus abest liquidumque plumbum.   20

te Spes et albo rara Fides colit
velata panno, nec comitem abnegat,
      utcumque mutata potentis
          veste domos inimica linquis.

at vulgus infidum et meretrix retro   25
periura cedit, diffugiunt cadis
      cum faece siccatis amici
          ferre iugum pariter dolosi.

serves iturum Caesarem in ultimos
orbis Britannos et iuvenum recens   30
      examen Eois timendum
          partibus Oceanoque rubro.

eheu, cicatricum et sceleris pudet
fratrumque. quid nos dura refugimus
      aetas? quid intactum nefasti   35
          liquimus? unde manum iuventus

Ahead of you there always goes ferocious
Necessity.[7] In her bronze hand she carries
  beam nails and wedges, nor does she leave out
   the unforgiving hook and molten lead. 20

With you go Hope and scarce-found Loyalty,
enveloped in white rags. They do not shirk
  companionship when you, your clothing changed,
   abandon mighty houses, now unfriendly.[8]

But the unfaithful mob—a lying whore— 25
shrinks back, and fleeing everywhere go friends
  who drain the wine jugs to the dregs and yet
   don't keep their word when asked to
    share the yoke.

Watch over Caesar, setting out against
the world's most distant Britons, and the latest 30
  swarm of young men, who will awaken terror
   within the eastern regions and Red Sea.[9]

Alas! How shameful are the scars, the crime,
the brothers![10] What do we, a hardened age,
  refuse? What have we left untouched in all 35
   our wickedness? From what have our young men

---

7. **ferocious Necessity:** The goddess Necessity represents what was simply inescapable and inevitable owing to the operations of Fortuna. She carries implements whose function is unclear. Some see them as devices of torture; others, as tools she will use to build an edifice that cannot be altered and from which escape is impossible.
8. **when you . . . unfriendly:** The meaning of this stanza, which West (1995, 170) calls "one of the most difficult passages in Horace," is much debated. One major point of contention is whose companions Hope and Faith continue to be when Fortune departs. Do they stay with Fortune and abandon the powerful with her, or do they remain with the powerful after she goes (unlike the faithless friends of the next stanza)?
9. **Britons . . . Red Sea:** Augustus seems to have made several plans to launch an expedition against Britain, but he never followed through on them. For Aelius Gallus's unsuccessful campaign in Arabia, see the note at *Odes* 1.29.3.
10. **scars . . . crimes . . . brothers:** Mayer (2012) sums up the thought here as "the criminal wounds brothers have inflicted upon each other in civil war."

metu deorum continuit? quibus
pepercit aris? o utinam nova
   incude diffingas retusum in
      Massagetas Arabasque ferrum!   40

held back their hands in fear of gods? What altars
have they not harmed? I wish you would remake
    your blunted sword upon a brand new anvil
        to strike the Massagetae[11] and the Arabs!   40

---

11. **Massagetae:** A tribe northeast of the Caspian Sea.

ODES 1.36

Et ture et fidibus iuvat
placare et vituli sanguine debito
    custodes Numidae deos,
qui nunc Hesperia sospes ab ultima

    caris multa sodalibus,   5
nulli plura tamen dividit oscula
    quam dulci Lamiae, memor
actae non alio rege puertiae

    mutataeque simul togae.
Cressa ne careat pulchra dies nota,   10
    neu promptae modus amphorae,
neu morem in Salium sit requies pedum,

    neu multi Damalis meri
Bassum Threicia vincat amystide,
    neu desint epulis rosae   15
neu vivax apium neu breve lilium.

ODES 1.36[1]

> With incense, lyre, and the promised
> blood of a calf[2] it's pleasing to appease
>   the guardian gods of Numida,
> who now, safe from the farthest western land,
>
>   gives many kisses to dear comrades,   5
> and yet to no one does he give more kisses
>   than his sweet Lamia,[3] recalling
> his boyhood passed with no one else his king[4]
>
>   and the togas they exchanged together.[5]
> Let this fair day not lack the Cretan mark.[6]   10
>   Let's fetch the wine and not refrain!
> Our feet should have no rest from Salian dances.[7]
>
>   Let Damalis—she downs neat wine—
> not conquer Bassus[8] in the Thracian guzzling.[9]
>   Let there be roses at the feasts   15
> and long-lived celery and fleeting lilies.

---

1. **Odes 1.36** (*Second Asclepiadean*): A poem extolling the return of a man named Numida (otherwise unknown), most likely from a campaign in Spain under Augustus from 27 to 25 B.C.E. The ode celebrates the friendship between Numida and another man named Lamia, whereupon Horace describes the festive banquets to come. The exuberant drinking and Salian dances anticipate the following ode on the defeat of Cleopatra.

2. **promised . . . calf**: A sacrifice had been vowed, probably by Lamia, in exchange for Numida's safe return.

3. **Lamia**: On Lamia, see note at *Odes* 1.26.8.

4. **no one else his king**: Mayer (2012) suggests this marks Lamia as "the acknowledged superior of the two." There were also childhood games, mentioned by Horace in *Epistles* 1.1.59, in which the leading boy was called "king."

5. **togas . . . together**: This suggests Lamia and Numida were age-mates and would have exchanged the *toga praetexta* (which had a purple border) for the *toga virilis* (which was all white) in the same year. This normally occurred at the age of fifteen or sixteen.

6. **Cretan mark**: Days of good fortune were marked on the calendar with white chalk (*creta*). Horace is punning on the similarity of *creta* (chalk) and *Creta* (Crete).

7. **Salian dances**: See note at *Odes* 1.37.3.

8. **Damalis . . . Bassus**: Otherwise unknown attendees at the symposium to come.

9. **Thracian guzzling**: A drinking game that involved draining cups as quickly as possible.

omnes in Damalin putris
deponent oculos, nec Damalis novo
divelletur adultero
lascivis hederis ambitiosior.   20

On Damalis will everyone
lay melting eyes, but Damalis will not
        be torn away from her new lover.
Tighter than lustful ivy she entwines him.   20

ODES 1.37

Nunc est bibendum, nunc pede libero
pulsanda tellus, nunc Saliaribus
    ornare pulvinar deorum
        tempus erat dapibus, sodales.

antehac nefas depromere Caecubum   5
cellis avitis, dum Capitolio
    regina dementis ruinas
        funus et imperio parabat

contaminato cum grege turpium
morbo virorum, quidlibet impotens   10
    sperare fortunaque dulci
        ebria. Sed minuit furorem

vix una sospes navis ab ignibus,
mentemque lymphatam Mareotico

ODES 1.37[1]

Now we must drink, now pound upon the earth
with a free foot.[2] Now it is past the time
    to ornament the couches of the gods
        with banquets of the Salii,[3] my comrades.[4]

Before, it was a sin to bring Caecuban[5]   5
out of ancestral cellars, while the queen
    was plotting for the Capitol insane[6]
        destruction and a funeral for the empire,

alongside her polluted herd of men
foul with disease.[7] She had no self-control   10
    to check her hopes, and on sweet fortune she
        was drunk. But having scarcely just one ship

safe from the flames diminished all her madness.
Her mind, diluted by Egyptian wine,

---

1. **Odes 1.37** (*Alcaic Strophe*): The ode celebrates Augustus's defeat of Cleopatra at Actium in 31 B.C.E. and her death by suicide the following year. Although Horace draws extensively on the negative propaganda directed toward Cleopatra in the years surrounding her defeat, he nevertheless paints a highly complex portrait of the Egyptian queen. She is at once a crazed woman, a trembling victim, and a worthy foe that bravely and fearlessly undertakes her own death. Horace significantly never mentions her ally and consort Mark Antony.
2. **free foot:** The foot is "free" (*liber*) for multiple reasons: (a) they are shoeless, (b) the dancing is unrestrained, (c) they are drunk (the god of wine, Bacchus, also went by the name Liber in Rome), and (d) Cleopatra's tyranny is no longer a threat.
3. **banquets of the Salii:** The Salii were priests of Mars, god of war, known for their lavish banquets and rhythmic dancing.
4. **Now we must drink . . . comrades:** Horace opens the poem with a rhetorical tour de force. The **alliterative** *pede . . . pulsanda* echoes the pounding of the earth in the dance. The triple **anaphora** of *nunc* (now) forms a **tricolon**, and Horace stresses the urgency of his demands with **asyndeton**.
5. **Caecuban:** A native Italian wine.
6. **insane:** A **transferred epithet**. She is the one "insane," but Horace applies the adjective to the destruction she would bring. Compare "pompous" in the last stanza.
7. **foul with disease:** Horace has in mind here the customary presence of eunuchs in the Egyptian court.

redegit in veros timores   15
    Caesar ab Italia volantem

remis adurgens, accipiter velut
mollis columbas aut leporem citus
    venator in campis nivalis
        Haemoniae, daret ut catenis   20

fatale monstrum; quae generosius
perire quaerens nec muliebriter
    expavit ensem nec latentis
        classe cita reparavit oras;

ausa et iacentem visere regiam   25
voltu sereno, fortis et asperas
    tractare serpentes, ut atrum
        corpore combiberet venenum,

deliberata morte ferocior,
saevis Liburnis scilicet invidens   30
    privata deduci superbo
        non humilis mulier triumpho.

was made to face the terrifying truth   15
    when Caesar,[8] as she flew from Italy,

chased after her with oars, just as an eagle
pursues soft pigeons or a speedy hunter
    a hare within the open fields of snowy
        Thessaly, so that he could put in chains   20

the deadly monster.[9] She, desiring
to die more nobly, neither like a woman
    grew frightened at the sword nor came ashore
        at hidden beaches with her speedy fleet.

She even dared to view her toppled palace   25
with a serene face and was brave enough
    to handle scaly serpents so she might
        drink into her own body their black poison,

fiercer because of her deliberate death—
begrudging to the cruel Liburnians[10]   30
    that she, a queen no longer, be paraded
        (no lowly woman!) in a pompous triumph.

---

8. **Caesar:** This refers to Augustus. His name is pointedly at the **pivot** or center of the poem.
9. **deadly monster:** The Latin *monstrum* suggests not only that Cleopatra was a "monster" Augustus had to conquer but also that she was a "portent" (*moneo* = to warn) of fatal danger. Portents were thought to be of unnatural origin; as Nisbet and Hubbard (1970) point out, Cleopatra's incestuous origins—her parents were most likely the brother-sister pair Ptolemy XI and Cleopatra V—would have qualified her as such.
10. **Liburnians:** The warships used by Augustus at Actium.

ODES 1.38

Persicos odi, puer, apparatus,
displicent nexae philyra coronae;
mitte sectari, rosa quo locorum
     sera moretur.

simplici myrto nihil allabores   5
sedulus curo: neque te ministrum
dedecet myrtus neque me sub arta
     vite bibentem.

ODES 1.38[1]

I loathe, slave-boy, the finery of Persia.[2]
Garlands entwined with linden[3] do not please me.
Stop looking for the places where a late
      rose is remaining.

That you not overwork the simple myrtle[4]   5
is my main care. Myrtle befits both you,
my slave, and me, while I drink underneath
      tightly packed vine-leaves.[5]

---

1. *Odes* 1.38 (*Sapphic Strophe*): A deceptively simple ode in which the speaker urges his slave to exercise restraint when preparing for a simple symposium at which Horace will be the only drinker. The solo drinking party offers a contrast with the communal drinking of the previous ode, and closes the book on a private rather than a public note.
2. **finery of Persia**: The east was often associated with luxury and wealth.
3. **entwined with linden**: The bark of the linden tree was used to weave together flowers into more elaborate arrangements.
4. **simple myrtle**: Myrtle was often interwoven with other plants, but Horace here requests myrtle alone.
5. **tightly packed vine-leaves**: As Garrison (1991) notes here, "Horace pictures himself outdoors under a trellis or *pergola* of vines that have been pruned to stimulate the growth of leaves for denser shade."

ODES 2

ODES 2.1

Motum ex Metello consule civicum
bellique causas et vitia et modos
        ludumque Fortunae gravisque
                principum amicitias et arma

ODES 2.1[1]

The civic turmoil since Metellus was consul,[2]
war's causes and its evils and its modes,
    the game of Fortune and the burdensome
        friendships among the foremost men,[3]
           the weapons

---

1. *Odes* 2.1 (*Alcaic Strophe*): This ode celebrates a (now lost) historical work by Gaius Asinius Pollio dealing with the civil wars that arose in the late republic. Pollio was also a tragedian and eminent Roman statesman, having held the position of consul in 40 B.C.E. He is named as a patron of Vergil's early poetry in *Eclogues* 3, 4, and 8. Throughout the poem, Horace contrasts his own unwarlike lyric with the weighty, even dangerous themes of history. The poem looks back to Horace's earlier poetic treatments of Actium and civil war, especially *Epodes* 7 and 16, as well as *Odes* 1.2. Throughout the second book my notes are indebted to the commentaries of Nisbet and Hubbard (1978), Garrison (1991), and Harrison (2017). West (1998) also offers a helpful reading of each poem.

2. **civic . . . consul:** Horace opens the second book with yet another untranslatable stylistic tour de force. The opening line combines **alliteration** (of *m, c, t*), **assonance** (of long *o*, "*mo̲tum Metello̲*"), and **chiasm** (*motum* ex Me̲te̲llo̲ co̲n̲su̲le̲ *civicum* = *abba*). Quintus Metellus Celer was consul in 60 B.C.E. This year marked the alliance between Julius Caesar and Pompey the Great that, when Crassus joined the following year, would become known as the First Triumvirate.

3. **friendships . . . men:** A reference to the alliance (often euphemistically referred to as "friendship") of the First Triumvirate.

nondum expiatis uncta cruoribus,   5
periculosae plenum opus aleae,
  tractas, et incedis per ignis
    suppositos cineri doloso.

paulum severae Musa tragoediae
desit theatris: mox ubi publicas   10
  res ordinaris, grande munus
    Cecropio repetes coturno,

insigne maestis praesidium reis
et consulenti, Pollio, curiae,
  cui laurus aeternos honores   15
    Delmatico peperit triumpho.

iam nunc minaci murmure cornuum
perstringis auris, iam litui strepunt,
  iam fulgor armorum fugaces
    terret equos equitumque vultus.   20

audire magnos iam videor duces
non indecoro pulvere sordidos,
  et cuncta terrarum subacta
    praeter atrocem animum Catonis.

covered with carnage not yet expiated—   5
a work abounding in precarious chance[4]—
    these are the themes you handle, and you walk
        through fires placed beneath deceptive ash.

May tragedy's stern Muse quit theaters
for just a while. When soon you have recorded   10
    public affairs, then you will seek once more
        your weighty duty in the Attic buskin,[5]

you famed protector of your sad defendants,
Pollio, and of the consulting senate.
    To you the laurel bore eternal honors   15
        during your triumph over the Dalmatians.[6]

Already with the threatening blasts of horns
you grate the ears, already trumpets roar,
    already now the flash of weapons panics
        the fleeing horses and the horsemen's faces.   20

Already now I seem to hear of mighty
leaders begrimed with dust not unbecoming
    and everything in all the world subdued—
        but not the unrelenting mind of Cato.[7]

---

4. **chance**: Horace suggests that writing contemporary history is a risky enterprise. Literally, *alea*, translated "chance," is a "die" used in gambling. Horace likely alludes to Caesar's famous phrase *alea iacta est* (the die has been cast), which Pollio's history no doubt recorded.

5. **Attic buskin**: That is, tragedy. Early tragedy was an especially Athenian phenomenon. The buskin was a boot worn by tragic actors and became a **metonymy** to indicate tragedy itself.

6. **laurel . . . Dalmatian triumph**: In October of 39/38 B.C.E., Pollio celebrated a triumph over the Parthini in Dalmatia. Triumphant generals wore a wreath of laurel, which became synonymous with victory.

7. **Cato**: Marcus Porcius Cato Uticensis killed himself in Utica (in North Africa) in 46 B.C.E. rather than submit to Julius Caesar. He became an exemplar of Stoic suicide and resistance for later Romans living under the empire.

Iuno et deorum quisquis amicior   25
Afris inulta cesserat impotens
    tellure victorum nepotes
        rettulit inferias Iugurthae.

quis non Latino sanguine pinguior
campus sepulcris impia proelia   30
    testatur auditumque Medis
        Hesperiae sonitum ruinae?

qui gurges aut quae flumina lugubris
ignara belli? quod mare Dauniae
    non decoloravere caedes?   35
        quae caret ora cruore nostro?

sed ne relictis, Musa procax, iocis
Ceae retractes munera neniae,
    mecum Dionaeo sub antro
        quaere modos leviore plectro.   40

Juno[8] and all the gods that were in favor   25
of Africa but, seething, left the land
    still unavenged[9] have now brought back the victors'
        grandsons as sacrifices to Jugurtha.[10]

What field, more fertile due to Latin blood,
does not bear witness with its graves to our   30
    impious battles and the loud collapse
        of Italy, which even Medes[11] could hear?

What whirlpools or what rivers do not know
about this mournful war? Is there a sea
    the slaughter of the Daunians[12] has not stained?   35
        Where is a shore that does not hold our carnage?

But, brazen Muse, do not abandon trifles,
handling instead the Cean dirge's rites.[13]
    With me beneath a grotto of Dione[14]
        seek out the modes that suit a lighter
            plectrum.[15]   40

---

8. **Juno**: Roman goddess identified with the Carthaginian Tanit. Her favoritism of Carthage features prominently in Vergil's *Aeneid*.

9. **still unavenged**: That is, in the Third Punic War, when, Horace states, the gods who had favored Carthage abandoned the city.

10. **Jugurtha**: Horace suggests that Roman civil bloodshed at the Battle of Thapsus and in the North African campaigns of 46 B.C.E. was atonement for the defeats suffered at the hands of the Romans by the North African king Jugurtha in 104 B.C.E.

11. **Medes**: The Parthians.

12. **Daunians**: Daunus was the legendary founder of Apulia, the Italian region of which Horace himself was a native. Horace uses the region as a **synecdoche** for all Italy but also suggests his own personal stake in the war.

13. **Cean dirge's rites**: Refers to Simonides of Ceos, whose lyric poems feature laments or **dirges**.

14. **grotto of Dione**: Dione was the mother of Venus. Horace thus suggests that his Muse resume amatory themes appropriate to lyric.

15. **plectrum**: The plectrum was the instrument used to strum the lyre and stands here for lyric itself.

ODES 2.2

Nullus argento color est avaris
abdito terris, inimice lamnae
Crispe Sallusti, nisi temperato
    splendeat usu.

vivet extento Proculeius aevo,   5
notus in fratres animi paterni;
illum aget pinna metuente solvi
    Fama superstes.

latius regnes avidum domando
spiritum, quam si Libyam remotis   10
Gadibus iungas et uterque Poenus
    serviat uni.

crescit indulgens sibi dirus hydrops,
nec sitim pellas, nisi causa morbi

ODES 2.2[1]

There is no sheen for silver when it's hidden[2]
beneath the greedy earth, Sallustius Crispus,
you enemy to coin unless it gleams with
    moderate spending.

With life prolonged will Proculeius[3] live,   5
known for paternal feeling toward his brothers.
On wings afraid to melt[4] will everlasting
    Glory convey him.

You'll rule a broader kingdom if you tame
your greedy soul than if you fastened Libya   10
to distant Gades and each Punic people[5]
    slaved for you only.

Dreadful edema[6] grows when it's indulged.
You can't be rid of thirst unless the source

---

1. **Odes 2.2** (*Sapphic Strophe*): An ethical meditation on the appropriate use of and attitude toward wealth addressed to Gaius Sallustius Crispus, the great-nephew and adopted heir of the historian Sallust. The pronounced Stoic flavor of the poem suggests that Sallustius was perhaps drawn to that particular philosophical school, though Horace's own famous concern with moderation ("the golden mean") runs through the poem as well.

2. **when it's hidden**: This probably refers to a miser's burial of treasure. The implication in these opening lines is that money must be put to proper use, subject to the extremes neither of greedy hoarding nor of lavish prodigality.

3. **Proculeius**: The ancient commentator Porphyrio says that Proculeius was an equestrian and a friend of Augustus who divided his property with his brothers after they lost their estate in civil war. His fraternal goodwill is noteworthy since brothers were thought to be prone to competitive and often violent wrangling, especially over issues of money and inheritance.

4. **afraid to melt**: Most commentators see an allusion here to the doomed flight of Icarus, who failed to observe the mean between the extremes of heaven and earth.

5. **Libya . . . Gades . . . each Punic people**: Libya is the home of Carthage, whose inhabitants were known as "Punic," and Gades (modern Cádiz) is a Carthaginian colony in southwest Spain.

6. **edema**: Once known as dropsy, this is a swelling caused by excess fluid. The ancients thought it was both caused by and resulted in thirst. It was often used as an analogy for avarice, which similarly feeds itself and cannot be sated.

fugerit venis et aquosus albo   15
    corpore languor.

redditum Cyri solio Phraaten
dissidens plebi numero beatorum
eximit Virtus, populumque falsis
    dedocet uti   20

vocibus, regnum et diadema tutum
deferens uni propriamque laurum,
quisquis ingentis oculo irretorto
    spectat acervos.

of sickness leaves the veins and watery   15
    sloth the pale body.

Phraates sits restored on Cyrus' throne,[7]
but Virtue, clashing with the plebs, expels
him from the number of the blessed and makes
    people unlearn how   20

to use false words. It gives a stable realm
and crown and lasting laurel[8] to just one:
he who can glimpse, his eye not turning back,[9]
    mountainous stockpiles.

---

7. **Phraates . . . Cyrus' throne**: Phraates was the newly restored king of the Persians/ Parthians (of whom Cyrus was a famous king), which dates the poem to after 25 B.C.E.

8. **laurel**: Triumphant victors wore a laurel wreath, so the word came to be synonymous with "victory." This is the third and therefore most emphasized element in an **ascending tricolon**.

9. **eye not turning back**: That is, not turning back to continue gazing at the riches.

ODES 2.3

Aequam memento rebus in arduis
servare mentem, non secus in bonis
    ab insolenti temperatam
        laetitia, moriture Delli,

seu maestus omni tempore vixeris,   5
seu te in remoto gramine per dies
    festos reclinatum bearis
        interiore nota Falerni.

quo pinus ingens albaque populus
umbram hospitalem consociare amant   10
    ramis? quid obliquo laborat
        lympha fugax trepidare rivo?

huc vina et unguenta et nimium brevis
flores amoenae ferre iube rosae,
    dum res et aetas et sororum   15
        fila trium patiuntur atra.

ODES 2.3[1]

In arduous circumstances don't forget
to keep a level head,[2] and in success
      one likewise that is tempered from extreme
          rejoicing, Dellius, since you're bound to die

whether you live each moment sorrowful   5
or else, stretched out upon secluded grass,
      you cheer yourself on every festive day
          with an expensive bottle of Falernian.[3]

Why do the massive pine tree and white poplar
love to unite their shade to welcome guests   10
      beneath their branches? Why in slanting banks
          does rushing water toil to go so fast?

Order that there be brought here wines and perfumes
and pleasant rose's all too fleeting flowers,
      as long as circumstances and our age   15
          and the three sisters' deadly threads allow.[4]

---

1. *Odes* 2.3 (*Alcaic Strophe*): A well-loved ode that combines many key Horatian themes: equanimity and moderation, the importance of focusing on the moment at hand, the inevitability of death, the common mortality of both rich and poor, and the symposium as a locus of present enjoyment. Like Pollio of 2.1, Dellius seems to have been a historian embroiled in the politics of civil war. Ancient sources record that he frequently switched sides between Antony and Octavian. Seneca the Elder, for example, refers to him as a *desultor bellorum civilium* (a trick-rider of civil wars)—a *desultor* specialized in leaping from one horse to the other. As such, he would be an appropriate recipient of Horation advice on the avoidance of dangerous extremes.
2. **level head**: *Aequa mens* (literally "balanced mind") is a variation of *aequus animus*, whence comes the English "equanimity."
3. **expensive . . . Falernian**: Translated literally, the Latin says "with an interior label of Falernian." The better, older wines were stored in the interior of the cellar, with a label recording their year of vintage. On Falernian, see note on 1.20.10.
4. **three sisters' . . . allow**: The three sisters are the Fates, each of whose woven threads represents the lifespan of one mortal. This stanza contains two **ascending tricolons**.

cedes coemptis saltibus et domo
villaque flavus quam Tiberis lavit;
    cedes, et exstructis in altum
        divitiis potietur heres.   20

divesne prisco natus ab Inacho
nil interest an pauper et infima
    de gente sub divo moreris,
        victima nil miserantis Orci.

omnes eodem cogimur, omnium   25
versatur urna serius ocius
    sors exitura et nos in aeternum
        exilium impositura cumbae.

You'll go from your bought pastureland and house
and villa[5] that the yellow Tiber washes.

    You'll go, and then your heir will be the master
        of riches that you heaped up to the sky.   20

Whether you're rich and born of old Inachus[6]
or, poor and from the lowest clan, you dwell
    beneath the sky[7]—it does not make a difference.
        You are the victim of unfeeling Orcus.[8]

To the same place we each are gathered, each   25
one's lot turns in the urn. Sooner or later
    it's bound to make its exit and will put
        us on the skiff[9] in everlasting exile.

---

5. **house and villa**: A *domus* (house) was technically an urban dwelling and the *villa* a country one.
6. **Inachus**: Early king of Argos in Greece. Descent from him would indicate an ancient ancestry indeed.
7. **beneath the sky**: Literally, "beneath god." The god here implies Jupiter, who stands **metonymically** for the sky.
8. **Orcus**: The Etruscan god of the underworld.
9. **skiff**: The ferry of Charon that carried the souls of the dead across the Styx.

ODES 2.4

Ne sit ancillae tibi amor pudori,
Xanthia Phoceu, prius insolentem
serva Briseis niveo colore
     movit Achillem;

movit Aiacem Telamone natum   5
forma captivae dominum Tecmessae;
arsit Atrides medio in triumpho
     virgine rapta,

barbarae postquam cecidere turmae
Thessalo victore et ademptus Hector   10

ODES 2.4[1]

Don't be embarrassed that you love a slave,[2]
Phocian Xanthias.[3] Before, the slave
Briseis[4] with her snowy hue aroused
      pompous Achilles.

Captive Tecmessa's[5] beauty stirred her master,   5
the Ajax who was born from Telamon.[6]
Atrides[7] burned mid-triumph for the virgin
      raped and abducted[8]

when the barbarian squadrons had collapsed
to the Thessalian victor[9] and dead Hector   10

---

1. *Odes* 2.4 (*Sapphic Strophe*): Horace here advises Xanthias, a seemingly elite Greek youth, not to feel ashamed that the object of his desire is his female slave or *ancilla* named Phyllis. What Horace and Xanthias call love would very likely be rape from Phyllis's perspective, a fact that comes through clearly in Horace's mythological parallels. One must recall that Roman male slaveholders had exclusive sexual access to their slaves, both male and female.
2. slave: The word *ancilla* here, like *serva* in line 3, indicates a woman of enslaved status. Although the two words differ in Latin and carry a slightly different nuance—*ancilla* indicates a slave that works in the home, whereas *serva* is more general—I translate them both with the English word "slave" so as to be clear about her lack of agency.
3. Xanthias: A Greek name. Phocis is an area near Delphi on the Greek mainland. It is therefore suitable that all of the mythological parallels for him are of Greek heroes.
4. Briseis: In Homer's *Iliad* the young woman Briseis is Achilles's war prize, a captive slave given to him in recognition of his martial excellence.
5. Captive Tecmessa's: Tecmessa was the daughter of the mythical Mysian king Teuthras. After Ajax killed her father, he took Tecmessa captive.
6. Ajax, . . . Telamon: There are two Ajaxes in Greek mythology, the "Greater" Ajax, whose father was the hero Telamon, and the "Lesser" Ajax, whose father was Oileus, the king of Locris.
7. Atrides: That is, the "son of Atreus." This is a patronymic for Agamemnon, who was the leader of the Greeks during the Trojan War.
8. virgin raped and abducted: This refers to Cassandra, the Trojan princess whose truthful prophecies were doomed by Apollo (whose love she rebuffed) to disbelief. Her rape and abduction could refer to two different incidents. After Troy fell, Agamemnon took her captive as his war prize, after which he would no doubt have raped her. Even before that, the Lesser Ajax (the son of Oileus) famously dragged her off as she was seeking sanctuary in the temple of Minerva, then raped her. This so enraged the goddess that she made the Greek homecomings difficult. The words "raped" and "abducted" both translate the one Latin word *rapta*, which suggests both of these acts.
9. Thessalian victor: Achilles

tradidit fessis leviora tolli
    Pergama Grais.

nescias an te generum beati
Phyllidis flavae decorent parentes:
regium certe genus et penatis   15
    maeret iniquos.

crede non illam tibi de scelesta
plebe dilectam, neque sic fidelem,
sic lucro aversam potuisse nasci
    matre pudenda.   20

bracchia et vultum teretesque suras
integer laudo; fuge suspicari
cuius octavum trepidavit aetas
    claudere lustrum.

had yielded to the weary Greeks a Troy
    easier to topple.

You never know—blonde Phyllis' wealthy parents
might do you credit as their son-in-law.
No doubt her birth is royal and she mourns   15
    hostile Penates.[10]

Don't think the one you love is from the vicious
masses or that a shameful mother could
have given birth to one so faithful, so
    hateful to profits.[11]   20

I praise her arms and face and shapely calves,
but I am unaffected. Don't suspect
a man whose age already has completed
    eight five-year timespans.[12]

10. **hostile Penates**: The *Penates* were one's household gods. Phyllis's are "hostile" since they allowed her to be taken away as a captive slave.
11. **shameful mother . . . profits**: Ancients tended to believe that character was inherited, so Phyllis's exemplary moral character is the best evidence for her elite status. Her hostility to money suggests that Phyllis does not display qualities stereotypically suited to a *meretrix* (prostitute).
12. **eight . . . timespans**: A *lustrum* was a period of five years. Now forty years old, Horace claims no longer to be suitable for youthful erotics, though some have rightly doubted his sincerity.

ODES 2.5

Nondum subacta ferre iugum valet
cervice, nondum munia comparis
    aequare nec tauri ruentis
        in venerem tolerare pondus.

circa virentis est animus tuae   5
campos iuvencae, nunc fluviis gravem
    solantis aestum, nunc in udo
        ludere cum vitulis salicto

praegestientis. tolle cupidinem
immitis uvae: iam tibi lividos   10
    distinguet Autumnus racemos
        purpureo varius colore.

iam te sequetur: currit enim ferox
aetas et illi quos tibi dempserit
    apponet annos; iam proterva   15
        fronte petet Lalage maritum,

dilecta, quantum non Pholoe fugax,
non Chloris albo sic umero nitens

ODES 2.5[1]

She's not yet strong enough to bear the yoke,
her neck subdued,[2] nor yet to match her partner's
      duties[3] or stand the burden[4] of the bull
         as he is rushing into acts of love.[5]

Upon the verdant fields your heifer's mind   5
is focused. Now in streams does she allay
      the stifling heat. Now she intensely yearns
         to play amid the dewy willow groves

with fellow calves. Get rid of your desire
for grapes that aren't yet ripened. Soon for you   10
      will Autumn with his many colors stain
         the darkened bunches with a crimson hue.

Soon she will follow you, for ruthless time
runs on. The years that it subtracts from you
      it will apply to her. Soon with a brazen   15
         brow will Lalage dash against a mate.

She'll be more loved than fleeing Pholoë,
or Chloris, luminous with her pale shoulder

---

1. **Odes 2.5** (*Alcaic Strophe*): Horace urges the unnamed addressee of this ode to put an end to his erotic longing for an inappropriately young girl, whom he compares to a young heifer. The poem is based on a sixth-century B.C.E. Greek ode by Anacreon, the so-called "Thracian filly" poem (fr. 417), in which the poet compares the young girl resisting his erotic advances to a horse not yet broken in by an experienced rider.
2. **yoke ... subdued**: Horace compares the act of sex to plowing. This is hardly an unusual **metaphor** for Horace to use—in the ancient Athenian betrothal ceremony, the bride's father would proclaim, "I give you this woman for the plowing of legitimate children."
3. **her partner's duties**: It was crucial that the team of oxen contribute equally to the work of the plow.
4. **burden**: *Pondus* (burden or weight) can refer to the weight of the bull as he mounts the cow, but the word more graphically suggests the bull's penis. For this use of *pondus*, see Adams (1982, 71).
5. **acts of love**: Literally *venerem* means "Venus," the goddess of love whose name often stands via **metonymy** for sex.

ut pura nocturno renidet
    luna mari, Cnidiusve Gyges,   20

quem si puellarum insereres choro,
mire sagaces falleret hospites
    discrimen obscurum solutis
        crinibus ambiguoque vultu.

just like the brilliant moon when it is shining
　　　upon the nighttime sea, or Cnidian Gyges[6]—   20

if you should place him in a dance of girls,
it would deceive amazingly shrewd strangers,[7]
　　　his difference nearly imperceptible[8]
　　　　　due to his flowing hair and girl-boy face.

---

6. **Pholoe . . . Chloris . . . Gyges:** In an **ascending tricolon**, Horace names three earlier beloveds of the addressee. Whereas Pholoe and Chloris are female, Gyges is a pederastic beloved from the eastern city of Cnidos in Asia Minor.
7. **shrewd strangers:** An allusion to a story of Diomedes and Odysseus. They came to Skyros to find the young Achilles, who was hiding in disguise as a girl among the daughters of the king. The disguise was so successful that Odysseus had to trick him into revealing himself.
8. **difference nearly imperceptible:** The Latin *discrimen obscurum* (imperceptible difference) is a striking *callida iunctura*.

***ODES* 2.6**

Septimi, Gadis aditure mecum et
Cantabrum indoctum iuga ferre nostra et
barbaras Syrtis, ubi Maura semper
     aestuat unda,

Tibur Argeo positum colono   5
sit meae sedes utinam senectae,
sit modus lasso maris et viarum
     militiaeque!

unde si Parcae prohibent iniquae,
dulce pellitis ovibus Galaesi   10
flumen et regnata petam Laconi
     rura Phalantho.

ille terrarum mihi praeter omnis
angulus ridet, ubi non Hymetto

ODES 2.6[1]

Septimius, you'd go with me to Gades,[2]
Cantabria[3] (not taught to wear our yoke), and
the barbarous Syrtes, where Moroccan[4] waves
    always are churning.

Let Tibur, founded by the Argive settler,[5]   5
be—how I wish!—the seat of my old age,
and end the sea and roads and service[6] that have
    left me exhausted.

If Fates unjustly keep me from that place,
I'll seek Galaesus,[7] river sweet to sheep   10
enwrapped in hides,[8] and fields in which the king was
    Spartan Phalanthus.[9]

That corner of the world smiles at me more
than all the rest. The honey there does not

---

1. ***Odes* 2.6** (*Sapphic Strophe*): Addressed to a friend named Septimius, *Odes* 2.6 describes Horace's desire to spend his final years in the Italian villages of Tibur or Tarentum, the former (modern Tivoli) located in the Sabine countryside outside of Rome where Horace had his famous farm, and the latter (modern Taranto) in the southern Italian region of Apulia, Horace's birthplace.
2. **Gades:** Modern Cádiz, it was a Carthaginian colony in southwest Spain on the very edge of the Roman Empire.
3. **Cantabria:** The northern Spanish region that contended with Rome numerous times in the 20s B.C.E.
4. **Syrtes . . . Moroccan:** The Syrtes were dangerous sandbanks off the coast of Libya in North Africa. For the term "barbarous," see note at *Epodes* 5.61. For "Moroccan," see the note at *Odes* 1.22.2.
5. **Argive settler:** According to legend, Tibur was settled by a man from Argos named either Tiburnus or Tiburtus.
6. **service:** The only known military service of Horace was at Philippi in 42 B.C.E., where he fought on the side of Brutus and Cassius against Antony and Octavian, though he may have been present at Actium as well, for which see *Epodes* 1.
7. **Galaesus:** The Galaesus (modern Galeso) is a river near Tarentum.
8. **enwrapped in hides:** The sheep wear covers of hide in order to protect their valuable fleeces.
9. **Spartan Phalanthus:** The legendary founder of Tarentum.

mella decedunt viridique certat   15
    baca Venafro,

ver ubi longum tepidasque praebet
Iuppiter brumas, et amicus Aulon
fertili Baccho minimum Falernis
    invidet uvis.   20

ille te mecum locus et beatae
postulant arces; ibi tu calentem
debita sparges lacrima favillam
    vatis amici.

yield to Hymettus,[10] and the olive rivals   15
    verdant Venafrum.[11]

There Jupiter bestows a lengthy spring
and tepid winters, and the valley Aulon,[12]
friendly to fertile Bacchus,[13] barely envies
    grapes of Falernum.[14]   20

That place and its blessed citadels request
both me and you. That is where you will shed
the tears required for your friend the bard's
    smoldering ashes.

---

10. **Hymettus**: The Athenian mountain where the best honey was produced.
11. **Venafrum**: Modern Venafro on the border of Latium, it was renowned in antiquity for its olives.
12. **Aulon**: The geographical reference here is unclear, but in Greek *aulon* simply means "valley."
13. **Bacchus**: Used **metonymically** for wine.
14. **grapes of Falernum**: Falernian was the most celebrated Italian wine.

ODES 2.7

O saepe mecum tempus in ultimum
deducte Bruto militiae duce,
      quis te redonavit Quiritem
         dis patriis Italoque caelo,

Pompei, meorum prime sodalium?   5
cum quo morantem saepe diem mero
      fregi coronatus nitentis
         malobathro Syrio capillos.

tecum Philippos et celerem fugam
sensi relicta non bene parmula,   10
      cum fracta virtus, et minaces
         turpe solum tetigere mento.

sed me per hostis Mercurius celer
denso paventem sustulit aere;
      te rursus in bellum resorbens   15
         unda fretis tulit aestuosis.

ODES 2.7¹

You, often led with me into great danger
when Brutus was the leader of our troops,
   who has restored you as a citizen
      to your paternal gods and Italy's sky?²

Pompeius, first and foremost of my comrades,   5
with you I often broke the lingering day
   with undiluted wine, wrapping a garland
      round hair made sleek with Syrian malobathrum.³

With you I suffered Philippi and quick
retreat, my shield ignobly left behind,⁴   10
   when virtue⁵ broke apart and those who threatened
      thumped their disgraceful chins upon the dirt.

But quickly Mercury, amid the foes,
carried me off, afraid, inside dense mist,
   whereas the wave sucked you back into war   15
      and carried you along the roiling straits.

1. **Odes 2.7** (*Alcaic Strophe*): Horace addresses an old friend named Pompeius, with whom he had served on the losing side under Brutus at Philippi (42 B.C.E.) against Antony and Octavian. Whereas this defeat brought an end to Horace's military service and perhaps the confiscation of his property (see *Epistles* 2.2.49–52), Pompeius's resistance continued, and he probably went on to serve in the navy of Sextus Pompey, to whom his name suggests he may have had some relation. Octavian defeated Sextus Pompey in 36 B.C.E. and, after the Battle of Actium in 31 B.C.E., extended a general amnesty the following year. It is perhaps under this amnesty that Pompeius's citizen standing has been restored.
2. **who . . . Italy's sky**: The implicit answer here is Octavian.
3. **malobathrum**: An eastern plant from which fragrant oils were produced.
4. **shield . . . behind**: The *parmula* was a small, round shield. Horace cites his loss of it as evidence for his martial incompetence, and if true it would have been thought disgraceful. It is, however, most likely a poetic fiction placing him in the literary lineage of earlier lyric poets. Alcaeus, according to Herodotus (5.95), wrote a poem about losing his shield in flight from battle; Anacreon (fr. 51) mentions throwing down his shield beside a river; and Archilochus (fr. 5) left his shield beside a bush, and it was taken by a Thracian. For a more political reading of the passage, see Smith (2015).
5. **virtue**: *Virtus* suggests both "manliness" and abstract "virtue." It was an entrenched republican value and may here evoke the republic itself or even, more specifically, the Stoic virtue of Brutus.

ergo obligatam redde Iovi dapem
longaque fessum militia latus
    depone sub lauru mea, nec
        parce cadis tibi destinatis.   20

oblivioso levia Massico
ciboria exple; funde capacibus
    unguenta de conchis. quis udo
        deproperare apio coronas

curatve myrto? quem Venus arbitrum   25
dicet bibendi? non ego sanius
    bacchabor Edonis: recepto
        dulce mihi furere est amico.

So pay to Jupiter the feast now due
and place your flank, weary with lengthy service,
    beneath my laurel tree, and do not spare
        the jars that I have set aside for you.   20

With Massic wine that brings forgetfulness[6]
fill up the polished cups. Pour out the perfumes
    from spacious vessels. Who is making sure
        to finish garlands of wet celery

or myrtle? Whom will Venus pick to be   25
judge of the drinking?[7] No more soberly
    than the Edonians[8] will I rave. To me
        it's sweet to lose my mind—my friend is back.

6. **brings forgetfulness**: The word *oblivioso* (forgetful/causing forgetfulness) recalls the Latin word for "amnesty" (*oblivio*), an official "forgetting" of past conduct.
7. **judge . . . drinking**: The *arbiter bibendi* set the drinking rules at the symposium, instructing the guests how much and when to drink. He was chosen by the *iactus Venerius* (the Venus throw) on a set of four dice, on which each showed a different number.
8. **Edonians**: The Edoni were a tribe in Thrace, an eastern region associated with Bacchic rites—Horace's word *bacchabor* literally means, "I will be a Bacchant." Bacchants, also called Maenads, worshipped the god by entering an enthusiastic state of raving madness.

ODES 2.8

Ulla si iuris tibi peierati
poena, Barine, nocuisset umquam,
dente si nigro fieres vel uno
      turpior ungui,

crederem. sed tu, simul obligasti   5
perfidum votis caput, enitescis
pulchrior multo iuvenumque prodis
      publica cura.

expedit matris cineres opertos
fallere et toto taciturna noctis   10
signa cum caelo gelidaque divos
      morte carentis.

ridet hoc, inquam, Venus ipsa, rident
simplices Nymphae, ferus et Cupido,
semper ardentis acuens sagittas   15
      cote cruenta.

adde quod pubes tibi crescit omnis,
servitus crescit nova, nec priores

ODES 2.8[1]

If ever for a perjured oath,[2] Barine,
some punishment had injured you at all,
if by a blackened tooth or single nail[3]
    you'd become fouler,

I would believe you. But, once you have bound   5
your faithless head with vows, you shine so much
more beautifully and turn into young men's
    national interest.

To bear false witness on your mother's buried
ash and the silent stars of night—the whole   10
of heaven—and the gods who lack cold death
    works in your favor.

I say that Venus laughs at this. And laughing
too are the guileless nymphs and savage Cupid,
who always whets upon a bloodstained stone his   15
    blistering arrows.

Plus, all young men are growing up[4] for you—
your brand new slaves are growing. And the former

---

1. ***Odes* 2.8** (*Sapphic Strophe*): An ode written to a woman named Barine, whose beauty defies cosmic justice as well as the view (seen for example in *Odes* 1.25) that a woman's sexual desirability belongs only to a brief, youthful moment. Barine's status is unknown, but she is most likely a prostitute. As Harrison (2017) points out, her name suggests a "carp" in Greek (*barinos*), and "several fish names were used by Greek *hetairai* as names or sobriquets, suggesting perhaps sexual 'delicacies' analogous to fish for eating." Horace plays throughout on the **tropes** of love elegy, especially that of ***servitium amoris*** (slavery of love).
2. **perjured oath**: It is a conventional **topos** that the gods do not enforce the oaths of lovers.
3. **single nail**: Nisbet and Hubbard (1978) cite here the ancient belief that lying caused white spots to appear on the fingernails. As they state, "Horace is proceeding from a black tooth to an even more trivial blemish."
4. **growing up**: Scholars suggest several images at work here. Most basically *crescit* means that the next generation are now "growing up." Harrison (2017) suggests that Horace evokes the agricultural image of a "growing" crop. Ancona (1994, 81) proposes a potential sexual double entendre; the word "suggests . . . their literal sexual response to Barine (they are 'growing big')."

impiae tectum dominae relinquunt,
    saepe minati.   20

te suis matres metuunt iuvencis,
te senes parci, miseraeque nuper
virgines nuptae, tua ne retardet
    aura maritos.

don't quit their impious mistress' house, although
　　often they've threatened.   20

It's you that mothers dread for their own young.
It's you that frugal old men dread[5] and wretched
virgins, just married, lest that breeze of yours[6]
　　hinder their bridegrooms.

---

5. **frugal . . . dread:** The old men's fear is most likely based in the potential that their
　sons may spend their inheritance on Barine.
6. **you . . . you . . . of yours:** The repetition of the second-person pronoun is a feature
　especially of **hymns.** Barine becomes, to quote Harrison (2017) a kind of "malign
　goddess."

ODES 2.9

Non semper imbres nubibus Histricos
manant in agros aut mare Caspium
      vexant inaequales procellae
          usque, nec Armeniis in oris,

amice Valgi, stat glacies iners   5
mensis per omnis aut Aquilonibus
      querqueta Gargani laborant
          et foliis viduantur orni:

tu semper urges flebilibus modis
Mysten ademptum, nec tibi Vespero   10
      surgente decedunt amores
          nec rapidum fugiente solem.

at non ter aevo functus amabilem
ploravit omnis Antilochum senex
      annos, nec impubem parentes   15
          Troilon aut Phrygiae sorores

flevere semper. desine mollium
tandem querelarum, et potius nova

ODES 2.9[1]

Not always do the rains drip down from clouds
onto the Histrian[2] fields, and storms do not
      unlevel and harass the Caspian Sea
          all of the time, nor during every month,

dear Valgius,[3] does sluggish ice stand still   5
upon Armenian shores nor do the oaks
      on Mount Garganus[4] vie with Aquilos[5]
          nor are the mountain ash bereft of leaves.

You always with your tearful verse beset
dead Mystes, and your love does not depart,   10
      not when the evening star is on the rise,
          nor when it's fleeing from the rapid sun.

But that old man who passed three spans of life[6]
did not lament his dear Antilochus
      all of his years. The parents of young Troilus[7]   15
          did not bewail him always; neither did his

Phrygian sisters. Put an end at last
to your soft lamentations and instead

---

1. ***Odes* 2.9** (*Alcaic Strophe*): Horace offers a poem on moderation to Valgius, who has
been mourning for a deceased Mystes, perhaps his younger lover. Valgius's unceasing
lamentations evoke the genre of elegy, whereas Horatian lyric embraces instead
restraint. The focus on moderation is a good lead-in to the following poem, the
"golden mean" ode.
2. **Histrian:** Histria was on the west coast of the Black Sea.
3. **dear Valgius:** Gaius Valgius Rufus would go on to be suffect consul in 12 B.C.E. In
Satires 1.10.81–82 Horace includes him in the ideal readership of his poetry.
4. **Mount Garganus:** A mountain in the southern Italian region Apulia, where Horace
was born.
5. **Aquilos:** The north winds, associated with winter storms.
6. **old man . . . three spans of life:** The proverbially long-lived Nestor, whose son
Antilochus was killed in the Trojan War.
7. **Troilus:** A son of Priam and Hecuba killed in the Trojan War.

cantemus Augusti tropaea
Caesaris et rigidum Niphaten,   20

Medumque flumen gentibus additum
victis minores volvere vertices,
intraque praescriptum Gelonos
exiguis equitare campis.

let's sing about Augustus Caesar's recent
   victories[8] and the frozen-stiff Niphates,[9]   20

and how the river of the Medes,[10] now added
to nations we have won, winds smaller waves,
  and how Geloni,[11] in the zone prescribed,
    gallop their horses over meager fields.

---

8. **recent victories:** Horace probably means the eastern victories of Augustus
 celebrated as part of his grand triple triumph in 29 B.C.E.
9. **Niphates:** An Armenian mountain range.
10. **river of the Medes:** The Euphrates.
11. **Geloni:** A remote nomadic tribe in Scythia. As Powell (2009, 145) points out, "no
 people of this name existed at the time Horace was writing." He identifies them
 instead with the Parthians, specifically the Parthian cavalry whose range was likely
 constricted by Augustus's peace negotiations with the Parthians in 29 B.C.E.

ODES 2.10

Rectius vives, Licini, neque altum
semper urgendo neque, dum procellas
cautus horrescis, nimium premendo
      litus iniquum.

auream quisquis mediocritatem   5
diligit, tutus caret obsoleti
sordibus tecti, caret invidenda
      sobrius aula.

saepius ventis agitatur ingens
pinus et celsae graviore casu   10
decidunt turres feriuntque summos
      fulgura montis.

sperat infestis, metuit secundis
alteram sortem bene praeparatum
pectus. informis hiemes reducit   15
      Iuppiter, idem

ODES 2.10[1]

Life will go smoother,[2] Licinius,[3] if you don't
press always on the deep nor, while you quake
at storms, cautiously hug against uneven
    shoreline too tightly.

Whoever prizes golden moderation[4]   5
in safety lacks the squalor of a rundown
shack, and he sanely lacks a palace that
    rouses up envy.

More often it's the mighty pine that wind
drives to and fro. The crash is heavier   10
when lofty towers fall, and lightning strikes
    summits of mountains.

The well-adapted heart in bad times hopes
its lot will change; in good times this is what
it fears. Jupiter brings about the grisly   15
    winters; he likewise

---

1. ***Odes* 2.10** (*Sapphic Strophe*): In this poem (which falls in the middle of the middle book of *Odes* 1–3) Horace coins yet another famous phrase, "golden moderation" or the "golden mean" (*aurea mediocritas*). Moderation involves not just standing midway between extremes but also in adapting when extremes are unavoidable and recognizing that they are temporary and will change. The formulation of virtue as a mean goes back to the philosophy of Aristotle, but it had an even earlier history in popular ethical thought. One of the two strictures inscribed on the temple of Apollo of Delphi was *meden agan* (nothing in excess).
2. **smoother:** *Rectius*, literally "straighter," from the Latin verb meaning "to guide in a straight line," can also simply mean "better." Ideas of evenness and levelness, however, are important throughout the poem because they suggest the equanimity (levelheadedness) that the golden mean helps one attain. I chose "smooth" to introduce the nautical **metaphor** (i.e., smooth sailing) that runs through the poem.
3. **Licinius:** This is perhaps Lucius Licinius Murena, the brother-in-law of Maecenas. He was put to death for involvement in a conspiracy against Augustus in 22 B.C.E. If this identification is correct, he is well chosen as the recipient of Horace's advice on safe living.
4. **golden moderation:** Horace's *aurea mediocritas* is an arresting ***callida iunctura***. As Nisbet and Hubbard (1978) note, *aurea* (golden) suggests exceptional worth, while *mediocritas* can imply "mediocrity." The word Horace normally uses to denote the "mean" is *medium*.

summovet. non, si male nunc, et olim
sic erit: quondam cithara tacentem
suscitat Musam neque semper arcum
      tendit Apollo.   20

rebus angustis animosus atque
fortis appare; sapienter idem
contrahes vento nimium secundo
      turgida vela.

removes them. If it's bad right now, it won't be
someday. At times Apollo[5] with his lyre
stirs up the silent Muse—he does not always
       tauten his bowstring.   20

In narrow circumstances show yourself
daring and brave. You also will be wise,
when breezes are too fair, to draw back in
       sails that are swollen.

---

5. **Apollo:** The god of archery and hunting as well as the lyre and other stringed instruments.

ODES 2.11

Quid bellicosus Cantaber et Scythes,
Hirpine Quincti, cogitet Hadria
    divisus obiecto, remittas
        quaerere, nec trepides in usum

poscentis aevi pauca: fugit retro   5
levis iuventas et decor, arida
    pellente lascivos amores
        canitie facilemque somnum.

non semper idem floribus est honor
vernis, neque uno Luna rubens nitet   10
    vultu: quid aeternis minorem
        consiliis animum fatigas?

cur non sub alta vel platano vel hac
pinu iacentes sic temere et rosa
    canos odorati capillos,   15
        dum licet, Assyriaque nardo

potamus uncti? dissipat Euhius
curas edaces. quis puer ocius
    restinguet ardentis Falerni
        pocula praetereunte lympha?   20

ODES 2.11[1]

Hirpinian Quinctius,[2] stop questioning
what bellicose Cantabrians[3] plot, and what
     the Scythians,[4] whom the Adriatic's hurdle
          divides from us. Don't fret about the needs

of a time of life that makes but few demands.   5
Into the past flee smooth-cheeked youthfulness
     and grace, while brittle white hair drives away
          lascivious love affairs and easy slumber.

The springtime's flowers do not keep their beauty
always, nor does the blushing moon forever   10
     shine with the selfsame face. Why do you weary
          your mind, too short-lived for eternal plans?

Why don't we lie down here beneath this tall
plane tree or pine and with no more ado
     drink while we can, once we have scented our   15
          white hair with rose oil and have
          smeared ourselves

with Syrian nard? Euhius[5] drives away
gnawing anxieties. What slave boy will
     more quickly douse the cups of burning-hot
          Falernian with the water as it passes?[6]   20

---

1. *Odes* 2.11 (*Alcaic Strophe*): Horace invites Quinctius to stop worrying about faraway actions over which he has no control and instead enjoy the sympotic friendship appropriate to his middle age.
2. **Hirpinian Quinctius**: The Hirpini were a Samnite people in central Italy. Nisbet and Hubbard (1978) connect Quinctius, who is also the addressee of *Epistles* 1.16, to a Gaius Quinctius Valgus, who in 85 B.C.E. was the patron of the Hirpinian town Aeclanum. Nothing specific, however, is reliably known of Horace's Quinctius.
3. **Cantabrians**: Augustus fought several campaigns against the Cantabrians, in northern Spain, during the 20s B.C.E.
4. **Sythians**: Scythia was an eastern locale unlikely to be plotting military action against Rome at this time.
5. **Euhius**: Bacchus, **metonymy** for wine.
6. **douse the cups . . . water as it passes**: Horace urges the slave to water the wine.

quis devium scortum eliciet domo
Lyden? eburna dic age cum lyra
   maturet in comptum Lacaenae
      more comas religata nodum.

Who'll lure from home, off of her beaten path,
Lyde, the whore?[7] Go tell her to make haste
and bring her ivory lyre,[8] with her hair
done Spartan style—bound in a simple knot.

---

7. **off her beaten path . . . whore:** Most commentators have taken *devium* as meaning "elite" or "selective," creating a ***callida iunctura*** with the brusque *scortum* (hooker, whore). Harrison (2017), however, convincingly points out that *devium* instead always indicates "wandering from a normal path" and translates "who will induce Lyde to make an exceptional journey far from her home?" We should understand that Horace and Quinctius are somewhere in the rustic outer suburbs of Rome, perhaps even on Horace's Sabine farm, whereas Lyde normally keeps to the city, where she has an urban house (*domus*).

8. **ivory lyre:** At symposia courtesans were expected to offer not just sexual but also musical entertainment.

ODES 2.12

Nolis longa ferae bella Numantiae
nec durum Hannibalem nec Siculum mare
Poeno purpureum sanguine mollibus
       aptari citharae modis,

nec saevos Lapithas et nimium mero   5
Hylaeum domitosque Herculea manu
Telluris iuvenes, unde periculum
       fulgens contremuit domus

Saturni veteris; tuque pedestribus
dices historiis proelia Caesaris,   10
Maecenas, melius ductaque per vias
       regum colla minacium.

ODES 2.12[1]

You would not want the lengthy wars of fierce
Numantia nor hardened Hannibal
nor Sicily's sea, dyed red with Punic blood,[2]
    matched to the cithara's[3] soft modes,

nor the ferocious Lapiths and Hylaeus[4]   5
who drank too much unwatered wine, nor Earth's
young sons subdued by Herculean hand—
    their danger shook the shining house

of ancient Saturn.[5] You, in histories
that walk on foot,[6] will better tell of Caesar's   10
battles, Maecenas, and the necks of threatening
    kings he paraded through the streets.[7]

---

1. *Odes* 2.12 (*Third Asclepiadean*): Horace explains why his lyric poems are more suited to the themes of erotic lyric than epic, particularly **panegyric** epic in honor of Augustus. After suggesting that Maecenas take it upon himself to praise Augustus in historical prose, Horace describes the subject matter appropriate for his poetry, a woman named Licymnia whose identification has been much debated. Some, such as Nisbet and Hubbard (1978), have suggested that she is romantically linked in the ode with Maecenas and identify her as Terentia, his wife (a problematic identification given the highly eroticized portrait of her), whereas others have paired her instead with Horace. Sutherland (2005) argues that she stands symbolically for the genre of lyric itself, "an embodiment of light, erotic literature." The poem diverges metrically from the preceding poems of book 2, which had all been written in either Alcaics (the odd-numbered poems) or Sapphics (the even-numbered poems).
2. **fierce Numantia's war . . . Punic blood**: Rejected topics, all from Roman history: the destruction of Numantia in 133 B.C.E., the Second Punic War fought against the Carthaginian general Hannibal in 218–201 B.C.E., and the naval battles of the First Punic War in 264–241 B.C.E.
3. **cithara's**: The cithara was a stringed instrument similar to the lyre.
4. **Hylaeus**: A centaur. Horace has in mind the mythical battle between the Lapiths and the Centaurs, which occurred after the Centaurs drank too much wine at the wedding of the Lapith king, Pirithous, and tried to steal the bride.
5. **Earth's young sons . . . ancient Saturn**: The Gigantomachy, in which the Giants, children of Earth, attempted to overthrow the gods. Hercules traditionally played a key role in their defeat.
6. **walk on foot**: That is, written in prose. Poetry, on the other hand, is sublime.
7. **threatening kings**: An allusion to Augustus's triple triumph in 29 B.C.E., in which enemy kings were paraded through Rome.

me dulcis dominae Musa Licymniae
cantus, me voluit dicere lucidum
fulgentis oculos et bene mutuis   15
    fidum pectus amoribus,

quam nec ferre pedem dedecuit choris
nec certare ioco nec dare bracchia
ludentem nitidis virginibus sacro
    Dianae celebris die.   20

num tu quae tenuit dives Achaemenes
aut pinguis Phrygiae Mygdonias opes
permutare velis crine Licymniae,
    plenas aut Arabum domos,

cum flagrantia detorquet ad oscula   25
cervicem aut facili saevitia negat,
quae poscente magis gaudeat eripi,
    interdum rapere occupet?

But me—the Muse wants me to speak of mistress
Licymnia's pleasant songs, me of her eyes
that brightly shine and heart that stays devoted   15
    in well requited love affairs.

It's brought her no disgrace to enter dances
or vie in games of wit or playfully
link arms with gleaming virgins on the sacred
    day when Diana's rites are crowded.[8]   20

Surely you[9] wouldn't take the goods of rich
Achaemenes[10] or all of Mygdon's[11] wealth
from fertile Phrygia or the brimming homes
    of Arabs for Licymnia's hair

when she inclines her neck toward burning kisses   25
or with good-natured harshness turns them down,
who likes them more when stolen, not requested,
    and sometimes is the first to steal?

---

8. **Diana's . . . crowded:** Diana's major festival was held on August 13 at her temple on the Aventine Hill.
9. **you:** There is disagreement about who the "you" here signifies, whether Maecenas or the hypothetical reader.
10. **Achaemenes:** The proverbially rich founder of the Achaemenid dynasty in Persia.
11. **Mygdon:** A legendary king of Phrygia in Asia Minor.

***ODES* 2.13**

Ille et nefasto te posuit die
quicumque primum, et sacrilega manu
    produxit, arbos, in nepotum
        perniciem opprobriumque pagi;

illum et parentis crediderim sui   5
fregisse cervicem et penetralia
    sparsisse nocturno cruore
        hospitis; ille venena Colcha

et quidquid usquam concipitur nefas
tractavit, agro qui statuit meo   10
    te triste lignum, te, caducum
        in domini caput immerentis.

quid quisque vitet numquam homini satis
cautum est in horas: navita Bosphorum
    Poenus perhorrescit neque ultra   15
        caeca timet aliunde fata;

ODES 2.13[1]

That man who planted you to start with did so
on an unlucky[2] day. With profane hand
    he propagated you, O tree, to plague
        his progeny and bring his precinct shame.[3]

That man—I would believe it—broke the neck   5
of his own father, and he splashed his home's
    shrine with nocturnal blood he spilled from his
        own guest. That man[4] laid hold of
        Colchian poisons[5]—

whatever sacrilege is conjured up
in any place—who placed you in my field,   10
    you wretched log, destined to fall one day
        onto your undeserving master's head.

A human cannot fully heed each danger
at any given hour. The Punic sailor
    quakes at the Bosporus,[6] but once beyond it   15
        is not afraid of unseen death from elsewhere.

---

1. *Odes* 2.13 (*Alcaic Strophe*): An ode addressed to a tree that nearly killed Horace when it fell on his head, an event whose historicity it is impossible to know but which Horace mentions repeatedly (see also *Odes* 2.17.27 and 3.8.7). It may be based at least in part on a story told of the Greek lyric poet Simonides, who was said to have escaped a falling house unscathed thanks to the protection of the gods Castor and Pollux (for which see Quintilian 11.2.11–16). In *Odes* 2.17.27 Horace claims that he was rescued by Faunus, the son of Mercury.

2. **unlucky:** Days labeled *nefasti* in the calendar were considered divinely inauspicious, and no business could be conducted on them.

3. **plant . . . precinct:** The **alliteration** of –*p* in the translation attempts to recreate the same feature in the Latin. The effect is to reproduce the vituperative sputtering of a curse.

4. **That man . . . that man . . . that man:** The triple **anaphora** with **polyptoton** (*ille, illum, ille*) is typical of prayers and curses.

5. **Colchian poisons:** The poisons are "Colchian" because of that area's association with Medea, the most infamous mythological witch.

6. **Bosporus:** A proverbially stormy strait that forms the southwestern entrance to the Black Sea.

miles sagittas et celerem fugam
Parthi, catenas Parthus et Italum
    robur; sed improvisa leti
        vis rapuit rapietque gentis.   20

quam paene furvae regna Proserpinae
et iudicantem vidimus Aeacum
    sedesque discriptas piorum et
        Aeoliis fidibus querentem

Sappho puellis de popularibus,   25
et te sonantem plenius aureo,
    Alcaee, plectro dura navis,
        dura fugae mala, dura belli.

utrumque sacro digna silentio
mirantur umbrae dicere; sed magis   30
    pugnas et exactos tyrannos
        densum umeris bibit aure vulgus.

quid mirum, ubi illis carminibus stupens
demittit atras belua centiceps

The soldier fears the Parthian's darts and quick
retreat;[7] the Parthian fears Italian chains
    and toughness, but the unanticipated
        violence of death has seized and will
            seize nations.   20

How close I came to seeing dark Proserpina's
kingdom[8] and Aeacus[9] as he passed judgment,
    the seat apportioned to the pious and
        Sappho complaining on Aeolian lyre

about the girls of her own population   25
and you, Alcaeus, who with golden plectrum[10]
    sang with more force the sorrows of the ship,[11]
        the evil sorrows of retreat,[12] war's sorrows.

The shades are struck with awe as each one tells
things fit for sacred silence. But the mob,   30
    its shoulders crowded tight, drinks with their ears
        the battles and the ousted tyrants[13] more.

Why is this wondrous when, stunned by those songs,
the hundred-headed beast[14] lets fall his black

---

7. **darts and quick retreat:** The most infamous Parthian military tactic was the backward shot—horsemen would feign retreat, then turn backward on horseback and shoot.

8. **dark Proserpina's kingdom:** Proserpina is the queen of the dead and wife of Pluto.

9. **Aeacus:** One of the mythological judges of the dead; the other two are Minos and Rhadamanthus.

10. **plectrum:** This was the stick used to play a lyre, but here it probably stands for the lyre itself.

11. **ship:** On Alcaeus's ship poems, see the introductory note to *Odes* 1.14.

12. **retreat:** *Fuga* is here sometimes taken not as "retreat" but "exile," as Alcaeus seems to have written about both topics.

13. **ousted tyrants:** Alcaeus's poetry was very involved with the Mytilenian tyrants Melanchrus and Myrsilus.

14. **hundred-headed beast:** Cerberus, who usually has a more modest three heads.

auris et intorti capillis   35
    Eumenidum recreantur angues?

quin et Prometheus et Pelopis parens
dulci laborum decipitur sono,
    nec curat Orion leones
        aut timidos agitare lyncas.   40

ears, and the snakes entangled in the hair   35
    of the Eumenides are livened up?[15]

Yes, and Prometheus and Pelops' father[16]
are charmed by that sweet sound to disregard
    their labors, and Orion[17] does not care
        for chasing lions and faint-hearted lynxes.   40

---

15. **are livened up**: The Latin word here (*recreantur*) is ambiguous. It could mean
(a) that the snakes are "lulled" and grow quiet or (b) that they are "enlivened" and thus
begin to move and stand up. The latter interpretation would make a nice contrast
with Cerberus's drooping ears and perhaps suggest the movement of a snake under
the influence of a charmer.
16. **Prometheus and Pelops' father**: Prometheus and Tantalus (the father of
Pelops) were two of the great sinners. Prometheus's continually regenerating liver
was eternally consumed by an eagle, and Tantalus stands in water that recedes when
he tries to drink and beneath a fruit tree that withdraws when he reaches to eat. On
Prometheus's presence in the Underworld, see note at *Epodes* 17.67.
17. **Orion**: Another sinner punished in the Underworld. He attempted to rape
Diana while he was hunting with her.

ODES 2.14

Eheu fugaces, Postume, Postume,
labuntur anni nec pietas moram
    rugis et instanti senectae
        adferet indomitaeque morti:

non si trecenis quotquot eunt dies,   5
amice, places illacrimabilem
    Plutona tauris, qui ter amplum
        Geryonen Tityonque tristi

compescit unda, scilicet omnibus,
quicumque terrae munere vescimur,   10
    enaviganda, sive reges
        sive inopes erimus coloni.

frustra cruento Marte carebimus
fractisque rauci fluctibus Hadriae,
    frustra per autumnos nocentem   15
        corporibus metuemus Austrum:

visendus ater flumine languido
Cocytos errans et Danai genus

ODES 2.14[1]

Alas, the years, Postumus, Postumus,
go gliding by, and piety[2] won't bring
    any delay to wrinkles or impending
        old age or death, which cannot be escaped—

not even if, on every passing day,   5
my friend, you sacrifice three hundred bulls[3]
    to placate heartless Pluto, who confines
        three-bodied Geryon and Tityos[4]

with that sad wave[5] which surely all of us,
whoever eats the bounty of the earth,   10
    will have to sail across—it does not matter
        whether we're kings or farmers without means.

In vain will we avoid blood-thirsty Mars
and the rough Adriatic's fractured flood;
    in vain each autumn will we be afraid   15
        of Auster and the harm he does to bodies.[6]

You'll have to go see dark Cocytos drifting
with its lethargic flow, the ill-reputed

---

1. *Odes* 2.14 (*Alcaic Strophe*): An ode on the inevitability of death addressed to a man Postumus, whose name fittingly suggests "after death." Nisbet and Hubbard (1978) propose he should be identified as Gaius Propertius Postumus, a relative of the poet Propertius, but this identification is not universally accepted. Death in the poem is a force that unites all humanity, whether rich or poor.
2. **piety**: The word suggests dutiful obedience to the gods as well as to one's state and family. It was a keyword of Augustan morality, seen most exemplarily in Vergil's Aeneas, who incidentally was bound not for death but for immortality.
3. **three hundred bulls**: A triple hecatomb (a sacrifice of a hundred bulls) performed on a daily basis is an outlandish hyperbole.
4. **Geryon and Tityos**: Geryon was a mythological giant defeated by Hercules. He had either three heads or (as here) three bodies. Tityos was a giant who tried to rape Leto, the mother of Apollo and Diana. The two are now confined in the Underworld.
5. **sad wave**: The wave refers to the Styx, the chief of the underworld's rivers.
6. **Auster . . . bodies**: Auster was the south wind associated with the autumn, a season thought to bring disease and death.

infame damnatusque longi
    Sisyphus Aeolides laboris: 20

linquenda tellus et domus et placens
uxor, neque harum quas colis arborum
    te praeter invisas cupressos
        ulla brevem dominum sequetur:

absumet heres Caecuba dignior   25
servata centum clavibus et mero
    tinget pavimentum superbo,
        pontificum potiore cenis.

daughters of Danaus, and Sisyphus,
      son of Aeolus, sentenced to long labor.[7]   20

You'll have to leave your land and home and pleasing
wife, and not any of those trees you tend—
      apart from those detested cypresses[8]—
         will follow after you, their short-lived master.

A worthier heir will squander that Caecuban[9]   25
you safeguard with a hundred keys. He'll stain
      the pavement with unmixed and pompous wine,
         better than what they drink at pontiffs' banquets.

---

7. **Cocytos . . . long labor**: Coctytos was one of the rivers of the Underworld. Danaus had fifty daughters, all but one of whom killed their grooms at his bidding on their wedding night; they were condemned to an eternity of trying to fill sieves with water. Sisyphus was another sinner whose crimes included divulging a secret of Zeus and various attempts to cheat death. His punishment consists of spending his days rolling a boulder up a hill only to watch it roll back down.

8. **trees . . . cypresses**: The stanza suggests that arboriculture is a hobby of Postumus, which he probably practiced at an elite villa outside of Rome. The cypress was associated with death because its branches were placed on the door of the bereaved as well as on the funeral pyre.

9. **Caecuban**: A very fine Italian wine.

ODES 2.15

Iam pauca aratro iugera regiae
moles relinquent, undique latius
    extenta visentur Lucrino
        stagna lacu, platanusque caelebs

evincet ulmos; tum violaria et   5
myrtus et omnis copia narium
    spargent olivetis odorem
        fertilibus domino priori;

tum spissa ramis laurea fervidos
excludet ictus. non ita Romuli   10
    praescriptum et intonsi Catonis
        auspiciis veterumque norma.

privatus illis census erat brevis,
commune magnum: nulla decempedis
    metata privatis opacam   15
        porticus excipiebat Arcton,

ODES 2.15[1]

Before long, kingly heaps will leave behind
few acres for the plow. And everywhere,
      stretched out more broadly than the Lucrine lake,[2]
          will pools be on display, and bachelor planes[3]

will overcrowd the elms. Then violets and   5
myrtles and every bounty for the nostrils
      will spread their odor in the olive groves
          that once were fruitful for their prior master.

The laurel,[4] thick with boughs, will then shut out
hot sunbeams. This was not established under   10
      the auspices of Romulus[5] and long-haired
          Cato,[6] nor by the custom of the ancients.

For those men private property was small,
but common wealth was great. No portico
      marked out by ten-foot measuring rods snatched up   15
          Arctos's chilly shade[7] for private persons.

---

1. *Odes* **2.15** (*Alcaic Strophe*): An ode with no addressee, this poem decries decadent private building practices, introducing a strong moralizing tone that runs through some of the final poems of book 2 (esp. also 2.16 and 2.18) in anticipation of the Roman Odes that open book 3. Romans habitually explained political and social crises as resulting from moral decline, and it is a common refrain in moralizing literature that contemporary men and women lack the principled hardiness of the early Romans, who they believed prioritized the state over the individual and adhered to a code of austere agrarian simplicity.
2. **Lucrine lake:** A lake in southern Italy that had recently been joined to Lake Avernus by Marcus Agrippa.
3. **pools . . . bachelor planes:** Artificial pools and landscapes, as well as ornamental rather than productive trees and plants (such as the plane), were sources of especial anxiety for Roman moralists. The plane trees are "bachelors" since they bore no fruit and were not used as trellises for (i.e., "wedded to") vines, as the elms of line 5 were.
4. **laurel:** Another ornamental tree, used for shade.
5. **Romulus:** The mythological founder of Rome.
6. **Long-haired Cato:** Cato the Elder (234–149 B.C.E.) was often cited as the ideal standard of Roman morality. His unshorn hair suggests old-fashioned as well as Stoic asceticism.
7. **Arctos's chilly shade:** The Big Bear constellation was associated with northern coolness.

nec fortuitum spernere caespitem
leges sinebant, oppida publico
    sumptu iubentes et deorum
        templa novo decorare saxo.   20

The laws did not allow them to despise
the turf[8] they happened on by chance, but ordered
them to adorn from public funds their towns
and temples of the gods with fresh-hewn stone. 20

---

8. **turf:** Turf was a very modest building material, used here for simple homes or altars.

ODES 2.16

Otium divos rogat in patenti
prensus Aegaeo, simul atra nubes
condidit lunam neque certa fulgent
    sidera nautis;

otium bello furiosa Thrace,   5
otium Medi pharetra decori,
Grosphe, non gemmis neque purpura ve-
    nale neque auro.

non enim gazae neque consularis
summovet lictor miseros tumultus   10
mentis et curas laqueata circum
    tecta volantis.

vivitur parvo bene, cui paternum
splendet in mensa tenui salinum
nec levis somnos timor aut cupido   15
    sordidus aufert.

ODES 2.16[1]

For peacefulness[2] the one caught on the wide
Aegean asks the gods, as soon as dark
clouds have obscured the moon and no fixed stars
    twinkle for sailors.

For peacefulness Thrace asks, raging with war,   5
for peacefulness the quiver-decked Medes[3] ask,
Grosphus, which not with gems nor purple nor
    gold can be purchased.

For neither riches[4] nor a consul's lictor[5]
remove the wretched turmoil of a mind   10
or the anxieties that flit around
    ceilings with coffers.

He lives well on a little, whose ancestral
salt-cellar gleams upon his slender table,[6]
whose gentle slumbers neither fear nor sordid   15
    passion dismisses.

---

1. **Odes 2.16** (*Sapphic Strophe*): This ode is addressed to Pompeius Grosphus, a wealthy Sicilian landowner mentioned also in *Epistles* 1.12.22. The main concern of the poem is how a human can acquire tranquility or peace of mind (*otium*), defined here as freedom from worry or anxiety (*cura*). This suggests the Epicurean concept of *ataraxia* (lack of mental disturbance), obtainable through a retired, apolitical life free of ambition, filled with simple enjoyments, and focused on the here-and-now.
2. **peacefulness:** The Latin *otium* (often translated "leisure") is a loaded word with both negative and positive connotations. On the one hand, it is the opposite of *negotium* (business), which was often held up as an ideal; Roman men thought it virtuous to keep busy and felt leisure corrupted one's moral vigor. On the other hand, *otium* has close connections with "peace," a matter of celebration in Horace's Rome, and with philosophical ideals such as *ataraxia* (see above).
3. **Medes:** That is, Parthians.
4. **riches:** The word *gazae* used here is a Persian loanword, which gives these riches an Eastern color.
5. **consul's lictor:** That is, political power. A lictor attended Roman magistrates while carrying the *fasces*, the bundles of rods and axes that symbolized the magistrate's power.
6. **slender table:** Here Horace's poetic and ethical principals align, with the slender compass of his table mirroring the slender compass of his poems.

quid brevi fortes iaculamur aevo
multa? quid terras alio calentis
sole mutamus? patriae quis exul
      se quoque fugit?   20

scandit aeratas vitiosa navis
Cura nec turmas equitum relinquit,
ocior cervis et agente nimbos
      ocior Euro.

laetus in praesens animus quod ultra est   25
oderit curare et amara lento
temperet risu; nihil est ab omni
      parte beatum.

abstulit clarum cita mors Achillem,
longa Tithonum minuit senectus,   30
et mihi forsan, tibi quod negarit,
      porriget hora.

te greges centum Siculaeque circum
mugiunt vaccae, tibi tollit hinnitum
apta quadrigis equa, te bis Afro   35
      murice tinctae

Why do we boldly aim in our brief span
for much? Why move to lands made warm by some
new sun? What exile has escaped his country
    and himself also?   20

Depraved Anxiety climbs up bronze ships,[7]
and she does not desert the troops of horsemen—
faster than deer she goes, faster than Eurus[8]
    chasing the rainclouds.

Glad in the present, let your mind be loath   25
to fret about what's next. Temper the bitter
with your unhurried smile. There's simply nothing
    blessed in each detail.

Swift death bore off illustrious Achilles,
a long senescence withered Tithonus,[9]   30
and what the hour denies to you perhaps
    I will be granted.

Around you low a hundred herds of cattle
from Sicily. For you there neighs a mare
fit for a four-horse team.[10] You're clothed in wool that   35
    African purple

---

7. **bronze ships:** Most likely designates naval warships.
8. **Eurus:** The southeast wind.
9. **withered Tithonus:** Tithonus was the mortal beloved of Aurora, goddess of the dawn. She persuaded Jupiter to grant him immortality but omitted to ask for everlasting youth. He eventually grew so old that his limbs withered into the form of a cicada.
10. **four-horse team:** The team of four horses that pulled a *quadriga* or racing chariot.

vestiunt lanae; mihi parva rura et
spiritum Graiae tenuem Camenae
Parca non mendax dedit et malignum
    spernere vulgus.   40

has dyed two times. Fate, who does not deceive,[11]
has granted me a modest farm, the slender
breath of a Greek Camena[12] and to shun the
       envious masses.   40

---

11. **Fate:** *Parca* is a native Italian word for Fate. Her name suggests she is "frugal" or "sparing," which is why Horace says she does not deceive—her modest gifts live up to what her name suggests.

12. **Camena:** *Camena* was a native Italian word for "Muse." The combination with "Greek" nicely illustrates Horace's mingling of Greek forms and Latin language in the *Odes*.

ODES 2.17

Cur me querelis exanimas tuis?
nec dis amicum est nec mihi te prius
      obire, Maecenas, mearum
          grande decus columenque rerum.

a! te meae si partem animae rapit   5
maturior vis, quid moror altera,
      nec carus aeque nec superstes
          integer? ille dies utramque

ducet ruinam. non ego perfidum
dixi sacramentum: ibimus, ibimus,   10
      utcumque praecedes, supremum
          carpere iter comites parati.

me nec Chimaerae spiritus igneae
nec, si resurgat, centimanus Gyas
      divellet umquam: sic potenti   15
          Iustitiae placitumque Parcis.

ODES 2.17[1]

Why are you killing me with your complaints?
It is not welcome to the gods or me
    that you die first, Maecenas, you, the lofty
        adornment and the capstone of my deeds.

Ah! If a force should seize you prematurely,   5
you half of my own soul,[2] why would I linger?
    My half is not as precious and would not
        survive you in one piece. That day will lead

us both to ruin. It is not a faithless
oath I have spoken: we will go, we'll go,   10
    whenever you will take the lead—we're ready
        to trek the final journey as companions.

Neither the burning-hot Chimaera's breath[3]
nor hundred-handed Gyges,[4] if he rises,
    will ever split me from you. Thus it's been   15
        decreed by mighty Justice and the Fates.

---

1. *Odes* 2.17 (*Alcaic Strophe*): Horace assures Maecenas of his willingness to follow him even into death itself. Horace's use of astrology in the poem may, as scholars suggest, teasingly allude to Maecenas's own astrological interests. Elsewhere (*Odes* 1.11) Horace urges his addressee to ignore astrology and focus on the present, an admonition implicit in this poem too as Horace redirects Maecenas from his fixation on the future toward thanksgiving for his life. The ancient Suetonian biography of Horace records that he died fifty-nine days after Maecenas, so the accidents of history in fact seem to coincide with Horace's promises.
2. **half of my own soul**: It is a traditional idea that a friend was a "second self" or shared a single soul. Cicero, for example, writes at *De Amicitia* 81 that a friend "seeks out another whose mind so mixes with his own that it nearly produces one out of two."
3. **Chimaera's breath**: The Chimaera was a fire-breathing amalgamation of a goat's body, a lion's head, and a serpent's tail. It was slain by Bellerophon.
4. **Gyges**: One of the Hundred-Handers, who joined the attempt of the Giants to overthrow the rule of Jupiter (the Gigantomachy). He was constrained in the Underworld after Jupiter's victory.

seu Libra seu me Scorpios aspicit
formidolosus, pars violentior
     natalis horae, seu tyrannus
         Hesperiae Capricornus undae,   20

utrumque nostrum incredibili modo
consentit astrum: te Iovis impio
     tutela Saturno refulgens
         eripuit volucrisque Fati

tardavit alas, cum populus frequens   25
laetum theatris ter crepuit sonum:
     me truncus illapsus cerebro
         sustulerat, nisi Faunus ictum

dextra levasset, Mercurialium
custos virorum. reddere victimas   30
     aedemque votivam memento:
         nos humilem feriemus agnam.

No matter if it's Libra[5] that beholds me
or dreadful Scorpio, my natal hour's
      more powerful degree,[6] or Capricorn,
          the tyrant of the waters in the west,[7]   20

it is amazing how the stars of both
of us are in alignment. As for you,
      Jove's bright protection[8] rescued you from impious
          Saturn[9] and slowed the flying wings of Fate.

The people, crowded in the theater,   25
then three times sounded out a joyful noise.[10]
      And as for me, the trunk that fell upon my
          skull would have finished me, if Faunus had

not eased the blow with his right hand—he is
the guard of Mercury's men.[11] Do not forget   30
      to pay the victims and the shrine you vowed.
          I'll deal the deathblow to a humble lamb.[12]

---

5. **Libra**: Horace reinforces his promise to die alongside Maecenas by claiming that their horoscopes are aligned. The accuracy of Horace's use of astrology here has been much debated. For the suggestion that Horace freely exploits astrological language with little concern for precision, see Kidd (1982); for arguments that Horace does in fact aim for accuracy, see West (1991) and Bradshaw (2002).

6. **more powerful degree**: Horace most likely means here that the sign of Scorpio (Oct. 23–Nov. 21) falls shortly before his birthday (Dec. 8).

7. **tyrant . . . west**: Capricorn was thought to have influence over the west. He was also associated with the sea and was depicted with a fish tail.

8. **Jove's bright protection**: Maecenas enjoys the protection of the planet/god Jupiter, who rescued Maecenas from an almost lethal sickness. Similarly, Horace is protected by the planet/god Mercury, who rescued him from the tree's fall (described in *Odes* 2.13).

9. **Saturn**: Saturn was "impious" because he castrated his father Cronus and attempted to consume his own children. In astrology the planet's influence was considered malevolent.

10. **joyful noise**: Horace twice mentions (here and at *Odes* 1.20.3–4) the rounds of applause given to Maecenas in the theater in celebration of his recovery from illness.

11. **Faunus . . . Mercury's men**: Faunus is aligned with Pan, the son of Hermes/Mercury. For Horace's associations with Mercury, see also *Odes* 2.7.13–16, where he rescues Horace at Philippi, as well as *Odes* 1.10, a **hymn** to the god.

12. **humble lamb**: In *Odes* 3.8 Horace says he makes thank-offerings annually on March 1 for surviving the fall of the tree; this humble sacrifice is most likely intended for that day.

ODES 2.18

Non ebur neque aureum
mea renidet in domo lacunar,
    non trabes Hymettiae
premunt columnas ultima recisas
    Africa, neque Attali   5
ignotus heres regiam occupavi,
    nec Laconicas mihi
trahunt honestae purpuras clientae:
    at fides et ingeni
benigna vena est, pauperemque dives   10
    me petit: nihil supra
deos lacesso nec potentem amicum
    largiora flagito,
satis beatus unicis Sabinis.
    truditur dies die,   15
novaeque pergunt interire lunae:
    tu secanda marmora
locas sub ipsum funus et sepulcri
    immemor struis domos
marisque Bais obstrepentis urges   20

ODES 2.18[1]

    No ivory nor gilded
coffers of ceilings shine inside my house,
      nor do Hymettian beams[2]
press columns hewn in farthest Africa.
    Nor as the unknown heir   5
of Attalus[3] have I usurped a palace,
      nor do distinguished women
drag along Spartan purple[4] as my clients.
    I do have loyalty,[5]
and a kindly vein of talent. Poor, a rich   10
      man[6] seeks me out. For nothing
else do I vex the gods, nor beg my mighty
      friend for more lavish things,
blessed amply by my matchless Sabine farm.
    Day is pressed on by day,   15
and moons that once were new proceed to wane.
      But you contract the cutting
of marble up till death itself. Forgetting
      the tomb,[7] you heap up houses
and strain to shift the coastline of the sea[8]   20

---

1. *Odes* 2.18 (*Hipponactaeans*): Horace offers another moralizing poem in preparation
   for the "Roman Odes" that open book 3. The ode has no specified addressee apart
   from a generalized "you" in line 17, a common feature of moralizing poetry. He
   contrasts his own satiety with the greed of those who try to cheat death through wealth.
2. **Hymettian beams:** These are architraves carved out of marble from Mt. Hymettus in
   Attica.
3. **unknown heir of Attalus:** The king of Pergamum, Attalus III, had no heir and
   bequeathed his wealthy kingdom to Rome in 133 B.C.E.
4. **Spartan purple:** Luxury fabrics colored purple with Spartan dye.
5. **loyalty:** Horace perhaps plays here on the connection between *fides* (loyalty) and
   fides (lyre), each of which make the humble Horace an attractive friend for Maecenas.
6. **rich man:** A reference most likely to Maecenas, who is widely credited as the
   benefactor of the Sabine farm. For an opposing view, see Bradshaw (1989).
7. **Forgetting the tomb:** Horace suggests his unnamed target should be thinking about
   the marble of the tomb rather than marble for his home.
8. **to shift the coastline of the sea:** The rich man builds an artificial coastline into the
   water. Transgression of natural boundaries was considered highly decadent, even
   impious.

summovere litora,
parum locuples continente ripa.
quid quod usque proximos
revellis agri terminos et ultra
limites clientium   25
salis avarus? pellitur paternos
in sinu ferens deos
et uxor et vir sordidosque natos.
nulla certior tamen
rapacis Orci fine destinata   30
aula divitem manet
erum. quid ultra tendis? aequa tellus
pauperi recluditur
regumque pueris, nec satelles Orci
callidum Promethea   35
revexit auro captus. hic superbum
Tantalum atque Tantali
genus coercet, hic levare functum
pauperem laboribus
vocatus atque non vocatus audit.   40

that loudly roars in Baiae,
not rich enough as long as shore restrains you.
     And what of how you always
tear up the neighboring farmstead's border stones
     and greedily leap past   25
your clients' limits? Holding in their arms
     their family gods and filthy
children, the man and wife are driven out.
     Nevertheless, no hall
more certain than the end ordained by grasping   30
     Orcus[9] awaits the wealthy
master. Why strive for more? The earth is opened
     equally for a pauper
and sons of kings. Orcus's escort,[10] bribed
     by gold, has not restored   35
clever Prometheus.[11] He shuts in pompous
     Tantalus and the race
of Tantalus.[12] Called on or not called on
     to bring ease to the pauper
whose labors all have been performed, he hears.   40

---

9. **Orcus:** Orcus is another name for Hades, god of the dead.
10. **Orcus's escort:** Refers most likely to Mercury, the god of boundary-crossing, who in his capacity as the psychopomp leads souls to and from the Underworld.
11. **Prometheus:** One of the great sinners, who challenged Zeus and gave fire to man. On his presence in the Underworld see the note at *Epodes* 17.67.
12. **Tantalus . . . Tantalus:** Tantalus fed his son Pelops to the gods, thereby introducing a curse to his descendants, particularly Atreus, who similarly killed the children of his brother Thyestes and fed them to him.

ODES 2.19

Bacchum in remotis carmina rupibus
vidi docentem—credite posteri—
    Nymphasque discentis et auris
        capripedum Satyrorum acutas.

Euhoe, recenti mens trepidat metu   5
plenoque Bacchi pectore turbidum
    laetatur: Euhoe, parce Liber,
        parce gravi metuende thyrso!

fas pervicaces est mihi Thyiadas
vinique fontem lactis et uberes   10
    cantare rivos atque truncis
        lapsa cavis iterare mella:

fas et beatae coniugis additum
stellis honorem tectaque Penthei

ODES 2.19[1]

I have seen[2] Bacchus on secluded bluffs
as he taught songs—trust me, posterity—
    and nymphs who were his students, and the ears,
        all pricked and pointed,[3] of goat-footed Satyrs.

Euhoe![4] My mind is jarred by fear still fresh.   5
It wildly revels, and my chest is brimming
    with Bacchus. Euhoe! Liber,[5] show me mercy,
        mercy—so dreadful with your heavy thyrsus![6]

Lawful[7] it is for me to sing the tireless
Thyades[8] and the spring of wine and rich   10
    rivers of milk and to recount anew
        the honey dripping out of hollow tree-trunks,

lawful to sing of how your blessed wife's beauty
was added to the stars,[9] of Pentheus's

---

1. **Odes 2.19** (*Alcaic Strophe*): This ode constitutes a dithyramb, a poem in praise of the wine-god Bacchus, the Roman version of Dionysus. Bacchus, who was also a god of ecstasy ("a standing outside of oneself") was long associated with poetic inspiration, likened to the frenzy of inebriation or the maddened state of Maenads, his mythical female followers. Horace's Bacchus is not, however, a god of mere violent mania. His guise is gentle to those who, like Cerberus at the poem's end, submit to his power.
2. **I have seen**: This suggests an epiphany (an "appearance") of the god to Horace.
3. **pricked and pointed**: Both of these descriptions translate the Latin word *acutas* (sharp). The satyrs' ears are "sharp" because of both their pointed shape and their acute hearing.
4. **Euhoe**: A ritual cry to Bacchus.
5. **Liber**: Another Roman name for Dionysus. It suggests the Latin word *liber* (free) and evokes his Greek cult title *Eleutheros* (the Liberator).
6. **thyrsus**: The ivy-covered staff carried by Bacchus and his followers.
7. **Lawful**: *Fas* signifies something sanctioned by divine law—these are not religious mysteries Horace is forbidden from divulging.
8. **Thyades**: Another name for Maenads.
9. **blessed wife's . . . stars**: A reference to the fate of Ariadne, who was rescued by and married to Bacchus after she was abandoned on Naxos by Jason. Her wedding-crown was catasterized, i.e., added to the heavens as a constellation. The "beauty" (*honorem*) of Ariadne refers to this crown, which was both an honor paid to her and a token of her beauty.

disiecta non leni ruina   15
    Thracis et exitium Lycurgi.

tu flectis amnis, tu mare barbarum,
tu separatis uvidus in iugis
    nodo coerces viperino
        Bistonidum sine fraude crinis: 20

tu, cum parentis regna per arduum
cohors Gigantum scanderet impia,
    Rhoetum retorsisti leonis
        unguibus horribilique mala;

quamquam choreis aptior et iocis   25
ludoque dictus non sat idoneus
    pugnae ferebaris: sed idem
        pacis eras mediusque belli.

te vidit insons Cerberus aureo
cornu decorum leniter atterens   30
    caudam et recedentis trilingui
        ore pedes tetigitque crura.

house, torn to pieces in no gentle fall,[10]   15
    and of Lycurgus's demise in Thrace.[11]

You divert rivers; you, barbarian sea.
You, tipsy, on the distant mountain ridges
    tie back the hair of the Bistonides[12]
        into a snaky knot—and are not hurt.   20

You, when the impious throng of Giants[13] climbed
along the heights up to your father's realm,
    took on your lion aspect and turned Rhoetus[14]
        back with your claws and horrifying jaw.[15]

Though you were called more suitable for dances   25
and jokes and play, and said not to be fit
    enough for battle, yet you were the same[16]
        when in the thick of peace and thick of war.

Cerberus[17] looked at you but did not harm you,
beautiful with your golden horns. He grazed   30
    you gently with his tail, and with his three-tongued
        mouth licked your feet and legs as they departed.

---

10. **Pentheus's house . . . no gentle fall**: Pentheus was the mythical Theban
    king who was destroyed when he rejected the god. His palace was "torn to pieces"
    (*disiecta*) by an earthquake, but this word in fact more properly alludes to the fate
    of Pentheus himself, who was torn limb from limb by his mother and other Theban
    women while they were under the god's inspiration.
11. **Lycurgus's . . . Thrace**: A mythical Thracian king, Lycurgus was blinded and killed
    when he denied Bacchus's power.
12. **Bistonides**: Thracian women, i.e., Maenads.
13. **Giants**: Bacchus is credited with fighting on Jupiter's side in the
    Gigantomachy, when the Giants attempted to ascend to heaven by piling mountain
    on mountain in order to usurp the Olympian throne.
14. **Rhoetus**: One of the Giants.
15. **claws and horrifying jaw**: Bacchus had the ability to appear in the shape of an
    animal, here a lion and below, with his golden horns in lines 29–30, a bull.
16. **The same**: That is, equally vigorous.
17. **Cerberus**: The guard dog of the Underworld. Horace alludes to the story of
    Bacchus's *katabasis* (descent) to the Underworld to rescue his mother Semele from
    death.

ODES 2.20

Non usitata nec tenui ferar
penna biformis per liquidum aethera
  vates, neque in terris morabor
    longius, invidiaque maior

urbis relinquam. non ego pauperum   5
sanguis parentum, non ego quem vocas,
  dilecte Maecenas, obibo
    nec Stygia cohibebor unda.

iam iam residunt cruribus asperae
pelles, et album mutor in alitem   10
  superne, nascunturque leves
    per digitos umerosque plumae.

iam Daedaleo notior Icaro
visam gementis litora Bosphori
  Syrtisque Gaetulas canorus   15
    ales Hyperboreosque campos.

ODES 2.20[1]

Not on a common or a slender wing
will I be borne through shining air, a bard[2]
    of double form, nor on the lands will I
        stay longer. I, superior to envy,

will leave behind the cities. I, the offspring   5
of parents who were poor,[3] I, whom you summon,
    beloved Maecenas, will not pass away
        or be imprisoned by the Stygian wave.[4]

Already on my legs the roughened skin
is shrinking, and I'm changed into a white   10
    bird[5] on my upper half. Soft feathers spring
        to life along my fingers and my shoulders.

More famed than Daedalean Icarus,[6]
I now will go to see the Bosporus's
    lamenting shores and the Gaetulian Syrtes   15
        and Hyperborean fields,[7] a bird of song.

---

1. *Odes* 2.20 (*Alcaic Strophe*): Horace closes *Odes* 2 with a prediction of his own poetic immortality. He recounts his transformation into a swan, a common symbol for poets, and claims that he will traverse the lengths of the Roman Empire acquiring fame. Although the poem has been read as an earnest celebration of his poetic achievement, there are some dubious or even humorous elements to it, especially the grotesque description of his partially complete metamorphosis.
2. **bard**: For "bard," see the note at *Odes* 1.1.35.
3. **parents who were poor**: In *Satires* 1.6 and *Epistles* 1.20, Horace claims that his father was a freedman, for which see the introduction.
4. **Stygian wave**: The Styx was the principal river of the Underworld.
5. **white bird**: The swan was a traditional figure for poets. In *Odes* 4.2, for example, Horace refers to the Greek lyric poet Pindar as the "swan of Dirce."
6. **famed . . . Icarus**: Icarus, whose doomed flight illustrates how art cannot equate us with the immortal gods, is a problematic parallel for Horace. *Notior* (more famous) can also mean more "infamous" or "notorious."
7. **Bosporus's lamenting shores . . . Hyperborean fields**: The Bosporus is the strait that forms the southwestern entrance to the Black Sea. The Syrtes are sandbanks off the coast of Libya in North Africa; they are called "Gaetulian" after a North African people. Hyperborea (the land "beyond the north wind") was a fanciful rather than actual location suggesting extreme remoteness.

me Colchus et qui dissimulat metum
Marsae cohortis Dacus et ultimi
    noscent Geloni, me peritus
        discet Hiber Rhodanique potor.   20

absint inani funere neniae
luctusque turpes et querimoniae;
    compesce clamorem ac sepulcri
        mitte supervacuos honores.

The Colchian and the Dacian[8] (who feigns fear
of Marsian troops[9]) and far-away Geloni[10]
    will come to know me, and the cultured Spaniard
        will study me, and he who drinks Rhodanus.[11]   20

And at my empty funeral let there be
no dirges or foul grief or lamentation.
    Contain all of your crying and dismiss
        the unnecessary honors of a tomb.

---

8. **Colchian and Dacian:** Colchis was on the eastern shore of the Black Sea, Dacia a
region in modern Romania.
9. **Marsian troops:** The Marsi were an ancient Italian people famous for their rugged
hardiness.
10. **Geloni:** A remote nomadic tribe in Scythia. See note on *Odes* 2.9.23.
11. **Rhodanus:** The Rhodanus is the modern Rhône in Gaul (i.e., France).

ODES 3

ODES 3.1

Odi profanum vulgus et arceo;
favete linguis: carmina non prius
    audita Musarum sacerdos
        virginibus puerisque canto.

regum timendorum in proprios greges,   5
reges in ipsos imperium est Iovis,

ODES 3.1[1]

I hate the common mob[2] and keep it back.
Be silent with your tongues. Songs never heard
    before this time I, as the Muses' priest,
        am singing to the virgins and the boys.

Dread kings have power over their own flocks—   5
over the kings themselves is Jupiter's,

---

1. *Odes* 3.1 (*Alcaic Strophe*): This is the first of the six poems (3.1–6) conventionally called the "Roman Odes" for their focus on the Roman state, in which Horace adopts the **persona** of a spokesman (or, as here, a priest) diagnosing the moral failures that have brought civil war to Rome and recommending ways in which these can now be corrected. These failures range from greed and political ambition to loss of traditional virtue and sexual impurity, and the solutions he puts forth in these problems vary and draw from a wide range of philosophical and ethical thought. In 3.1, contentment suited to our mortal lot offers the appropriate antidote for political ambition. Throughout the third book my notes are indebted to the commentaries of Garrison (1991) and especially Nisbet and Rudd (2004). West (2002) also offers a helpful reading of each poem.
2. **common mob**: Horace, figured as a priest, excludes from his poetic rites the common mob, preferring an exclusive audience of young boys and girls.

　　　　clari Giganteo triumpho,
　　　　　　cuncta supercilio moventis.

est ut viro vir latius ordinet
arbusta sulcis, hic generosior　　　　　　　　　　　　　　10
　　　　descendat in Campum petitor,
　　　　　　moribus hic meliorque fama

contendat, illi turba clientium
sit maior: aequa lege Necessitas
　　　　sortitur insignis et imos;　　　　　　　　　　　　15
　　　　　　omne capax movet urna nomen.

destrictus ensis cui super impia
cervice pendet, non Siculae dapes
　　　　dulcem elaborabunt saporem,
　　　　　　non avium citharaeque cantus　　　　　　20

somnum reducent: somnus *agrestium*
lenis *virorum* non humilis domos
　　　　fastidit umbrosamque ripam,
　　　　　　non Zephyris agitata Tempe.

illustrious for his triumph over Giants,[3]
who sets all things in motion with his brow.

One man more broadly than another lines
his trees in furrows. This man, higher born,   10
climbs down into the Campus to get votes;[4]
this one campaigns with better character

and fame. Another has a bigger throng
of clients. With fair law Necessity
selects by lot the lofty and the low;   15
her spacious urn sets every name in motion.

The man above whose impious neck there hangs
an unsheathed sword[5]—for him Sicilian banquets
do not produce a gratifying flavor,
nor does the song of birds or of the lyre   20

restore his sleep. Untrouble<u>d sleep</u> does not
hold in contempt the humble homes of *rustic*
men[6] nor the riverbank suffused with shade
nor the valley driven to and fro by Zephyrs.

---

3. **triumph over Giants**: Jupiter's victory in the Gigantomachy (Battle with the Giants) was an important moment in the myth outlining his rise to power, signaling his supreme position in the cosmos. The Giants came to represent those who impiously sought to rival the gods.

4. **votes**: Elections in Rome took place in the flat plain of the Campus Martius. The candidate "climbs down" from the hills of Rome (such as the Palatine) inhabited by the city's elite.

5. unsheathed **sword**: This alludes to the famous story of Damocles, a courtier of the Sicilian tyrant Dionysius II, who ruled in Syracuse from 367 to 357 B.C.E. According to Cicero (*Tusculan Disputations* 5.61–62), Damocles praised the "happiness" (*beatitas*) that enormous wealth brought to Dionysius, who in turn invited Damocles to experience it for himself. Dionysius had Damocles placed on a golden couch in the midst of an elaborate feast. Then, to illustrate the tyrant's constant fear of assassination, ordered a sword to be hung above Damocles's head, suspended by a single horsehair.

6. **Untroubled sleep . . . rustic men**: *Somnus agrestium / lenis virorum* is a lovely (and untranslatable) example of **interlocking word order** (ABAB), with which Horace illustrates how *somnus levis* (gentle sleep) intertwines the "rustic men" (*agrestium virorum*).

desiderantem quod satis est neque   25
tumultuosum sollicitat mare
    nec saevus Arcturi cadentis
        impetus aut orientis Haedi,

non verberatae grandine vineae
fundusque mendax, arbore nunc aquas   30
    culpante, nunc torrentia agros
        sidera, nunc hiemes iniquas.

contracta pisces aequora sentiunt
iactis in altum molibus; huc frequens
    caementa demittit redemptor   35
        cum famulis dominusque terrae

fastidiosus: sed Timor et Minae
scandunt eodem quo dominus, neque
    decedit aerata triremi et
        post equitem sedet atra Cura.   40

quodsi dolentem nec Phrygius lapis
nec purpurarum sidere clarior

Whoever wants what is sufficient, neither   25
does the unruly sea cause him distress,
    nor does the savage onslaught of Arcturus
        when it is setting or of rising Haedus.[7]

He's not disturbed when hail has thrashed his vineyards,
nor by a lying farm, the fruit tree blaming   30
    now the excessive rain, now stars[8] that burn
        and parch the fields, now detrimental winters.

Fish can perceive when seas have been contracted
by masses thrown into the deep.[9] Here often
    the contractor, beside the slaves, casts down   35
        cement. So does the master—of the land

he is contemptuous.[10] But Fear and Threats
climb up to meet the master. Likewise, gloomy
    Anxiety does not depart the bronze
        trireme, and she sits down behind the
        horseman.[11]   40

But if to one who grieves not Phrygian marble
nor wearing purple brighter than a star

---

7. **Arcturus . . . Haedus:** Horace refers to the evening setting of Arcturus in October and the evening rising of Haedus in September and thus the close of the sailing season owing to stormy weather.
8. **stars:** Probably a reference to Sirius, the "Dog Star," that brought with it the hot "dog days" of summer.
9. **masses . . . deep:** Horace has in mind here the building of villas that extended over the shoreline. Crossing such natural boundaries was a hallmark of those who impiously transgress divine law.
10. **master—of the land / . . . contemptuous:** Horace offers here a brilliant use of **enjambment** that I have tried (perhaps inelegantly) to preserve. By postponing *fastidiosus* "contemptuous) until line 36, Horace unexpectedly and pointedly rewrites the syntax of line 35. The owner imagines himself to be "master of the land" (*dominus terrae*) but is really contemptuous of it (*terrae / fastidiosus*).
11. **horseman:** Technically an "equestrian" or *eques*. Equestrians originally made up the Roman cavalry but came to designate the social rank just below senators. Horace's focus on excessively luxurious building may have shifted to a military context, or Horace may be using the word to indicate the equestrian pastimes of the wealthy.

delenit usus nec Falerna
    vitis Achaemeniumque costum,

cur invidendis postibus et novo   45
sublime ritu moliar atrium?
    cur valle permutem Sabina
        divitias operosiores?

can bring relief, nor can Falernian
    vines and the perfume of Achaemenes,[12]

why would I build a lofty atrium   45
with posts to envy and in modern style?
    Or why would I exchange my Sabine valley
        for riches that exact too many pains?

---

12. **perfume of Achaemenes**: That is, Persian perfume. Achaemenes was a
seventh-century B.C.E. Persian king who gave his name to the Achaemenids, the
dynasty that ruled Persia from around 550 to 330 B.C.E.

ODES 3.2

Angustam amice pauperiem pati
robustus acri militia puer
    condiscat et Parthos feroces
        vexet eques metuendus hasta

vitamque sub divo et trepidis agat   5
in rebus. illum ex moenibus hosticis
    matrona bellantis tyranni
        prospiciens et adulta virgo

suspiret, "eheu, ne rudis agminum
sponsus lacessat regius asperum   10
    tactu leonem, quem cruenta
        per medias rapit ira caedis."

dulce et decorum est pro patria mori:
mors et fugacem persequitur virum,

ODES 3.2[1]

The boy that soldiering has toughened up
should learn to suffer pinching poverty
  on friendly terms. Let him, on horseback, plague
    ferocious Parthians,[2] dreadful with his spear,

and pass his life beneath the open sky[3]   5
in tense conditions. As they gaze at him
  from hostile ramparts,[4] let the warring tyrant's
    wife and their virgin daughter, now grown-up,

sigh out, "Alas! My royal fiancé[5]
is new to battle-lines. May he not rouse   10
  the lion, rough when touched,[6] whom bloody wrath
    carries along throughout the midst of slaughter."

It's sweet and seemly to die for one's own country.[7]
But death pursues as well the man who flees

---

1. *Odes* 3.2 (*Alcaic Strophe*): In this second of the Roman Odes, Horace extols
Virtus—an impossible-to-define word that can suggest "manliness," "excellence" of
character or morality, "virtue," or more specific virtues such as "steadfastness" or
"battle prowess." In the ode, one wins wars, honors, and heaven itself through *virtus*.
Horace's formulation of virtue as a route to heaven is particularly indebted to Stoic
thought.
2. **ferocious Parthians**: See note at *Odes* 1.2.23.
3. **beneath the open sky**: Literally, "beneath the god," with the "god" standing
metonymically for the sky.
4. **hostile ramparts**: Horace envisions an epic *teichoscopia*, a scene in which citizens of a
besieged city survey the enemy from the walls. The most famous of these is in *Iliad* 3.
5. **My royal fiancé**: The quotation suits the daughter rather than her mother. I have
followed those editors who make these lines a direct quotation rather than a
subordinate clause.
6. **rough when touched**: The words, as Nisbet and Rudd (2004) note, suggest both that
the "lion" (i.e., the enemy soldier) grows rough when provoked and that he is literally
rough to the touch.
7. **It's sweet . . . own's country**: The notion that it is *decorum* (seemly, noble, or even
beautiful) to die for one's country is paralleled in Greek writers, e.g., Tyrtaeus fr. 10
("To fall and die among the fore-fighters is a beautiful thing / for a brave man who is
doing battle on behalf of his country," trans. Miller [1996]). Wilfred Owen's "Dulce et
Decorum Est," published posthumously in 1920, offers a pointed rebuke to Horace's
line in the context of World War I.

nec parcit imbellis iuventae   15
    poplitibus timidove tergo.

Virtus repulsae nescia sordidae
intaminatis fulget honoribus,
    nec sumit aut ponit securis
        arbitrio popularis aurae.   20

Virtus, recludens immeritis mori
caelum, negata temptat iter via
    coetusque vulgaris et udam
        spernit humum fugiente penna.

est et fideli tuta silentio   25
merces: vetabo, qui Cereris sacrum
    vulgarit arcanae, sub isdem
        sit trabibus fragilemque mecum

solvat phaselon: saepe Diespiter
neglectus incesto addidit integrum: 30
    raro antecedentem scelestum
        deseruit pede Poena claudo.

and does not spare the hamstrings or the timid   15
    back of the youth who is not fit for war.

Virtue is ignorant of base defeat. *Possible* *arose*
It gleams with honors[8] that are undefiled,
    not picking up or putting down the axes[9]
        according to the fickle people's whim.   20

Virtue, unlocking heaven to those not
deserving death, attempts to walk a path
    denied to others. It rejects the mob's
        assemblies and dank earth on fleeing wings.

There is for faithful silence too a safe   25
reward.[10] I will not let whoever has
    divulged the holy rite of secret Ceres[11]
        be under my same roof beams or unmoor

a fragile boat with me. Jupiter often,
if slighted, joins the pure to the defiled.   30
    It's rare that when a wicked man precedes her
        lame-footed Punishment does not catch up.

---

8. **base defeat . . . honors:** *Repulsa* (defeat) suggests in particular defeat at the polls. *Honores* (honors) were not just abstract honors but also political offices. As Nisbet and Rudd (2004) put it, "the good man who has been denied *honores* (magistracies) shines with *honores* (of a less material sort)."

9. **axes:** The axes that formed part of the *fasces*. They were wrapped in bundles as symbols of a magistrate's power.

10. **There is . . . safe reward:** This turn in thought has puzzled readers, but Horace seems to be transitioning to the idea that virtue is found also in religious piety. Those who do not divulge the secret rites of mystery religions also have a share of it. The idea that silence brings no risks is found in the Greek lyric poet Simonides, who was known for his **panegyrics**. There may therefore be a hint in Horace's poem of the dangers of panegyric poetry, for which reading see Bleisch (2001).

11. **secret Ceres:** A reference to the Eleusinian Mysteries, which initiates were prohibited from revealing.

ODES 3.3

Iustum et tenacem propositi virum
non civium ardor prava iubentium,
    non vultus instantis tyranni
        mente quatit solida neque Auster,

dux inquieti turbidus Hadriae,   5
nec fulminantis magna manus Iovis:
    si fractus illabatur orbis,
        impavidum ferient ruinae.

hac arte Pollux et vagus Hercules
enisus arces attigit igneas,   10
    quos inter Augustus recumbens
        purpureo bibet ore nectar.

hac te merentem, Bacche pater, tuae
vexere tigres indocili iugum
    collo trahentes; hac Quirinus   15
        Martis equis Acheronta fugit,

ODES 3.3[1]

The man who's just and steadfast to his purpose—
neither the zeal of citizens who order
      crimes nor the visage of a threatening tyrant
          can shake his fixed resolve, nor can the Auster,[2]

the restless Adriatic's[3] raging leader,   5
nor the colossal hand of thundering Jove.
      If the whole sky should break and tumble down,
          the falling shards would strike him unafraid.

Pollux and roving Hercules rose up
and gained the fiery heights due to this trait.   10
      Augustus will recline together with them
          and drink down nectar with his crimson mouth.[4]

Due to this trait your tigers, father Bacchus,[5]
rightly transported you—they pulled the yoke
      with untamed necks. Quirinus,[6] due to this,   15
          fled Acheron upon the steeds of Mars,[7]

---

1. **Odes 3.3** (*Alcaic Strophe*): The third Roman ode begins by praising the qualities
of character (namely, justice and resolve) through which great heroes attain
divinity—including Pollux, Hercules, Bacchus, Romulus, and (in the future) Augustus.
Romulus provides the hinge to the next section, in which Horace records Juno's
speech conceding to his deification and thus the rise of Rome. She agrees only on the
condition that Troy not be rebuilt, a compromise found also in her concession speech
in *Aeneid* 12. The poem has many points of contact with Vergil's epic, particularly
with the idea that Rome may enjoy *imperium sine fine* (empire without end).
2. **Auster**: The south wind.
3. **Adriatic's**: The Adriatic is the sea to the east of Italy.
4. **crimson mouth**: His mouth is crimson most likely because the nectar is the same
color as wine. Nisbet and Rudd (2004) also suggest it is a sign of eternal youthfulness.
5. **father Bacchus**: Although Bacchus was traditionally born a god, he was a latecomer
who had to work to spread his worship.
6. **Quirinus**: A cult name of Romulus.
7. **Acheron . . . steeds of Mars**: Acheron is the Underworld, i.e., death. Romulus rode
the steeds of Mars to heaven because the god was his father.

gratum elocuta consiliantibus
Ionone divis: "Ilion, Ilion
  fatalis incestusque iudex
    et mulier peregrina vertit   20

in pulverem, ex quo destituit deos
mercede pacta Laomedon, mihi
  castaeque damnatum Minervae
    cum populo et duce fraudulento.

iam nec Lacaenae splendet adulterae   25
famosus hospes nec Priami domus
  periura pugnaces Achivos
    Hectoreis opibus refringit,

nostrisque ductum seditionibus
bellum resedit. protinus et gravis   30
  iras et invisum nepotem,
    Troica quem peperit sacerdos,

Marti redonabo; illum ego lucidas
inire sedes, discere nectaris
  sucos et adscribi quietis   35
    ordinibus patiar deorum.

dum longus inter saeviat Ilion
Romamque pontus, qualibet exules

once Juno spoke in their assembly words
that pleased the gods: "Ilion, Ilion![8]
    That judge, so catastrophic and unchaste,
        together with his foreign wife,[9] has turned it   20

to ashes. Ever since Laomedon[10]
cheated the gods of pay he had agreed to,
    it has been doomed by me and chaste Minerva—
        it and its people and its lying leader.

The ill-famed guest no longer gleams for his   25
Spartan adulteress.[11] No longer does
    the perjured house of Priam pound to bits
        warlike Acheans with the might of Hector.

All of the strife among us drew it out,
but war has now subsided. Straight away   30
    I will surrender my excessive wrath
        and grant to Mars the grandson I despise,

the one born to the Trojan priestess.[12] Let
him come into these shining realms and learn
    about the juice of nectar and be classed   35
        among the tranquil ranks of gods—I'll bear it.

As long as, separating Ilion
from Rome, a wide sea rages, let the exiles

---

8. **Ilion, Ilion**: This is another name for Troy.
9. **The judge ... foreign wife**: The judge is Paris, who arbitrated the famous beauty contest between Minerva, Juno, and Venus. His wife is Helen, whom Venus offered to him as a bribe.
10. **Laomedon**: A king of Troy and father of Priam. He promised payment to Neptune and Apollo for building the walls of Troy and then reneged on paying.
11. **ill-famed guest ... Spartan adulteress**: Paris and Helen again. He was a guest in Menelaus and Helen's house in Sparta when he either seduced or seized her.
12. **grandson ... Trojan priestess**: The grandson is Romulus, the Trojan priestess his mother Rhea Silvia. The god Mars raped her, whereupon she gave birth to Romulus and Remus. Romulus later killed Remus for mocking his walls.

in parte regnanto beati;
    dum Priami Paridisque busto   40

insultet armentum et catulos ferae
celent inultae, stet Capitolium
    fulgens triumphatisque possit
        Roma ferox dare iura Medis.

horrenda late nomen in ultimas   45
extendat oras, qua medius liquor
    secernit Europen ab Afro,
        qua tumidus rigat arva Nilus,

aurum irrepertum et sic melius situm,
cum terra celat, spernere fortior   50
    quam cogere humanos in usus
        omne sacrum rapiente dextra.

quicumque mundo terminus obstitit,
hunc tanget armis, visere gestiens,
    qua parte debacchentur ignes,   55
        qua nebulae pluviique rores.

sed bellicosis fata Quiritibus
hac lege dico, ne nimium pii
    rebusque fidentes avitae
        tecta velint reparare Troiae.   60

rule anywhere they'd like, and be successful.
As long as cattle stomp on Priam's tomb   40

and Paris's, and wild beasts hide their whelps
there unavenged, the shining Capitol[13]
may stand and ruthless Rome possess the power
to triumph over Medes[14] and give them laws.

Feared the world over, let her spread her name   45
to farthest shores, where water flows between
Europe and Africa, dividing them,[15]
and where the Nile swells up and wets the fields.

She's stronger if she spurns still buried gold,
best left where earth can cover over it,   50
than if she forces it to human uses,
her right hand grasping every sacred thing.

Whatever boundary line confines the world,
she'll touch it with her weapons, keen to see
that zone where fire rages like a Bacchant,[16]   55
that zone where there are clouds and
rain and dew.[17]

But to the warlike Quirites[18] I speak
these fates on this condition: that they not,
too pious or too sure in their good luck,
desire to build once more ancestral Troy.   60

---

13. **shining Capitol:** A reference to the temple of Jupiter on the Capitoline, which had a gilded roof.
14. **Medes:** That is, the Persians. See the note on *Odes* 1.2.23.
15. **dividing them:** The Strait of Gibraltar, which separates Africa and Asia in the west, where the Mediterranean Sea meets the Atlantic Ocean.
16. **that zone . . . Bacchant:** This fiery zone runs around the equator.
17. **that zone . . . dew:** The zone running across the extreme north.
18. **Quirites:** A name for the citizens of Rome, derived from Cures, a Sabine town that was incorporated into it in its early history.

Troiae renascens alite lugubri
fortuna tristi clade iterabitur,
    ducente victrices catervas
        coniuge me Iovis et sorore.

ter si resurgat murus aeneus   65
auctore Phoebo, ter pereat meis
    excisus Argivis, ter uxor
        capta virum puerosque ploret."

non hoc iocosae conveniet lyrae:
quo, Musa, tendis? Desine pervicax   70
    referre sermones deorum et
        magna modis tenuare parvis.

Troy's lot will once more end in mournful ruin
if it's reborn beneath a dire omen.
>   And I myself will lead the conquering throngs—
>   the sister and the wife of Jupiter.

If three times there should rise a wall of bronze,   65
Phoebus its builder, three times it would topple,
>   felled by my Argives. Three times will a wife,
>   made captive, mourn her husband and
>   her children."

This is not suited to the playful lyre.
Where are you headed, Muse? Stop stubbornly   70
>   reporting conversations of the gods and
>   degrading mighty themes with small-
>   scale measures.

ODES 3.4

Descende caelo et dic age tibia
regina longum Calliope melos,
     seu voce nunc mavis acuta,
         seu fidibus citharave Phoebi.

auditis an me ludit amabilis   5
insania? audire et videor pios
     errare per lucos, amoenae
         quos et aquae subeunt et aurae.

me fabulosae Vulture in Apulo
nutricis extra limen Apuliae   10

ODES 3.4[1]

Descend[2] from heaven and perform a lengthy
song on your flute,[3] O queen Calliope,
    or with your high-pitched voice, if you prefer,
        or on the lyre or cithara[4] of Phoebus.

Do you too hear her or is there a lovely   5
madness deluding me? I seem to hear her
    and stroll through holy groves while into them
        the pleasant winds and waters make their way.

I was a boy[5] when on Apulian Vultur[6]
just past the threshold of Apulia,   10

---

1. **Odes 3.4** (*Alcaic Strophe*): The fourth Roman Ode, in the words of Garrison (1991), is "Horace's longest and most difficult ode," an opinion shared by many scholars who have attempted to trace and explicate its thought. The poem's first half (roughly) focuses on the poet—his particular relationship with the Muses and the landscapes that give rise to his poetry. Horace then turns his attention to Augustus, who himself has a special connection to the Muses. The final stanzas of the poem focus on Jupiter, Augustus's celestial counterpart, and his establishment of order in the cosmos through his defeat of numerous foes. The praise poetry of the Greek lyric poet Pindar has especially influenced Horace's ode, for which see the commentary of Nisbet and Rudd (2004).
2. **Descend . . . Calliope:** Calliope was one of the Muses. In Hesiod's *Theogony* 80, she is called the companion of kings. The invocation and request that she "descend" give the opening the flavor of a **cletic hymn**.
3. **flute:** The tibia was a double reed flute.
4. **cithara:** A stringed instrument much like a lyre.
5. **I was a boy:** Horace describes a divine encounter he had with the gods when he was just a boy. This is a common **topos** poets employ to establish their special relationship with the divine, especially the Muses. Hesiod, for instance, describes in the *Theogony* how he, while a shepherd, encountered the Muses on Mt. Helicon. Pindar was supposed to have been fed honey by bees in his childhood.
6. **Apulian Vultur:** Vultur was a mountain near Venosa, in the southern Italian region of Apulia, where Horace was born.

ludo fatigatumque somno
　　fronde nova puerum palumbes

texere, mirum quod foret omnibus,
quicumque celsae nidum Aceruntiae
　　saltusque Bantinos et arvum   15
　　　　pingue tenent humilis Forenti,

ut tuto ab atris corpore viperis
dormirem et ursis, ut premerer sacra
　　lauroque collataque myrto,
　　　　non sine dis animosus infans.   20

vester, Camenae, vester in arduos
tollor Sabinos, seu mihi frigidum
　　Praeneste seu Tibur supinum
　　　　seu liquidae placuere Baiae.

vestris amicum fontibus et choris   25
non me Philippis versa acies retro,

my nurse,[7] the doves of legend[8] covered me,
     exhausted by my play and sleep, with fresh

foliage. It astonished everyone,
all those who dwell within the lofty nest
     of Aceruntia and Bantium's glades   15
          or on the fertile plain of low Forentum,[9]

how I was sleeping with my body safe
from glossy snakes and bears, how heaps of holy
     laurel and myrtle were concealing me,
          a baby dauntless through the aid of gods.   20

As yours, O Muses, yours, I'm borne aloft
into the Sabine hills, or to Praeneste,
     if drawn there by its chill, or to the slopes
          of Tibur, or the crystal air of Baiae.[10]

Since I am friendly to your springs and dances,   25
neither the routed line at Philippi

---

7. **Apulia, my nurse:** There is significant disagreement here as to what the Latin text should say. Some manuscripts have, as printed here, *limen Apuliae* (threshold of Apulia), in which case Horace has wandered outside the bounds of Apulia (which he refers to as his "nurse"). Mt. Vultur was on the border with Lucania. Scholars protest that a *limen* must be the threshold of a house and that the repetition *Apulo . . . Apuliae* (with differing metrical quantities) is awkward. Other manuscripts have *limina Pulliae* (the thresholds of Pullia), which some have taken as the name of Horace's wet nurse. Conjectures include *limina pergulae* (the cottage's thresholds) and *limina villulae* (the little farmhouse's thresholds).

8. **doves of legend:** It is not clear exactly which legend Horace has in mind here, but in myth doves are associated both with Venus (as the drivers of her chariot) and Zeus (as those who delivered his ambrosia while he was hidden in Crete as an infant).

9. **Aceruntia . . . Bantium . . . Forentum:** Three towns near Mt. Vultur. Aceruntia (modern Acerenza) is at a high elevation, as "nest" implies; Bantium (Banzi) in the hills, and Forentum (Forenza) in the low-lying plain.

10. **Praeneste . . . Tibur . . . Baiae:** Praeneste and Tibur were towns in the Sabine hills, near Horace's farm. Baiae was a beach resort town on the bay of Naples. As in lines 14–16, these are arranged in order of descending altitude.

devota non extinxit arbos,
    nec Sicula Palinurus unda.

utcumque mecum vos eritis, libens
insanientem navita Bosphorum   30
    temptabo et urentis harenas
        litoris Assyrii viator,

visam Britannos hospitibus feros
et laetum equino sanguine Concanum,
    visam pharetratos Gelonos   35
        et Scythicum inviolatus amnem.

vos Caesarem altum, militia simul
fessas cohortes abdidit oppidis,
    finire quaerentem labores
        Pierio recreatis antro.   40

vos lene consilium et datis et dato
gaudetis almae. scimus ut impios
    Titanas immanemque turbam
        fulmine sustulerit caduco,

nor the accursed tree extinguished me,
 nor the Sicilian wave of Palinurus.[11]

Whenever you are with me, as a sailor
I gladly will attempt the Bosporus,   30
 despite its rage, or as a traveler
  the burning sands upon the Syrian shore.[12]

I'll go to see the Britons, fierce to guests,
and the Concanian glad in horse's blood.
 I'll go to see the quiver-clad Geloni,   35
  and Scythia's river[13]—all while safe from harm.

Now that exalted Caesar has retired
his service-weary troops throughout the towns[14]
 and seeks to bring his labors to an end,
  in your Pierian grotto[15] you restore him.   40

You give him gentle counsel and rejoice
once it's been given. We know how the impious
 Titans and their enormous throng[16] were crushed
  by the descending thunderbolt of him

---

11. **Philippi ... Palinurus**: Three instances when Horace almost lost his life. He fought on the losing side of Brutus and Cassius at the Battle of Philippi in 42 B.C.E. A tree later fell on him while he was at his Sabine farm, for which see *Odes* 2.13. The last incident is unknown, but it happened at sea near Cape Palinuro in southwest Italy.
12. **Bosporus ... Syria**: The Bosporus was the entrance to the Black Sea. Syria probably refers generally to the east.
13. **Britons ... Concanian ... river**: Foreign tribes considered ferocious by the Romans. The Concani in northern Spain were thought to drink horse blood. The Geloni were a Scythian tribe, and "Scythia's river" is the Don.
14. **retired ... towns**: A reference to Augustus's settlement of his soldiers throughout Italy after the Battle of Actium, which he achieved through a series of land confiscations.
15. **Pierian grotto**: Pieria was the Greek location of Mt. Helicon, the home of the Muses.
16. **Titans and their enormous throng**: Horace describes the Titanomachy, the battle between Jupiter/the Olympians and the preceding generation of Titans, led by Saturn (Jupiter's father), through which Jupiter acquired his supreme position. He seems to conflate this with the Gigantomachy, the attempt by the Giants to overthrow Jupiter once his rule was established.

qui terram inertem, qui mare temperat   45
ventosum, et umbras regnaque tristia
    divosque mortalisque turmas
        imperio regit unus aequo.

magnum illa terrorem intulerat Iovi
fidens iuventus horrida bracchiis   50
    fratresque tendentes opaco
        Pelion imposuisse Olympo.

sed quid Typhoeus et validus Mimas,
aut quid minaci Porphyrion statu,
    quid Rhoetus evulsisque truncis   55
        Enceladus iaculator audax

contra sonantem Palladis aegida
possent ruentes? hinc avidus stetit
    Vulcanus, hinc matrona Iuno et
        numquam umeris positurus arcum,   60

qui rore puro Castaliae lavit
crinis solutos, qui Lyciae tenet
    dumeta natalemque silvam,
        Delius et Patareus Apollo.

who regulates the sluggish earth and windy   45
sea and who rules the shades and gloomy kingdoms
    as well as all the gods and mortal throngs
        with his impartial sovereignty—alone.

They struck a mighty terror into Jove—
young and horrendous, trusting in their arms[17]—   50
    as did the brothers who aspired to pile
        Pelion onto shady Mount Olympus.[18]

And yet what could Typhoeus or the mighty
Mimas, what could Porphyrion with his threatening
    stature, or Rhoetus or Enceladus,[19]   55
        that daring thrower of uprooted trees—

rushing against Minerva's blaring aegis,
what could they do? Keen Vulcan stood beside her
    on one side; on the other, matron Juno
        and him whose shoulders always wear
            the bow,   60

who washes in Castalia's spotless stream
his loosened hair, who occupies the thickets
    of Lycia and the forests of his birth,[20]
        Apollo, Delian and Patarean.[21]

---

17. **young . . . arms:** This may refer to either the Giants or to the Hundred-Handers. Though Horace pits the latter against Zeus/Jupiter, in Hesiod's *Theogony* they fight on his side.

18. **brothers . . . Mount Olympus:** Otis and Ephialtes, giants who piled up the mountains in order to ascend to heaven.

19. **Typhoeus . . . Mimas . . . Porphyrion . . . Rhoetus . . . Enceladus:** More monstrous opponents of Jupiter. Typhoeus was a man/bird/snake giant to whom Gaia gave birth to challenge Jupiter's established power. The others are Giants and were part of the Gigantomachy.

20. **Forests . . . birth:** Apollo was famously born on the island of Delos.

21. **Castalia's . . . Delian . . . Patarean:** Castalia was a spring near Delphi, Delos was the Aegean island where Apollo was born, and Patara was a city in Lycia.

vis consili expers mole ruit sua: 65
vim temperatam di quoque provehunt
    in maius; idem odere viris
        omne nefas animo moventis.

testis mearum centimanus Gyges
sententiarum, notus et integrae   70
    temptator Orion Dianae,
        virginea domitus sagitta.

iniecta monstris Terra dolet suis
maeretque partus fulmine luridum
    missos ad Orcum; nec peredit   75
        impositam celer ignis Aetnen,

incontinentis nec Tityi iecur
reliquit ales, nequitiae additus
    custos; amatorem trecentae
        Pirithoum cohibent catenae.   80

Force without counsel falls by its own weight.   65
But regulated force the gods advance
    and amplify. Likewise they hate the force
        that ponders every kind of sinfulness.

Let hundred-handed Gyges be the witness
to these my maxims. And Orion,[22] too,   70
    ill-famed assailant of untouched Diana—
        but by her virgin's arrow he was vanquished.

The Earth is grieving, piled with her own monsters.
She mourns her offspring sent to ghastly Orcus
    by thunderbolt. Nor has the nimble fire   75
        eaten its way through Aetna piled on top.[23]

The bird—the one assigned to be the guard
over his mischief—has not quit the liver
    of lustful Tityus. Three hundred chains
        are hemming in Pirithous, the lover.[24]   80

---

22. **Gyges . . . Orion**: Gyges was one of the Hundred-Handers and is now
    imprisoned in Tartarus. Orion (in this version) tried to rape Diana, whereupon
    she killed him.
23. **Aetna piled on top**: Aetna here has been piled on top of Tartarus to keep all of
    the defeated foes of Jupiter locked away. This would describe its volcanic fury.
24. **Tityus . . . Pirithous, the lover**: Tityus tried to rape Leto, the mother of
    Apollo and Diana, for which he is eternally punished in the Underworld by having an
    eagle consume his perpetually regenerating liver. Pirithous came to the Underworld
    in an attempt to rape Persephone, for which he is kept eternally chained.

ODES 3.5

Caelo tonantem credidimus Iovem
regnare: praesens divus habebitur
    Augustus adiectis Britannis
        imperio gravibusque Persis.

milesne Crassi coniuge barbara   5
turpis maritus vixit et hostium—
    pro curia inversique mores!—
        consenuit socerorum in armis

sub rege Medo Marsus et Apulus,
anciliorum et nominis et togae   10
    oblitus aeternaeque Vestae,
        incolumi Iove et urbe Roma?

hoc caverat mens provida Reguli
dissentientis condicionibus
    foedis et exemplo trahenti   15
        perniciem veniens in aevum,

ODES 3.5[1]

Because he thunders we believe that Jove
rules in the sky. Augustus will be deemed
    a god on earth when Britons and the grievous
        Parthians[2] have been added to our empire.

Has Crassus' soldier lived, a shameful husband   5
to a barbarian[3] wife? Has he grown old
    (woe for the senate and inverted morals!)
        amid the hostile army of his in-laws?

Have the Marsian and Apulian[4] forgotten,
under the Parthian king, about the shields,[5]   10
    their name, the toga, and eternal Vesta,[6]
        while Jove[7] and Rome the city are intact?

Regulus' prescient mind had warned of this
when he dissented from disgraceful terms
    and from a precedent that would have brought   15
        destruction to the coming generation

---

1. *Odes* 3.5 (*Alcaic Strophe*): The fifth Roman Ode pits the behavior of Marcus Licinius Crassus's soldiers, ten thousand of whom were captured in the Battle of Carrhae in 53 B.C.E. and whom Horace envisions as willingly integrating into Parthian culture, against the Roman hero Regulus, a Roman consul and statesmen who was captured by the Carthaginians in 255 B.C.E. during the First Punic War. Regulus was sent back to the Romans to negotiate peace and the ransom of the prisoners, but he instead urged them to continue fighting and allow the prisoners to be executed. He then voluntarily returned to Carthage to be tortured to death.
2. **Parthians:** For the Parthians, see the note at *Odes* 1.2.23.
3. **barbarian:** See note at *Epodes* 5.61.
4. **Marsian and Apulian:** Two native Italian peoples renowned for their prowess in war. Apulia was Horace's birthplace.
5. **shields:** The *ancilia* were twelve shields kept by the Salii, priests of Mars. One of them was thought to have fallen from heaven during the time of the legendary king Numa Pompilius, who ordered eleven identical ones to be made to guard the original from theft.
6. **eternal Vesta:** A reference to the eternal flame of Vesta, kept alight by the Vestal Virgins.
7. **Jove:** Standing **metonymically** for the temple of Jupiter Optimus Maximus on the Capitoline.

si non periret immiserabilis
captiva pubes. "signa ego Punicis
    adfixa delubris et arma
        militibus sine caede" dixit   20

"derepta vidi; vidi ego civium
retorta tergo bracchia libero
    portasque non clausas et arva
        Marte coli populata nostro.

auro repensus scilicet acrior   25
miles redibit. flagitio additis
    damnum: neque amissos colores
        lana refert medicata fuco,

nec vera virtus, cum semel excidit,
curat reponi deterioribus.   30
    si pugnat extricata densis
        cerva plagis, erit ille fortis

qui perfidis se credidit hostibus,
et Marte Poenos proteret altero,
    qui lora restrictis lacertis   35
        sensit iners timuitque mortem.

hic, unde vitam sumeret inscius,
pacem duello miscuit. o pudor!
    o magna Carthago, probrosis
        altior Italiae ruinis!"   40

fertur pudicae coniugis osculum
parvosque natos ut capitis minor

if the young prisoners were not allowed
to die with no tears shed for them. "I've seen
    our standards fastened onto Punic temples,"
        he said, "and weapons snatched away
            from soldiers   20

amid no bloodshed. I have seen the arms
of citizens twisted behind free backs,
    the gates left open, and the fields that we
        once spoiled in war now being cultivated.

I guess[8] the soldier ransomed with his weight   25
in gold will come back fiercer. You are adding
    financial loss to shame. The wool, once dyed,
        never gets back the color it has lost.

Nor is true virtue, once it has departed,
eager to be restored in lesser men.   30
    If a doe attacks when it has broken free
        of close-mesh nets,[9] then that man will be brave

who lent himself to faithless enemies.
And he will crush the Carthaginians
    when he reenters war, who, arms tied back,   35
        timidly felt the whips and dreaded death.

This man, not knowing how one saves one's life,
confounded war and peace. O shamefulness!
    O mighty Carthage, raised up even higher
        by the disgraceful fall of Italy!"   40

It's said that he rebuffed his chaste wife's kiss
and drove his own small children from himself,

---

8. **I guess**: The word *scilicet* introduces heavily ironic statements. Regulus's point is that of course a ransomed soldier will not come back braver.

9. **doe attacks . . . close-mesh nets**: A caught deer will of course *not* be aggressive but will run away, as deer are proverbially timid.

ab se removisse et virilem
    torvus humi posuisse vultum,

donec labantis consilio patres   45
firmaret auctor numquam alias dato,
    interque maerentis amicos
        egregius properaret exsul.

atqui sciebat quae sibi barbarus
tortor pararet; non aliter tamen   50
    dimovit obstantis propinquos
        et populum reditus morantem

quam si clientum longa negotia
diiudicata lite relinqueret,
    tendens Venafranos in agros   55
        aut Lacedaemonium Tarentum.

like one deprived of civil rights, and sternly
    focused his manly gaze upon the ground,

until he steeled the wavering senators   45
by giving them unprecedented counsel.
    And in the midst of his lamenting friends
        he hurried forth, a most distinguished exile.

He knew just what the barbarous torturer
prepared for him, and yet he moved aside   50
    the relatives who stood to block his way
        and the large crowd delaying his return

as though he'd left behind his clients' lengthy
business, his lawsuit now adjudicated,
    and made his way into Venafrum's fields[10]   55
        or into Lacedaemonian Tarentum.[11]

---

10. **Venafrum's fields:** Venafrum was rural area one hundred miles outside of
Rome on the Latium-Samnium border. In other words, Regulus exits as though en
route to a country holiday at his villa rather than to death by torture.
11. **Tarentum:** Another popular area in southern Italy that was associated with villas in
Horace's day. It was founded by Spartan (i.e., Lacedaemonian) colonists.

ODES 3.6

Delicta maiorum immeritus lues,
Romane, donec templa refeceris
        aedesque labentis deorum et
            foeda nigro simulacra fumo.

dis te minorem quod geris, imperas: 5
hinc omne principium, huc refer exitum:
        di multa neglecti dederunt
            Hesperiae mala luctuosae.

iam bis Monaeses et Pacori manus
non auspicatos contudit impetus   10
        nostros et adiecisse praedam
            torquibus exiguis renidet.

paene occupatam seditionibus
delevit urbem Dacus et Aethiops,
        hic classe formidatus, ille   15
            missilibus melior sagittis.

ODES 3.6[1]

Though guiltless, Roman, you'll atone for your
ancestors' crimes until you have restored
      the temples and the gods' collapsing shrines and
          their images[2] begrimed with murky smoke.

Since you subject yourselves to gods, you rule.[3]   5
Ascribe to them each start, from them each outcome.
      The gods, since they've been scorned, have given many
          evils to sorrowful Hesperia.[4]

Already twice Monaeses and the band
of Pacorus[5] have crushed the strikes we made   10
      without the auspices. They beam with joy
          to add our booty to their little torques.[6]

The city, seized by civil strife, was almost
crushed by the Dacian and the Ethiopian,[7]
      the latter terrifying with his fleet,   15
          the former better at propelling arrows.

---

1. *Odes* 3.6 (*Alcaic Strophe*): In this last Roman Ode, Horace connects the health of the Roman state with the morality of its people, particularly their religious piety and the sexual chastity of its women. The poem must be read in the context of Augustus's moral revival, in the course of which the emperor restored or built numerous temples and inaugurated legislation aimed at curbing women's extramarital sexuality and encouraging instead marriage and fertility.

2. **images:** The cult statues of the gods.

3. **Since you subject . . . you rule:** This articulates the *pax deorum* (the peace of the gods), i.e., the good will of the gods (which ensured the Roman empire) in exchange for the Romans' religious piety.

4. **Hesperia:** Italy.

5. **Monaeses . . . band of Pacorus:** Monaeses and Pacorus were both Parthian leaders at whose hands the Romans suffered defeats. Pacorus's troops defeated Lucius Decidius Saxa in 40 B.C.E., and those of Monaeses defeated Oppius Statianus in 36 B.C.E. Both Saxa and Statianus were legates of Mark Antony.

6. **torques:** A kind of necklace that the Romans associated with easterners and Gauls.

7. **Dacian and Ethiopian:** A reference to the troops that served Antony and Cleopatra. "Ethiopian" here stands for Cleopatra's Egyptian forces.

fecunda culpae saecula nuptias
primum inquinavere et genus et domos;
    hoc fonte derivata clades
        in patriam populumque fluxit.   20

motus doceri gaudet Ionicos
matura virgo et fingitur artibus
    iam nunc et incestos amores
        de tenero meditatur ungui;

mox iuniores quaerit adulteros   25
inter mariti vina, neque eligit
    cui donet impermissa raptim
        gaudia luminibus remotis,

sed iussa coram non sine conscio
surgit marito, seu vocat institor   30
    seu navis Hispanae magister,
        dedecorum pretiosus emptor.

non his iuventus orta parentibus
infecit aequor sanguine Punico,

Ages abounding in depravity
first sullied marriage, family, and the home.
> This was the font from which disaster gushed
>> and poured out on the fatherland and people.   20

The virgin, now grown up,[8] takes joy in learning
Ionian dance[9] and trains herself in arts
> already as she ponders sinful trysts
>> all the way to her tender fingernail.[10]

Before long she looks out for younger lovers   25
at the symposia of her husband, not
> selecting one on whom she might bestow
>> illicit joys in haste with lamps removed.

But up she rises, summoned openly—
her husband her accomplice[11]—if a peddler   30
> calls or the captain of a Spanish ship,
>> a lavish buyer of indecency.

Young men not born from parents such as these
once stained the sea with Carthaginian blood.[12]

---

8. **now grown up:** That is, at a marriageable age. This would put her perhaps in her
   mid-teens.
9. **Ionian dance:** Dancing was never a respectable activity for a Roman woman, much
   less dancing in an Ionian Greek style.
10. **all the way ... fingernail:** That is, with every fiber of her being. Some
    commentators suggest this refers instead to the soft fingernails of young children and
    means "from childhood."
11. **her husband her accomplice:** Horace is implying that her husband acts as her
    pimp. Under the Julian law on adultery, husbands could be charged with *lenocinium*
    (pimping) if they were thought to be too compliant in their wives' extramarital
    affairs. On this, see McGinn (1998, 171–94).
12. **Young men ... Carthaginian blood:** Horace contrasts the current generation
    with the earlier one that fought the Carthaginians in the Punic Wars.

Pyrrhumque et ingentem cecidit   35
    Antiochum Hannibalemque dirum,

sed rusticorum mascula militum
proles, Sabellis docta ligonibus
    versare glebas et severae
        matris ad arbitrium recisos   40

portare fustis, sol ubi montium
mutaret umbras et iuga demeret
    bobus fatigatis, amicum
        tempus agens abeunte curru.

damnosa quid non imminuit dies?   45
aetas parentum peior avis tulit
    nos nequiores, mox daturos
        progeniem vitiosiorem.

They cut down Pyrrhus and magnificent   35
      Antiochus and dreadful Hannibal.[13]

But they were rustic soldiers' manly sons
and had been taught to turn the clods of earth
      using Sabellian hoes and at a stern
          mother's directive to chop down and haul   40

firewood at that time when sun transforms
the mountains' shadows and removes the yokes
      from weary oxen, heralding the welcome
          hour with its departing chariot.

What's not diminished by destructive time?   45
Our parents' age, worse than our grandfathers',
      produced us poorer still. We soon will bear
          a generation even more corrupt.

---

13. **Pyrrhus . . . Antiochus . . . Hannibal**: Three enemies of Rome in earlier
generations. Pyrrus was the king of Epirus whom the Romans (under Manius Curius)
defeated in 275 B.C.E. Antiochus was a Syrian king defeated in 190 B.C.E. Hannibal
was the famed Carthaginian general who marched on Italy in the Second Punic War
but was finally defeated at the Battle of Zama in 202 B.C.E.

ODES 3.7

Quid fles, Asterie, quem tibi candidi
primo restituent vere Favonii
    Thyna merce beatum,
        constantis iuvenem fide

Gygen? ille Notis actus ad Oricum   5
post insana Caprae sidera frigidas
    noctes non sine multis
        insomnis lacrimis agit.

atqui sollicitae nuntius hospitae,
suspirare Chloen et miseram tuis   10
    dicens ignibus uri,
        temptat mille vafer modis.

ut Proetum mulier perfida credulum
falsis impulerit criminibus nimis
    casto Bellerophontae   15
        maturare necem refert:

ODES 3.7[1]

Why weep, Asterie, for one whom shining
Zephyrs[2] will carry back to you come spring,
    wealthy in Thynian[3] merchandise,
        a youth of steadfast loyalty—

Gyges? Once Capra's raging stars[4] arose   5
the Noti carried him to Oricus.[5]
    And there he passes chilly nights,
        awake and crying many tears.

And yet the envoy of his pining hostess,
saying that wretched Chloe[6] sighs and burns   10
    with flames like yours, adroitly tempts
        him in a thousand different ways.

He tells him how a lying woman[7] crafted
charges to force the unsuspecting Proetus
    quickly to carry out the murder   15
        of much too chaste Bellerophon.

---

1. *Odes* 3.7 (*Fourth Asclepiadean*): The change of meter signals that the sequence of Roman Odes has come to and end and, with them, the patriotic themes they espoused. Horace turns now to private, amatory concerns, addressing a woman named Asterie, distraught about the absence of her lover Gyges, who is abroad.
2. **Zephyrs:** The winds that signaled the start of spring.
3. **Thynian:** The Thynians were a people in Bithynia.
4. **Capra's raging stars:** The stars of Capra (part of the constellation Auriga) rose in late September, a time when sailing was considered dangerous.
5. **Noti . . . Oricus:** The Noti were the south winds. Oricus was a town in the Greek region of Epirus.
6. **envoy . . . Chloe:** Chloe is the hostess (presumably the wife of his host) who is attempting to seduce her young guest through a go-between.
7. **lying woman:** Anteia/Sthenoboea, the wife of the mythical king Proetus, tries to seduce Bellerophon but fails. She accuses him of rape to her husband, whereupon Proetus has Bellerophon sent to Iobates, his father-in-law, bearing a sealed message requesting that the bearer be slain. Iobates instead sends Bellerophon to fight the Chimaera.

narrat paene datum Pelea Tartaro,
Magnessam Hippolyten dum fugit abstinens;
    et peccare docentis
        fallax historias monet.   20

frustra: nam scopulis surdior Icari
vocis audit adhuc integer. at tibi
    ne vicinus Enipeus
        plus iusto placeat cave;

quamvis non alius flectere equum sciens   25
aeque conspicitur gramine Martio,
    nec quisquam citus aeque
        Tusco denatat alveo.

prima nocte domum claude neque in vias
sub cantu querulae despice tibiae,   30
    et te saepe vocanti
        duram difficilis mane.

He speaks of prudish Peleus, nearly sent
to Tartarus while fleeing from Magnesian
      Hippolyte.[8] He cleverly
          recalls the stories that teach sin.   20

In vain—for deafer than Icarian cliffs[9]
does Gyges hear his voice, still pure. But you—
      make sure your neighbor Enipeus
          does not appeal to you too much,

though no one else knows how to turn his horse   25
so well while on display in Mars's grass,[10]
      and nobody can swim as fast
          as he does down the Tuscan river.[11]

At nightfall shut your door, and when he plays
his mournful pipe don't look down to the streets.   30
      And even if he often calls
          you harsh, remain intractable.

---

8. **Peleus . . . Hippolyte:** Hippolyte was the wife of the Magnesian king Acastus. As in the previous story, she tries and fails to seduce Peleus, whereupon she accuses him of rape to her husband. The centaurs rescue Peleus after Acastus leaves him to die on Mount Pelion.
9. **Icarian cliffs:** The cliffs off the island Icaria in the Aegean.
10. **in Mars's grass:** The Campus Martius, where military exercises took place.
11. **Tuscan river:** The Tiber.

ODES 3.8

Martiis caelebs quid agam Kalendis,
quid velint flores et acerra turis
plena miraris positusque carbo in
    caespite vivo,

docte sermones utriusque linguae?   5
voveram dulcis epulas et album
Libero caprum prope funeratus
    arboris ictu.

hic dies anno redeunte festus
corticem adstrictum pice dimovebit   10
amphorae fumum bibere institutae
    consule Tullo.

sume, Maecenas, cyathos amici
sospitis centum et vigilis lucernas
perfer in lucem: procul omnis esto   15
    clamor et ira.

mitte civilis super urbe curas:
occidit Daci Cotisonis agmen,

ODES 3.8[1]

You ask what I, a bachelor, am doing
on March's Kalends,[2] what the flowers mean,
the box of incense and the charcoal placed
    onto the fresh turf—

you who have learned both languages' discourses?[3]   5
I'd vowed delicious banquets and a white
he-goat to Liber[4] when the falling tree
    nearly destroyed me.

Each time the year comes round, this festive day
will take the pitch-sealed cork out of the jar   10
that was appointed to imbibe the smoke[5] when
    Tullus was consul.[6]

Take up, Maecenas, a hundred ladles full
to toast your rescued friend, and keep the lamps
awake till morning light. Away with all   15
    shouting and anger.

Dismiss your civic cares about the city:
the troops of Dacian Cotiso[7] have fallen.

---

1. ***Odes* 3.8** (*Sapphic Strophe*): Horace invites Maecenas to drink with him to celebrate his survival of the tree's fall (for which see esp. *Odes* 2.13). Horace urges him to set aside his excessive anxiety over public life by withdrawing to a private symposium.
2. **bachelor . . . March's Kalends:** March 1 was the Matronalia, a festival to Juno celebrated by Roman matrons (i.e., married women). Horace, a single man, would have little reason to take part in this, which leaves Maecenas puzzled. Instead, it's a purely private ritual of thanksgiving that the two men will enjoy.
3. **both language's discourses:** The philosophical writings by both Greek and Latin authors, which often took dialogue form.
4. **Liber:** Bacchus. The banquets in his honor would suggest this is the god to whom Horace credits his survival. In 2.17.28 he mentions instead Faunus and in 3.4.27 the Muses.
5. **imbibe the smoke:** Wine was stored in attics above smoke-filled kitchens. It was thought that the smoke mellowed the wine.
6. **Tullus was consul:** Lucius Volcatius Tullus was consul in 66 B.C.E., the year before Horace was born, although Nisbet and Rudd (2004) suggest he means instead the son's consulship in 33 B.C.E.
7. **Dacian Cotiso:** Cotiso was a Dacian king who was defeated in a campaign of 29 B.C.E.

Medus infestus sibi luctuosis
    dissidet armis,   20

servit Hispanae vetus hostis orae
Cantaber sera domitus catena,
iam Scythae laxo meditantur arcu
    cedere campis.

neglegens ne qua populus laboret   25
parce privatus nimium cavere et
dona praesentis cape laetus horae ac
    linque severa.

The hated Medes fight civil wars with arms that
    cause themselves sorrow.[8]   20

Our old Cantabrian rival from Spain's coast,[9]
tamed by a recent fetter, slaves for us.
The Scythians[10] plan to leave behind their plains,
    bows now unbended.

Forget what troubles might befall the people.   25
You hold no office,[11] so don't fret too much.
Happily seize the present hour's gifts and
    part with all sternness.

---

8. **Medes ... sorrow:** In 26 B.C.E. a Parthian named Tiridates challenged Phraates for the throne, leading to a civil conflict.
9. **Cantabrian rival ... coast:** In 26 B.C.E. Augustus had launched an inconclusive campaign against the Cantabrians in Spain. Horace's statement that they have been enslaved is hyperbolic.
10. **Scythians:** The Scythians occupied the Eurasian steppes. There was no active campaign against them, leading Garrison to suggest that their inclusion here is meant to round out the picture because they lived at the opposite end of the empire from the Cantabrians.
11. **You hold no office:** Despite his powerful connections with Augustus, Maecenas is officially a *privatus* or private citizen.

ODES 3.9

Donec gratus eram tibi
nec quisquam potior bracchia candidae
    cervici iuvenis dabat,
Persarum vigui rege beatior.

"donec non alia magis   5
arsisti neque erat Lydia post Chloen,
    multi Lydia nominis
Romana vigui clarior Ilia."

me nunc Thraessa Chloe regit,
dulcis docta modos et citharae sciens,   10
    pro qua non metuam mori,
si parcent animae fata superstiti.

"me torret face mutua
Thurini Calais filius Ornyti,
    pro quo bis patiar mori,   15
si parcent puero fata superstiti."

quid si prisca redit Venus
diductosque iugo cogit aeneo,
    si flava excutitur Chloe
reiectaeque patet ianua Lydiae?   20

"quamquam sidere pulchrior
ille est, tu levior cortice et improbo
    iracundior Hadria,
tecum vivere amem, tecum obeam libens."

ODES 3.9[1]

As long as I delighted you
and no young man, preferred to me, was putting
his arms around your gleaming neck,
I thrived, happier than the Persian king.

"As long as there was no one else   5
you burned for more and Lydia bested Chloe,
I, Lydia, was of great renown
and thrived, more famed than Roman Ilia.[2]"

Now Thracian Chloe is my queen.
She knows sweet songs, an expert on the lyre.   10
For her I would not dread to die
if only fates would let her live—my soul.

"Calais, son of Ornytus
the Thurian,[3] burns me with a mutual torch.
For him I'd bear a double death   15
if only fates would let him live—my boy."

What if the former Venus[4] comes
and drives old flames back under her bronze yoke,
if blond-haired Chloe is cast out,
the door reopened for rejected Lydia?   20

"Though he's more lovely than a star
and you are lighter than a cork and rage
more than the shameless Adriatic,[5]
I'd gladly live with you and die with you."

---

1. **Odes 3.9** (*Second Asclepiadean*): This poem presents a dialogue between two former lovers, a man (perhaps Horace) and a woman named Lydia, a name Horace has already used in *Odes* 1.8, 1.13, and 1.25. We learn that rivals had come between the speaker and Lydia, but by the end they are ready to resume their love affair. On Horace's Lydia, see, for example, Johnson (2003–4).
2. **Roman Ilia**: Ilia was the mother of Romulus and Remus.
3. **Thurian**: Thurii was a Greek colony in southern Italy.
4. **Venus**: The goddess stands here **metonymically** for sexual desire.
5. **Adriatic**: The sea on Italy's eastern coast.

ODES 3.10

Extremum Tanain si biberes, Lyce,
saevo nupta viro, me tamen asperas
porrectum ante foris obicere incolis
⠀⠀⠀⠀plorares Aquilonibus.

audis quo strepitu ianua, quo nemus⠀⠀⠀⠀⠀⠀⠀⠀5
inter pulchra satum tecta remugiat
ventis, et positas ut glaciet nives
⠀⠀⠀⠀puro numine Iuppiter?

ingratam Veneri pone superbiam,
ne currente retro funis eat rota.⠀⠀⠀⠀⠀⠀⠀⠀10
non te Penelopen difficilem procis
⠀⠀⠀⠀Tyrrhenus genuit parens.

o quamvis neque te munera nec preces
nec tinctus viola pallor amantium
nec vir Pieria paelice saucius⠀⠀⠀⠀⠀⠀⠀⠀15
⠀⠀⠀⠀curvat, supplicibus tuis

ODES 3.10[1]

If you drank from the distant Don,[2] O Lyce,
wed to a brutal husband, you'd still weep
to cast me, stretched before your ruthless doors,
    out to the local Aquilos.[3]

Do you hear how the door shakes, how the trees   5
planted between the lovely buildings howl
with winds, how Jupiter with cloudless sway[4]
    freezes already fallen snows?

Cast off the haughtiness that Venus hates,
lest on the running wheel the rope reverse.[5]   10
Not like Penelope, unkind to suitors,
    did your Etruscan father sire you.

Although your lovers' presents and entreaties
and crimson-tinted pallor cannot bend you,
nor can the wounds your husband feels toward your   15
    Pierian rival,[6] please do spare

---

1. *Odes* 3.10 (*Third Asclepiadean*): This ode constitutes a *paraclausithyron* sung to a young woman named Lyce by an *exclusus amator*. This Lyce is clearly a married woman, which means the young lover is flouting Augustus's strictures against adultery. Some scholars have wanted to downplay this aspect of the poem. Nisbet and Rudd (2004), for example, suggest that "condemnation mattered [little] except where the highest classes were concerned." There is no suggestion, though, that Lyce is lower class—in fact the opposite. That the woman is not poor (and so perhaps elite) is clear from her elegant house, which has a wooded area inside a central portico (lines 5–6).
2. **drank . . . Don**: The Don (the ancient Tanaïs) is a river in south Russia. This line is Horace's way of saying, "If you were a Scythian . . . ." The Scythians were stereotypically harsh, but even a Scythian woman, he states, would pity him.
3. **Aquilos**: The north winds.
4. **cloudless sway**: Jupiter represents **metonymically** the weather in general. Here, the snows freeze even further beneath the cloudless sky.
5. **Running . . . reverse**: The meaning of this line has been much debated. The most likely interpretation is that the lover envisions himself as cranking a rope hoist, but if she continues to rebuff him he will simply let go, and it will drop its weight.
6. **Pierian rival**: Lyce's husband is enamored of a woman from Pieria in Macedonia. There may be a hint that the rival is learned, since the Muses were associated with this area.

parcas, nec rigida mollior aesculo
nec Mauris animum mitior anguibus.
non hoc semper erit liminis aut aquae
    caelestis patiens latus.   20

your suppliants—you, no softer than stiff oak,
your heart less gentle than Moroccan snakes.
My flank won't always tolerate the threshold
     or water falling from the sky.   20

ODES 3.11

Mercuri—nam te docilis magistro
movit Amphion lapides canendo—
tuque testudo resonare septem
     callida nervis,

nec loquax olim neque grata, nunc et   5
divitum mensis et amica templis,
dic modos, Lyde quibus obstinatas
     applicet auris,

quae velut latis equa trima campis
ludit exsultim metuitque tangi,   10
nuptiarum expers et adhuc protervo
     cruda marito.

tu potes tigris comitesque silvas
ducere et rivos celeres morari;
cessit immanis tibi blandienti   15
     ianitor aulae,

ODES 3.11[1]

O Mercury—for since you were his teacher
shrewd Amphion[2] could move the stones with song—
and you, O tortoise shell,[3] on seven strings
    artfully ringing—

previously you could not speak or please,   5
but now you're prized at rich men's feasts and temples.
Sing measures to which Lyde might apply her
    ears so unbending.

Just like a filly three years old,[4] she plays
in spacious fields and shrinks at being touched.   10
Untried in marriage, she is still not ripe
    for a bold husband.

You[5] have the skill to lead as your companions
tigers and forests and to slow fast streams.
There yielded to your flattery the huge   15
    palace's door guard,

---

1. *Odes* 3.11 (*Sapphic Strophe*): This ode begins as a **hymn** to Mercury and the lyre.
Horace then requests the lyre's aid in singing a song that might win the attention of a
young woman named Lyde, who has no interest yet in sexuality. The poem then ends
with a recounting of the myths of the Danaids, the fifty daughters of Danaus who—apart
from one—killed their bridegrooms on their wedding night at the behest of their
father. The young women were sentenced to eternal torture in the underworld, where
they now spend their days attempting to fill up a leaky jar. The complex connection of
the myth to the rest of the ode has constituted the chief scholarly focus of the poem.
It certainly seems to urge Lyde to be more yielding to the man (i.e., the narrator)
attempting to woo her. It is worth noting that Augustus's newly built Temple of Apollo
on the Palatine included sculptural depictions of the Danaids in its portico.
2. **Amphion**: Amphion and his brother Zethus built the walls of Thebes. Amphion used
Mercury's lyre to charm the stones so they would fall into place of their own accord.
3. **tortoise shell**: The lyre, which Mercury as an infant made by hollowing a tortoise
shell.
4. **filly . . . old**: The comparison of a young girl to a filly goes back especially to
Anacreon fr. 417, the "Thracian filly" fragment.
5. **You**: Horace here recounts the various marvels the lyre can perform, and the story of
Orpheus is lurking in the background. He used the lyre to enchant lions and tigers, to
transform nature, and to charm the denizens of the Underworld.

Cerberus, quamvis furiale centum
muniant angues caput eius atque
spiritus taeter saniesque manet
      ore trilingui.   20

quin et Ixion Tityosque vultu
risit invito, stetit urna paulum
sicca, dum grato Danai puellas
      carmine mulces.

audiat Lyde scelus atque notas   25
virginum poenas et inane lymphae
dolium fundo pereuntis imo,
      seraque fata,

quae manent culpas etiam sub Orco.
impiae—nam quid potuere maius?—   30
impiae sponsos potuere duro
      perdere ferro.

una de multis face nuptiali
digna periurum fuit in parentem
splendide mendax et in omne virgo   35
      nobilis aevum,

"surge," quae dixit iuveni marito,
"surge, ne longus tibi somnus, unde
non times, detur; socerum et scelestas
      falle sorores,   40

Cerberus,[6] though his head, just like a fury's,
is covered with a hundred snakes and he
exhales disgusting breath and gore from his
    triple-tongued muzzle.   20

Yes, even Ixion and Tityos[7] smiled
on wary faces. Briefly did the urn
stand dry while with your pleasant song you soothed
    Danaus' daughters.

Let Lyde hear about the virgins' crime   25
and famous punishment—the vessel empty
due to the water flowing through its bottom,
    and the deferred fates

that even down in Orcus[8] wait for sins.
Impious ones! What worse could they have done?   30
Those impious women could with solid iron
    slaughter their bridegrooms!

Out of so many there was one[9] who earned
the nuptial torch—amazingly deceitful
against her father, and a virgin famous   35
    now and forever,

who to her youthful husband said, "Arise.
Arise, or one you do not fear will grant
you lasting sleep. You must escape my wicked
    father and sisters.   40

6. **Cerberus:** The three-headed dog with snaky hair that guards the entrance to the Underworld.
7. **Ixion and Tityos:** Two of the great sinners in the Underworld. The former is turned constantly on a wheel, while the latter's regenerating liver is forever consumed by an eagle.
8. **Orcus:** The Underworld.
9. **there was one:** Hypermnestra, who alone of the daughters refused to kill her groom, usually named Lynceus.

quae velut nactae vitulos leaenae
singulos eheu lacerant: ego illis
mollior nec te feriam neque intra
    claustra tenebo.

me pater saevis oneret catenis,   45
quod viro clemens misero peperci:
me vel extremos Numidarum in agros
    classe releget.

i pedes quo te rapiunt et aurae,
dum favet nox et Venus, i secundo   50
omine et nostri memorem sepulcro
    scalpe querellam."

They, just as lions meet with calves and then
rip them apart (woe!) one by one—but I,
softer than they, will neither strike nor keep you
      bound in a prison.

Let my own father weigh me down with chains   45
because I kindly spared my wretched husband.
Or let him send me in a boat to distant
      fields in Numidia.[10]

Now go wherever feet and breezes take you
while night and Venus are propitious. Go—   50
good luck. And in my memory carve a dirge
      onto my tombstone."

---

10. **Numidia**: In North Africa.

ODES 3.12

Miserarum est neque amori dare ludum neque dulci
mala vino lavere aut exanimari metuentis
      patruae verbera linguae.

tibi qualum Cythereae puer ales, tibi telas
operosaeque Minervae studium aufert, Neobule,   5
      Liparaei nitor Hebri,

simul unctos Tiberinis umeros lavit in undis,

eques ipso melior Bellerophonte, neque pugno
      neque segni pede victus:

catus idem per apertum fugientis agitato   10
grege cervos iaculari et celer arto latitantem
      fruticeto excipere aprum.

ODES 3.12[1]

Miserable girls[2] cannot indulge their love or drink sweet wine
to wash their ills away—or else, senseless with fright, they dread
   the thrashing of an uncle's tongue.

The winged son of Venus[3] takes your basket,[4] and your weaving
and zeal for careful wool-work[5] are borne off, Neobule,   5
   by Liparean[6] Hebrus' gleam

when he has washed his oil-smeared shoulders in the Tiber's
   waves,
a horseman better than Bellerophon[7] himself, unconquered
   due to a sluggish fist or foot.

Likewise he's skilled at throwing javelins at deer in flight,   10
the herd alarmed, and quick to take his stand against a boar
   lurking inside the close-knit thickets.

---

1. **Odes 3.12** (*Ionic a minore*): Horace addresses a young woman named Neobule, in love with an otherwise unknown Hebrus. The plight of lovesick girls is the poem's focus—they cannot indulge their romantic feelings due to the cultural expectations of modesty and chastity, signified here by the characteristically feminine duty of wool-work. This is Horace's only poem in this meter.
2. **Miserable girls**: "Miserable" is almost a technical word here indicating "love-sick," as in much Roman love poetry.
3. **winged son of Venus**: Cupid, who stands here **metonymically** for sexual desire.
4. **basket**: The wicker basket that held the girl's allotment of wool.
5. **wool-work**: Literally, "Minerva." She stands **metonymically** here for one sphere over which she presided.
6. **Liparean**: Lipara was an island north of Sicily.
7. **Bellerophon**: A hero who in myth rode the winged horse Pegasus.

ODES 3.13

O fons Bandusiae splendidior vitro
dulci digne mero non sine floribus,
    cras donaberis haedo,
        cui frons turgida cornibus

primis et venerem et proelia destinat;   5
frustra: nam gelidos inficiet tibi
    rubro sanguine rivos
        lascivi suboles gregis.

te flagrantis atrox hora Caniculae
nescit tangere, tu frigus amabile   10
    fessis vomere tauris
        praebes et pecori vago.

fies nobilium tu quoque fontium,
me dicente cavis impositam ilicem
    saxis, unde loquaces   15
        lymphae desiliunt tuae.

ODES 3.13[1]

Bandusian spring, more shimmering than glass,
deserving of sweet wine and flowers, too—
    tomorrow you'll receive a kid
        whose forehead, swollen with new horns,

marks him for sensuality and battles[2]—   5
but all in vain, for with his ruby blood
    the offspring of the lusty herd
        will stain your streams, as cold as ice.

The blazing Dog Star's unrelenting hour[3]
cannot assault you. You grant lovely coolness   10
    to bulls exhausted by the plow
        and to the flock as it meanders.

You too will be among the famous springs[4]
because I sing about the holm-oak placed
    atop the hollow cave from where   15
        your babbling waters frolic down.

---

1. **Odes** 3.13 (*Fourth Asclepiadean*): This is one of Horace's most celebrated odes, in which he **hymns** a spring located most likely on his Sabine farm. The occasion is perhaps the festival of the Fontinalia in mid-October, during which sacrifices (normally libations and garlands) are offered to springs and wells. The sweltering Dog Star, however, suggests a summer date. Horace plans to offer the spring a sacrifice of a young goat, whose red blood, he poignantly describes, will stain the clear, bright water.
2. **sensuality and battles:** Male goats were proverbially lusty and prone to fighting. "Sensuality" is literally "Venus" here, with the goddess standing **metonymically** for the sphere over which she presides.
3. **Dog Star . . . hour:** Canicula, the Dog Star, rose in late July.
4. **famous springs:** Such springs include Castalia (at Delphi) and Dirce (near Thebes), both associated with poetic inspiration.

ODES 3.14

Herculis ritu modo dictus, o plebs,
morte venalem petiisse laurum,
Caesar Hispana repetit penatis
    victor ab ora.

unico gaudens mulier marito   5
prodeat iustis operata divis,
et soror clari ducis et decorae
    supplice vitta

virginum matres iuvenumque nuper
sospitum. vos, o pueri et puellae   10
non virum expertae, male nominatis
    parcite verbis.

hic dies vere mihi festus atras
eximet curas; ego nec tumultum
nec mori per vim metuam tenente   15
    Caesare terras.

ODES 3.14[1]

O plebs,[2] though lately rumored to have sought
the laurel won by death,[3] Caesar—a victor
from Spanish shores, like Hercules[4]—again
    seeks his Penates.[5]

Glad in her matchless husband, may his wife   5
worship the righteous gods and come; so too
the famous leader's sister and, adorned with
    suppliant fillets,[6]

the mothers of the virgins and young men
just rescued.[7] You, O boys, and you, O girls,   10
who have not known a husband,[8] cease from any
    words of ill omen.

This festive day will truly take from me
gloomy anxieties. I will not fear
sedition or a violent death while Caesar   15
    rules all the nations.

---

1. *Odes* **3.14** (*Sapphic Strophe*): A celebration of Augustus's return from Spain in 24 B.C.E. after several years of campaigning. Augustus had spent some of this time ill in Tarroco, and rumors of his sickness had reached Rome. After victory was declared in late 25 B.C.E., the doors of the Temple of Janus were closed, signaling that the empire was at peace. Augustus declined a triumph but was voted celebratory honors. In the ode, the public celebration—including the procession of Augustus's wife Livia and sister Octavia—gives way, in the second half, to the poet's private celebration, which a woman named Neaera (who is probably a prostitute) is invited to attend.
2. **O plebs:** The plebs were the common people of Rome.
3. **laurel won by death:** That is, it had been rumored that Augustus had died.
4. **like Hercules:** Hercules laid low the monster Geryon in Spain and then returned to Greece via Rome (where he defeated the monster Cacus).
5. **Penates:** The Penates were household gods but also had a public guise as ancestral gods of the Romans. They stand here for Rome itself via **metonomy**.
6. **suppliant fillets:** Woolen bands worn around the head. This indicates that a *supplicatio* (prayer of thanksgiving) took place at the celebration.
7. **virgins ... rescued:** The young men are the returned soldiers, the virgins their fiancées.
8. **O boys ... husband:** Horace urges the children attending the ceremony to be quiet so they do not botch the religious rites.

i pete unguentum, puer, et coronas
et cadum Marsi memorem duelli,
Spartacum si qua potuit vagantem
     fallere testa.   20

dic et argutae properet Neaerae
murreum nodo cohibere crinem;
si per invisum mora ianitorem
     fiet, abito.

lenit albescens animos capillus   25
litium et rixae cupidos protervae;
non ego hoc ferrem calidus iuventa
     consule Planco.

Go and get perfume, slave boy, and some garlands,
a jug that can recall the Marsian War[9]—
if anywhere a wine jar could escape
    Spartacus' rampage.[10]   20

And tell clear-voiced Neaera[11] to be quick
at binding in a knot her copper[12] hair.
But if her nuisance of a doorman[13] makes her
    tarry, just leave her.

My graying hair now mollifies a spirit   25
once eager for disputes and shameless quarrels.
I'd not have borne this, hot with youth, the year
    Plancus was consul.[14]

---

9. **Marsian War**: The Social War between Rome and its allies, which took place from 91 to 88 B.C.E. The Marsi were among the chief Italian allies and were the first to take up arms against Rome.

10. **Spartacus' rampage**: Spartacus led the slave revolt of 73–71 B.C.E.

11. **Neaera**: This was a frequent name for prostitutes in literature going back to the speech (attributed to Demosthenes) *Against Neaera* from fourth-century B.C.E. Athens.

12. **copper**: The word could also mean "perfumed." It either means "myrrh-scented" or "the color of myrrh."

13. **doorman**: The doorman (*ianitor*) was a slave placed there to control access to the woman. Her husband, pimp/madam, or she herself could place him there.

14. **the year . . . consul**: Plancus was consul in 42 B.C.E., when Horace was in his early twenties and fighting in the army of Brutus against the future Augustus (see introductory note to *Odes* 2.7). At the time the *Odes* were published, he was in his early forties. His erotic (and perhaps political) temper has mellowed, or so he claims, with age.

ODES 3.15

Uxor pauperis Ibyci,
tandem nequitiae fige modum tuae
famosisque laboribus:
maturo propior desine funeri

inter ludere virgines   5
et stellis nebulam spargere candidis.
non, si quid Pholoen satis,
et te, Chlori, decet: filia rectius

expugnat iuvenum domos,
pulso Thyias uti concita tympano.   10
illam cogit amor Nothi
lascivae similem ludere capreae:

te lanae prope nobilem
tonsae Luceriam, non citharae decent
nec flos purpureus rosae   15
nec poti vetulam faece tenus cadi.

ODES 3.15[1]

Wife of the poor man Ibycus,
at long last place a limit on your vice
    and on your now notorious labors.
You're all too close to timely death—refrain

from prancing in the midst of virgins   5
and scattering a cloud on gleaming stars.
    What's suited well to Pholoe[2]
does not suit you, too, Chloris. It's your daughter

who better storms the young men's homes,
incited by the drumbeat like a Bacchant.[3]   10
    Her love for Nothus[4] urges her
to prance around just like a lusty she-goat.[5]

What's suitable for you, old woman,
is wool shorn in renowned Luceria,[6]
    not lyres nor the rose's purple   15
flower, nor wine jars guzzled to the dregs.

---

1. *Odes* 3.15 (*Second Asclepiadean*): Horace addresses an older woman named Chloris, who longs still to take part in the activities appropriate to youth. The poet combines ethical advice (on propriety and age, a recurrent theme) with **invective** against an older woman (as seen, though in a coarser tone, in *Epodes* 8 and 12). Chloris's age is difficult to determine, but she most likely qualifies as "middle-aged" (but probably younger than Horace himself, given the age at which women married and began childbearing).
2. **Pholoe:** Presumed by most commentators to be the daughter of the following line.
3. **Bacchant:** A female follower of Bacchus, who worshipped the god in an ecstatic state.
4. **Nothus:** This name in Greek means "illegitimate" and can designate someone, such as the child of a slave or concubine, whose birth does not bring them respectable citizenship. The name therefore suggests that Pholoe's Nothus is not elite.
5. **lusty she-goat:** Goats were proverbially lusty. The word *caprea* could, alternatively, be a "roe deer," but deer are known for their timidity, not lustfulness.
6. **wool . . . Luceria:** Wives such as Chloris were expected to stay at home and work wool, symbolic of female chastity. Luceria was a southern Italian town known for producing fine wool.

ODES 3.16

Inclusam Danaen turris aenea
robustaeque fores et vigilum canum
tristes excubiae munierant satis
    nocturnis ab adulteris,

si non Acrisium virginis abditae   5
custodem pavidum Iuppiter et Venus
risissent: fore enim tutum iter et patens
    converso in pretium deo.

aurum per medios ire satellites
et perrumpere amat saxa potentius   10
ictu fulmineo: concidit auguris
    Argivi domus ob lucrum

demersa exitio: diffidit urbium
portas vir Macedo et subruit aemulos
reges muneribus; munera navium   15
    saevos illaqueant duces.

ODES 3.16[1]

When Danaë was shut away,[2] the bronze
tower and oaken doors and wakeful dogs'
unfriendly watches would have shielded her
　　　from lovers sneaking in at night,

if Jupiter and Venus had not laughed   5
at Acrisius, the locked-up virgin's fearful
guard, for the god would have a safe and open
　　　passage when he became a bribe.[3]

Gold loves to travel through the midst of henchmen
and force its way through rock more powerfully   10
than lightning strikes. Because of avarice,
　　　the Argive seer's[4] home collapsed,

plunged into death.[5] The man of Macedon[6]
split open city gates and undermined
his rival kings with gifts. Gifts can ensnare   15
　　　the ruthless admirals of ships.

---

1. **Odes 3.16** (*Third Asclepiadean*): A moralizing ode on wealth, the corrupting
   influence of which compromises everyone except the person satisfied with what is
   enough. Horace weaves through the poem the Stoic paradox that only the wise man
   is free and every fool a slave. Kings, he says, are slaves to their own avarice, whereas
   the person happy with modest means is more truly a master of himself. The poem is
   addressed to Maecenas, but that is only revealed halfway through.
2. **Danaë ... shut away**: Danaë's father Acrisius was told by an oracle that his grandson
   would kill him, so he locked his daughter in a bronze tower. Jupiter turned into a
   shower of gold and impregnated her, whereupon she gave birth to Perseus, who later
   kills Acrisius.
3. **became a bribe**: We expect Jupiter to metamorphose into gold, but "bribe" points
   to an alternate tradition in which Jupiter bribed the guards. The change suggests the
   corrupting influence of money, the idea of the next stanzas.
4. **Argive seer**: Amphiaraus was a seer and one of the "Seven against Thebes." His
   wife, Eriphyle, persuaded him to join the war after Polynices bribes her with a gold
   necklace to do so.
5. **plunged into death**: An oblique reference to Amphiaraus's fate. While he was on
   the battlefield, the earth opened up and swallowed him and his chariot into the
   Underworld.
6. **man of Macedon**: Alexander the Great (356–323 B.C.E.). Horace's exempla here move
   from the mythological to the historical.

crescentem sequitur cura pecuniam
maiorumque fames. iure perhorrui
late conspicuum tollere verticem,
     Maecenas, equitum decus.   20

quanto quisque sibi plura negaverit,
ab dis plura feret: nil cupientium
nudus castra peto et transfuga divitum
     partis linquere gestio,

contemptae dominus splendidior rei   25
quam si quidquid arat impiger Apulus
occultare meis dicerer horreis,
     magnas inter opes inops.

purae rivus aquae silvaque iugerum
paucorum et segetis certa fides meae   30
fulgentem imperio fertilis Africae
     fallit sorte beatior.

quamquam nec Calabrae mella ferunt apes
nec Laestrygonia Bacchus in amphora
languescit mihi nec pinguia Gallicis   35
     crescunt vellera pascuis,

importuna tamen pauperies abest
nec, si plura velim, tu dare deneges.

Once money grows, anxiety ensues,
the appetite for more. Rightly I've shuddered
to raise a head conspicuous far and wide,
Maecenas, adornment of the knights.[7]   20

The more that one denies oneself, the more
the gods will give him. Stripped,[8] I seek the camp
of those desiring nothing and, deserter,
I long to leave the rich men's faction,

a finer master of the wealth I spurn   25
than if alleged to hide inside my barns
all that the diligent Apulian plows,[9]
a pauper though amid great wealth.

A stream of spotless water and a forest
of a few acres and my crop's sure harvest—   30
this is a better lot than his who rules
rich Africa, though this escapes him.

Although Calabrian[10] bees don't make my honey
nor in a Laestrygonian jar does Bacchus[11]
mature for me and I possess no fleeces   35
now growing fat in Gallic pastures,[12]

yet I am free of grievous poverty,
and if I wanted more you'd not say no.

---

7. **adornment of the knights**: A reminder that Maecenas had not sought senatorial status (remaining instead an equestrian) and a suggestion that he, like Horace, is free of ambition.
8. **Stripped**: The military **metaphor** suggests "stripped of weapons," but the claim to desert the rich suggests "stripped of wealth."
9. **diligent Apulian plows**: Apulia is the Italian region in which Horace was born and where the inhabitants were proverbially hardworking.
10. **Calabrian**: Calabria in southern Italy produced fine honey.
11. **Laestrygonian ... Bacchus**: "Laestrygonian" refers to Formiae in southern Italy, which was associated with Homer's Laestrygonians. Bacchus stands here **metonymically** for wine. Formian wine was celebrated—see for example 1.20.11.
12. **Gallic pastures**: A reference to the famously thick wool of Cisalpine Gaul.

contracto melius parva cupidine
    vectigalia porrigam,   40

quam si Mygdoniis regnum Alyattei
campis continuem. multa petentibus
desunt multa: bene est, cui deus obtulit
    parca quod satis est manu.

I will stretch out my meager income better
    if I diminish my desire   40

than if I should combine the fields of Mygdon
with Alyattes' realm.[13] They who want much
lack much. All's well for him on whom the god
    with frugal hand bestows enough.

---

13. **Mygdon ... Alyattes' realm:** Mygdon was a legendary Phrygian king, and Alyattes the father of the Lydian king Croesus.

ODES 3.17

Aeli vetusto nobilis ab Lamo,—
quando et priores hinc Lamias ferunt
     denominatos et nepotum
        per memores genus omne fastus,

auctore ab illo ducis originem,   5
qui Formiarum moenia dicitur
     princeps et innantem Maricae
        litoribus tenuisse Lirim

late tyrannus:—cras foliis nemus
multis et alga litus inutili   10
     demissa tempestas ab Euro
        sternet, aquae nisi fallit augur

annosa cornix. dum potes, aridum
compone lignum: cras Genium mero
     curabis et porco bimestri   15
        cum famulis operum solutis.

ODES 3.17[1]

Aelius, noble[2] sprung from ancient Lamus—
(Since they report through all recording archives
    that early Lamiae and that whole race
        of progeny derive their name from him,

you trace your line from that progenitor   5
who was the first, as it is told, to hold
    the city walls of Formiae and the Liris,
        which flows upon the shores of Marica.[3]

He was a ruler far and wide)—tomorrow,
storms sent by Eurus[4] will bestrew the grove   10
    with foliage and the shore with useless seaweed,
        unless the aged crow, water's diviner,[5]

is tricking me. While you are able, gather
dry logs. Tomorrow you'll restore your Genius[6]
    with full-strength wine and a piglet two months old, 15
        together with your slaves released from work.[7]

---

1. *Odes* 3.17 (*Alcaic Strophe*): An ode addressed to Lucius Aelius Lamia, a member
of an elite family from Formiae. The poem's first half celebrates his illustrious
line, founded supposedly by Lamus, who in Homer's *Odyssey* was the king of the
Laestrygonians (associated by the Romans with the Formians). In the second half,
Horace urges Aelius to make the most out of a coming storm by staying inside and
enjoying himself.
2. **noble:** Aelius was not technically a *nobilis*, as he had no direct ancestor who had held
the consulship. As Nisbet and Rudd (2004) suggest, Horace "gives him *nobilitas* in a
non-technical sense through his descent from Lamus."
3. **Liris . . . Marica:** The Liris was a river near Formiae. Marica was a local goddess who
had a nearby shrine.
4. **Eurus:** The southeast wind.
5. **crow, water's diviner:** Birds were of fundamental importance to Roman augury. The
crow was thought to signal rain.
6. **Genius:** A man's guardian spirit—a woman had a Juno. Individuals would make
offerings to them, particularly on birthdays. Here, however, the occasion is simply a
day indoors.
7. **slaves:** *Famuli* (household slaves) were part of the *familia* of the *paterfamilias* and so
participated in his family religion.

ODES 3.18

Faune, Nympharum fugientum amator,
per meos finis et aprica rura
lenis incedas abeasque parvis
    aequus alumnis,

si tener pleno cadit haedus anno,   5
larga nec desunt Veneris sodali
vina craterae, vetus ara multo
    fumat odore.

ludit herboso pecus omne campo,
cum tibi Nonae redeunt Decembres;   10
festus in pratis vacat otioso
    cum bove pagus;

inter audaces lupus errat agnos;
spargit agrestis tibi silva frondis;
gaudet invisam pepulisse fossor   15
    ter pede terram.

ODES 3.18[1]

Faunus, you lover of the fleeing nymphs,[2]
pass gently through my land and sunny fields,
and as you take your leave be kindly toward my
    delicate nurslings,[3]

if every year a young goat dies for you   5
and lavish wine fills up the mixing bowl
(that friend of Venus) and the ancient altar
    smokes with much incense.

The whole herd frolics in the grassy field
when in your name December's Nones return.[4]   10
The festive district and the idle oxen
    laze in the meadows.

Amid the daring lambs the wolf goes roaming.
For you the forest strews its rustic leaves.
The digger feels delight to pound three times[5]   15
    earth he despises.

---

1. *Odes* 3.18 (*Sapphic Strophe*): A **hymn** to the god Faunus, a god of the countryside often identified with the Greek Pan. The poem centers upon the ancient religious concept of *do ut des* (I give so that you will give), i.e., the exchange of reciprocal goods and favors between humans and gods. Here, Horace's regular worship of Faunus through annual sacrifices and festivals should ensure that the god treats his lands and animals with kindness whenever he passes through Horace's farm.
2. **lover . . . nymphs**: The god is presented on a note that hints at his dangerous aspect—he regularly chases nymphs in an attempt to rape them.
3. **delicate nurslings**: The young animals on Horace's farm.
4. **December's Nones return**: The annual festival to Faunus, the Faunalia, occurred every December 5.
5. **pound three times**: That is, in his celebratory dancing.

ODES 3.19

      Quantum distet ab Inacho
Codrus pro patria non timidus mori,
      narras et genus Aeaci,
et pugnata sacro bella sub Ilio:

      quo Chium pretio cadum   5
mercemur, quis aquam temperet ignibus
      quo praebente domum et quota
Paelignis caream frigoribus, taces.

      da lunae propere novae,
da noctis mediae, da, puer, auguris   10
      Murenae: tribus aut novem
miscentur cyathis pocula commodis.

      qui Musas amat imparis,
ternos ter cyathos attonitus petet

ODES 3.19[1]

The span from Inachus to Codrus,[2]
who was not scared to die for his own country—
   you talk of this and Aeacus's
line[3] and the wars fought under sacred Troy.

   But what's the price to buy a jar   5
of Chian wine,[4] who warms with flame the water,[5]
   who lends his house, what hour I
will shed Paelignian cold[6]—of this you're silent.

   Pour quickly to the brand new moon.
Pour to the midnight, slave, pour to the augur   10
   Murena.[7] Cups are being mixed
with three or nine full ladles, as suits each.[8]

   Whoever loves the Muses, odd
in number,[9] will seek out the thrice three ladles,

1. *Odes* **3.19** (*Second Asclepiadean*): An ode urging that a symposium get underway. The addressee, Telephus, keeps wanting to discuss recherché mythological topics, whereas Horace's interest is rather in the wine, music, and women that accompany the symposium. The occasion for the poem seems to be the new augurship of a man named Murena, either the Licinius Murena to whom *Odes* 2.10 is addressed or his brother, Aulus Terentius Varro Murena.
2. **The span . . . Codrus:** Telephus is trying to sort out the chronology of legendary kings. Inachus was the first king of Argos, and Codrus was the last king of Athens—he sacrificed himself to save his people in a war against the Dorians.
3. **Aeacus's line:** Aeacus was the son of Zeus, father of Peleus, grandfather of Achilles, and great-grandfather of Neoptolemus.
4. **Chian wine:** Wine from Chios was considered exceptional.
5. **warms . . . water:** The water mixed with the wine was first heated.
6. **Paelignian cold:** The Paeligni lived in the central Apennines. As Nisbet and Rudd (2004) suggest, this is not where the symposium is taking place but simply indicative of cold weather.
7. **Pour . . . pour . . . pour . . . Murena:** Every ladle of wine that goes into the mixing bowl is given in honor of something or someone. Water would go first into the mixing bowl, then wine was added to it. The new moon here suggests the start of the month in which Murena's consulship began (at midnight).
8. **three or nine . . . each:** The wine is being mixed at two strengths, one weaker and one stronger.
9. **odd in number:** There were traditionally nine Muses.

vates; tris prohibet supra   15
rixarum metuens tangere Gratia

nudis iuncta sororibus.
insanire iuvat: cur Berecyntiae
        cessant flamina tibiae?
cur pendet tacita fistula cum lyra?   20

parcentis ego dexteras
odi: sparge rosas: audiat invidus
        dementem strepitum Lycus
et vicina seni non habilis Lyco.

spissa te nitidum coma,   25
puro te similem, Telephe, Vespero
        tempestiva petit Rhode:
me lentus Glycerae torret amor meae.

a bard enthused.[10] The Grace, afraid   15
of quarreling, bans taking more than three—

she links her arms with her nude sisters.[11]
It's fun to lose one's mind. Why are no blasts
    coming from Berecyntian[12] flutes?
Why do the pipe and lyre hang in silence?   20

How I detest right hands that are
tightfisted. Scatter roses! Lycus[13] ought
    to hear the senseless noise with envy,
and she next door, not suited to old Lycus.

Rhode,[14] whose age is ripe for yours,   25
seeks you out, Telephus, your thick hair sleek,
    you, like the brilliant evening star.
My love for Glycera consumes me slowly.

---

10. **bard enthused:** For *vates* (bard), see note at *Odes* 1.1.35.
11. **nude sisters:** The three Graces were often depicted in sculpture linked arm in arm.
12. **Berecyntian:** That is, Phrygian—in Asia Minor.
13. **Lycus:** Presumably an old man who lives next door and hates the noise only,
as Horace claims, because he is envious of it. The woman "next door" in line 24 is
presumably his much younger wife.
14. **Rhode:** She is perhaps a prostitute attending the symposium—as is true of
Glycera in line 28 as well.

ODES 3.20

Non vides quanto moveas periclo,
Pyrrhe, Gaetulae catulos leaenae?
Dura post paulo fugies inaudax
      proelia raptor,

cum per obstantis iuvenum catervas   5
ibit insignem repetens Nearchum,
grande certamen, tibi praeda cedat
      maior, an illi.

interim, dum tu celeris sagittas
promis, haec dentis acuit timendos,   10
arbiter pugnae prosuisse nudo
      sub pede palmam

fertur et leni recreare vento
sparsum odoratis umerum capillis,
qualis aut Nireus fuit aut aquosa   15
      raptus ab Ida.

ODES 3.20¹

Do you not see, Pyrrhus, at what great risk
you steal a Gaetulian² lioness's cubs?
A gutless kidnapper,³ you soon will flee
    difficult battles

when through the troops of young men in her way   5
she'll go to seek back beautiful Nearchus,
a mighty test of whether you or she will
    seize the more plunder.

Meanwhile, as you are taking out swift arrows
and she is sharpening her dreadful teeth,   10
the combat's judge with his bare foot, it's said,
    stands on the palm branch

and with the gentle breeze restores his shoulders,
on top of which his perfumed hair is fanned—
like Nireus⁴ or the boy who once from rainy   15
    Ida was kidnapped.⁵

---

1. **Odes 3.20** (*Sapphic Strophe*): The addressee, a man named Pyrrhus, is pursuing a young man named Nearchus, who is also the object of an unnamed woman's affection. The woman is like a lioness whose cub has been stolen, and she will challenge Pyrrhus to get him back. Nearchus, meanwhile, stands on the sidelines, beautiful and not interested in either. It is unclear what agency he has, and the prospect of rape runs throughout the poem.
2. **Gaetulian**: The Gaetuli lived in north Africa.
3. **kidnapper**: The Latin *raptor* suggest a "robber" or "predator," but the idea of "rapist" lurks behind it as well.
4. **Nireus**: One of the Greek warriors in the Trojan War. He was renowned for his beauty.
5. **boy . . . kidnapped**: A reference to Ganymede, whom Jupiter kidnapped and raped. The word *raptus* (kidnapped) looks back to the *raptor* (kidnapper) in the first stanza and, as there, carries the additional suggestion of rape.

ODES 3.21

O nata mecum consule Manlio,
seu tu querelas sive geris iocos
     seu rixam et insanos amores
        seu facilem, pia testa, somnum,

quocumque lectum nomine Massicum   5
servas, moveri digna bono die,
     descende, Corvino iubente
        promere languidiora vina.

non ille, quamquam Socraticis madet
sermonibus, te negleget horridus: 10
     narratur et prisci Catonis
        saepe mero caluisse virtus.

tu lene tormentum ingenio admoves
plerumque duro; tu sapientium
     curas et arcanum iocoso   15
        consilium retegis Lyaeo;

tu spem reducis mentibus anxiis,
virisque et addis cornua pauperi

ODES 3.21[1]

O born with me in Manlius' consulship,[2]
whether you bring complaints or raillery
    or quarreling and frenzied love affairs
      or, holy wine jar, easygoing slumber,

under whatever name you keep the choice   5
Massic[3] worth fetching on a lucky day,
    come down,[4] because Corvinus is entreating
      me to go get a more full-flavored wine.

He, though he's dripping in the dialogues
of Socrates,[5] will not neglect you rudely.   10
    Even the virtue of old-fashioned Cato,[6]
      it's said, was often warmed by unmixed wine.

You mete out gentle torture to a mind
that's normally severe. You bring to light
    wise men's anxieties and secret plans—   15
      all with the cheerful Loosener's[7] assistance.

You lead back hope and strength to minds beset
with troubles, and you give a poor man horns.

---

1. **Odes 3.21** (*Alcaic Strophe*): A **hymn** to a wine jar that Horace intends to enjoy at a symposium with his friend Marcus Valerius Messalla Corvinus, whom Nisbet and Rudd (2004) refer to as "the most versatile aristocrat in Augustan Rome." He was a soldier, consul, city prefect, augur, orator, and poet. The poem has many formal elements of a **hymn**, including an invocation, **Du-Stil**, and a request. On the many facets of wine in the *Odes*, see Commager (1957).
2. **Manlius' consulship**: Lucius Manlius Torquatus was consul in 65 B.C.E.
3. **Massic**: Massic wine was a fine wine from the Italian region of Campania.
4. **come down**: Wine was stored in an attic over the kitchen, but the word also resembles the call for gods to "descend" from heaven in **cletic hymns**.
5. **dialogues of Socrates**: Philosophical writings that feature Socrates as an interlocutor, such as those written by Plato and Xenophon.
6. **virtue of old-fashioned Cato**: Cato the Elder (234–149 B.C.E.). *Virtus* can suggest abstract or philosophical "virtue," but it also indicates old-fashioned rugged masculinity.
7. **Loosener's**: This was a cult name of Bacchus, god of wine.

post te neque iratos trementi
regum apices neque militum arma.   20

te Liber et, si laeta aderit, Venus
segnesque nodum solvere Gratiae
vivaeque producent lucernae,
dum rediens fugat astra Phoebus.

Following you, he quakes no more in fear
>> at angry crowns of kings and soldiers'
>>> weapons.   20

Liber and Venus—if she'll gladly come—
and Graces, slow to disconnect their knot,[8]
>> and brightly burning lamps will make you last
>>> till Phoebus comes again and routs the stars.

---

8. **disconnect their knot**: A reference to the arm-in-arm pose in which the Graces were
often depicted in art.

ODES 3.22

Montium custos nemorumque, Virgo,
quae laborantis utero puellas
ter vocata audis adimisque leto,
      diva triformis,

imminens villae tua pinus esto,   5
quam per exactos ego laetus annos
verris obliquum meditantis ictum
      sanguine donem.

ODES 3.22[1]

Virgin, you guardian of peaks and woods,
you who attend to girls in labor pangs
when called three times and rescue them from death,
    triple-formed goddess,[2]

have as your own the pine above my villa   5
to which I'll gladly give, when every year
is done, blood from a boar still practicing its
    sideways offensive.[3]

---

1. *Odes* **3.22** (*Sapphic Strophe*): A short **hymn** to the virgin goddess Diana, to whom
   Horace dedicates a pine tree on his farm. In addition to hunting and wild animals,
   she was a goddess of childbirth and was especially associated with girls at moments
   of transition—whether into puberty, motherhood, or death.
2. **triple-formed goddess**: Diana had three aspects. She was Luna (the moon) in
   heaven, Diana on earth, and Hecate in the underworld.
3. **sideways offensive**: Boars attacked from the side to better utilize their tusks. The
   fact that the boar is "practicing" this maneuver indicates that it is still quite young.

ODES 3.23

Caelo supinas si tuleris manus
nascente Luna, rustica Phidyle,
    si ture placaris et horna
        fruge Lares avidaque porca,

nec pestilentem sentiet Africum   5
fecunda vitis nec sterilem seges
    robiginem aut dulces alumni
        pomifero grave tempus anno.

nam quae nivali pascitur Algido
devota quercus inter et ilices   10
    aut crescit Albanis in herbis
        victima pontificum securis

cervice tinget: te nihil attinet
temptare multa caede bidentium
    parvos coronantem marino   15
        rore deos fragilique myrto.

immunis aram si tetigit manus,
non sumptuosa blandior hostia
    mollivit aversos Penatis
        farre pio et saliente mica.   20

ODES 3.23[1]

If you raise outstretched hands up to the heavens
at Luna's birth,[2] my rustic Phidyle,
    if you appease your household gods with incense,
        with this year's fruits, and with a greedy pig,[3]

your fertile vineyard will not feel the harmful   5
Africus,[4] nor your harvests suffer mildew
    that sterilizes plants, nor your sweet nurslings
        the sickly climate in the apple season.

Now pasturing on snowy Algidus[5]
between the oaks and ilex trees or growing   10
    on Alban grasses is a victim vowed
        for sacrifice, which with its neck will stain

the axes of the priests. It's not for you
by slaying many sheep to try to sway
    the little gods around whose heads you wreath   15
        delicate sprigs of rosemary and myrtle.

And if a giftless hand has touched an altar,
a lavish victim won't make it more pleasing
    than if it mollifies adverse Penates[6]
        by sprinkling pious grain and crackling salt.[7]   20

---

1. *Odes* 3.23 (*Alcaic Strophe*): Horace instructs a countrywoman named Phidyle
(Thrifty) on the proper worship of the Lares, the household gods, whose likenesses
were normally kept within a shrine inside the home. Through pious (rather than
ostentatious) worship, Phidyle will ensure the gods remain propitious and make her
farm thrive.
2. **at Luna's birth**: At the new moon, which marks the start of the lunar month.
3. **greedy pig**: Pigs were common victims in private cult. This contrasts with the
grander sheep described in lines 9–13.
4. **Africus**: The southwest wind, which was thought to bring bad weather.
5. **Algidus**: A mountain in the Alban Hills.
6. **Penates**: Another name for household gods.
7. **pious grain . . . salt**: The salted meal (*mola salsa*) used often in acts of simple
sacrifice.

ODES 3.24

Intactis opulentior
thesauris Arabum et divitis Indiae
    caementis licet occupes
Tyrrhenum omne tuis et mare Apulicum,

si figit adamantinos   5
summis verticibus dira Necessitas
    clavos, non animum metu,
non mortis laqueis expedies caput.

campestres melius Scythae,
quorum plaustra vagas rite trahunt domos,   10
    vivunt et rigidi Getae
immetata quibus iugera liberas

fruges et Cererem ferunt,
nec cultura placet longior annua,
    defunctumque laboribus   15
aequali recreat sorte vicarius.

illic matre carentibus
privignis mulier temperat innocens,

ODES 3.24[1]

Though you are richer than the Arabs'
unlooted treasure troves and India's wealth[2]
    and with your building stones you fill
the whole Tyrrhenian and Apulian sea,[3]

    if dire Necessity[4] should hammer   5
into your roof her adamantine nails,
    you will not free your mind from fear
nor extricate death's nets from round your head.

The Scythians on the grasslands live
better, whose carts by custom pull their rambling   10
    houses, as do the hardy Getae,
for whom unparcelled acres yield their fruits

    and harvests, free for all to take.
To till for more than one year does not please them,[5]
    and a replacement with an equal   15
portion relieves the one who's done his work.

    No woman in that place mistreats
or harms her stepchildren who've lost their mother.

---

1. *Odes* 3.24 (*Second Asclepiadean*): A long moralizing ode, with no addressee, on the dangers and negative influence of wealth, in which Horace (once again) blames Roman civic upheavals on the moral degradation of its citizens. Here it is the northern Scythians and Getae that by contrast provide behavior worthy of emulation. These groups, as presented here, are a product of the Roman imagination, inhabiting a quasi-Golden Age. It belongs to Augustus to restore the state's moral order and religious piety.
2. **Arabs' . . . India's wealth**: Unlike the Scythians and Getae, who inhabited the far north, the Romans considered these Eastern peoples as decadent and softened by wealth.
3. **Tyrrhenian . . . Apulian sea**: The Tyrrhenian was on the western coast of Italy, the Apulian on its southeastern coast. In other words, the imagined addressee surrounds the peninsula with his luxury homes built out into the ocean.
4. **Dire Necessity**: For this portrait of Necessity, see note on *Odes* 1.35.16–20.
5. **till . . . please them**: The Scythians and Getae are nomadic, so take turns harvesting the land.

nec dotata regit virum
coniunx nec nitido fidit adultero.   20

    dos est magna parentium
virtus et metuens alterius viri
    certo foedere castitas;
et peccare nefas aut pretium est mori.

    o quisquis volet impias   25
caedis et rabiem tollere civicam,
    si quaeret PATER VRBIUM
suscribi statuis, indomitam audeat

    refrenare licentiam,
clarus postgenitis: quatenus—heu nefas!—   30
    virtutem incolumem odimus,
sublatam ex oculis quaerimus invidi.

    quid tristes querimoniae,
si non supplicio culpa reciditur,
    quid leges sine moribus   35
vanae proficiunt, si neque fervidis

    pars inclusa caloribus
mundi nec Boreae finitimum latus
    durataeque solo nives
mercatorem abigunt, horrida callidi   40

    vincunt aequora navitae,
magnum pauperies opprobrium iubet
    quidvis et facere et pati
virtutisque viam deserit arduae?

No dowered wife commands her husband
or trusts an elegant adulterer.   20

    Their parents' virtue is their great
dowry, and chastity that shirks another
      man in unwavering alliance.
To sin[6] is sacrilege and death its price.

    Whoever wants to do away   25
with impious massacres and civic madness,
      if he will want "Father of Cities"[7]
inscribed upon his statues, let him dare

    to check untamed licentiousness—
famed among those to come,[8] since (sacrilege!)   30
      we jealously hate living virtue
but seek it when it's taken from our eyes.

    What good are bitter lamentations
if guilt is not excised through punishment?
      What good are laws if they are void   35
of morals, if the region of the world

    obstructed by the searing heat[9]
and that zone which is next to Boreas,[10]
      where snows are packed upon the ground,
do not deter the merchant, and ingenious   40

    sailors subdue the dreadful sea,
and poverty, a great disgrace, compels us
      to do and suffer anything,
even desert the lofty path toward virtue?

---

6. **To sin:** "To sin" here suggests sexual misconduct in particular.

7. **Father of Cities:** Augustus would be given the title *pater patriae* (father of the
fatherland) in 2 B.C.E., a couple decades after the publication of *Odes* 1–3.

8. **famed . . . to come:** It was a common idea that the great, while alive, attracted envy,
which fell away after their death.

9. **region . . . heat:** The hot equatorial zone.

10. **zone . . . Boreas:** The arctic north. Boreas was the north wind.

vel nos in Capitolium,   45
quo clamor vocat et turba faventium,
    vel nos in mare proximum
gemmas et lapides, aurum et inutile,

    summi materiem mali,
mittamus, scelerum si bene paenitet.   50
    eradenda cupidinis
pravi sunt elementa et tenerae nimis

    mentes asperioribus
formandae studiis. nescit equo rudis
    haerere ingenuus puer   55
venarique timet, ludere doctior

    seu Graeco iubeas trocho
seu malis vetita legibus alea,
    cum periura patris fides
consortem socium fallat et hospites,   60

    indignoque pecuniam
haredi properet. scilicet improbae
    crescunt divitiae; tamen
curtae nescio quid semper abest rei.

Let us cast down our gems and stones   45
and useless gold—the source of highest evil—
    either atop the Capitol,[11]
where shouting crowds are calling their approval,

or down into the nearest sea,
if we are truly sorry for our crimes.   50
    We must uproot the first beginnings
of vicious avarice and fashion minds

that are too tender with pursuits
that make them hardier. The freeborn boy,
    untrained, cannot stay on his horse   55
and is afraid to hunt, more skilled in playing

with a Greek hoop,[12] if you should bid him,
or with the dice that are against the law,[13]
    all while his father's perjured trust
deceives his business partner and his guests.   60

He hurries to build up his money
for his unworthy heir. Without a doubt
    do shameless riches grow. Yet never
are they enough, and wealth is always lacking.

---

11. **Capitol**: Horace suggests that the Romans dedicate all their luxury items to Jupiter
    Optimus Maximus in his temple on the Capitoline.
12. **Greek hoop**: A metal hoop used in athletic activities. These are often found on
    Greek vases that depict pederastic scenes, so Horace may be disparaging the boy's
    sexuality—a citizen boy should not, according to Roman norms, be a pederastic
    beloved.
13. **dice . . . against the law**: Gambling with dice was generally illegal, except
    during the Saturnalia. Nisbet and Rudd (2004) note, however, that the law was
    barely enforced.

ODES 3.25

Quo me, Bacche, rapis tui
plenum? quae nemora aut quos agor in specus
    velox mente nova? quibus
antris egregii Caesaris audiar

    aeternum meditans decus   5
stellis inserere et consilio Iovis?
    dicam insigne recens adhuc
indictum ore alio. non secus in iugis

    exsomnis stupet Euhias
Hebrum prospiciens et niue candidam   10
    Thracen ac pede barbaro
lustratam Rhodopen, ut mihi devio

    ripas et vacuum nemus
mirari libet. o Naiadum potens
    Baccharumque valentium   15
proceras manibus vertere fraxinos,

    nil parvum aut humili modo,
nil mortale loquar. dulce periculum est,
    o Lenaee, sequi deum
cingentem viridi tempora pampino.   20

ODES 3.25[1]

Where, Bacchus, do you seize me, full
of you? I'm led into what groves or caves,
      sped by my strange, new[2] mind? In what
grottos will I be heard while practicing

    to place distinguished Caesar's lasting   5
glory among the stars and in Jove's council?
      My song will be superb and new,
unspoken by another's mouth. Just as

    the sleepless Bacchant is amazed
while gazing at the Hebrus and at Thrace,   10
      gleaming with snow, and Rhodope,[3]
tramped by barbarian feet, so I am pleased

    to gape in awe at banks and empty
woods in untrodden places. You who rule
      over the Naiads and the Bacchants,   15
who can upturn tall ash trees with their hands,[4]

    my song will not be small or low
in style, nor mortal. It's a pleasant danger,[5]
      Lenaeus,[6] to pursue a god
while wreathing verdant vines[7] around my temples.   20

---

1. *Odes* **3.25** (*Second Asclepiadean*): A **hymn** to Bacchus, in which Horace presents himself as being in the throes of divine inspiration. As Horace rushes through the wilderness associated with Bacchic inspiration, a political aspect enters the poem—while there he will practice **encomiastic** songs for the *princeps*, Augustus, in which he foretells the emperor's future deification.

2. **strange, new:** Both of these words translate the Latin *nova*—the two ideas were yoked in the Roman mind.

3. **Hebrus . . . Thrace . . . Rhodope:** Hebrus was a river and Rhodope a mountain in Thrace.

4. **upturn . . . hands:** Those inspired by Bacchus performed amazing feats of strength such as ripping up trees or killing animals by tearing them limb from limb.

5. **pleasant danger:** A famous Horatian *callida iunctura* brilliantly summing up the worship of Bacchus. Some have suggested that the phrase applies also to the practice of **encomium**.

6. **Lenaeus:** A cult name of Bacchus.

7. **verdant vines:** A plant sacred to Bacchus in his guise as god of wine.

ODES 3.26

Vixi puellis nuper idoneus
et militavi non sine gloria;
       nunc arma defunctumque bello
          barbiton hic paries habebit,

laevum marinae qui Veneris latus   5
custodit. hic, hic ponite lucida
       funalia et vectis et arcus
          oppositis foribus minaces.

o quae beatam diva tenes Cyprum et
Memphin carentem Sithonia nive,   10
       regina, sublimi flagello
          tange Chloen semel arrogantem.

ODES 3.26[1]

Until just lately I was fit[2] for girls
and was a soldier not without renown.
    But now my weapons and my barbiton,[3]
        discharged from battle, this wall will support,

the one that guards the left-hand flank of Venus,   5
born from the sea. Here, here put down the torches,
    still glowing,[4] and the crowbars and the bows.
        menaces to the doors that stood against them.

O goddess, you who occupy rich Cyprus
and Memphis,[5] always lacking Thracian snow,   10
    O queen, raise up your whip and just one time
        thwack Chloe the contemptuous with it.

---

1. ***Odes* 3.26** (*Alcaic Strophe*): Horace has retired from the upheavals of erotic life, likened, via the **metaphor** of ***militia amoris***, to warfare. He hangs up the instruments of erotic war in Venus's temple before making a prayer that suggests he may not be as far removed from the throes of love as he would have us believe.
2. **fit**: The word *idoneus* is the first of several military terms that appear in the poem. It is normally used to indicate suitability in martial contexts, as in Propertius 1.6.29: *idoneus armis* (fit for weapons).
3. **barbiton**: A stringed instrument much like a lyre. Horace suggests he used it to compose amatory poetry, but now he's retiring from that genre.
4. **still glowing**: Like his wet clothes in *Odes* 1.5, the still-glowing torches suggest that Horace's retirement is only very recent and perhaps impromptu.
5. **Cyprus ... Memphis**: Cyprus in the Mediterranean and Memphis in Egypt were important cult sites of Aphrodite/Venus.

ODES 3.27

Impios parrae recinentis omen
ducat et praegnans canis aut ab agro
rava decurrens lupa Lanuvino
     fetaque vulpes:

rumpat et serpens iter institutum   5
si per obliquum similis sagittae
terruit mannos: ego cui timebo
     providus auspex,

antequam stantis repetat paludes
imbrium divina avis imminentum,   10
oscinem corvum prece suscitabo
     solis ab ortu.

sis licet felix ubicumque mavis,
et memor nostri, Galatea, vivas,

ODES 3.27[1]

May the omen of a screeching owl escort
the impious, or a pregnant dog or she-wolf
hurrying down Lanuvium's field[2] or vixen
    fresh from her labor.[3]

May a snake disrupt their journey as they leave,   5
if crosswise like a dart it scares the ponies.
To help the one for whom I'm frightened, I,
    provident augur—

before the raven, who predicts the coming
rain, can return to stagnant swamps—will use   10
my prayers to make that seer bird fly forth
    from the sun's rising.[4]

May you find joy wherever you prefer
and live remembering me, O Galatea.

---

1. **Odes 3.27** (*Sapphic Strophe*): Horace opens this complex ***propempticon*** in the
persona of an augur, a reader of bird signs, hoping to receive (and produce) good
omens as a woman named Galatea sets out on a sea voyage. The relationship between
Horace and Galatea is unclear, but many assume they have been lovers, and some
suggest that Galatea is now leaving him for another man. Rather than simply ask for
propitious omens and make wishes for a safe journey, the augur-poet underscores
the journey's dangerous risks. The poem then moves on to the long mythological
exemplum of Europa, whom Jupiter kidnapped and raped in the guise of a bull,
sweeping her across the ocean on his back. One interpretive crux in the poem is
whether Jupiter has raped Europa at this point or if that still lies in the future.
2. **Lanuvium's field**: Lanuvium was twenty miles to the southeast of Rome.
3. **owl ... labor**: Horace lists a number of events that would be considered bad omens
for anyone departing on a dangerous journey. He hopes, or claims to hope, that these
befall the impious rather than Galatea—all the while reminding her of their possibility.
4. **before the raven ... sun's rising**: Horace says he will attempt to manipulate
the raven's flight in order to prevent it from returning to the marshes, where its
appearance would foretell bad weather. "The sun's rising" is the east. As Nisbet and
Rudd (2004) point out, Roman augurs faced south, so a bird flying from the east
would appear on the augur's left, generally taken as a favorable sign.

teque nec laevus vetet ire picus   15
    nec vaga cornix.

sed vides quanto trepidet tumultu
pronus Orion? ego quid sit ater
Hadriae novi sinus et quid albus
    peccet Iapyx.   20

hostium uxores puerique caecos
sentiant motus orientis Austri et
aequoris nigri fremitum et trementis
    verbere ripas.

sic et Europe niveum doloso   25
credidit tauro latus et scatentem
beluis pontum mediasque fraudes
    palluit audax.

nuper in pratis studiosa florum et
debitae Nymphis opifex coronae,   30
nocte sublustri nihil astra praeter
    vidit et undas.

quae simul centum tetigit potentem
oppidis Creten, "pater, o relictum
filiae nomen, pietasque" dixit   35
    "victa furore!

May no woodpecker on the left[5] or roving   15
    crow slow your journey.

But don't you see with what a storm Orion
quakes as he's setting?[6] I myself know how
the Adriatic's bay turns black and cloudless
    Iapyx[7] makes trouble.   20

Let our foes' wives and children feel the blind
churning of Auster[8] as he rises up,
the darkened water's rumble, and the shore
    trembling with lashes.

So too Europa lent the crafty bull   25
her snow-white flank and, though she was courageous,
blanched at the monster-gushing sea and dangers
    lurking around her.

The girl who just was seeking meadow flowers[9]
to make a garland she had promised Nymphs,   30
saw nothing in the night's low light except
    stars and the water.

As soon as she arrived in Crete, a mighty
land with a hundred cities, she said, "Father,
I've lost the name of daughter! Duty's[10] been   35
    conquered by madness!

---

5. **woodpecker on the left**: In Roman practice, a bird on the left, as noted above, would generally be taken as a good sign. Garrison (1991) suggests on this passage that Horace has switched abruptly to the Greek practice, where the augur faced north. Horace's inconsistent language is most likely "a parody of impressive-sounding magical jargon" (Garrison) rather than a consistent portrait of augural practice.

6. **Orion . . . setting**: The constellation Orion's November setting brought storms.

7. **Adriatic . . . Iapyx**: The Adriatic is the sea to the east of Italy, suggesting that Galatea is sailing to Greece. Iapyx was the west-northwest wind.

8. **Auster**: The south wind.

9. **meadow flowers**: It is a traditional part of the myth that the bull/Jove appears to Europa while she is picking flowers.

10. **Duty**: *Pietas* indicated not just "duty" to the gods but also duty to one's parents.

unde quo veni? levis una mors est
virginum culpae. vigilansne ploro
turpe commissum, an vitiis carentem
     ludit imago   40

vana, quae porta fugiens eburna
somnium ducit? meliusne fluctus
ire per longos fuit, an recentis
     carpere flores?

si quis infamem mihi nunc iuvencum   45
dedat iratae, lacerare ferro et
frangere enitar modo multum amati
     cornua monstri.

impudens liqui patrios Penatis,
impudens Orcum moror. o deorum   50
si quis haec audis, utinam inter errem
     nuda leones!

antequam turpis macies decentis
occupet malas teneraeque sucus
defluat praedae, speciosa quaero   55
     pascere tigris.

'vilis Europe,' pater urget absens:
'quid mori cessas? potes hac ab orno
pendulum zona bene te secuta
     laedere collum.   60

I've come from where to where? One death is mild
for guilty virgins. Do I, wide awake,
bewail a shameful crime, or am I guiltless,
    tricked by an empty   40

image, which flees the gate of ivory
and brings a dream?[11] Which was the better choice—
to go across the distant waves or pluck
    newly grown flowers?

If anyone should hand that ill-famed bull   45
to me, enraged, how I would strive to mangle
it with a sword and break its horns—that monster
    just so beloved.[12]

Shameless, I left my father's household gods.
Shameless, I'm making Orcus wait. O if   50
there's any god who hears this, let me wander
    nude among lions!

Before foul gauntness falls upon my lovely
cheeks and the tender plunder's sap all flows
away—while I'm still beautiful—I pray,   55
    feed me to tigers.

'Worthless Europa,' my absent father urges,
'Why wait to die? It's possible to smash
your neck and hang it from the girdle[13] you
    luckily brought here.   60

---

11. **gate of ivory . . . dream**: Europa wonders if perhaps she is dreaming. Traditionally,
false dreams came from the Underworld, exiting through an ivory gate.
12. **just so beloved**: Europa was smitten by the beauty of the bull and voluntarily
climbed onto his back, whereupon he dashed off, kidnapping her. There is perhaps
also a suggestion here that sexual intercourse has already taken place, while Jupiter
was still in the guise of a bull.
13. **girdle**: The girdle was a long belt that went around the waist. For women, it
was often thought of as a symbol of virginity.

sive te rupes et acuta leto
saxa delectant, age te procellae
crede veloci, nisi erile mavis
   carpere pensum

regius sanguis dominaeque tradi   65
barbarae paelex.'" aderat querenti
perfidum ridens Venus et remisso
   filius arcu.

mox, ubi lusit satis: "abstineto"
dixit "irarum calidaeque rixae,   70
cum tibi invisus laceranda reddet
   cornua taurus.

uxor invicti Iovis esse nescis:
mitte singultus, bene ferre magnam
disce fortunam; tua sectus orbis   75
   nomina ducet."

Or if the cliffs and boulders, sharp for death,
delight you, come and lend yourself to headlong
breezes, unless you'd rather pluck a mistress'
    wool and be given

to a barbarian lady, though you're royal—   65
her rival.'"[14] While she wept, Venus appeared,
perfidiously laughing, with her son, whose
    bow was now slackened.

When soon she'd finished mocking her, she said,
"Be sure to end your rage and fiery quarrels   70
when the detested bull brings back to you his
    horns to be mangled.[15]

You do not know that you're the wife of Jove
unconquered.[16] End your sobbing. Learn to bear
great fortune rightly. You will have as namesake   75
    half of the planet."[17]

---

14. **you'd rather ... rival**: If Europa does not commit suicide, she imagines, the
    only fate left to her is to be taken prisoner as a slave, in which position she would
    work wool for the mistress and provide sex to the master.
15. **Be sure ... mangled**: Venus's words are not entirely clear here, but they
    certainly mock Europa's earlier desire to mangle the bull's horns—Venus has been
    eavesdropping. If Jupiter has not yet raped Europa, this may be a reference to this
    impending event.
16. **You do not know ... unconquered**: Venus's words here could also be
    translated, "You do not know how to be the wife of Jove unconquered."
17. **half of the planet**: Europe was thought to have been named after Europa.

ODES 3.28

Festo quid potius die
Neptuni faciam? prome reconditum,
    Lyde, strenua Caecubum
munitaeque adhibe vim sapientiae.

    inclinare meridiem   5
sentis ac, veluti stet volucris dies,
    parcis deripere horreo
cessantem Bibuli consulis amphoram.

    nos cantabimus invicem
Neptunum et viridis Nereidum comas;   10
    tu curva recines lyra
Latonam et celeris spicula Cynthiae,

    summo carmine, quae Cnidon
fulgentisque tenet Cycladas et Paphum
    iunctis visit oloribus;   15
dicetur merita Nox quoque nenia.

ODES 3.28[1]

What would I like to do on Neptune's
festival day? Go fetch the stored away
    Caecuban,[2] Lyde, and be quick.
Make an assault on wisdom's citadel.[3]

You know that noon is sinking now,   5
yet you, as if the winged day stood still,
    are slow to snatch that jar from storage
that's rested since Bibulus' consulship.[4]

In alternation we will sing
of Neptune and the Nereids'[5] green hair.   10
    You on your curving lyre will hymn
Latona[6] and the darts of swift Diana.

The final song will be of her
who holds the gleaming Cyclades and Cnidus,
    who visits Paphos on yoked swans.[7]   15
Night also will be sung a worthy tune.

---

1. **Odes 3.28** (*Second Asclepiadean*): Horace outlines his plans for celebrating a festival
   to Neptune, most likely the Neptunalia on July 23. He urges a woman named Lyde to
   join him in the celebration, imbibing fine wine and taking turns in lyric performance.
2. **Caecuban**: A superior Italian wine.
3. **Make an assault . . . citadel**: That is, allow yourself to relax a little.
4. **Bibulus' consulship**: Consul in 59 B.C.E., which would make the wine more than
   thirty years old.
5. **Nereids**: The daughters of the sea god Nereus.
6. **Latona**: The mother of Apollo and Diana.
7. **who holds . . . yoked swans**: Venus. The Cyclades are a group of Aegean islands.
   Cnidus was a city in Asia Minor with strong associations with Venus/Aphrodite. It is
   where Praxiteles's famous statue of Aphrodite stood.

ODES 3.29

Tyrrhena regum progenies, tibi
non ante verso lene merum cado
      cum flore, Maecenas, rosarum et
          pressa tuis balanus capillis

iamdudum apud me est. eripe te morae,   5
nec semper udum Tibur et Aefulae
      declive contempleris arvum et
          Telegoni iuga parricidae.

fastidiosam desere copiam et
molem propinquam nubibus arduis;   10
      omitte mirari beatae
          fumum et opes strepitumque Romae.

plerumque gratae divitibus vices
mundaeque parvo sub lare pauperum
      cenae sine aulaeis et ostro   15
          sollicitam explicuere frontem.

iam clarus occultum Andromedae pater
ostendit ignem, iam Procyon furit
      et stella vesani Leonis,
          sole dies referente siccos: 20

ODES 3.29[1]

Descendant of Etruscan kings, Maecenas,
a mellow wine inside an untipped jar,
    together with the buds of roses and
        pressed perfume for your hair, has long awaited

you at my house. You need to stop delaying—   5
do not just always gaze at watered Tibur
    and at the sloping fields of Aefula and
        the heights of Telegonus, father-killer.[2]

Abandon that repulsive opulence and
the heap that goes up to the lofty clouds.   10
    No longer be in awe of all the smoke,
        the riches, and the noise of blessed Rome.

Changes are mostly pleasant for the rich,
and modest dinners in a poor man's humble
    home with no coverlets or purple cloth   15
        have smoothed the wrinkles from an
        anxious brow.

Now does Andromeda's bright father show
his hidden fire. Now Procyon is raging,
    as is the star of Leo, full of fury—
        the sun is bringing back the arid days.[3]   20

---

1. **Odes** 3.29 (*Alcaic Strophe*): This is perhaps the grandest of all of the poems to
Maecenas, and in it Horace again (as in 1.20) invites his patron to visit his Sabine farm.
In preparation to close the collection, Horace weaves together many of the ethical
strands running through the odes, such as the moral superiority of the countryside
and moderate poverty, the reciprocal benefits of friendship, the unknowability of the
future, and contentment with the present moment as the key to peace of mind.
2. **Tibur . . . Aefula . . . heights of Telegonus**: Tibur (modern Tivoli) and Aefula are in
the Sabine countryside northeast of Rome where Horace's celebrated farm is located,
and Tusculum is in the Alban Hills to the east. Telegonus was the legendary son of
Odysseus and Circe and the founder of Tusculum. He accidentally killed his father.
3. **Andromeda . . . arid days**: The astronomical information gives the poem a dramatic
date of mid-July, since Andromeda's father is Cepheus, a constellation that rises at
that time. Procyon is the Dog Star, also rising in mid-July, and the sun enters the
zodiac sign of Leo on July 21.

iam pastor umbras cum grege languido
rivumque fessus quaerit et horridi
     dumeta Silvani, caretque
          ripa vagis taciturna ventis.

tu civitatem quis deceat status   25
curas et Vrbi sollicitus times
     quid Seres et regnata Cyro
          Bactra parent Tanaisque discors.

prudens futuri temporis exitum
caliginosa nocte premit deus,   30
     ridetque si mortalis ultra
          fas trepidat. quod adest memento

componere aequus; cetera fluminis
ritu feruntur, nunc medio alveo
     cum pace delabentis Etruscum   35
          in mare, nunc lapides adesos

stirpesque raptas et pecus et domos
volventis una non sine montium
     clamore vicinaeque silvae,
          cum fera diluvies quietos   40

irritat amnis. ille potens sui
laetusque deget, cui licet in diem
     dixisse "vixi: cras vel atra
          nube polum Pater occupato

Now does the shepherd with his languid flock
seek out in weariness the shade, the stream,
    the thickets of the shaggy god Silvanus.
       No wind is wandering on the quiet bank.

You are concerned about what constitution   25
befits the state and, worried for the city,
    fear what the Chinese and the Cyrus-ruled
       Bactrians plot, and what the feuding Don.[4]

God in his wisdom hides away the outcome
of future time inside the misty darkness   30
    and laughs when mortals fret more than is right.
       Remember to attend to what's at hand

with equanimity. The rest is borne
along just like a river, now serenely
    flowing within its channel down into   35
       the sea of Tuscany,[5] now whirling round

eroded stones and torn-up stumps of trees,
cattle and houses, all together, while
    the mountains and the nearby forest shout,
       whenever an unruly flood incites   40

the quiet flow. He will be his own master
and pass life happily who every day
    says: "I have lived.[6] Tomorrow let the Father
       fill up the heavens with a gloomy cloud

---

4. **Don:** Used to designate Scythia. Maecenas is worried about highly unlikely threats from the eastern edges of the empire.

5. **sea of Tuscany:** The Tyrrhenian on the western coast of Italy.

6. **I have lived:** Some editors end the quotation here. This would perhaps be a more powerfully succinct way to assert a well-lived life than continuing the quotation to line 48.

vel sole puro; non tamen irritum,   45
quodcumque retro est, efficiet neque
    diffinget infectumque reddet,
        quod fugiens semel hora vexit."

Fortuna saevo laeta negotio et
ludum insolentem ludere pertinax   50
    transmutat incertos honores,
        nunc mihi, nunc alii benigna.

laudo manentem; si celeris quatit
pennas, resigno quae dedit et mea
    virtute me involvo probamque   55
        pauperiem sine dote quaero.

non est meum, si mugiat Africis
malus procellis, ad miseras preces
    decurrere et votis pacisci,
        ne Cypriae Tyriaeque merces   60

addant avaro divitias mari.
tunc me biremis praesidio scaphae
    tutum per Aegaeos tumultus
        aura feret geminusque Pollux.

or with pure sunlight. Yet he cannot render   45
invalid what is in the past, nor can
    he shape anew and make undone whatever
        the fleeing hour has carried off for good."

Fortune, delighting in her ruthless task and
relentless as she plays her pompous game,   50
    switches around her vacillating honors—
        she's kindly now to me, now to another.

I praise her while she stays. But if she beats
her speedy wings, I hand back what she's given,
    wrap up in my own virtue,[7] and pursue   55
        upstanding but undowered poverty.

It's not my way, if violent southwest winds
have made the ship's mast bellow, to have recourse
    to wretched prayers and to make deals with vows
        so that my goods from Cyprus and from Tyre   60

won't add their riches to the greedy sea.
Then, in the shelter of a two-oared skiff,
    the breeze and Pollux, with his twin,[8] will bear
        me safely through the storms of the Aegean.

---

7. **wrap up . . . virtue:** Horace here alludes to the tattered cloak associated with Cynic and Stoic philosophers, who espoused virtue as the highest good.
8. **with his twin:** Castor and Pollux formed the Gemini or Dioscuri, tutelary deities of sailors.

ODES 3.30

Exegi monumentum aere perennius
regalique situ pyramidum altius,
quod non imber edax, non Aquilo impotens
possit diruere aut innumerabilis
annorum series et fuga temporum.   5
non omnis moriar, multaque pars mei
vitabit Libitinam: usque ego postera
crescam laude recens, dum Capitolium
scandet cum tacita virgine pontifex.
dicar, qua violens obstrepit Aufidus   10

ODES 3.30[1]

I've made a monument more lasting than bronze,
more lofty than the king-built pyramids.
Devouring rain and Aquilo's[2] wild rage
cannot demolish it, nor can the years'
countless succession and the flight of time.   5
I won't die wholly—much of me will flee
from Libitina.[3] I'll grow ever fresh
with future praise, however long the pontiff[4]
and silent virgin[5] climb the Capitol.[6]
I will be spoken of, where Aufidus[7]   10

---

1. **Odes 3.30** (*First Asclepiadean*): In this final poem of *Odes* 1–3, published as a unit in
23 B.C.E., Horace invites us to see himself and his text as one. His body will die, but he
will live on through his immortal poetry. The poem forms a signature (traditionally
called a *sphragis* [seal]) that neatly closes the collection. Its meter is used elsewhere
in the first three books only in 1.1.
2. **Aquilo's:** The north wind.
3. **Libitina:** A goddess of death, specifically funerals.
4. **pontiff:** The Pontifex Maximus, the chief priest of Rome.
5. **silent virgin:** This refers to the Vestal Virgins, priests of Vesta who were to keep her
hearth fire constantly lit.
6. **Capitol:** The Capitoline Hill was the religious center of the city. It was the site of
several temples, including that of Jupiter Optimus Maximus ("Greatest and Best").
7. **Aufidus:** A river in Apulia, the southern Italian region in which Horace was born.

et qua pauper aquae Daunus agrestium
regnavit populorum, ex humili potens
princeps Aeolium carmen ad Italos
deduxisse modos. sume superbiam
quaesitam meritis et mihi Delphica   15
lauro cinge volens, Melpomene, comam.

violently roars, where Daunus,[8] poor in water,
ruled rustic folks, as lowly born but mighty,
the first[9] to have brought back[10] Aeolian song[11]
to poems of Italy. Take up the pride
attained through merit, and with Delphic laurel,[12]   15
Melpomene,[13] joyfully wreath my hair.

8. **Daunus:** A mythical Apulian king. He is called "poor in water" because the region was prone to drought.
9. **first:** Horace uses a loaded term to describe himself as "first" (*princeps*). This word, whence comes the word "prince" and "principate," was the title Augustus adopted for himself to designate his position as "first" among equals.
10. **to have brought back:** This translates *deduxisse*, a word with important associations. First, it is a weaving term designating "fine-spun" poetry, and Horace uses it to indicate the refined excellence of his verse. Second, it is a word used in contexts of the Roman triumph to describe the bringing back of captives and booty, as in 1.37.31, where Cleopatra refuses "to be paraded" (*deduci*) in Augustus's triumph.
11. **Aeolian song:** A reference to Lesbos (where the Aeolian Greek dialect was spoken). The island's most famous residents were Sappho and Alcaeus.
12. **laurel:** Again alludes to the Roman triumph, as the *triumphator* was crowned with a laurel wreath. The laurel is Delphic because of its connection with Apollo, god of Delphi.
13. **Melpomene:** One of the Muses.

CARMEN SAECULARE

Phoebe silvarumque potens Diana,
lucidum caeli decus, o colendi
semper et culti, date quae precamur
    tempore sacro,

CARMEN SAECULARE[1]

Phoebus and she who rules the woods, Diana,
bright beauty of the sky,[2] worshipped and to be
worshipped forever, grant[3] our prayer on this
    sacred occasion,

---

1. *Carmen Saeculare* (*Sapphic Strophe*): Horace wrote this difficult poem as a **hymn** for
   the Secular Games that Augustus held in June of 17 B.C.E. to inaugurate a new *saeculum,*
   a period of roughly 100 years (or, in this case, it was argued to occur every 110 years).
   Previous games had been held in 249 B.C.E. and 146 B.C.E. Civil war had prevented the
   games from being held in the 40s B.C.E. The games took place over a period of three
   days and involved sacrifices, prayers, plays, athletic games, chariot races, hunts, and
   various other ritual events. On the third day, bloodless sacrifices were made to Apollo
   and Diana on the Palatine, where Augustus had dedicated a new temple to Apollo in
   28 B.C.E. It was on this day that the *Carmen Saeculare* was performed by a chorus of
   twenty-seven boys and twenty-seven girls, all with still living mothers and fathers.
   It was then re-sung on the Capitoline. Thomas (2011) refers to the Secular Games
   as "the most notable ritual of the Augustan principate." Those interested in a fuller
   reconstruction of the games and the events leading up to them should consult Thomas's
   commentary. For a nice overview of the games and reading of Horace's poem, see esp.
   Miller (2009, 276–88). For a much fuller consideration, see Putnam (2000).
2. **bright beauty . . . sky:** It is unclear which god this indicates. Apollo was associated
   with the sun, and Diana the moon.
3. **grant:** In the Latin the word *dati* (grant) follows immediately after the word *culti*
   (worshipped). This suggests the reciprocal quid quo pro nature of Roman religion,
   whereby gods grant benefactions in exchange for devotion and dedications.

quo Sibyllini monuere versus   5
virgines lectas puerosque castos
dis, quibus septem placuere colles,
    dicere carmen.

alme Sol, curru nitido diem qui
promis et celas aliusque et idem   10
nasceris, possis nihil urbe Roma
    visere maius.

rite maturos aperire partus
lenis, Ilithyia, tuere matres,
sive tu Lucina probas vocari   15
    seu Genitalis:

diva, producas subolem, patrumque
prosperes decreta super iugandis
feminis prolisque novae feraci
    lege marita,   20

certus undenos deciens per annos
orbis ut cantus referatque ludos
ter die claro totiensque grata
    nocte frequentis.

when verses of the Sibyl[4] have advised   5
virgins and boys, select and undefiled,
to sing a song for gods to whom the seven
    hills[5] have been pleasing.

You, kindly Sun, who bring and hide the day
with your bright car, reborn both new and yet   10
the same, may Rome the city be the greatest
    object you look on.

Gentle at solemnly unsealing ready
childbirth, Ilithyia, protect our mothers,
whether you favor being called Lucina   15
    or Genitalis.[6]

Goddess, may you deliver progeny
and champion the senators' decrees
on wedding women and the marriage law,
    rich in new offspring,[7]   20

so, fixed at every ten times eleven years,
the cycle may bring back the songs and games,
crowded three times in daylight and in pleasant
    night just as often.

---

4. **verses of the Sibyl:** Oracles attributed to the prophetic Sybil that were kept in the temple of Palatine Apollo. The originals had been lost, but a second set was produced in 18 B.C.E. by the *quindecimviri sacris faciundis*, a priestly college tasked with keeping the oracles, of which Augustus was a member.

5. **the seven hills:** Rome's seven hills stand via **metonomy** for the city itself.

6. **Ilithyia ... Lucina ... Genitalis:** Diana is here aligned with the Greek goddess of childbirth, Ilithyia, who also went by the names Lucina and Genitalis. The variant names ensure that one has the ear of the correct divinity. The stanza introduces the preoccupation with fertility and childbirth running through the poem. The civil wars had depleted Rome's population, and Augustus in both his building program and legislation emphasized marriage and childbirth.

7. **senators' decrees ... new offspring:** On Augustus's marriage legislation, see the introduction. This line clearly refers to the *Lex Iulia de maritandis*, enacted the previous year.

vosque veraces cecinisse, Parcae,   25
quod semel dictum est stabilisque rerum
terminus servet, bona iam peractis
　　　iungite fata.

fertilis frugum pecorisque Tellus
spicea donet Cererem corona;   30
nutriant fetus et aquae salubres
　　　et Iovis aurae.

condito mitis placidusque telo
supplices audi pueros, Apollo;
siderum regina bicornis, audi,   35
　　　Luna, puellas:

Roma si vestrum est opus, Iliaeque
litus Etruscum tenuere turmae,
iussa pars mutare Lares et urbem
　　　sospite cursu,   40

cui per ardentem sine fraude Troiam
castus Aeneas patriae superstes
liberum munivit iter, daturus
　　　plura relictis:

di, probos mores docili iuventae,   45
di, senectuti placidae quietem,
Romulae genti date remque prolemque
　　　et decus omne.

And you, O Fates,[8] who tell the truth in singing   25
what has been spoken (may the end of things
preserve it firmly), add good fates to those
      brought to fruition.

Fertile in fruits and livestock, may the Earth[9]
bestow a garland made of corn on Ceres.   30
May wholesome wind and water sent by Jove
      nourish the produce.

Your weapon stored away, be calm and mild
while listening to the suppliant boys, Apollo,
and listen to the girls, you queen of stars,   35
      double-horned Luna.

If Rome is of your[10] making and if throngs
from Ilium[11] reached the Tuscan shore, the part
that, ordered to give up their homes and city,
      journeyed to safety   40

when undefiled Aeneas, who outlived
his country, paved for them a harmless path
to freedom through Troy's flames—he'd grant them more than
      they had relinquished:

gods, grant good morals to the docile youth,   45
gods, grant tranquility to calm old age,
grant to the Roman people wealth and children,
      every adornment.

---

8. **Fates**: The Fates received sacrifices on the first night of the Games.
9. **Earth**: Tellus received sacrifice on the third night of the Games.
10. **your**: This looks ahead to the "gods" of line 45 but probably more specifically
    refers to Jupiter and Juno as the founding gods of Rome.
11. **throngs from Ilium**: This triad focuses on the foundation of the city by Aeneas and
    those who fled from Troy with him, events narrated in Vergil's *Aeneid*, published
    upon the poet's death not even two years before the Secular Games.

quaeque vos bubus veneratur albis
clarus Anchisae Venerisque sanguis,   50
impetret, bellante prior, iacentem
      lenis in hostem.

iam mari terraque manus potentis
Medus Albanasque timet securis,
iam Scythae responsa petunt superbi   55
      nuper et Indi.

iam Fides et Pax et Honos Pudorque
priscus et neglecta redire Virtus
audet, apparetque beata pleno
      Copia cornu.   60

augur et fulgente decorus arcu
Phoebus acceptusque novem Camenis,
qui salutari levat arte fessos
      corporis artus,

si Palatinas videt aequus aras,   65
remque Romanam Latiumque felix
alterum in lustrum meliusque semper
      prorogat aevum,

All that the famous bloodline of Anchises
and Venus[12] asks of you with pure white steers,   50
may they obtain—foremost in war, but mild toward
    foes they've defeated.[13]

The Persian now is frightened of our troops,
mighty on land and sea, and Alba's axes.[14]
The Scythians and the Indians, lately proud, now   55
    seek our responses.[15]

Now Loyalty and Peace, Honor and antique
Shame and neglected Virtue dare to come
again. Rich Plenty is appearing with her
    horn of abundance.   60

Phoebus, the augur lovely with his shining
bow and the darling of the nine Camenae,
who with his healing art relieves the weary
    limbs of the body,[16]

may he with favor look on Palatine altars   65
and stretch out Roman might and Latin fortune
into another cycle and an age
    always improving,

---

12. **bloodline ... Venus**: Romans are presented as the descendants of Venus and
Anchises, the parents of Aeneas.

13. **foremost ... defeated**: This line alludes to Vergil's famous injunction, spoken
by Anchises in *Aeneid* 6: *tu . . . Romane, memento . . . parcere subiectis et debellare
superbos* (Remember Roman, to spare the conquered and war down the proud).

14. **Alba's axes**: A reference to the *fasces*, the bundle of rods wrapped around an
ax, which symbolized Roman power.

15. **seek our responses**: This is the technical language of diplomacy. As Thomas
(2011) notes, this is "the regular term for envoys or individuals consulting a leader or
governing body."

16. **Phoebus ... body**: This stanza enumerates various spheres over which Apollo
presided: prophecy, hunting, music, and medicine. "Camena" is a Latin term for a
Muse.

quaeque Aventinum tenet Algidumque,
quindecim Diana preces virorum   70
curat et votis puerorum amicas
    applicat auris.

haec Iovem sentire deosque cunctos
spem bonam certamque domum reporto,
doctus et Phoebi chorus et Dianae   75
    dicere laudes.

may she, the ruler of the Aventine
and Algidus,[17] Diana, hear the pleas   70
of the Quindecimviri[18] and give friendly
    ears to boys praying.

That Jove and all the gods perceive these prayers
I bring back to my home good, certain hope—
I, chorus taught to sing the praise of Phoebus   75
    and of Diana.

---

17. **Aventine and Algidus:** Diana had a temple on the Aventine. The Algidus is
a mountain southeast of Rome, where Diana Nemorensis (Diana of the groves) was
worshipped.
18. **Quindecimviri:** The *quindecimviri sacris faciundis*, for which see note on line 5.

ODES 4

ODES 4.1

> Intermissa, Venus, diu
> rursus bella moves? Parce precor, precor.
> non sum qualis eram bonae
> sub regno Cinarae. desine, dulcium

ODES 4.1[1]

 O Venus, long ago suspended
wars—you revive them?[2] Stop! I beg, I beg.
 I am not what I used to be
when good Cinara ruled me.[3] Quit attempting,

---

1. *Odes* 4.1 (*Second Asclepiadean*): Horace opens this fourth book of *Odes*, published in
   13 B.C.E. (around a decade after the publication of books 1–3) with an address not to
   Maecenas (as in all the other opening odes), but to Venus, goddess of erotic love and
   sexuality. Horace protests that Venus is spurring him on to erotic activity—not only
   love but also the writing of erotic lyric poetry—that is now inappropriate for his age.
   Horace thus resumes lyric with reluctance in this book, and his thematic concerns
   shift away from the light and erotic toward the imperial household and the power of
   poetry. Throughout the fourth book my notes are indebted to the commentaries of
   Garrison (1991) and Thomas (2011).
2. **long ago suspended / revive them**: As Thomas (2011) notes, the Latin syntax of
   the opening two lines "entraps the reader in a momentary ambiguity." *Intermissa*
   (suspended) seems at first to modify Venus, who often stands **metonymically** for sexual
   activity. When the reader reaches the **enjambed** *bella* (wars) in line two, the syntax must
   be rethought, although the original impression remains. Horace is therefore too old both
   for sex and for all of the metaphorical "wars" (see *militia amoris*) that go along with it.
3. **Cinara ruled me**: Cinara appears several times in Horace's later poetry, twice in
   the *Epistles* (1.7.28 and 1.14.33) and twice in *Odes* 4 (here and 4.13.21–22, in the latter
   of which he speaks of her as being dead), always in passages describing his current
   unsuitability for sexuality. Horace alludes here to another metaphor of erotic poetry,
   servitium amoris.

mater saeva Cupidinum,   5
circa lustra decem flectere mollibus
        iam durum imperiis: abi
quo blandae iuvenum te revocant preces.

        tempestivius in domum
Pauli purpureis ales oloribus   10
        comissabere Maximi,
si torrere iecur quaeris idoneum:

        namque et nobilis et decens
et pro sollicitis non tacitus reis
        et centum puer artium   15
late signa feret militiae tuae,

        et, quandoque potentior
largi muneribus riserit aemuli,
        Albanos prope te lacus
ponet marmoream sub trabe citrea.   20

        illic plurima naribus
duces tura, lyraeque et Berecyntiae
        delectabere tibiae
mixtis carminibus non sine fistula;

you ruthless mother of sweet Cupids, 5
to bend a nearly fifty-year-old man,
who's harsh now to your soft commands.
Go back where coaxing prayers of young men call you.

More suitably you'll bring your revels
into the house of Paullus Maximus[4] 10
while taking wing on radiant swans,[5]
if you desire a liver fit for burning.[6]

For he is nobly born and seemly,
and vocal in support of anxious clients.
A young man of a hundred arts, 15
he'll carry far the standards of your warfare.

Whenever he has overpowered
his lavish rival's presents[7] he will laugh
and place you, made of marble, near
the Alban Lake beneath a citron roof-beam.[8] 20

There you'll inhale the most abundant
incense and be delighted by the mingled
tunes of the lyre and Berecyntian
flute,[9] not without a panpipe joining in.

---

4. **Paullus Maximus**: Paullus Fabius Maximus, nearly two decades younger, is a more appropriate object for Venus's commands. Paullus would become consul in 11 B.C.E.

5. **radiant swans**: Swans are strongly associated with Aphrodite, and she is often depicted riding on them on Greek vases. Horace actually calls these swans "purple" (*purpureis*), but this term in Latin can designate anything with sparkling radiance.

6. **liver fit for burning**: In ancient humoral theory, the liver was considered the seat of passionate emotions.

7. **rival's presents**: The lover's rival is a **stock figure** of ancient love poetry.

8. **citron roof-beam**: Horace suggests Paullus will erect a shrine (made of citron wood), complete with cult statue, to Venus on his suburban property in the Alban hills.

9. **Berecyntian / flute**: The flute (*tibia*) was a wind instrument made of reed similar to an oboe and was associated with the orgiastic worship of Cybele, the Phrygian earth goddess. Mt. Berecyntus is a mountain in Phrygia.

illic bis pueri die   25
numen cum teneris virginibus tuum
    laudantes pede candido
in morem Salium ter quatient humum.

me nec femina nec puer
iam nec spes animi credula mutui   30
    nec certare iuvat mero
nec vincire novis tempora floribus.

sed cur heu, Ligurine, cur
manat rara meas lacrima per genas?
    cur facunda parum decoro   35
inter verba cadit lingua silentio?

nocturnis ego somniis
iam captum teneo, iam volucrem sequor
    te per gramina Martii
campi, te per aquas, dure, volubilis.   40

There two times every day will boys   25
together with young virgins praise your godhead,
        and with their gleaming feet they'll shake
the earth in triple time like Salian priests,[10]

Woman or boy[11] no longer pleases
me, nor a wide-eyed hope for mutual feelings,   30
        nor contests of unwatered wine,
nor garlanding my temples with fresh flowers.

But why (woe!), Ligurinus, why
does a sporadic tear drip down my cheeks?
        Why does my fluent tongue break down   35
mid-sentence in a too unseemly silence?

During the night while dreaming, I
now hold you captured, now pursue you fleeing
        across the grass of Mars's field
and you, harsh boy, across the rolling waters.[12]   40

---

10. **Salian priests:** The Salii were priests of Mars whose rhythmic dancing is
    alluded to also in the opening lines of *Odes* 1.37.
11. **boy:** Suggests the ancient Greek practice of pederasty, whereby an adult male and
    teenage boy formed an erotic pair. This prepares us for the introduction in line 33 of
    the youthful male Ligurinus as the object of Horace's desire.
12. **Mars's field . . . flowing waters:** Mars's field is the Campus Martius, where
    athletic and military exercises took place. The "flowing waters" of the final line
    indicate the river Tiber, where Horace envisions Ligurinus swimming.

ODES 4.2

Pindarum quisquis studet aemulari,
Iulle, ceratis ope Daedalea
nititur pinnis vitreo daturus
     nomina ponto.

monte decurrens velut amnis, imbres   5
quem super notas aluere ripas,
fervet immensusque ruit profundo
     Pindarus ore,

laurea donandus Apollinari,
seu per audaces nova dithyrambos   10
verba devolvit numerisque fertur
     lege solutis,

seu deos regesque canit, deorum
sanguinem, per quos cecidere iusta

ODES 4.2[1]

Whoever is intent to rival Pindar,
Iullus,[2] relies on wings secured with wax
through Daedalean art[3]—he'll give his name
    to the bright ocean.

Just like a river rushing down a mountain,   5
which rains have swelled above familiar banks,
measureless Pindar with his boundless mouth
    surges and rushes.

He is deserving of Apollo's laurel,
whether[4] he rolls down novel words through daring   10
dithyrambs[5] and is borne along by meters
    freed from convention,[6]

or if he sings of gods and kings,[7] the sons
of gods, through whom the Centaurs[8] were extinguished

---

1. ***Odes* 4.2** (*Sapphic Strophe*): This poem forms something of a ***recusatio***, with Horace refusing the grand Pindaric style, especially the Pindaric **encomium**, both of which he suggests his addressee is better suited to. Horace is not, like Pindar, a swan of Dirce, a figure for elevated lyric praise poetry, but rather the Matine bee, i.e., the highly refined but small-scale Callimachean lyric poet. At the same time, however, Horace undercuts the ***recusatio***, demonstrating a facility with Pindaric praise and style even as he eschews it. The poem introduces the pronounced influence of Pindar in book 4. For Pindar in Horace, see especially Race (2010).
2. **Iullus**: Iullus Antonius, the son of Mark Antony and Fulvia. He had been raised by his stepmother Octavia and was married to her daughter, Claudia Marcella. He would be consul in 10 B.C.E. but would later be implicated in the adultery of Julia, the daughter of Augustus, whereupon he was sentenced to death for treason.
3. **wings . . . Daedalean art**: An allusion to the story of Icarus. Daedalus, his artisan father, fashioned wings for him, but when he flew too close to the sun, the wax holding them together melted and he fell into the sea.
4. **whether**: Horace here begins a catalog of Pindar's poetic genres starting with the most elevated types in celebration of gods to the lighter genres eulogizing mortal men.
5. **dithyrambs**: **Hymns** in celebration of the god Dionysus (the Roman Bacchus).
6. **freed from convention**: Horace attributes metrical license to Pindaric dithyramb, but it is much debated exactly what this means. For a full consideration, see Freis (1983, 30–31n7).
7. **kings**: That is, heroes.
8. **Centaurs**: Half-men, half-horse creatures, fought by Hercules and Theseus.

morte Centauri, cecidit tremendae   15
    flamma Chimaerae,

sive quos Elea domum reducit
palma caelestis pugilemve equumve
dicit et centum potiore signis
    munere donat,   20

flebili sponsae iuvenemve raptum
plorat et viris animumque moresque
aureos educit in astra nigroque
    invidet Orco.

multa Dircaeum levat aura cycnum,   25
tendit, Antoni, quotiens in altos
nubium tractus: ego apis Matinae
    more modoque

grata carpentis thyma per laborem
plurimum circa nemus uvidique   30
Tiburis ripas operosa parvus
    carmina fingo.

concines maiore poeta plectro
Caesarem, quandoque trahet feroces

in well-earned death, through whom the dread Chimaera's[9]   15
    flame was extinguished,

or if he tells of those whom Elean palm[10]
brings home as gods, a boxer or a horseman,
and with a gift that's better than a hundred
    statues rewards them,   20

or he bewails[11] a youth seized from his crying
bride and uplifts his strength and mind and golden
character to the stars, not letting dark
    Orcus[12] possess him.

A mighty breeze lifts Dirce's swan[13] whenever,   25
Antonius, he stretches toward the clouds'
high tracts. But I—as is a Matine[14] bee's
    manner and method

while harvesting the pleasant thyme with massive
labor around the groves and riverbanks   30
of watered Tibur[15]—fashion, though I'm small,
    painstaking poems.

A greater lyric poet,[16] you will sing
of Caesar when, adorned with leaves that he

---

9. **Chimaera:** The Chimaera was a hybrid monster that breathed fire, often an admixture of a lion, snake, and goat. It was defeated by the hero Bellerophon.
10. **Elean palm:** The prize of the Olympian victor. Horace refers here to epinician, poetry in praise of victors in athletic games, which is the main type of Pindaric poetry that survives.
11. **bewails:** The final Pindaric genre is the *threnos*, the **dirge** of lamentation for the dead.
12. **Orcus:** God of the Underworld.
13. **Dirce's swan:** Dirce was a spring in Thebes, Pindar's birthplace.
14. **Matine:** That is, from Matinus, a mountain in Apulia near Horace's birthplace.
15. **Tibur:** A town in the Sabine hills near which Horace had his farm.
16. **A greater lyric poet:** Pindar, like Horace, is a lyric poet, but of a grander sort, and it is with this grander type of lyric that Horace here associates Iullus Antonius.

per sacrum clivum merita decorus
    fronde Sygambros,   35

quo nihil maius meliusve terris
fata donavere bonique divi
nec dabunt, quamvis redeant in aurum
    tempora priscum.   40

concines laetosque dies et Vrbis
publicum ludum super impetrato
fortis Augusti reditu forumque
    litibus orbum.

tum meae, si quid loquar audiendum,   45
vocis accedet bona pars, et: "o sol
pulcher! o laudande!" canam, recepto
    Caesare felix.

tuque dum procedis, io Triumphe,
non semel dicemus, io Triumphe,   50
civitas omnis, dabimusque divis
    tura benignis.

te decem tauri totidemque vaccae,
me tener solvet vitulus, relicta
matre qui largis iuvenescit herbis   55
    in mea vota,

has earned, he drags along the sacred hill[17]   35
    ruthless Sygambri.[18]

The fates and kindly gods have given nothing
bigger or better to the lands than him,
nor will they give, though time become again
    ancient and golden.[19]   40

You'll sing too of the happy days, the public
games of the City to observe the prayed-for
return of brave Augustus, and the forum
    emptied of lawsuits.

I'll add, if I say anything worth hearing,   45
a good part of my voice: "O lovely day!
O warranting our praise!" I'll sing, in joy at
    Caesar's arrival.

While you[20] are marching forth, "Io Triumphe,"
we'll say, and not just once. "Io, Triumphe,"   50
all of the state together, and we'll give
    kindly gods incense.

Ten bulls or just as many cows will fill
your pledges; mine a young calf that has left
its mother and, to pay my vows, now grows   55
    strong on lush grasses.

---

17. **the sacred hill:** The Capitoline. The reference is to a triumphal parade, which
made its way to the temple of Jupiter Optimus Maximus on the Capitoline.
18. **Sygambri:** A Germanic tribe defeated in 16 B.C.E., though they would be twice
more defeated in 12 and 8 B.C.E. and would remain defiant.
19. **ancient and golden:** A reference to mankind's mythical Golden Age, which
the poets frequently suggested was returning under Augustus.
20. **you:** Presumably Iullus Antonius as he participates in the triumph.

fronte curvatos imitatus ignis
tertius lunae referentis ortum,
qua notam duxit, niveus videri,
    cetera fulvus.   60

Its forehead looks just like the crescent fires
of the new moon its third night after rising.[21]
And where it has that mark, it looks like snow—
    elsewhere it's tawny.   60

---

21. **Its forehead ... rising:** The subcutaneous horns on the calf's head are creating
   a crescent shape similar to that of the moon on the third night after it was completely
   new.

ODES 4.3

Quem tu, Melpomene, semel
nascentem placido lumine videris,
   illum non labor Isthmius
clarabit pugilem, non equus impiger

   curru ducet Achaico   5
victorem, neque res bellica Deliis
   ornatum foliis ducem,
quod regum tumidas contuderit minas,

   ostendet Capitolio:
sed quae Tibur aquae fertile praefluunt   10
   et spissae nemorum comae
fingent Aeolio carmine nobilem.

   Romae principis urbium
dignatur suboles inter amabilis
   vatum ponere me choros,   15
et iam dente minus mordeor invido.

   o, testudinis aureae
dulcem quae strepitum, Pieri, temperas,

ODES 4.3[1]

The one, Melpomene, that you
once looked upon at birth with friendly eyes,
    no Isthmian labor will exalt
him as a boxer,[2] nor spry horses bear him

    in an Achaean[3] chariot   5
as victor, nor a military feat
    display him to the Capitol,[4]
a general adorned with foliage

    for crushing swollen threats of kings.
But waters flowing next to fertile Tibur[5]   10
    and leaves dense-packed inside of groves
will make him famous with Aeolian song.[6]

    The youth of Rome, the chief of cities,
thinks I am worthy to be placed among
    the lovely choruses of bards,[7]   15
and now I'm gnawed less by the tooth of envy.

    O you, who modulate the sweet
sound of the golden lyre, Pierian,[8]

---

1. ***Odes* 4.3** (*Second Asclepiadean*): A poem of thanksgiving addressed to the Muse Melpomene, to whom Horace attributes his success as a lyric poet. It presents a variation on the **priamel** and has many connections with *Odes* 1.1. The poem takes as its starting point a well-known line from Hesiod, *Theogony* 81–88: "Whomever among Zeus-nourished kings the daughters of great Zeus honor and behold when he is born, they pour sweet dew upon his tongue, and his words flow soothingly from his mouth" (translated by Glenn Most, Loeb).
2. **Isthmian . . . boxer:** A reference to the Isthmian games, one of the major Panhellenic athletic contests.
3. **Achaean:** Greek.
4. **Capitol:** The end-point of a triumphal procession.
5. **Tibur:** A town in the Sabine hills, near Horace's farm.
6. **Aeolian song:** See note to *Odes* 3.30.13–14.
7. **bards:** For *vates* (bard), see note at *Odes* 1.1.35.
8. **Pierian:** Another word for "Muse." Mt. Pierus in Greece was traditionally a home of the Muses.

o mutis quoque piscibus
donatura cycni, si libeat, sonum,   20

totum muneris hoc tui est,
quod monstror digito praetereuntium
Romanae fidicen lyrae;
quod spiro et placeo, si placeo, tuum est.

O you, who'd even grant mute fish
the music of the swan if you so wished,   20

it is entirely your gift
that people walking past me point me out
        as player of the Roman lyre.
I breathe and please (if I do please) through you.

ODES 4.4

Qualem ministrum fulminis alitem,
cui rex deorum regnum in avis vagas
      permisit expertus fidelem
          Iuppiter in Ganymede flavo,

olim iuventas et patrius vigor   5
nido laborum protulit inscium,
      vernique iam nimbis remotis
          insolitos docuere nisus

venti paventem, mox in ovilia
demisit hostem vividus impetus,   10
      nunc in reluctantis dracones
          egit amor dapis atque pugnae,

qualemve laetis caprea pascuis
intenta fulvae matris ab ubere

ODES 4.4[1]

Just like[2] the winged attendant of the lightning
whom Jupiter, the king of gods, gave power
    over the roving birds once he had tested
        its loyalty with blond-haired Ganymede[3]

(Once,[4] youthfulness and its paternal vigor   5
propelled it from the nest, unversed in labors,
    and soon spring breezes, when the clouds withdrew,
        trained it in new exertions, though it still

trembled in fear, but soon a lively urge
sent it against the sheepfolds as a foe,   10
    and now its love of feasting and of battle
        launches it into wrestling bouts with snakes.)

or like a lion weaned now from the rich
milk of its tawny mother, which a deer

---

1. **Odes 4.4** (*Alcaic Strophe*): An ode in praise of Tiberius and especially Drusus, the sons of Augustus's wife Livia with her prior husband, Tiberius Claudius Nero. Drusus would die while on campaign in 9 B.C.E., whereas Tiberius would go on to become the second emperor of Rome. The ode's high **encomium** is strongly evocative of Pindar, to whom Horace alludes throughout the poem. In *Odes* 4.2 Horace had claimed to be a Matine bee rather than a Pindaric swan, but here he seems to take up exactly the kind of poetry he had earlier avoided. As Harrison (1990, 34) states, "In this fourth book of odes Horace is turning the victory-ode of Pindar into a celebration of Roman military success.". Quite a few scholars have found the high praise of the poem unsatisfying. Thomas (2011, 11) writes, for example, "what is admirable patriotism and loyalty for one person will be despicable propaganda and jingoism for another."
2. **Just like**: This starts a tour de force of a sentence, imitating Pindaric style, that continues on for twenty-six lines, climaxing with the word "Neros." The poem starts here with two **similes** describing Drusus, the first of an eagle and the second a lion. We do not discover whom the similes are describing until line 18.
3. **Ganymede**: In the regular version of the myth, Jupiter seizes Ganymede in the form of an eagle, but here the eagle seems to have delivered the boy to Jupiter. Ganymede was a young Trojan prince whom Jupiter kidnapped and raped and who subsequently became his cupbearer in heaven.
4. **Once**: Horace outlines the various stages of the eagle's life (infancy, childhood, youth, and adulthood) in order to suggest Drusus's new maturity.

   iam lacte depulsum leonem   15
     dente novo peritura vidit,

 videre Raetis bella sub Alpibus
 Drusum gerentem Vindelici—quibus
   mos unde deductus per omne
     tempus Amazonia securi   20

 dextras obarmet, quaerere distuli,
 nec scire fas est omnia—sed diu
   lateque victrices catervae
     consiliis iuvenis revictae

 sensere, quid mens rite, quid indoles   25
 nutrita faustis sub penetralibus
   posset, quid Augusti paternus
     in pueros animus Nerones.

 fortes creantur fortibus et bonis;
 est in iuvencis, est in equis patrum   30
   virtus, neque imbellem feroces
     progenerant aquilae columbam;

 doctrina sed vim promovet insitam,
 rectique cultus pectora roborant;

engrossed in fertile pasturage has spotted,   15
    destined to perish under its new tooth[5]—

so Drurus looked when the Vendelici[6] saw him,
while he waged war beneath the Raetian Alps[7]—
    I have put off inquiring[8] from where
        there sprang the ancient custom that they arm   20

their right hands with an Amazonian ax,
nor is it right to know all things—and yet
    their troops, longstanding victors far and wide,
        were vanquished by the young man's stratagems

and realized what a mind and talent rightly   25
nurtured within a house divinely favored
    can bring about, what too Augustus's
        paternal feelings toward the youthful Neros.[9]

Brave men are fathered by the brave and good.
In bullocks and in horses there exists   30
    the virtue of the father, nor do ruthless
        eagles engender the unwarlike dove.

But training amplifies one's inborn might,
and proper education strengthens hearts;

---

5. **new tooth:** That is, with the adult teeth that replace the milk teeth the lion had as a baby.
6. **Vendelici:** A northern tribe in the Alps. This marks the celebratory occasion as Drusus and Tiberius's northern campaigns in 15 B.C.E.
7. **Raetian Alps:** The Raeti were another Alpine tribe.
8. **I have . . . inquiring:** This aside seems oddly included (and the custom to which Horace refers is obscure), but, as Thomas (2011) points out, it imitates Pindar, *Nemean* 5.14–19: "I shrink from telling of a mighty deed, one ventured not in accord with justice, how in fact they left the glorious island and what fortune drove the brave men from Oenona. I will halt, for not every exact truth is better for showing its face" (translated by W. Race, Loeb).
9. **mind and talent . . . youthful Neros:** Drusus and Tiberius were the legal sons of their father, Tiberius Claudius Nero, but after his death in 33 B.C.E. they were raised in the house of Augustus. Horace focuses in these lines not only on the innate character Drusus and Tiberius inherited from their father's Claudian line but also on how Augustus developed and nourished these intrinsic qualities.

> utcumque defecere mores,   35
> indecorant bene nata culpae.

quid debeas, o Roma, Neronibus,
testis Metaurum flumen et Hasdrubal
> devictus et pulcher fugatis
> ille dies Latio tenebris,   40

qui primus alma risit adorea,
dirus per urbis Afer ut Italas
> ceu flamma per taedas vel Eurus
> per Siculas equitavit undas.

post hoc secundis usque laboribus   45
Romana pubes crevit, et impio
> vastata Poenorum tumultu
> fana deos habuere rectos,

dixitque tandem perfidus Hannibal
"cervi, luporum praeda rapacium,   50
> sectamur ultro, quos opimus
> fallere et effugere est triumphus.

gens, quae cremato fortis ab Ilio
iactata Tuscis aequoribus sacra
> natosque maturosque patres   55
> pertulit Ausonias ad urbis,

whenever customs have not been sufficient,   35
    failings degrade the assets one was born with.[10]

How greatly, Rome, you're in the Neros' debt
the river of Metaurus[11] testifies,
    and vanquished Hasdrubal, and that exquisite
        day when the darkness was repelled
            from Latium,   40

which was the first to smile with kindly glory
since that dread African charged through the cities
    of Italy like fire galloping
        through pines or Eurus[12] through Sicilian waves.

Following this, the youth of Rome grew strong   45
with ever-fruitful labors, and the shrines
    which Carthaginians had razed in their
        impious riot held the gods upright.

At last the faithless Hannibal declared:
"We are like stags, the prey of greedy wolves,   50
    and we in fact pursue those whom it is
        the highest triumph to escape and flee.

The race that, buffeted on Tuscan waters,[13]
bravely conveyed from Ilium's inferno
    its holy gods, its children, and its aged   55
        fathers to cities in Ausonia[14]

---

10. **customs ... one was born with:** The idea is that if one does not have the proper nurture ("customs"), then one's intrinsic potential ("nature") cannot be met.
11. **river of Metaurus:** The ancestor of Drusus and Tiberius, Gaius Claudius Nero, was one of the generals who defeated the Carthaginian general Hasdrubal (the brother of Hannibal) at the Metaurus River in central Italy in 207 B.C.E. According to Livy (23.51.11), the Romans beheaded Hasdrubal and threw his head into the Carthaginian camp.
12. **Eurus:** The southeast wind.
13. **Tuscan waters:** The Tyrrhenian Sea.
14. **bravely conveyed ... cities in Ausonia:** These lines take us from the fires of Troy to the shores of Italy (Ausonia) and owe a great debt to Vergil's *Aeneid*, which

duris ut ilex tonsa bipennibus
nigrae feraci frondis in Algido,
      per damna, per caedes, ab ipso
            ducit opes animumque ferro.   60

non hydra secto corpore firmior
vinci dolentem crevit in Herculem,
      monstrumve submisere Colchi
            maius Echioniaeve Thebae.

merses profundo: pulchrior evenit: 65
luctere: multa proruet integrum
      cum laude victorem geretque
            proelia coniugibus loquenda.

Carthagini iam non ego nuntios
mittam superbos: occidit, occidit   70
      spes omnis et fortuna nostri
            nominis Hasdrubale interempto."

nil Claudiae non perficient manus,
quas et benigno numine Iuppiter
      defendit et curae sagaces   75
            expediunt per acuta belli.

is like an oak tree cut by sturdy axes
on Algidus[15] where shady leaves are lush—
 amid the harm and chopping it derives
  its strength and spirit from the iron itself.   60

Hydra's slashed body[16] did not grow this strong
when fighting Hercules, who loathed defeat.
 The Colchians never brought forth any monster
  this massive, nor the Thebes of Echion.[17]

Plunge it down deep, it comes out more outstanding.   65
Wrestle it—with great praise it will knock down
 an undefeated victor and will wage
  battles that must be talked about with wives.[18]

No more will I dispatch to Carthage pompous
envoys. There disappeared, there disappeared   70
 our every hope and all our name's good fortune
  when Hasdrubal was taken from our midst."

There's nothing Claudian hands will not accomplish.
Jupiter with his kindly majesty
 protects them, and their skillful management   75
  releases them from war's adversities.[19]

---

treats this voyage. The "sacred objects," "children," and "elderly fathers" strongly
 allude to *Aeneid* 2, in which Aeneas flees from Troy with his son Ascanius, elderly
 father Anchises, and the Penates, the household gods.
15. **Algidus:** An Alban mountain.
16. **Hydra's slashed body:** The Lernean Hydra was a monster with many heads,
 and each time Hercules cut one off, two more would spring up in its place.
17. **Colchians . . . Echion:** In Colchis Jason fought men sprung from the earth out
 of the seeds of dragon teeth. In Thebes, Cadmus similarly killed a dragon and sowed
 men from its teeth, who became the city's founders.
18. **with wives:** Or "by wives."
19. **There's nothing . . . adversities:** This last stanza is sometimes given to
 Hannibal as the speaker, sometimes to the poet.

ODES 4.5

Divis orte bonis, optime Romulae
custos gentis, abes iam nimium diu;
maturum reditum pollicitus patrum
    sancto consilio, redi.

lucem redde tuae, dux bone, patriae: 5
instar veris enim vultus ubi tuus
adfulsit populo, gratior it dies
    et soles melius nitent.

ut mater iuvenem, quem Notus invido
flatu Carpathii trans maris aequora   10
cunctantem spatio longius annuo
    dulci distinet a domo,

votis ominibusque et precibus vocat,
curvo nec faciem litore dimovet:
sic desideriis icta fidelibus   15
    quaerit patria Caesarem.

tutus bos etenim rura perambulat,
nutrit rura Ceres almaque Faustitas,
pacatum volitant per mare navitae,
    culpari metuit fides,   20

ODES 4.5¹

Sprung from the noble gods,² best guardian
of Romulus's race,³ you've been gone far
too long. You promised to the Fathers' sacred
    council⁴ you'd come back soon—come back.

Restore, good leader, light to your own country.   5
For when your countenance, just like the spring,
has gleamed upon your people, day goes by
    more pleasantly and suns shine brighter.

Just as the mother of a young man kept
away from his sweet home more than a year   10
beyond the plains of the Carpathian Sea⁵
    by Notus's unfriendly breeze⁶

summons him back with vows and signs and prayers
and does not move her gaze from the curved shore—
stricken with faithful longing just like this,   15
    the fatherland is seeking Caesar.

For in the fields the oxen stroll in safety,
Ceres and kindly Richness tend the fields,
the sailors fly across the peaceful sea,
    fidelity fears being blamed,⁷   20

---

1. **Odes 4.5** (*Third Asclepiadean*): An ode describing the fatherland's urgent desire that Augustus, who had been away in Gaul from 16 to 13 B.C.E., return to Rome. Horace describes the peaceful state of the fatherland, a feat for which he credits Augustus's moral and legislative program. DuQuesnay (1995) suggests the poem was written to be performed at Augustus's return in July of 13 B.C.E., although there is no direct evidence for this.
2. **Sprung . . . gods**: Augustus traced his lineage back to Aeneas and thus to Venus.
3. **Romulus's race**: Romulus was the legendary founder of Rome.
4. **Fathers' sacred council**: The Senate.
5. **Carpathian Sea**: The sea around the island Carpathos, between Crete and Rhodes.
6. **Notus's unfriendly breeze**: Notus is the south wind.
7. **fidelity . . . blamed**: *Fides* (fidelity) was valued not only in friendship but also in marriage, so the implication is that neither friends nor spouses break their fidelity to one another.

nullis polluitur casta domus stupris,
mos et lex maculosum edomuit nefas,
laudantur simili prole puerperae,
    culpam poena premit comes.

quis Parthum paveat, quis gelidum Scythen,   25
quis Germania quos horrida parturit
fetus, incolumi Caesare? quis ferae
    bellum curet Hiberiae?

condit quisque diem collibus in suis,
et vitem viduas ducit ad arbores;   30
hinc ad vina redit laetus et alteris
    te mensis adhibet deum;

te multa prece, te prosequitur mero
defuso pateris et Laribus tuum
miscet numen, uti Graecia Castoris   35
    et magni memor Herculis.

"longas o utinam, dux bone, ferias
praestes Hesperiae!" dicimus integro
sicci mane die, dicimus uvidi,
    cum sol Oceano subest.   40

no shameful sex[8] pollutes the spotless house,
custom and law[9] have vanquished tainted sin,
new mothers garner praise for young like fathers,[10]
    punishment follows guilt, its partner.

Who'd fear the Parthian,[11] who the icy Scythian,   25
who'd fear the brood that shaggy[12] Germany
brings forth, while Caesar is unharmed? Who'd worry
    about a war in brutal Spain?[13]

Each man concludes his day in his own hills
and weds the vine to trees that have no mate.   30
Joyous, he then comes home to wine and hails
    you as a god in his dessert course.[14]

With many prayers, with unmixed wine poured out
of bowls he honors you. He worships you
beside his household gods, as Greece remembers   35
    Castor and mighty Hercules.[15]

"May you, good leader, grant long holidays
to Italy!" We say this in the morning
while we are sober, and we say it drunk
    when the sun sinks beneath the ocean.   40

---

8. **shameful sex**: This translates the difficult Latin word *stuprum*, which is used to describe any type of illicit sexual activity and here indicates adultery in particular.
9. **custom and law**: The law is especially the *lex Iulia de adulteriis coercendis* of 18 B.C.E., which made adultery a crime. See the introduction.
10. **like fathers**: Horace does not specify "like fathers," but it is implicit in the designation that the offspring is *simili*, "similar" or "matching." The baby's likeness to its father is evidence that no adultery has taken place.
11. **Parthian**: In 20 B.C.E., Augustus had recovered the standards lost to the Parthians by Crassus at Carrhae three decades earlier.
12. **shaggy**: Probably a reference to the belief that Germans (and other non-Romans) wore long, unkempt hair. Another possibility is that this refers to the dense forests of Germany.
13. **brutal Spain**: Rome had conquered the Spanish Concani and Cantabri in 19 B.C.E.
14. **you as a god ... course**: Augustus, Horace suggests, is being worshipped alongside the *Lares*, the household gods, to whom it was customary to make an offering during the "second" or dessert course.
15. **Castor ... Hercules**: In myth, these were two mortal heroes who attained immortality.

ODES 4.6

Dive, quem proles Niobea magnae
vindicem linguae Tityosque raptor
sensit et Troiae prope victor altae
    Pthius Achilles,

ceteris maior, tibi miles impar,   5
filius quamvis Thetidis marinae
Dardanas turris quateret tremenda
    cuspide pugnax.

ille, mordaci velut icta ferro
pinus aut impulsa cupressus Euro,   10
procidit late posuitque collum in
    pulvere Teucro.

ille non inclusus equo Minervae
sacra mentito male feriatos
Troas et laetam Priami choreis   15
    falleret aulam;

ODES 4.6[1]

God[2] who took vengance on Niobe's children
(for her proud tongue)[3] and Tityos the rapist[4]
and he who almost conquered lofty Troy,
    Phthian Achilles,

who outdid everyone but you in war,[5]   5
though he, the son of briny Thetis, shook
Dardanian[6] towers with his lofty spear,
    eager for battle.

That man, just like a pine tree struck by biting
iron or a cypress overthrown by Eurus,[7]   10
plunged forward, splayed, and plunked his neck down into
    Teucrian[8] ashes.

That man would not have lurked inside the horse,
a feigned gift to Minerva,[9] nor deceived
the Trojans' ill-timed fetes and Priam's hall,   15
    happy with dancing.

---

1. *Odes* 4.6 (*Sapphic Strophe*): This ode begins as a **hymn** to Apollo but moves into an address to the girls and boys who sang the *Carmen Saeculare* in 17 B.C.E. The poem's first half focuses on Apollo as the warrior god of martial epic, whereas the second half takes up his guise as god of the lyre who favors Horace's poetic projects.
2. **God**: Apollo.
3. **Niobe's . . . tongue**: Niobe bragged that she had more children than Latona/Leto, whereupon the goddess had her children, Apollo and Diana, kill all of Niobe's offspring.
4. **Tityos the rapist**: Tityos attempted to rape Leto, a crime for which he is eternally punished in the Underworld by having vultures eat his constantly regenerating liver.
5. **everyone . . . in war**: Achilles died when Apollo helped Paris shoot him in his vulnerable heel.
6. **Dardanian**: Trojan.
7. **Eurus**: the southeast wind.
8. **Teucrian**: Trojan.
9. **horse . . . Minerva**: The Trojan horse, devised as a trick by Odysseus. The Greeks hid inside the horse, decked out as an offering to the goddess Minerva. After the Trojans let it inside the city and held victory celebrations, the Greeks leaped out and took the city. Unlike Odysseus, Achilles (who was dead by the time of the horse) is not disposed to such trickery or deception.

sed palam captis gravis, heu nefas! heu!
nescios fari pueros Achivis
ureret flammis, etiam latentem
     matris in alvo,   20

ni tuis victus Venerisque gratae
vocibus divum pater adnuisset
rebus Aeneae potiore ductos
     alite muros.

doctor argutae fidicen Thaliae,   25
Phoebe, qui Xantho lavis amne crines,
Dauniae defende decus Camenae,
     levis Agyieu.

spiritum Phoebus mihi, Phoebus artem
carminis nomenque dedit poetae.   30
virginum primae puerique claris
     patribus orti,

Deliae tutela deae fugaces
lyncas et cervos cohibentis arcu,
Lesbium servate pedem meique   35
     pollicis ictum,

But openly cruel to captives—woe! a sin!—
he would have burned up children not yet speaking
in the Greek fires, even one whose mother's
    womb still concealed it,   20

if your and pleasing Venus's entreaties[10]
had not convinced the father of the gods[11]
to give Aeneas city walls that better
    omens had guided.[12]

Lyre-teacher of the clear-voiced Thalia,[13]   25
Phoebus, who wash your hair in Xanthus'stream,[14]
defend the glory of the Daunian Muse,[15]
    beardless Agyieus.[16]

Phoebus gave inspiration to me. Phoebus
gave me the art of song and name of poet.   30
You foremost virgins and you boys,[17] the sons of
    prominent fathers,

wards of the Delian goddess,[18] who restrains
the flight of deer and lynxes with her bow,
observe the Lesbian meter and the beat   35
    kept by my finger

---

10. **your . . . Venus's entreaties**: Apollo and Venus were on the side of the Trojans.
11. **father of the gods**: Jupiter.
12. **Aeneas . . . guided**: Aeneas would flee Troy and found what would eventually become Rome, which forms the subject matter of Vergil's *Aeneid*.
13. **Thalia**: One of the Muses.
14. **Xanthus' stream**: Xanthus was a river that ran through Patara, one of Apollo's major cult centers.
15. **Daunian Muse**: *Camena* was a native Italian word for "Muse," and "Daunian" refers to Apulia, the birthplace of Horace.
16. **beardless Agyieus**: Apollo was eternally youthful and beardless. "Agyieus" is an **epithet** of Apollo that means "god of the streets."
17. **virgins . . . boys**: The *Carmen Saeculare* was sung by a chorus of girls and boys in praise of Apollo and Diana.
18. **Delian goddess**: Diana.

rite Latonae puerum canentes,
rite crescentem face Noctilucam,
prosperam frugum celeremque pronos
    volvere mensis.   40

nupta iam dices "ego dis amicum,
saeculo festas referente luces,
reddidi carmen, docilis modorum
    vatis Horati."

while singing duly of Latona's son,
duly of Nightshiner[19] whose brightness waxes,
who aids the crops and swiftly rolls around
      months as they gallop.   40

Soon you, a bride, will say, "I sang a song,
as the cycle[20] carried back its festive lights,
that pleased the gods, when I'd been taught the measures
      of the bard Horace."[21]

---

19. **Nightshiner: Epithet** of Diana in her guise as goddess of the moon.
20. **cycle:** The *saeculum*, a cycle of about a hundred years. Augustus's Secular
    Games, at which the *Carmen Saeculare* was performed, celebrated the inauguration
    of a new *saeculum*.
21. **bard Horace:** This is the only time that Horace names himself in the *Odes*. For
    vates (bard), see the note at *Odes* 1.1.35.

ODES 4.7

Diffugere nives, redeunt iam gramina campis
      arboribusque comae;
mutat terra vices, et decrescentia ripas
      flumina praetereunt;

Gratia cum Nymphis geminisque sororibus audet   5
      ducere nuda choros.
immortalia ne speres, monet annus et almum
      quae rapit hora diem:

frigora mitescunt Zephyris, ver proterit aestas,
      interitura simul   10
pomifer Autumnus fruges effuderit, et mox
      bruma recurrit iners.

damna tamen celeres reparant caelestia lunae:
      nos ubi decidimus
quo pius Aeneas, quo Tullus dives et Ancus,   15
      pulvis et umbra sumus.

ODES 4.7[1]

The snow has scattered. Grass returns now to the fields,
    and to the trees their foliage.
The Earth is switching out her changes, and receding
    rivers are flowing by their banks.

The Grace, along with Nymphs and her twin sisters, dares   5
    to lead the dancing in the nude.[2]
Don't hope for things immortal: this the year instructs,
    and the hour that robs the fruitful day.

Cold softens with the Zephyrs,[3] spring is crushed by summer,
    certain to die itself as soon as   10
fruit-bringing autumn has poured forth its crops, and shortly
    the idle winter hastens back.

And yet moons quickly reacquire their heavenly losses:
    when we descend to that place where
pious Aeneas,[4] where rich Tullus and Ancus[5] went,   15
    we're nothing more than dust and shadow.

---

1. *Odes* 4.7 (*First Archilochian*): In this poem, Horace again takes up the theme of seasonal change and develops it into a reflection on human mortality. It is something of a companion piece to *Odes* 1.4, with each poem contrasting the annually renewing cycle of seasons with the single cycle of human life. A. E. Housman is said to have ended a lecture on Horace in 1914 by pronouncing this "the most beautiful poem in ancient literature."
2. **Grace . . . nude:** The three Graces (who are sisters) and Nymphs are minor female deities whose dances Horace describes also in 1.4.6–7. The Graces are often depicted nude with interlocking arms in art.
3. **Zephyrs:** Warm, springtime winds.
4. **pious Aeneas:** Aeneas is the legendary founder of Rome celebrated in Vergil's *Aeneid*, in which "piety" (*pietas*) is his greatest attribute. Piety involves not just reverence toward the gods but a sense of duty that leads one to prioritize one's gods, state, and family above oneself. Horace may have in mind Vergil's account of Aeneas's descent into the Underworld in *Aeneid* 6, or he may be disputing the eventual deification of him promised to his mother Venus in *Aeneid* 1. Even great Aeneas, Horace suggests, was just a mortal like us.
5. **Tullus and Ancus:** Tullus Hostilius and Ancus Marcius are respectively the third and fourth kings of early Rome.

quis scit an adiciant hodiernae crastina summae
    tempora di superi?
cuncta manus avidas fugient heredis, amico
    quae dederis animo.   20

cum semel occideris et de te splendida Minos
    fecerit arbitria,
non, Torquate, genus, non te facundia, non te
    restituet pietas;

infernis neque enim tenebris Diana pudicum   25
    liberat Hippolytum,
nec Lethaea valet Theseus abrumpere caro
    vincula Pirithoo.

Who can be certain if the gods above are adding
    tomorrow's time to this day's total?
All of the things that you bestow to your own heart
    will flee your heir's rapacious hands.   20

When you have passed away—once and for all—and Minos
    has made his splendid judgments on you,[6]
Torquatus,[7] not your pedigree nor eloquence
    nor piety will bring you back.

Even Diana cannot liberate the chaste   25
    Hippolytus[8] from nether darkness,
and Theseus lacks the strength to break apart Lethean
    chains from his dear Pirithous.[9]

6. **Minos . . . judgments on you:** Minos was a mythical king of Crete who after death was thought to pass judgment on souls in the Underworld.
7. **Torquatus:** This is probably the son of the ex-consul Lucius Manlius Torquatus. This is a family of extremely long standing, his most famous ancestor being the Manlius Torquatus who was thrice consul in 347, 344, and 340 B.C.E. Horace addresses this Torquatus also in *Epistles* 1.5.
8. **Hippolytus:** The son of Theseus who was punished by Venus for his excessive devotion to the virgin goddess Diana. Venus caused his stepmother, Phaedra, to fall in love with him. Rebuffed, she killed herself after writing a letter accusing Hippolytus of rape. Theseus cursed his son, whereupon Neptune sent a bull from the sea to trample the young man to death. The most famous account of this myth is Euripides's *Hippolytus* from 428 B.C.E.
9. **Pirithous:** He attempted, with Theseus's help, to kidnap Proserpina from the Underworld, for which crime he remains chained to a rock as punishment. Despite the impiety suggested by this story, Theseus and Pirithous are often used as an exemplum of loyal friendship.

ODES 4.8

Donarem pateras grataque commodus,
Censorine, meis aera sodalibus,
donarem tripodas, praemia fortium
Graiorum, neque tu pessima munerum
ferres, divite me scilicet artium   5
quas aut Parrhasius protulit aut Scopas,
hic saxo, liquidis ille coloribus
sollers nunc hominem ponere, nunc deum.
sed non haec mihi vis, non tibi talium
res est aut animus deliciarum egens.   10
gaudes carminibus; carmina possumus
donare et pretium dicere muneri.
non incisa notis marmora publicis,
per quae spiritus et vita redit bonis
post mortem ducibus, non celeres fugae   15
reiectaeque retrorsum Hannibalis minae,
non incendia Carthaginis impiae
eius, qui domita nomen ab Africa

ODES 4.8[1]

I'd gladly give[2] libation bowls and prized

bronze statues to my comrades, Censorinus.

I would give tripods, those rewards of brave

Greeks,[3] and you wouldn't carry off the worst

of gifts if I were rich, that is, in arts   5

Parrhasius or Scopas[4] once produced—

the first in paint, the last in stone, each clever

at crafting now a human, now a god.

But I don't have this power, nor does your

estate or mind require such luxuries.   10

You take delight in poetry. I can

give poems and define their worth to you.

Not marble carved with public lettering,

through which the spirit and the life returns

to good men after death, nor Hannibal's[5]   15

hasty retreat and threats that he hurled back,

nor the inferno of unholy Carthage[6]

could render that man's praises, who returned

---

1. *Odes* 4.8 (*First Asclepiadean*): An ode celebrating the immortalizing power of poetry, a theme that connects it back to *Odes* 3.30, with which it shares its meter. The addressee is either Lucius Marcius Censorinus, the consul of 39 B.C.E., or his son, Gaius Marcius Censorinus, the consul of 8 B.C.E. Thomas (2011) calls it "an intensely Pindaric ode," and its Pindaric aspects have been illuminated by Harrison (1990), chief among which is the idea that poetry can confer enduring fame.

2. **I'd gladly give:** The poem opens with a **priamel** rejecting various types of gifts, with Horace finally stating that his proper gift is poetry. The rejection of art, especially sculpture, in favor of poetry, as Harrison (1990, 34) points out, is a Pindaric motif, for which see *Nemean* 5.

3. **rewards . . . Greeks:** Bowls, bronzes, and tripods were frequent prizes won by Greek heroes in epic and were also the prizes won by athletic victors in the Panhellenic games, the latter of whom were the celebrants of Pindaric epinician.

4. **Parrhasius or Scopas:** Parrhasius of Ephesus was a fifth-century B.C.E. painter, and Scopas of Paros was a fourth-century B.C.E. sculptor.

5. **Hannibal's:** The Carthaginian general who fought the Romans in the Second Punic War.

6. **inferno . . . Carthage:** Carthage was razed at the end of the Third Punic War in 146 B.C.E.

lucratus rediit, clarius indicant
laudes quam Calabrae Pierides: neque,   20
si chartae sileant quod bene feceris,
mercedem tuleris. quid foret Iliae
Mavortisque puer, si taciturnitas
obstaret meritis invida Romuli?
ereptum Stygiis fluctibus Aeacum   25
virtus et favor et lingua potentium
vatum divitibus consecrat insulis.
dignum laude virum Musa vetat mori:
caelo Musa beat. sic Iovis interest
optatis epulis impiger Hercules,   30
clarum Tyndaridae sidus ab infimis
quassas eripiunt aequoribus ratis,
ornatus viridi tempora pampino
Liber vota bonos ducit ad exitus.

with a name he won from conquered Africa,[7]
more clearly than Calabrian Muses.[8] Nor,   20
if pages did not speak of your good deeds,
would you reap your reward. What would the son
of Ilia and Mars[9] be now if spiteful
silence were barring Romulus's honors?
Virtue and favor[10] and the tongue of mighty   25
bards rescued Aeacus[11] from Stygian waves,[12]
immortalizing him on blessed isles.[13]
The Muse won't let him die who has earned praise.
The Muse grants him the heavens. So the tireless
Hercules sits among Jove's longed-for feasts.   30
And the Tyndaridae, the shining stars,
snatch shattered boats out of the deepest seas,
and, with his temples decked with verdant vines,
Liber[14] brings vows to prosperous conclusions.

---

7. **that man's praises . . . Africa:** Horace conflates two men here: Scipio Africanus
(236–183 B.C.E.), who defeated Hannibal at Zama in 202 B.C.E., and Scipio
Aemilianus (185–129 B.C.E.), who destroyed Carthage in 146 B.C.E.

8. **Calabrian Muses:** A reference to Ennius, a Roman poet from Calabria whose epic
Annales covered early Roman history, including the Second Punic War.

9. **Ilia and Mars:** Ilia is another name for Rhea Silvia, the Vestal Virgin raped by Mars
who then gave birth to Romulus and Remus.

10. **Virtue and favor:** It is unclear to whose virtue and favor this refers. The most
likely scenario is that Aeacus's own virtue earned him the favor of the bards, whose
tongue then immortalized him in song.

11. **Aeacus:** The father of Peleus and Telamon. He was the king of the island Aegina.

12. **Stygian waves:** The Styx was the principal river of the Underworld.

13. **blessed isles:** For the Isles of the Blessed, see the introduction to *Epodes* 16.

14. **Hercules . . . Tyndaridae . . . Liber:** Heroes who became gods. Hercules was
immortalized after his famous labors. The Tyndaridae are Castor and Pollux, the sons
of Tyndareus, who in their guise as St. Elmo's Fire rescue sailors on the sea. Liber is
the god Bacchus, sometimes included among deified heroes since he was thought of
as a young god who traveled throughout the world spreading his own worship.

ODES 4.9

Ne forte credas interitura, quae
longe sonantem natus ad Aufidum
    non ante vulgatas per artis
        verba loquor socianda chordis:

non, si priores Maeonius tenet   5
sedes Homerus, Pindaricae latent
    Ceaeque et Alcaei minaces
        Stesichorive graves Camenae;

nec, si quid olim lusit Anacreon,
delevit aetas; spirat adhuc amor   10
    vivuntque commissi calores
        Aeoliae fidibus puellae.

non sola comptos arsit adulteri
crinis et aurum vestibus illitum

ODES 4.9[1]

So that you don't by chance believe these words
will die, which I, born by the wide-resounding
   Aufidus,[2] sing in harmony with strings
      through art unknown before now by the people:

Maeonian[3] Homer holds first place, but Pindar's   5
songs have not vanished, nor have those of Ceos.[4]
   The threatening poems of Alcaeus live,[5]
      as do Stesichorus's weighty ones.[6]

The lapse of time has not destroyed the erstwhile
play of Anacreon.[7] The love still breathes,   10
   the passion still is living, which the girl[8]
      of Lesbos once entrusted to her lyre.

Helen of Sparta[9] is not the only woman
who burned while gazing at her lover's[10] stylish

---

1. ***Odes* 4.9** (*Alcaic Strophe*): Like 4.8, this ode celebrates the power of poetry. In the first half Horace outlines how not only epic but also lyric immortalizes poet and celebrant alike and suggests that without a poet brave deeds are lost in everlasting obscurity. The second half turns to the praises of Marcus Lollius, the consul of 21 B.C.E., whose son or younger relative Horace addresses in *Epistles* 1.2 and 1.18. This Lollius had a glorious military career under Augustus but in 17 B.C.E. lost his legion's standards to defeat in Gaul. Scholars have suggested that this well-known loss blunts the force of Horace's praise. Others, e.g., Williams (1968, 80) and Garrison (1991), see the poem as an attempt at "rehabilitation."
2. **Aufidus:** A river near Horace's native Venusia.
3. **Maeonian:** Homer was thought to be from Maeonia in Lydia.
4. **Ceos:** The Aegean island of Ceos was the home of the lyric poets Simonides and Bacchylides.
5. **threatening poems of Alcaeus:** Alcaeus's poetry was heavily involved in the fractious politics of Mytilene, on the island of Lesbos.
6. **weighty ones:** Stesichorus, although a lyric poet, adopted the mythological themes suited to epic.
7. **Anacreon:** A Greek lyric poet who was well-known for his erotic and symposiastic lyric.
8. **the girl:** Sappho.
9. **Helen of Sparta:** Here begins a long list of well-known epic figures. Horace argues that none of them are unique in what they experienced. They simply had a bard to record their deeds.
10. **her lover's:** That is, Paris's.

mirata regalisque cultus   15
      et comites Helene Lacaena,

primusve Teucer tela Cydonio
direxit arcu; non semel Ilios
      vexata; non pugnavit ingens
          Idomeneus Sthenelusve solus   20

dicenda Musis proelia; non ferox
Hector vel acer Deiphobus gravis
      excepit ictus pro pudicis
          coniugibus puerisque primus.

vixere fortes ante Agamemnona   25
multi; sed omnes illacrimabiles
      urgentur ignotique longa
          nocte, carent quia vate sacro.

paulum sepultae distat inertiae
celata virtus. non ego te meis   30
      chartis inornatum silebo,
          totve tuos patiar labores

impune, Lolli, carpere lividas
obliviones. est animus tibi
      rerumque prudens et secundis   35
          temporibus dubiisque rectus,

vindex avarae fraudis et abstinens
ducentis ad se cuncta pecuniae,
      consulque non unius anni,
          sed quotiens bonus atque fidus   40

hair and the gold embellishing his garments,   15
    his royal elegance and his companions.

Teucer[11] was not the first to aim his arrows
with a Cydonian[12] bow. Not only once
    was Troy assailed. Mighty Idomeneus
       and Sthenelus[13] did not alone fight battles   20

worthy of being sung by Muses. Warlike
Hector and fierce Deiphobus[14] were not
    the first to suffer grievous injuries
       on the behalf of their chaste wives and children.

Prior to Agamemnon[15] many brave   25
men lived. But all of them, now unlamented
    and nameless, are oppressed by everlasting
       darkness because they lacked a sacred bard.[16]

There's little difference between hidden virtue
and buried indolence. I will not keep   30
    you silent and unsung of in my pages
       nor suffer envious oblivion

to steal scot-free your praises, Lollius,
so great in number. You possess a mind
    wise in the way of things and principled   35
       in times both prosperous and dangerous,

a punisher of greedy fraud, abstaining
from money that draws all things to itself,
    a consul not just for one year alone
       but every time that as a good and faithful   40

11. **Teucer:** The foremost Greek with the bow and arrows. He fought in the Trojan War.
12. **Cydonian:** Cydonia was a city in Crete.
13. **Idomeneus and Sthenelus:** Warriors who fought with the Greeks at Troy.
14. **Hector . . . Deiphobus:** Two sons of Priam, both of whom were killed.
15. **Agamemnon:** The chief Greek king at Troy.
16. **bard:** For *vates* (bard) see the note at *Odes* 1.1.35.

iudex honestum praetulit utili,
reiecit alto dona nocentium
    vultu, per obstantis catervas
        explicuit sua victor arma.

non possidentem multa vocaveris   45
recte beatum: rectius occupat
    nomen beati, qui deorum
        muneribus sapienter uti

duramque callet pauperiem pati
peiusque leto flagitium timet,   50
    non ille pro caris amicis
        aut patria timidus perire.

judge he[17] preferred the noble to the useful,
rejected with a scornful face the bribes
    of guilty men, and flaunted his own weapons
        as victor through the troops opposing him.

You would not rightly call him happy[18] who   45
possesses many things. More rightly does
    he have the name of happy who knows how
        to use the gifts the gods have given him

with wisdom and to bear harsh poverty,
who fears disgrace as something worse than death.   50
    That man is not afraid to lose his life
        on the behalf of his dear friends or country.

17. **he**: The syntax of this line is difficult and debated. It is unclear here whether Horace is still describing Lollius's mind or if he is describing the man himself (but now in the third person rather than the second).
18. **happy**: The poem ends with a consideration of what constitutes true happiness, a question taken up by many different philosophical schools. Horace's formulation here sounds decidedly Stoic, with its focus on ennobling poverty, fear of disgrace, and willingness to die for the fatherland.

ODES 4.10

O crudelis adhuc et Veneris muneribus potens,
insperata tuae cum veniet †pluma superbiae
et, quae nunc umeris involitant, deciderint comae,

nunc et qui color est puniceae flore prior rosae,
mutatus, Ligurine, in faciem verterit hispidam,   5
dices "heu" quotiens te speculo videris alterum,
"quae mens est hodie, cur eadem non puero fuit,
vel cur his animis incolumes non redeunt genae?"

ODES 4.10[1]

O you who still are cruel and mighty with the gifts of Venus,
when unexpected down[2] arises on your arrogance
and those long locks, which float around your
    shoulders, fall away[3]
and that complexion, now surpassing roses' crimson flowers,
is altered, Ligurinus, changed into a prickly face,   5
you'll say, "Alas," when you see your new self inside a mirror,
"Why did I not possess the mind I have today in boyhood,
or why do flawless cheeks not come again with these desires?"

---

1. **Odes 4.10** (*Fifth Asclepiadean*): A follow-up to *Odes* 4.1 addressed to Ligurinus, the young man drawing the older Horace back into pederastic desire. Horace predicts that, once Ligurinus's youthful looks have deteriorated with age, he will rue his present disdain. The tables will turn, and Ligurinus will become a frustrated older lover rather than a beautiful, coy beloved.
2. **unexpected down**: That is, when puberty creeps up on him and his cheeks begin to grow a beard. This traditionally marked the end of desirability for a pederastic beloved.
3. **fall away**: That is, his youthful locks have been cut off by the barber.

ODES 4.11

Est mihi nonum superantis annum
plenus Albani cadus; est in horto,
Phylli, nectendis apium coronis;
    est hederae vis

multa, qua crinis religata fulges;   5
ridet argento domus; ara castis
vincta verbenis avet immolato
    spargier agno;

cuncta festinat manus, huc et illuc
cursitant mixtae pueris puellae;   10
sordidum flammae trepidant rotantes
    vertice fumum.

ut tamen noris quibus advoceris
gaudiis, Idus tibi sunt agendae,
qui dies mensem Veneris marinae   15
    findit Aprilem,

iure sollemnis mihi sanctiorque
paene natali proprio, quod ex hac
luce Maecenas meus affluentis
    ordinat annos.   20

ODES 4.11[1]

I have a jar that's full of Alban wine[2]
past nine years old. I have inside my garden,
Phyllis, some celery for weaving garlands.
        There is abundant

ivy, with which you'll wreath your hair and shine.   5
With silver my house gleams. An altar, wreathed
in holy boughs, is longing for a slaughtered
        lamb to imbue it.

All of the workers bustle. Here and there
the slave girls and the slave boys dart about.   10
The flames are flickering while whirling dirty
        smoke in a spiral.

Yet, so you know to what festivity
you are invited, you'll observe the Ides
of sea-born[3] Venus' month, the day that splits   15
        April asunder.[4]

To me it's rightly solemn, holier
almost than my own birthday, since from this
date my Maecenas tallies his own years,
        richly abundant.   20

---

1. **Odes 4.11** (*Sapphic Strophe*): Horace invites to his home a woman he desires, named Phyllis, who in turn loves a young man out of her league, named Telephus, who himself wants a woman of a higher social class than Phyllis. Horace advises that Phyllis be content with what (and who) suits her, i.e., Horace himself. The occasion for the invitation is a birthday party for Maecenas, whom Horace mentions with great praise in the fifth stanza. This is the only reference to Maecenas in the fourth book of *Odes*, which has been read as a sign that Maecenas was out of favor or that Augustus himself was now the more directly involved in literary patronage.
2. **Alban wine**: This was considered one of the finest Italian wines.
3. **sea-born**: Venus was traditionally born from the sea from the castrated genitals of her father Uranus.
4. **Ides . . . April asunder**: The Ides of April fell on the thirteenth.

Telephum, quem tu petis, occupavit
non tuae sortis iuvenem puella
dives et lasciva tenetque grata
    compede vinctum.

terret ambustus Phaethon avaras   25
spes, et exemplum grave praebet ales
Pegasus terrenum equitem gravatus
    Bellerophontem,

semper ut te digna sequare et ultra
quam licet sperare nefas putando   30
disparem vites. age iam, meorum
    finis amorum—

non enim posthac alia calebo
femina—condisce modos, amanda
voce quos reddas: minuentur atrae   35
    carmine curae.

Telephus, that young man whom you pursue,
is mastered[5] by a girl not of your rank—
she's rich and lewd, and with her pleasant chain she
    keeps him her captive.

The burned-up Phaethon[6] scares away our greedy   25
hopes, and a weighty lesson can be found
in Pegasus,[7] who dropped Bellerophon, his
    earthly bound rider:

always to seek what suits you and, by thinking
it wrong to hope beyond what is allowed,   30
to keep away from those above you. Come now,
    last of my lovers[8]—

no other woman after this will heat
me up—learn well the tunes you'll sing with your
exquisite voice. Gloomy anxieties   35
    mellow with music.

---

5. **is mastered**: Horace has in mind the erotic **trope** of *servitium amoris*.

6. **Phaethon**: In myth, especially as recounted in Ovid's *Metamorphoses*, Phaethon asked the Sun to prove he was his father by handing over his chariot. The boy could not control it and so was burned up in a thunderbolt sent by Jupiter. He exemplifies the pursuit of what is beyond one's capabilities.

7. **Pegasus**: The mythical winged horse. When Bellerophon tried to ride him to heaven to challenge the gods, Jupiter sent a gadfly to sting Pegasus, whereupon the horse dropped Bellerophon back to earth.

8. **last of my lovers**: This marks the poem as Horace's last with erotic themes.

ODES 4.12

Iam veris comites, quae mare temperant,
impellunt animae lintea Thraciae;
iam nec prata rigent nec fluvii strepunt
     hiberna nive turgidi.

nidum ponit Ityn flebiliter gemens   5
infelix avis et Cecropiae domus
aeternum opprobrium, quod male barbaras
     regum est ulta libidines.

dicunt in tenero gramine pinguium
custodes ovium carmina fistula   10
delectantque deum cui pecus et nigri
     colles Arcadiae placent.

adduxere sitim tempora, Vergili;
sed pressum Calibus ducere Liberum
si gestis, iuvenum nobilium cliens,   15
     nardo vina merebere.

ODES 4.12[1]

Now Thracian winds,[2] which usher in the spring
and calm the sea, are driving forth the sails.
No more are meadows frozen, nor do rivers,
    swollen with winter snow, resound.

Weeping for Itys tearfully, the wretched   5
bird[3] builds her nest—she brought enduring shame
on Cecrops' house[4] since she took dreadful vengeance
    against the barbarous[5] lusts of kings.

Reclining in soft grass, the guardians
of fattened sheep play songs upon their pipe   10
and cheer the god to whom the flock and shady
    hills of Arcadia are pleasing.[6]

This season, Vergil, has engendered thirst.
But if, you client of the noble youth,
you yearn to drink the vintage pressed in Cales,[7]   15
    you'll have to buy your wine with nard.

---

1. *Odes* **4.12** (*Third Asclepiadean*): This invitation to a springtime symposium is addressed to a man named Vergil, most likely the famous poet (although he had died before the publication of *Odes* 4). In support of this identification, there are many echoes of Vergilian poetry, particularly of the *Eclogues*, running through the poem, outlined well by Thomas (2011).
2. **Thracian winds**: This most likely refers to the Zephyrs, the winds of springtime.
3. **the wretched bird**: This stanza refers to the story of Procne, Philomela, and Tereus, told most famously in Ovid's *Metamorphoses*. After Tereus rapes his sister-in-law Philomela and cuts out her tongue, the sisters take vengeance on him by killing and cooking Itys, the son of Procne and Tereus, and feeding him to his father. To Horace, the crimes of filicide and cannibalism evidently trump Tereus's crime of rape. The "wretched bird" refers either to the swallow or the nightingale, into which the two sisters transformed. It was not always strictly maintained which sister became which bird, but in *Epistles* 1.7.12–13 Horace associates the springtime with the swallow.
4. **Cecrops' house**: Athens, where Cecrops was an early mythical king. In the myth, Procne and Philomela were the daughters of the Athenian king Pandion.
5. **barbarous**: See note at *Epodes* 5.61.
6. **Reclining . . . pleasing**: The pastoral setting of this stanza strongly recalls Vergil's pastoral *Eclogues*, wherein shepherds often play songs on their panpipes.
7. **vintage . . . Cales**: Calenian wine was considered especially fine.

nardi parvus onyx eliciet cadum,
qui nunc Sulpiciis accubat horreis,
spes donare novas largus amaraque
      curarum eluere efficax.   20

ad quae si properas gaudia, cum tua
velox merce veni: non ego te meis
immunem meditor tingere poculis,
      plena dives ut in domo.

verum pone moras et studium lucri,   25
nigrorumque memor, dum licet, ignium
misce stultitiam consiliis brevem:
      dulce est desipere in loco.

A little box of nard will lure the jar
that now reclines inside Sulpician cellars;[8]
it grants new hopes aplenty and can wash
      away the bitter taste of worries.   20

If you are eager for these joys, then quickly
come with your fee. I don't intend to soak
you with my goblets at no cost to you,
      as rich men do in well-stocked homes.

But put aside delay and zeal for profit.   25
Remembering, while you can, the gloomy fires,
mix in a bit of folly with your wisdom—
      it's fun to be a fool sometimes.

---

8. **Sulpician cellars**: These were warehouses near the Tiber where expensive wines
could be bought. Horace is jokingly suggesting that Vergil will need to bring fine
nard in order to purchase the jar of wine.

ODES 4.13

Audivere, Lyce, di mea vota, di
audivere, Lyce: fis anus, et tamen
      vis formosa videri
          ludisque et bibis impudens

et cantu tremulo pota Cupidinem   5
lentum sollicitas. ille virentis et
      doctae psallere Chiae
          pulchris excubat in genis.

importunus enim transvolat aridas
quercus et refugit te, quia luridi   10
      dentes te, quia rugae
          turpant et capitis nives.

nec Coae referunt iam tibi purpurae
nec cari lapides tempora quae semel
      notis condita fastis   15
          inclusit volucris dies.

quo fugit Venus, heu, quove color? decens
quo motus? Quid habes illius, illius,
      quae spirabat amores,
          quae me surpuerat mihi,   20

ODES 4.13[1]

The gods, Lyce,[2] have heard my prayers. The gods,
Lyce, have heard. You're getting old, and yet
    you wish to seem still beautiful.
        You prance and drink immodestly,

and when you're drunk you try to stir up flaccid   5
Cupid with wobbly singing. He keeps watch
    on Chia's lovely cheeks—she's green
        with youth and skillful on the lyre.

For impolitely he flies past the withered
oak trees, avoiding you because your yellow   10
    teeth make you foul, as do your wrinkles
        and all that snow atop your head.

Purple of Cos[3] and precious gems no longer
bring back to you those days that winged time
    once and for all has locked away,   15
        deposited in public records.[4]

Alas! Where has your charm gone? Where your glow?
Where are your lovely movements? What do you
    possess of her, of her who breathed
        out love, who stole me from myself?   20

---

1. *Odes* 4.13 (*Fourth Asclepiadean*): Horace revisits once again the theme of **invective** against aging women, as seen previously in *Epodes* 8 and 12 as well as *Odes* 1.25 and 3.15. His current target, Lyce, is a former lover whose efforts to preserve her attractiveness meet only with the mockery of Horace and the young men around her.
2. **Lyce:** Her Greek name suggests the word for "she-wolf." The Latin *lupa* (she-wolf) also designated a prostitute, so her name may point to this as her profession.
3. **Purple of Cos:** Fabrics from the island of Cos were renowned for their translucence. The mistresses of elegiac poetry often wear such garments.
4. **public records:** These recorded the deeds of public men. Lyce has her own set of public records that chronicle her famous love affairs.

felix post Cinaram notaque et artium
gratarum facies? sed Cinarae brevis
 annos fata dederunt,
  servatura diu parem

cornicis vetulae temporibus Lycen,   25
possent ut iuvenes visere fervidi
 multo non sine risu
  dilapsam in cineres facem.

After Cinara[5] you were favored, you,
a beauty known for pleasing arts. But fate
      gave just a few years to Cinara,
           yet will save Lyce long enough

to match the lifespan of an ancient crow,[6]   25
all so the lusty youth can feast their eyes,
      not checking their excessive laughter,
           upon a torch dissolved to ash.

---

5. **After Cinara:** It is unclear if Horace means that Lyce was the favorite second only to Cinara or following Cinara's death, described in the following lines. Cinara does not show up in the earlier *Odes* 1–3, but Horace mentions her as a past lover at *Odes* 4.1.4, *Epistles* 1.7.28, and *Epistles* 1.14.33.

6. **ancient crow:** Crows proverbially had long lives.

ODES 4.14

Quae cura patrum quaeve Quiritium
plenis honorum muneribus tuas,
      Auguste, virtutes in aevum
           per titulos memoresque fastus

aeternet, o, qua sol habitabilis   5
illustrat oras, maxime principum?
      quem legis expertes Latinae
           Vindelici didicere nuper,

quid Marte posses. milite nam tuo
Drusus Genaunos, implacidum genus,   10
      Breunosque velocis et arces
           Alpibus impositas tremendis

deiecit acer plus vice simplici;
maior Neronum mox grave proelium
      commisit immanisque Raetos   15
           auspiciis pepulit secundis,

spectandus in certamine Martio,
devota morti pectora liberae

ODES 4.14[1]

What[2] efforts of the senate and the people
with lavish gifts of honors, through inscriptions
    and unforgetting records[3] can, Augustus,
        grant to your virtues everlasting life

always, you greatest of the foremost men,[4]   5
wherever sun lights up the peopled shores?
    Untouched by Latin law, the Vindelici
        just recently discovered who you are,

what you can do in war. For with your soldiers
Drusus cut down the fierce race of Genauni,   10
    and the swift Breuni with their citadels
        placed high upon the fear-inspiring Alps—

he harshly dealt out more than simple vengeance.
Soon afterward the elder Nero[5] entered
    upon a weighty battle and struck down   15
        the fearsome Raeti[6] under lucky omens.

He was a sight amid that martial strife—
with such immense destruction he tormented

---

1. *Odes* 4.14 (*Alcaic Strophe*): An ode in praise of the military exploits of the imperial family, in particular Augustus's stepsons Drusus and Tiberius, whose Alpine victories reflect not so much their own accomplishments as those of Augustus himself. The poem is a companion piece to 4.4, also a Pindaric **encomium** in praise of Drusus and Tiberius.
2. **What:** The interrogative opening is a Pindaric feature.
3. **unforgetting records:** The *fasti* were public accounts of festivals and magistrates. The records chronicling Augustus's heroic deeds here contrast sharply with those recording Lyde's amorous adventures in the previous poem (4.13.15).
4. **foremost men:** *Princeps* (the "chief" or "foremost" man) indicated a leading man of the state during the republic, but during the empire it was used to designate the men of the imperial family and especially the emperor himself.
5. **elder Nero:** Tiberius.
6. **Vindelici . . . Raeti:** Horace lists here various Alpine tribes that Drusus and Tiberius defeated in 15 B.C.E.

> quantis fatigaret ruinis,
> > indomitas prope qualis undas   20

exercet Auster, Pleiadum choro
scindente nubes, impiger hostium
> vexare turmas et frementem
> > mittere equum medios per ignis.

sic tauriformis volvitur Aufidus,   25
qui regna Dauni praefluit Apuli,
> cum saevit horrendamque cultis
> > diluviem meditatur agris,

ut barbarorum Claudius agmina
ferrata vasto diruit impetu   30
> primosque et extremos metendo
> > stravit humum sine clade victor,

te copias, te consilium et tuos
praebente divos. nam tibi, quo die
> portus Alexandrea supplex   35
> > et vacuam patefecit aulam,

fortuna lustro prospera tertio
belli secundos reddidit exitus,
> laudemque et optatum peractis
> > imperiis decus arrogavit.   40

hearts that were resolute to die with freedom.
So similar to Auster[7] when he shakes   20

the frenzied waves while dancing Pleiades
cut through the clouds, he tirelessly harassed
the throngs of enemies and hurled their snorting
steeds through the very middle of the flames.

Just as the bull-formed Aufidus[8] streams forth,   25
which flows beside Apulian Daunus's realms,[9]
when he is full of rage and contemplates
a horrifying flood upon the farmland—

so Claudius[10] destroyed the iron-clad
barbarian[11] troops with his colossal strike,   30
and, mowing down the ones in front and back,
he strewed the ground, a victor without losses.

You[12] were the one who gave the troops, you gave
the strategy and your own gods. Yes, fifteen
years from that day when Alexandria   35
in supplication opened up to you

its harbor and its empty hall,[13] good fortune
again has brought a happy end to war
and added praise and coveted distinction
to the campaigns that you've already finished. 40

---

7. **Auster:** The south wind.
8. **Aufidus:** A river that ran through the Italian region of Apulia, Horace's birthplace.
9. **Daunus's realms:** Daunus was a legendary Apulian king.
10. **Claudius:** That is, Tiberius (Tiberius Claudius Nero).
11. **barbarian:** See the note at *Epodes* 5.61.
12. **You:** Throughout the poem's conclusion Horace addresses Augustus with the second-person pronoun (**Du-Stil**), a feature common to **hymns** and prayers. This is one of the various features that conspire here to elevate Augustus's status to that of a deity.
13. **that day when Alexandria . . . empty hall:** Alexandria fell to Octavian/Augustus on August 1, 31 B.C.E. Horace dates the victory of Tiberius and Drusus to the same date fifteen years later.

te Cantaber non ante domabilis
Medusque et Indus, te profugus Scythes
   miratur, o tutela praesens
      Italiae dominaeque Romae.

te, fontium qui celat origines,   45
Nilusque et Hister, te rapidus Tigris,
   te beluosus qui remotis
      obstrepit Oceanus Britannis,

te non paventis funera Galliae
duraeque tellus audit Hiberiae,   50
   te caede gaudentes Sygambri
      compositis venerantur armis.

You fill with awe the formerly untamed
Cantabrian, the Mede and Indian,
    the Scythian nomad[14]—you, savior on earth
        of Italy and Rome, the whole world's mistress.

To you the Nile, which hides its waters' source,   45
to you the Danube and the rushing Tigris,[15]
    to you the beast-abounding Ocean that
        reechoes to the Britons far away,

to you the lands of Gaul, not terrified
of death,[16] and hardy Spain all lend their ears.   50
    You are revered by the Sygambri[17]—they
        rejoice in slaughter but have stored their
            weapons.

---

14. **Cantabrian . . . Scythian nomad**: Horace attributes various accomplishments
to Augustus. He was in Cantabria/Spain in 26–25 B.C.E. and recovered the standards
lost by Crassus to the Medes/Parthians in 20 B.C.E. The references to the Indians and
Scythians are probably more fanciful.
15. **Danube . . . Tigris**: Rivers in Dacia and Parthia, respectively. This list of
bodies of water stand via **metonymy** for the people who live around them.
16. **not terrified of death**: Probably a reference to the Druidic belief in the
afterlife.
17. **Sygambri**: A Germanic tribe. Thomas (2011) points out that their "uprising . . .
is in part the reason or pretext for the activities of Tiberius and Drusus in the Alps."

ODES 4.15

Phoebus volentem proelia me loqui
victas et urbes increpuit lyra,
    ne parva Tyrrhenum per aequor
        vela darem. tua, Caesar, aetas

fruges et agris rettulit uberes,   5
et signa nostro restituit Iovi
    derepta Parthorum superbis
        postibus et vacuum duellis

Ianum Quirini clausit et ordinem
rectum evaganti frena licentiae   10
    iniecit emovitque culpas
        et veteres revocavit artis,

per quas Latinum nomen et Italae
crevere vires, famaque et imperi
    porrecta maiestas ad ortus   15
        solis ab Hesperio cubili.

custode rerum Caesare non furor
civilis aut vis exiget otium,

ODES 4.15[1]

Phoebus[2] rang out upon his lyre when
I wished to sing of wars and conquered cities,
    and stopped me spreading out my little sails
        upon the Tuscan Sea.[3] Caesar, your age

has brought again rich produce to the fields   5
and[4] has restored to our own Jupiter
    the standards wrested from the pompous doors
        of Parthians[5] and has closed the temple doors

of Janus Quirinus,[6] free of wars, and has
thrown reins on license, which had overstepped   10
    the proper bound. It has removed our faults
        and called back once again the ancient arts

through which the name of Latium and Italian
might and the fame and greatness of our empire
    increased, extending from the sun's far western   15
        bed all the way to where it makes its rising.

While Caesar safeguards our affairs, not rage
nor civic violence will drive out peace,

---

1. *Odes* **4.15** (*Alcaic Strophe*): In this final ode, Horace one last time reaffirms his commitment to the lyric form while simultaneously broadening its compass to include **encomium** of Augustus—as he has done throughout the fourth book. The poem is a celebration of the peace ushered in by Augustus after a century of civil strife and celebrates the accomplishments of the *princeps* that have made it possible.
2. **Phoebus**: In a *recusatio*, Horace describes how Apollo prevented him from setting out on the great sea of epic in his small lyric boat.
3. **Tuscan Sea**: The Tyrrhenian Sea, off the west coast of Italy.
4. **and**: The **polysyndeton** running throughout these next three stanzas, which form one unusually long sentence, creates a piling-on effect of Augustus's achievements.
5. **Standards . . . Parthians**: These are the standards that Crassus had lost to the Parthians in the Battle of Carrhae in 53 B.C.E. and which Horace imagines the Parthians had hung on their temples as war prizes. Augustus retrieved these standards diplomatically in 20 B.C.E.
6. **Temple . . . Quirinus**: The doors of Janus's temple were closed to signify Rome was at peace throughout its empire. Augustus closed the doors three times, in 29 B.C.E., 25/24 B.C.E., and in either 13 or 8/7 B.C.E.

non ira, quae procudit enses
    et miseras inimicat urbis.   20

non qui profundum Danuvium bibunt
edicta rumpent Iulia, non Getae,
    non Seres infidive Persae,
        non Tanain prope flumen orti.

nosque et profestis lucibus et sacris   25
inter iocosi munera Liberi
    cum prole matronisque nostris,
        rite deos prius apprecati,

virtute functos more patrum duces
Lydis remixto carmine tibiis   30
    Troiamque et Anchisen et almae
        progeniem Veneris canemus.

nor wrath, which hammers swords upon the forge
and fosters enmity in wretched cities.   20

Those who drink deeply of the Danube[7] will
not break the Julian laws, nor will the Getae,[8]
nor will the Chinese[9] or the faithless Persians,
nor will those born beside the river Don.[10]

And we, on working days and holidays,   25
amid the gifts of laughter-loving Liber,[11]
together with our children and our wives,
will solemnly invoke the gods, and then

in song accompanied by Lydian flutes
we'll sing, just as our fathers did, of leaders   30
who demonstrated virtue and Anchises
and the descendants of the kindly Venus.[12]

---

7. **Danube**: The river marked the northeastern border of the Roman Empire.
8. **Getae**: A Thracian tribe.
9. **Chinese**: Rudd (2004, 261) remarks here that "Chinese silk was imported by the Romans, but the idea of political submission is fanciful hyperbole."
10. **Don**: A river in modern Russia.
11. **Liber**: Bacchus, the god of wine.
12. **Anchises . . . kindly Venus**: Anchises and Venus were the parents of Aeneas, the legendary founder of Rome, but also the ancestors of Augustus. The subject matter of Horace's future song is familiar from Vergil's *Aeneid*. The last word, *canemus* (we will sing), sounds another Vergilian note, since it is also the final word of Vergil's *Eclogues* 9. The appearance of Venus in this final line, moreover, forms a ring with the opening line of the book.

GLOSSARY OF RHETORICAL
AND LITERARY TERMS

The following rhetorical and literary terms appear in bold in the notes, although it is neither possible nor desirable to point out every single occurrence of these features. This glossary's primary purpose is to enable readers to search out and identify these features on their own. It is not, moreover, meant to be an exhaustive catalog of every device Horace employs, but it does try to outline some of the more prominent stylistic and literary features of Horatian lyric.

adynaton: An "impossibility," used to illustrate that some stated thing cannot possibly occur or that something unbelievable is occurring. In *Epodes* 5.79, Canidia claims that "heaven will sooner sink below the sea" than Varus will cease to love her, where the impossibility of the heavens collapsing illustrates the impossibility that Varus will resist her magic.

alliteration: The repetition of consonant sounds, often for some specific effect. In the opening of *Odes* 2.13, Horace's barrage of *p* sounds vividly illustrates his disdain: "With **p**rofane hand / he **p**ro**p**agated you, O tree, to **p**lague / his **p**rogeny and bring his **p**recinct shame."

anaphora: The repetition of words for emphasis. In *Odes* 3.4, for example, Horace repeats the key words *vester . . . vester* (yours . . . yours, 21) and *visam . . . visam* (I'll go to see . . . I'll go to see, 33–35). Hymns often display emphatic anaphora, particularly of the second-person pronoun "you." *See also* Du-Stil.

ascending tricolon: A tricolon whose third item is given special emphasis, as in "life, liberty, and the pursuit of happiness." In *Odes* 2.5.17–24, for example, Horace lists three former beloveds of his addressee but develops most fully the final one, Gyges. *See also* tricolon.

assonance: The repetition of vowel sounds in close proximity, and often in combination with alliteration. In the opening of *Odes* 2.1, for example, Horace includes a series of *o* sounds with alliteration of *m* and *c*: *Motum ex Metello consule civicum* (the civic turmoil since Metellus was consul). *See also* alliteration.

asyndeton: The omission of conjunctions such as "and" and "but," the latter of which creates "adversative" asyndeton. In the final couplet of *Epodes* 2, Horace writes *omnem redegit idibus pecuniam, / quaerit Kalendis ponere*, which literally means "he collected all his money on the Ides, on the Kalends he seeks to lend it," and here an adversative aspect is implied. The connectives are at times reintroduced in English translation for clarity.

callida iunctura: A "clever joining," usually wherein antithetical or oxymoronic ideas are combined to create a novel effect. Horace excels at this device, seen for example at *Odes* 1.5.5 (*simplex munditiis* [simply elegant]) and *Odes* 2.5.23 (*discrimen obscurum* [an imperceptible difference]). Horace himself coined the phrase *callida iunctura* at *Ars Poetica* 47–48.

chiasm: Named from the Greek letter chi (X), chiasm is a pattern that creates a ring, such as ABBA or ABCBA, as in JFK's famous phrase, "Ask not what your country can do for you—ask what you can do for your country" ("country" . . ."you" . . ."you" . . ."country"). Because of its inflected nature, whereby word ending rather than word order determines grammar, Latin can exploit this device much more fully than English. For example, in *Odes* 1.5 Horace uses an ABCBA pattern: *multa*

<u>gracilis</u> **te** <u>puer</u> in *rosa*. Here, the "slender boy" (*gracilis puer*) surrounds the addressee Pyrrha, "you" (*te*), and both of them are surrounded by "many roses" (*multa rosa*). The effect is to produce a word picture of the two lovers embracing in a bed of roses—an effect that is unfortunately impossible to replicate in translation.

cletic hymn: A hymn in which a god is asked to appear to the speaker or another character. *Odes* 1.30, for example, constitutes a short cletic hymn to the goddess Venus, who is asked to come to the shrine of a woman named Glycera. *See also* hymn.

dirge: A song of lament (in Greek a "threnody") over the death of a loved one. *Odes* 1.24, for example, is a dirge for the death of Quintilius, a cherished friend of Vergil.

Du-Stil: A prominent feature of hymns—as well as curses and oaths—in which the second-person pronoun is repeated. In *Odes* 3.11, for example, Horace uses various inflections of "you" (*te . . . tu . . . tu . . . tibi*) while hymning Mercury and the lyre. In *Odes* 4.14.33–52, the use of Du-Stil (*te . . . te . . . te . . . te . . . te . . . te . . . te . . . te . . . te*) suggests that Horace's praise of Augustus has reached truly (and perhaps exaggeratedly) hymnic proportions. *See also* hymn *and* anaphora.

elegy: A genre of poetry popular in Rome at the same time Horace was writing his *Odes* and *Epodes*. Written in elegiac couplets, it regularly takes up the topic of erotic love. Although Horace does not write elegiac poetry, he is fully aware of its conventions and frequently alludes to the various metaphors popular in elegy. *See also* exclusus amator, paraclausithyron, militia amoris, *and* servitium amoris.

encomium: A literary work, originally an ode, designed to praise an individual, normally a human. The form goes back especially to Pindar, whose odes were often written in praise of victorious athletes, and Horace takes up this mode especially in book 4 of the *Odes,* wherein the imperial family are frequent objects of praise. *See also* panegyric.

enjambment: When a thought or sentence does not stop at the end of the verse but continues into the next line, often with an interesting or surprising effect. In the Cleopatra Ode (1.37), for example, Horace

enjambs *fatale monstrum* (deadly monster) in line 21 in order to empha-
size Cleopatra's threat and Augustus's heroism.

epic: A genre of poetry that usually consisted of works of great length on
either mythological or historical topics, always written in dactylic hexameter. Vergil's *Aeneid*, regarded by many as the greatest epic written in
Latin, was published in 19 B.C.E., just four years prior to the publication
of *Odes* 1–3. Although Horace often refuses to write epic and defines his
own lyric in opposition to it, he clearly understands its conventions and
frequently alludes to them. *See also* recusatio.

epithet: Adjectives used regularly to describe particular individuals,
especially gods. The practice goes back to Homer (e.g., "rosy fingered
Dawn" and "swift-footed Achilles") and is taken up by Roman poets to
lend a sense of epic gravity to an individual. In *Epodes* 17.12, for example,
Horace refers to Hector as *homicida* (man-slaying), a Latinization of his
common Homeric epithet.

***exclusus amator*:** "Locked-out lover," a trope seen frequently in elegy,
wherein a lover is shut out from his beloved's house and laments on her
threshold or outside of her windows. In *Odes* 1.25.1–4, for example, Lydia
keeps her windows locked to her would-be lovers, but Horace threatens
they will stop performing this role soon. The narrator of *Odes* 3.10 is an
exclusus amator. *See also* paraclausithyron.

golden line: A term coined by John Dryden in the seventeenth century.
This is a line arranged either chiastically or in interlocking word order
around a central verb (ABVerbBA or ABVerbAB). It was popular especially in epic, although Horace creates some lovely examples in his lyric
verse. In 3.1.16, for example, Horace writes, <u>omne</u> **capax** *movet* **urna**
<u>nomen</u> (her spacious urn sets every name in motion), where *capax urna*
(spacious urn) surrounds the verb and in turn is surrounded by *omne
nomen* (every name). The arrangement is unfortunately usually untranslatable. *See also* chiasm *and* interlocking word order.

hymn: A song sung in celebration of or in prayer to a god. Ancient
prayers usually involve typical elements, such as naming the god, giving
his or her epithets, providing the god's parentage and a list of his or her

powers, listing the god's cult sites, and making a request. Hymns are also notable for their frequent use of relative clauses and the use of the second-person singular (Du-Stil). Horace's hymns to Mercury (*Odes* 1.10 and 3.11), for example, exhibit many of these features.

hypallage: See *transferred epithet.*

hyperbaton: The separation of an adjective from the word it modifies, a phenomenon much more common in Latin, owing to its inflected nature, than in English. In 1.4.15, for example, Horace warns his addressee not to hope for the impossible: *vitae summa brevis spem nos vetat inchoare longam* (the short extent of life keeps us from taking up long hope). The separation between "long" (*longam*) and "hope" (*spes*) here perhaps illustrates how we extend our hopes beyond our allotted span. Horace frequently uses hyperbaton to create word pictures, as discussed under "chiasm" above.

interlocking word order: An interlocking pattern of words, usually in an ABAB arrangement. In *Epodes* 13.11, for example, Horace uses interlocking word order to create a golden line: **nobilis** *ut grandi* cecinit **Centaurus** *alumno* (just as the **noble Centaur** sang to his grown pupil). The effect is nearly impossible to reproduce in English. *See also* golden line.

invective: Literature meant to attack individuals, whether real or imaginary. Attack was a regular feature of oratory, as in Cicero's *Philippics* against Antony. Horace adopts it particularly in the *Epodes,* such as 8 and 12, which consist of harsh verbal attacks against women, or *Epodes* 4, which abuses an upstart freedman. Invective is not, however, confined to the *Epodes.* In *Odes* 4.13, for example, Horace harshly derides a woman named Lyce.

litotes: An expression of an affirmative through a double negative, as in "not unkind" to suggest "kind." In *Epodes* 5.50, for example, Canidia refers to Night and Diana as her "not faithless witnesses" (*non infideles arbitrae*), i.e., as her faithful witnesses.

locus amoenus: An idealized landscape, featuring a temperate climate, gently flowing water, shade trees, bird song, and other sensory pleasures.

Horace's farm often takes on the features of a *locus amoenus*, as, for example, in *Odes* 1.17. Such landscapes afford to Horace an alternative to the hubbub of the city, a place where he can produce poetry and practice the moderate lifestyle of rustic poverty he so frequently praises.

metaphor: A comparison between two things that have something in common but are not the same. So, for example, Horace frequently, as in *Odes* 1.4, uses the metaphor of the natural seasons to capture the fleeting quality of human life. In *Odes* 4.2, to give another example, he employs the metaphor of the rushing river to describe Pindar's poetry while figuring himself as a painstaking bee.

metonymy: A "change of name" whereby something is replaced with an item or idea closely associated with it, as in "the pen is mightier than the sword," wherein "pen" stands for "writing" or "reason," and "sword" stands for "war" or "violence." Horace and other ancient poets often use the names of gods metonymically as substitutes for things associated with them. In *Odes* 1.7.22–23, for example, Teucer wears *uda Lyaeo . . . populea . . . corona* (a poplar crown sprinkled with Bacchus), where the god's name stands in for "wine." *See also* synecdoche.

militia amoris: A metaphor, developed especially by love elegists, whereby the lover rejects obedience to a military leader in favor of obedience to his mistress or replaces the battles of war with the erotic battles of the bedroom. This elegiac trope makes frequent appearances in Horace's lyric poetry, as, for example, at *Odes* 1.13.17, where Horace says he writes about the *proelia virginum* (battles virgins wage) against young men instead of traditionally martial epic. Although Horace does not normally figure himself as a fighter on the battlefield of love or as serving a dominating mistress, his descriptions of himself as unwarlike (as, e.g., in *Epodes* 1.15–16) are related to this metaphor. *See* trope.

palinode: A poem written to recant or retract an earlier poem. The most famous palinode was written by the seventh- to sixth-century Greek lyric poet Stesichorus to repudiate an earlier poem in which he blamed Helen for the Trojan War. Horace likely models his palinode in *Odes* 1.16 on this poem.

panegyric: A literary expression of praise, closely related to "encomium." *See* encomium.

paraclausithyron: A song sung by an *exclusus amator* in front of a closed door. This is normally an elegiac trope, but it finds its way into Horatian lyric, as for example in the paraclausithyron that constitutes *Odes* 3.10. *See* exclusus amator.

persona: A "mask" or character adopted by an author to narrate or otherwise speak his or her work. The poet's voice is in many ways a self-constructed work of fiction, created for the needs of a particular work or even a poem. Horace creates a variety of personae throughout the *Epodes* and *Odes,* from the vituperative but impotent iambicist of the former to the Epicurean idler or patriotic spokesman of the latter.

pivot: The middle line or stanza of an ode, which often constitutes an important turning point. Horace's best known pivot comes in the Cleopatra Ode (*Odes* 1.37), where Caesar appears at the exact center of the poem, changing the queen from a destructive, emasculating threat to a victim of Caesar's heroic masculinity.

polyptoton: The repetition of the same word in different inflections, as in "strong" and "strength" or "sing" and "song." In *Odes* 3.4.65–68, for example, Horace repeats the word "force" in three different cases: *vis, vim, vires.*

polysyndeton: The opposite of "asyndeton," this is the repetition of conjunctions such as "and." In *Odes* 4.15.5–14, for example, Horace uses "and" no less than eight times to create a piling-on effect of Augustus's achievements.

priamel: A list wherein a number of options are rejected in preference to an alternative that comes at the climax of the list. *Psalms* 20:7 provides a nice example: "Some trust in chariots, and some in horses; but we will remember the name of the Lord our God." Horace's most elaborate priamel comes in *Odes* 1.1.

propempticon: A "sending forth." This is a poem written on the departure of someone on a journey, usually wishing them a safe trip and asking the gods to protect them. *Odes* 1.3 is a long *propempticon* to Vergil, addressed to the ship carrying him. A reversal of the form can be found in *Epodes* 10, where Horace wishes Maevius a dangerous journey.

recusatio: A nonancient term nowadays used to describe the trope wherein a poet turns down one type of poetic composition (usually epic) in favor of a different genre (usually lighter genres such as elegy or lyric). The topos goes back to Callimachus, who in his *Aetia* prologue describes how Apollo prevented him from taking up a long poem on kings and heroes, and is taken up by Roman poets such as Vergil, Propertius, and Horace. Two examples are offered by *Odes* 1.6 (a refusal to write epic celebrating Augustus) and *Odes* 4.15.1–4 (where Apollo prevents Horace from writing of "wars and conquered cities").

rhetorical question: A question not meant to elicit a response but to heighten the emotional effect of the passage or make some other point. Horace opens *Epodes* 7, for example, with two emotionally charged questions to underscore his exasperation at the possible renewal of civil war: *Quo, quo scelesti ruitis? aut cur dexteris / aptantur enses conditi?* (Where, where are you depraved men rushing? Why / do your right hands hold swords just sheathed?).

servitium amoris: "The slavery of love," a metaphor whereby a lover declares himself the metaphorical slave of his beloved, often likened to a *domina*, his "mistress." The metaphor recurs regularly in elegy, although Horace frequently exploits it in his lyric poems as well. In *Odes* 2.8, for example, Barine's seductive powers are such that all of Rome's youth are growing up to be her "new slave-band," *servitus nova*.

simile: A comparison using "like" or "as." Extended similes are found frequently in epic poetry going back to Homer, and Horace incorporates them often into his lyric verse. They often, but not always, compare some character to a phenomenon from the world of nature. In *Epodes* 1.19–22, for example, Horace compares himself to a protective mother bird, and in *Odes* 4.14 he likens Tiberius to the south wind and the river Aufidus.

stock figure: A character type that recurs frequently in certain genres of literature, such as the prostitute or stern father in Roman comedy.

Horace's stock characters are often borrowed from the worlds of comedy or elegy; for example, in *Epodes* 1.33–34 he mentions Chremes, a comedic stock miser, and in 4.1.18 he mentions an erotic rival, a frequent elegiac stock type.

synecdoche: A device whereby a part of something is meant to stand for the whole. In *Odes* 1.1.13, for example, the *trabe Cypria* (Cyprian ship-beam) is meant to stand for the whole ship. *See also* metonymy.

topos: A "commonplace," a topos is a recurring scene, situation, or motif in a particular genre of literature. In Horatian lyric, examples of recurring topoi include the *recusatio* or the *locus amoenus,* both of which mark his poetry as light and nonepic. In *Odes* 2.7, to name another example, we find the lyric topos of the lost shield, wherein Horace drops his shield in battle just as the lyric poets Alcaeus, Archilochus, and Anacreon before him had done—an incident that legitimizes him as a lyric poet. The term's use often overlaps with that of "trope," although the latter is more focused on recurring rhetorical devices rather than type scenes or situations. *See* recusatio, locus amoenus, *and* trope.

transferred epithet: Also called hypallage, this is when an adjective is transferred from the noun it logically goes with to another noun. In the Cleopatra Ode (1.37), for example, the queen plots "insane destruction," but the adjective "insane" more appropriately describes the queen herself.

tricolon: A common rhetorical technique wherein a list of three words or clauses is given, as in Caesar's famous phrase "I came, I saw, I conquered" (*veni, vidi, vici*). These appear throughout Horatian poetry and ancient literature in general. *Odes* 2.5, for example, opens with a stanza consisting of a tricolon—the girl is not strong enough (a) to bear the yoke, (b) to match her partner's duties, and (c) to stand the burden of the bull. *See also* ascending tricolon.

trope: A "turning," a trope is a figure of speech such as a metaphor, simile, image, or other rhetorical device that recurs across a particular genre or work of literature. The metaphors of *militia amoris* and *servitium amoris,* for example, are frequent elegiac tropes that Horace deploys in his lyric poems. Another frequent trope used across numerous ancient genres, for example, is the use of gods' names in metonymy to represent spheres or items over which they preside. The use of the word "trope" has some overlap with that of "topos," although the former is focused more on figures of speech and the latter on recurring situations or subjects. *See* topos, metaphor, simile, *and* metonymy.

BIBLIOGRAPHY

Adams, J. N. 1982. *The Latin Sexual Vocabulary.* Baltimore: Johns Hopkins University Press.

Ancona, Ronnie. 1994. *Time and the Erotic in Horace's* Odes. Durham: Duke University Press.

Anderson, William S. 1966. "Horace *Carm.* 1.14: What Kind of Ship?" *Classical Philology* 61: 84–98.

Armstrong, David. 1986. "*Horatius Eques et Scriba:* Satires 1.6 and 2.7." *Transactions of the American Philological Association* 116: 255–88.

———. 1989. *Horace.* New Haven: Yale University Press.

———. 2010. "The Biographical and Social Foundations of Horace's Poetic Voice." In *A Companion to Horace,* edited by Gregson Davis, 7–33. Chichester: Wiley-Blackwell.

Barchiesi, Alessandro. 2001. "Horace and Iambos: The Poet as Literary Historian." In *Iambic Ideas: Essays on a Poetic Tradition from Archaic Greece to the Late Roman Empire,* edited by Alberto Cavarzere, Antonio Aloni, and Alessandro Barchiesi, 141–64. Lanham: Rowman & Littlefield.

Bather, Philippa, and Claire Stocks, eds. 2016. *Horace's* Epodes*: Context, Intertexts, and Reception.* Oxford: Oxford University Press.

Bleisch, Pamela R. 2001. "Silence Is Golden: Simonides, Callimachus, and Augustan Panegyric at the Close of Horace, *Carm.* 3.2." *Quaderni Urbinati Di Cultura Classica* 68: 21–40.

Bowditch, Phoebe Lowell. 2001. *Horace and the Gift Economy of Patronage.* Berkeley: University of California Press.

Bowra, C. M. 1928. "Horace, *Odes* IV.12." *Classical Review* 42: 165–67.

Bradshaw, A. 1989. "Horace *in Sabinis*." In *Studies in Latin Literature and Roman History* V, edited by Carl Deroux, 160–86. Brussels: Latomus.

———. 2002. "Horace's Birthday and Deathday." In *Traditions and Contexts in the Poetry of Horace*, edited by Tony Woodman and Denis Feeney, 1–16. Cambridge: Cambridge University Press.

Clay, Jenny Strauss. 2010. "Horace and Lesbian Lyric." In *A Companion to Horace*, edited by Gregson Davis, 128–46. Chichester: Wiley-Blackwell.

———. 2015. "Horace *c.* 1.11: Wintry Thoughts on a Winter's Day . . . and a Hint of Spring." *Philologus* 159: 112–17.

Commager, Steele. 1957. "The Function of Wine in Horace's *Odes.*" *Transactions of the American Philological Association* 88: 68–80.

Davis, Gregson. 1987. "*Carmina/Iambi:* The Literary-generic Dimension of Horace's *Integer Vitae.*" *Quaderni Urbinati Di Cultura Classica* 27: 67–78.

———. 1989. "*INGENII CUMBA?* Literary *Aporia* and the Rhetoric of Horace's *O navis referent.*" *Rheinisches Museum für Philologie* 132: 331–45.

———. 1991. *Polyhymnia: The Rhetoric of Horatian Lyric Discourse.* Berkeley: University of California Press.

———. 2010. "Defining a Lyric Ethos: Archilochus *lyricus* and Horatian *melos.*" In *A Companion to Horace,* edited by Gregson Davis, 105–27. Chichester: Wiley-Blackwell.

Dixon, Suzanne. 1988. *The Roman Mother.* Norman: University of Oklahoma Press.

DuQuesnay, I. M. Le M. 1984. "Horace and Maecenas: The Propaganda Value of *Sermones* 1." In *Poetry and Politics in the Age of Augustus,* edited by Tony Woodman and David West, 19–58. Cambridge: Cambridge University Press.

———. 1995. "Horace, *Odes* 4.5: *Pro reditu imperatoris Caesaris divi filii Augusti.*" In *Homage to Horace: A Bimillenary Celebration,* edited by Stephen J. Harrison, 128–87. Oxford: Clarendon Press.

Eder, Walter. 2005. "Augustus and the Power of Tradition." Translated by Karl Galinsky. In *The Cambridge Companion to the Age of Augustus,* edited by Karl Galinsky. 13–32. Cambridge: Cambridge University Press.

Edmunds, Lowell. 2010. "The Reception of Horace's *Odes.*" In *A Companion to Horace,* edited by Gregson Davis, 337–66. Chichester: Wiley-Blackwell.

Edwards, Catharine. 1993. *The Politics of Immorality in Ancient Rome.* Cambridge: Cambridge University Press.

Fain, Gordon L. 2006. "Fortune and Thunder in Horace, *Odes* I, 34." *Latomus* 65: 88–96.

Fitzgerald, William. 1988. "Power and Impotence in Horace's *Epodes.*" *Ramus* 17: 176–91.

Freis, Richard. 1983. "The Catalogue of Pindaric Genres in Horace *Ode* 4.2." *Classical Antiquity* 2: 27–36.

Garrison, Daniel H. 1991. *Horace: Epodes and Odes.* Norman: University of Oklahoma Press.

Gowers, Emily. 2016. "Girls Will Be Boys and Boys Will Be Girls, Or, What Is the Gender of Horace's *Epodes?*" In *Horace's* Epodes*: Context, Intertexts, and Reception,* edited by Philippa Bather and Claire Stocks, 103–30. Oxford: Oxford University Press.

Griffin, Jasper. 2007. "Gods and Religion." In *The Cambridge Companion to Horace,* edited by Stephen Harrison, 181–94. Cambridge: Cambridge University Press.

Gruen, Erich S. 2005. "Augustus and the Making of the Principate." In *The Cambridge Companion to the Age of Augustus,* edited by Karl Galinsky, 33–51. Cambridge: Cambridge University Press.

Günther, Hans-Christian. 2013a. "Horace's Life and Work." In *Brill's Companion to Horace,* edited by Hans-Christian Günther, 1–62. Leiden: Brill.

———. 2013b. "The Book of *Iambi.*" In *Brill's Companion to Horace,* edited by Hans-Christian Günther, 169–210. Leiden: Brill.

Hawkins, Julia Nelson. 2014. "The Barking Cure: Horace's 'Anatomy of Rage' in *Epodes* 1, 6, and 16." *American Journal of Philology* 135: 57–85.

Harrison, Stephen. 1990. "The Praise Singer: Horace, Censorinus, and *Odes* 4.8." *Journal of Roman Studies* 80: 31–43.

———. 2001. "Some Generic Problems in Horace's *Epodes*: Or, on (Not) Being Archilochus." In *Iambic Ideas: Essays on a Poetic Tradition from Archaic Greece to the Late Roman Empire,* edited by Alberto Cavarzere, Antonio Aloni, and Alessandro Barchiesi, 165–86. Lanham: Rowman & Littlefield.

———, ed. 2007a. *The Cambridge Companion to Horace.* Cambridge: Cambridge University Press.

———. 2007b. "Horatian Self-Representations." In *The Cambridge Companion to Horace,* edited by Stephen Harrison, 22–35. Cambridge: Cambridge University Press.

———. 2007c. "Town and Country." In *The Cambridge Companion to Horace,* edited by Stephen Harrison, 235–47. Cambridge: Cambridge University Press.

———. 2017. *Horace:* Odes, *Book II.* Cambridge: Cambridge University Press.

Hejduk, Julia D. 2008. *Clodia: A Sourcebook.* Norman: University of Oklahoma Press.

Houghton, L. B. T., and Maria Wyke, eds. 2009. *Perceptions of Horace: A Roman Poet and His Readers.* Cambridge: Cambridge University Press.

Hutchinson, Gregory. 2007. "Horace and Archaic Greek Poetry." In *The Cambridge Companion to Horace,* edited by Stephen Harrison, 36–49. Cambridge: Cambridge University Press.

Johnson, Timothy S. 2003–4. "Locking-in and Locking-out Lydia: Lyric Form and Power in Horace's *C.* I. 25 and III. 9." *Classical Journal* 99: 113–34.

———. 2012. *Horace's Iambic Criticism.* Leiden: Brill.

Kennedy, Duncan. 1992. "'Augustan' and 'Anti-Augustan': Reflections on Terms of Reference." In *Roman Poetry and Propaganda in the Age of Augustus,* edited by Anton Powell, 26–58. Bristol: Bristol Classical Press.

Kidd, D. A. 1982. "Astrology for Maecenas." *Antichthon* 16: 88–96.

Knorr, Ortwin. 2006. "Horace's Ship Ode (*Odes* 1.14) in Context: A Metaphorical Love-Triangle." *Transactions of the American Philological Association* 136: 149–69.

Lewis, C. T., and C. Short. 1962. *A Latin Dictionary.* Oxford: Clarendon Press.

Lowrie, Michèle. 1997. *Horace's Narrative Odes.* Oxford: Clarendon Press.

———. 2007. "Horace and Augustus." In *The Cambridge Companion to Horace,* edited by Stephen Harrison, 77–89. Cambridge: Cambridge University Press.

Mankin, David. 1995. *Horace:* Epodes. Cambridge Greek and Latin Classics. Cambridge: Cambridge University Press.

———. 2010. "The *Epodes:* Genre, Themes, and Arrangement." In *A Companion to Horace,* edited by Gregson Davis, 93–104. Chichester: Wiley-Blackwell.

Martindale, Charles, and David Hopkins, eds. 1993. *Horace Made New: Horatian Influences on British Writing from the Renaissance to the Twentieth Century.* Cambridge: Cambridge University Press.

Mayer, Roland. 2012. *Horace:* Odes, *Book I.* Cambridge: Cambridge University Press.

Miralles, Carlos. 1983. "The Iambic Poet as a Wolf." In *Archilochus and the Iambic Poetry,* edited by Carlos Miralles and Jaume Pòrtulas, 53–60. Rome: Edizioni dell'Ateneo.

McCarter, Stephanie. 2015. *Horace between Freedom and Slavery: The First Book of* Epistles. Madison: University of Wisconsin Press.

McGinn, Thomas A. J. 1998. *Prostitution, Sexuality, and the Law in Ancient Rome.* Oxford: Oxford University Press.

Mette, Hans Joachim. 2009. "'Slender Genre' and 'Slender Table' in Horace." In *Horace:* Odes *and* Epodes. Oxford Readings in Classical Studies, edited by Michèle Lowrie, 50–55. Oxford: Oxford University Press. Originally published as "'Genus tenue' und 'mensa tenuis' bei Horaz." *Museum Helveticum* 18: 136–39 (1961).

Miller, Andrew M. 1996. *Greek Lyric: An Anthology in Translation.* Indianapolis: Hackett.

Miller, John. 2009. *Apollo, Augustus, and the Poets.* Cambridge: Cambridge University Press.

Moles, John. 2002. "Reconstructing Plancus (Horace, *C.* 1.7)." *Journal of Roman Studies* 92: 86–109.

———. 2007. "Philosophy and Ethics." In *The Cambridge Companion to Horace,* edited by Stephen Harrison, 165–80. Cambridge: Cambridge University Press.

Morrison, A. D. 2016. *"Lycambae Spretus Infido Gener | aut Acer Hosis Bupalo*: Horace's *Epodes* and the Greek Iambic Tradition." In *Horace's* Epodes: *Context, Intertexts, and Reception,* edited by Philippa Bather and Claire Stocks, 31–62. Oxford: Oxford University Press.

Murray, Oswyn. 1993. "Symposium and Genre in the Poetry of Horace." In *Horace 2000,* edited by Niall Rudd, 89–105. Ann Arbor: University of Michigan Press.

Nagel, Rebecca. 2000. "The Lyric Lover in Horace *Odes* 1.15 and 1.17." *Phoenix* 54: 53–63.

Nisbet, Robin. 1984. "Horace's *Epodes* and History." In *Poetry and Politics in the Age of Augustus,* edited by Tony Woodman and David West, 1–18. Cambridge: Cambridge University Press.

———. 2007. "Horace: Life and Chronology." In *The Cambridge Companion to Horace,* edited by Stephen Harrison, 7–21. Cambridge: Cambridge University Press.

Nisbet, Robin, and Margaret Hubbard. 1970. *A Commentary on Horace:* Odes *Book I.* Oxford: Clarendon Press.

———. 1978. *A Commentary on Horace:* Odes *Book II.* Oxford: Clarendon Press.

Nisbet, Robin, and Niall Rudd. 2004. *A Commentary on Horace:* Odes *Book III.* Oxford: Oxford University Press.

Oliensis, Ellen. 1991. "Canidia, Canicula, and the Decorum of Horace's *Epodes.*" *Arethusa* 24: 107–38.

———. 1998. *Horace and the Rhetoric of Authority.* Cambridge: Cambridge University Press.

———. 2002. "Feminine Endings, Lyric Seductions." In *Traditions and Contexts in the Poetry of Horace,* edited by Tony Woodman and Denis Feeney, 93–106. Cambridge: Cambridge University Press.

———. 2007. "Erotics and Gender." In *The Cambridge Companion to Horace,* edited by Stephen Harrison, 221–34. Cambridge: Cambridge University Press.

———. 2016. "Scenes from the Afterlife of Horace's *Epodes* (c. 1600–1900)." In *Horace's* Epodes*: Context, Intertexts, and Reception,* edited by Philippa Bather and Claire Stocks, 219–40. Oxford: Oxford University Press.

Pandey, Nandini. 2013. "Caesar's Comet, the Julian Star, and the Invention of Augustus." *Transactions of the American Philological Association* 143: 405–49.

Paschalis, Michael, ed. 2002. *Horace and Greek Lyric Poetry.* Rethymnon: University of Crete.

Paule, Maxwell Teitel. 2017. *Canidia: Rome's First Witch.* London: Bloomsbury.

Phillips, Tom. 2014. "A New Sapphic Intertext in Horace." *Archiv für Papyrusforschung und verwandte Gebiete* 60: 283–89.

Powell, J. G. F. 2009. "Horace, Scythia, and the East." *Papers of the Langford Latin Seminar* 14: 137–90.

Putnam, Michael C. J. 1969. "Horace *c.* 1.20." *Classical Journal* 64: 153–7.

———. 1992–93. "The Languages of Horace *Odes* 1.24." *Classical Journal* 88: 123–35.

———. 2000. *Horace's* Carmen Saeculare*: Ritual Magic and the Poet's Art.* New Haven: Yale University Press.

Race, William H. 1978. "*Odes* 1.20: An Horatian *Recusatio.*" *California Studies in Classical Antiquity* 11: 179–96.

———. 2010. "Horace's Debt to Pindar." In *A Companion to Horace,* edited by Gregson Davis, 147–73. Chichester: Wiley-Blackwell.

Riggsby, Andrew M. 2006. *Caesar in Gaul and Rome: War in Words.* Austin: The University of Texas Press.

Roller, Matthew. 2001. *Constructing Autocracy.* Princeton: Princeton University Press.

Rudd, Niall. 2004. *Horace:* Odes *and* Epodes. Loeb Classical Library 33. Cambridge, Mass.: Harvard University Press.

Saller, Richard P. 1982. *Personal Patronage under the Early Empire.* Cambridge: Cambridge University Press.

Schlegel, Catherine. 2000. "Horace and His Fathers: *Satires* 1.4 and 1.6." *American Journal of Philology* 121: 93–119.

Smith, Joshua M. 2015. "Horace *Odes* 2.7 and the Literary Tradition of *Rhipsaspia.*" *American Journal of Philology* 136: 243–80.

Stocks, Claire. 2016. "Monsters in the Night: Hannibal, *prodigia,* and the Parallel Worlds of *Epode* 16 and *Ode* 4.4." In *Horace's* Epodes*: Context, Intertexts, and Reception,* edited by Philippa Bather and Claire Stocks, 153–74. Oxford: Oxford University Press.

Sutherland, Elizabeth H. 2003. "How (Not) to Look at a Woman: Bodily Encounters and the Failure of the Gaze in Horace's *C.* 1.19." *American Journal of Philology* 124: 57–80.

———. 2005. "Literary Women in Horace's *Odes* 2.11 and 2.12." In *Defining Genre and Gender in Latin Literature,* edited by William W. Batstone and Garth Tissol, 193–210. New York: Peter Lang.

Syndikus, Hans Peter. 2010. "The Roman Odes." In *A Companion to Horace,* edited by Gregson Davis, 193–209. Chichester: Wiley-Blackwell.

Talbot, John. 2004. "Tennyson's Alcaics: Greek and Latin Prosody and the Invention of English Meters." *Studies in Philology* 101: 200–31.

Thomas, Richard F. 2011. *Horace:* Odes *Book* IV *and* Carmen Saeculare. Cambridge: Cambridge University Press.

von Ungern-Sternberg, Jürgen. 2014. "The Crisis of the Republic." Translated by Harriet I. Flower. In *The Cambridge Companion to the Roman Republic,* 2nd edition, edited by Harriet I. Flower, 78–98. Cambridge: Cambridge University Press.

Watson, Lindsay C. 1995. "Horace's *Epodes:* The Impotence of *Iambos?*" In *Homage to Horace,* edited by Stephen Harrison, 188–202. Oxford: Clarendon Press.

———. 2003. *A Commentary on Horace's* Epodes. Oxford: Oxford University Press.

———. 2007. "The *Epodes:* Horace's Archilochus?" In *The Cambridge Companion to Horace,* edited by Stephen Harrison, 93–104. Cambridge: Cambridge University Press.

West, David. 1991. "*Cur Me Querelis* (Horace, *Odes* 2.17)." *American Journal of Philology* 112: 45–52.

———. 1995. *Horace* Odes *I: Carpe Diem.* Clarendon Press: Oxford.

———. 1998. *Horace* Odes *II: Vatis Amici.* Clarendon Press: Oxford.

———. 2002. *Horace* Odes *III: Dulce Periculum.* Oxford University Press: Oxford.

Wickham, Edward C., and H. W. Garrod. 1901. *Q. Horati Flacci Opera.* Oxford: Clarendon Press.

White, Peter. 1991. "Maecenas' Retirement." *Classical Philology* 86: 130–38.

Williams, Gordon. 1968. *Tradition and Originality in Roman Poetry.* Oxford: Clarendon Press.

———. 1990. "Did Maecenas 'Fall from Favor'? Augustan Literary Patronage." In *Between Republic and Empire: Interpretations of Augustus and His Principate,* edited by Kurt A. Raaflaub and Mark Toher, 258–75. Berkeley: University of California Press.

———. 1995. "*Libertino Patre Natus:* True or False?" In *Homage to Horace,* edited by Stephen J. Harrison, 296–313. Oxford: Clarendon Press.

Woodman, Tony. 2017. "Vinous Voices: Horace's Ninth Epode." In *Word and Context in Latin Poetry: Studies in Memory of David West,* 43–60. Cambridge: Cambridge Philological Society.

Zanker, Paul. 1988. *The Power of Images in the Age of Augustus.* Translated by Alan Shapiro. Ann Arbor: University of Michigan Press.

Zumwalt, N. K. 1977. "Horace's *Navis* of Love Poetry." *Classical World* 71: 249–54.

9 780806 164878